D1714869

JAMES JOYCE AND CENSORSHIP

James Joyce and Censorship

The Trials of *Ulysses*

Paul Vanderham

NEW YORK UNIVERSITY PRESS
Washington Square, New York

First published in the U.S.A. in 1998 by
NEW YORK UNIVERSITY PRESS
Washington Square
New York, N.Y. 10003

This book is printed on paper suitable for recycling and
made from fully managed and sustained forest sources.

Library of Congress Cataloging-in-Publication Data
Vanderham, Paul.
James Joyce and censorship : the trials of Ulysses / Paul
Vanderham.
p.   cm.
Includes index.
ISBN 0–8147–8790–8
1. Joyce, James, 1882–1941. Ulysses.   2. Joyce, James, 1882–1941–
–Censorship.   3. Fiction—Censorship—History—20th century.
I. Title.
PR6019.O9U756 1997
823'.912—dc21   97–10873
                                                         CIP

Printed in Great Britain

For Ellen

Contents

Acknowledgements

This book, my first, would never have come to be without the efforts of those teachers who kindled within me a desire for understanding when the wood they had to work with was green: my grandmother, Eugenie Suttle; my parents, Rob and Mariette Vanderham; one of my high school English teachers, Mrs E. Ranson; and two of my English professors at the University of British Columbia, Frank Newby and John Hulcoop.

When I first proposed the subject of this book as a dissertation topic at the University of Virginia, E.D. Hirsch, Jr was enthusiastic in his support and confident that my labours would lead one fine day to publication. That day has now arrived, bringing with it many blessings, including the chance to thank him in print, not only for helping me to believe in myself but also for providing me with a model of gracious intellectual integrity. I am also grateful for the encouragement and insight of my other advisors at the University of Virginia: Paul Cantor, Michael Levenson, and George Rutherglen. I thank the University itself for giving me the opportunity to work with such fine scholars and for providing me with financial asistance. For other valuable financial support during my studies in Charlottesville, I am grateful to my parents and the Social Sciences and Humanities Research Council of Canada. I would also like to thank the English Department staff, especially Ruth Estep, for their cheerful help. While at the University of Virginia I also benefitted from the assistance of John Kidd, who generously gave me access to his personal library and provided me with valuable Joycean conversation. My friend Tim Spurgin faithfully read all the draft material I produced. Jim Gibson, another friend, kindly designed a cover for my typescript and bolstered my confidence when I needed it.

Many librarians and archivists have also contributed to this book. I am particularly grateful to staff at the following institutions: the National Archives in Washington and Sutland, Maryland; the Golda Meir Library (Special Collections), University of Wisconsin–Milwaukee; the University Libraries (Poetry/Rare Books Collection), State University of New York at Buffalo; the Harvard Law Library; and the New York Public Library (Rare Books and Manuscripts Division). My understanding of the historical circumstances of the trials of *Ulysses* has also been enriched by persons unaffiliated with educational institutions, including Anne Freedgood, Judge Jeffrey Atlas, Dr Roy Coleman, Stephanie Goldstein, John R. Horan, John M. Woolsey, Jr, and Alexis Leon.

My current employer, The King's University College, has supported me during the completion of this project by providing me with financial assistance and by giving me the opportunity to work in a community of Christian scholars.

From the beginning of this project, I have tried to write a book that could be enjoyed by readers outside the academic world. Several persons fitting that description have generously read my typescript and made useful suggestions. I would therefore like to thank my mother, my father-in-law, Henry Fulton, and especially my cousin Maarten Ingen-Housz.

My greatest debt of gratitude is to my immediate family. To my children, Thomas, Julia, and Ryan, for the joy they have brought into my life. To Ellen, my wife, for accepting the burdens that my studies have placed on her, for supporting me in good times and bad, for reading everything I have written, and for teaching me that love is indeed patient. For all those who have made this book possible, and especially for her, I thank God.

The author gratefully acknowledges the permission of the following to include material in this book: the Estate of James Joyce, for excerpts from *Ulysses* and the published letters of James Joyce, copyright © the Estate of James Joyce; the Rosenbach Museum and Library, for passages from its fair manuscript copy of *Ulysses*; Alexis L. Leon, for excerpts from the letters of Paul Léon; Jonathan Hand Churchill, for material from the papers of Judge Learned Hand at the Harvard Law School Library; Phyllis Cerf Wagner, for quotations from the letters of Bennet Cerf; Division of Rare and Manuscript Collections, Cornell University Library, for the excerpt from Jane Heap's letter to James Joyce; A.P. Watt Ltd, agents, on behalf of Anne Yeats and Michael Yeats, for a passage from John Butler Yeats's correspondence with John Quinn; the Yale Collection of America Literature, Beinecke Rare Book and Manuscript Library, Yale University, for material from John Quinn's legal documents; New Directions Publishing Corporation, agents, on behalf of the Trustees of the Ezra Pound Literary Property Trust, for the quotation from Ezra Pound's letter to John Quinn, copyright © 1995 by the Trustees of the Ezra Pound Literary Property Trust; New Directions Publishing Corporation and Faber and Faber Ltd, for quotations from *The Letters of Ezra Pound to James Joyce*, copyright © 1967 by Ezra Pound; Judge Jeffrey Atlas, for material from an interview with the author; Penguin USA, for excerpts from the Viking edition of the *Letters of James Joyce*; the Estate of T.S. Eliot, for a quotation from Eliot's correspondence with John Quinn; Stephanie Goldstein, for material from the Morris L. Ernst Papers; Anne Freedgood, for the quotation from her letter to the author; Special Collections, Morris Library, Southern Illinois University at Carbondale, for material from the John Quinn papers in its Harley Croessmann Collection of James Joyce; Harvard Law School Library, for excerpts from the papers of Manley O. Hudson and Learned Hand; John R. Horan, for material from his correspondence with the author; John M. Woolsey, Jr, for excerpts from the letters of Judge John Woolsey in the Manley O. Hudson Papers, Harvard Law School Library; Rare Books and Manuscripts Division, The New York Public Library, for quotations from the letters of John Quinn in the John Quinn Memorial Collection.

Part of Chapter 5 has appeared in *Mosaic: A Journal for the Interdisciplinary Study of Literature*, ADVERSARIA: *Literature and Law* 27.4 (1994); part of Chapter 2 has appeared in the *James Joyce Quarterly* 32.3 (1995). Permission to reprint material from these articles is gratefully acknowledged.

Abbreviations

D&C	*The United States of America* vs. *One Book Entitled 'Ulysses' by James Joyce: Documents and Commentary – A 50-year Retrospective*, edited by Michael Moscato and Leslie LeBlanc (Maryland: University Publications of America, 1984).
JJ	Richard Ellmann, *James Joyce*, rev. edn (New York: Oxford, 1982).
LI	*Letters of James Joyce*, vol. I, ed. Stuart Gilbert (New York: Viking, 1957).
LII/III	*Letters of James Joyce*, vols II and III, ed. Richard Ellmann (New York: Viking, 1966).
MS	*Ulysses*: A Facsimile of the Manuscript, 3 vols (New York: Octagon, with the Philip H. and A.S.W. Rosenbach Foundation, 1975).
LR	*The Little Review* (New York).
P	*A Portrait of the Artist as a Young Man* (Middlesex: Penguin, 1981).
P/J	*The Letters of Ezra Pound to James Joyce, with Pound's Essays on Joyce*, ed. Forrest Read (New York: New Directions, 1965).
P 1930	*Ulysses* (Paris: Shakespeare & Company, 1930).
RH 1934	*Ulysses* (New York: Random House, 1934).
SH	*Stephen Hero*, ed. Theodore Spencer (New Directions, 1944).
U	*Ulysses* (New York: Random House, 1961).

List of Illustrations

Introduction

Ulysses, as James Joyce observed, was one of the world-disturbing sailors.[1] The episodes of the novel that appeared serially in New York in *The Little Review* commencing in March 1918 shocked many readers, provoking some to denounce Joyce and his publishers. According to the magazine's founding editor, Margaret Anderson, the following reaction was common:

> I think this is the most damnable slush and filth that ever polluted paper in print. ... There are no words I know to describe, even vaguely, how disgusted I am; not with the mire of his effusion but with all those whose minds are so putrid that they dare allow such muck and sewage of the human mind to besmirch the world by repeating it – and in print, through which medium it may reach young minds. Oh my God, the horror of it.[2]

Offense at *Ulysses* was by no means confined to philistines, vice-society crusaders, and government officials. Indeed, one of the great ironies of the trials of *Ulysses* is that the first censor of the novel was none other than Ezra Pound. As foreign editor of *The Little Review*, Pound had ostensibly sound practical reasons for deleting certain passages from the 'Calypso' episode of *Ulysses*, which describes in unprecedented detail Leopold Bloom's visit to the jakes (outhouse). After all, Pound did not want Joyce's work to be suppressed by Post Office officials. But he had other, more personal, reasons. In his correspondence with Joyce, he presented these as essentially esthetic. Underneath every esthetic, however, lie ethical, political, philosophical, or religious convictions, and Pound's was no exception: when Pound's objections to *Ulysses* are examined in light of the expurgations they were intended to justify, they appear to be little more than thinly disguised religious objections to Joyce's tendency to subvert hierarchies cherished by Pound, especially that which separates the erotic and excremental aspects of human sexuality.

Eventually, of course, came the Post Office suppressions that Pound wanted to avoid. On three occasions between March 1918 and January 1920, US Postal authorities in New York denied *The Little Review* access to the mails by revoking the magazine's second-class postage privileges. The Post Office censors struck first in January 1919 when *The Little Review* published the first section of the 'Lestrygonians' episode, which begins with a poke at the King of England – 'God. Save. Our. Sitting on his throne, sucking jujubes.'[3] – and proceeds to Leopold Bloom's recollections of an early amorous encounter with Molly, recollections

1

framed by Bloom's vision of two flies stuck copulating on the window-pane of the restaurant in which he has stopped to eat lunch. *Ulysses* crossed into forbidden territory once again in May 1919 with the appearance of the second half of the 'Scylla and Charybdis' episode, in spite of Margaret Anderson's attempt to evade the censors by expurgating its most controversial passages, which deal with incest, bestiality, and masturbation. *Ulysses* ran afoul of the Post Office authorities a third time in January 1920 when *The Little Review* published its third instalment of the 'Cyclops' episode, containing more derisive comments about British Royalty, notably King Edward VII – 'There's a bloody sight more pox than pax about that boyo'[4] – and an incisive condemnation of British imperialism, in particular its sinister use of Christianity.

According to Jackson R. Bryer,[5] the Post Office suppressed *The Little Review* a fourth time, some time after the appearance of the magazine's July–August 1920 number containing the portion of the 'Nausicaa' episode in which Bloom, sexually aroused in the course of his stroll on the beach by the provocations of Gertrude MacDowell, masturbates in his pants. Ironically, if the Post Office *had* suppressed the July–August number altogether, the prosecution of the magazine's editors – not to mention the banning of *Ulysses* – might have been averted. There can be no doubt, however, that Post Office officials allowed some copies of the number to slip through the mails unmolested. In doing so, they sent *Ulysses* to encounter its most formidable enemy yet, John Sumner, the Secretary of the New York Society for the Suppression of Vice.

Responsibility for that encounter rests squarely with Margaret Anderson. Desirous of increasing subscriptions, she sent an unsolicited copy of the July–August number to the daughter of a prominent New York lawyer. Thus, just as Homer's storm-tossed hero was welcomed on the shores of Phaecia by the daughter of King Alcinous, Princess Nausicaa, so Joyce's *Ulysses* was received into the domestic realm by a privileged young woman. Unlike Homer's heroine, however, the lawyer's daughter was offended by the stranger's nakedness. She complained to her father, who drew the case to the attention of the District Attorney of New York County, Joseph Forrester, who in turn sought the advice of the expert in such matters: *Ulysses* was thus brought to the exacting moral attention of John Sumner.

Sumner was not amused. As Secretary of the Vice Society, he must have believed that the episode of *Ulysses* before him constituted a double violation of the young person he was sworn to protect. The first offence was committed when the July–August instalment of *Ulysses* penetrated the domestic realm to corrupt the lawyer's daughter with a story of sexual perversity. The second had been perpetrated earlier, when Joyce wrote an episode dramatizing an encounter between another young person, Gerty MacDowell, and another man of the world, Leopold Bloom. The gravity of this second offense undoubtedly lay not so much in Bloom's immorality as in the young person's impurity: she was not the innocent of the Victorian imagination. Thus, Sumner objected explicitly to the passage explaining that Gerty knows about the passion of men like Bloom because her friend Bertha has told her about 'the gentleman lodger that ... had pictures ... of those skirt dancers and ... used to do something not very nice that you could imagine sometimes in the bed.'[6] Likewise he took offence at Bloom's claim that Gerty was aware that Bloom was masturbating as she swung her legs to and fro: 'Did she know what I? Course.'[7] In other words, Sumner must have recognized that Joyce was assaulting the very foundation of the Vice Society's existence. And he acted accordingly, by advising the Assistant District Attorney to prosecute the editors of *The Little Review* for publishing obscenity.

John Quinn, legal counsel for the editors, strove to convince first Sumner and then the courts that *Ulysses*, or rather the offending portion of 'Nausicaa,' was not guilty as charged. Sumner, however, was not to be moved. As for the courts, Quinn made his first defense of *Ulysses* on 21 October 1920 at a preliminary hearing in Magistrate's Court before Judge Joseph E. Corrigan. Corrigan was interested in Quinn's argument, which included the claim that 'an innocent person would not understand the sex allusions and therefore could not be corrupted by them'; none the less, the judge ruled that '"the episode where the man went off in his pants, which no one could misunderstand,"' was '"smutty, filthy within the meaning of the statute."'[8] He was therefore obliged to hold the defendants over for trial in the Court of Special Sessions.

The judges there, Frederick Kernochan, James McInerney, and Joseph Moss, were more hostile than Corrigan and less interested in Quinn's arguments. Even so, Quinn believed at one point in the proceedings that he had won them over. The District Attorney had just finished reading the passages that Sumner had previously deemed unfit for the ear of the court (censorship trials abound with such irony). '"*I offer*,"' said Quinn, '"*Mr. Forrester in evidence as the defendants' chief exhibit.* Just look at him, still gasping for breath at the conclusion of his denunciation, his face distorted with rage, his whole aspect apoplectic. Is he filled with lewd desires? ... Not at all."'[9] The judges laughed ... then convicted Anderson and Heap, fining each $50 and enjoining them from publishing any more of *Ulysses*. Thus on 21 February 1921 Joyce's novel was effectively banned from the United States.

Since *Ulysses* could not be published in the United States, or for that matter in England, where the printers had steadfastly refused to set type for the novel, Joyce accepted Sylvia Beach's offer to have Shakespeare & Company publish it in Paris. In light of his previous difficulties with the censors, the Paris publication of *Ulysses* represented a major victory for Joyce, but the trials of *Ulysses* were still far from over: soon after the appearance of the novel in France (in February 1922), the US ban was duplicated by England, Ireland, Canada, and Australia. By the end of 1922 virtually the entire English-speaking world was united in opposition to *Ulysses*, a state of affairs which prompted Joyce to claim that he deserved a Nobel peace prize. In the following years, customs officials in those countries actively confiscated and destroyed Joyce's novel. Officials in the United States and England were especially vigilant: of the 2000 copies of the Egoist Press's 1922 edition, some 500 were confiscated by Post Office authorities in New York; and of the 500 copies of the second edition (printed to replace the copies lost to the US Post Office) 499 were seized and eventually destroyed by English Customs officials in Folkestone.

US Customs and British Home Office records indicate that individual attempts to import copies of *Ulysses* were routinely frustrated by government authorities. F.R. Leavis discovered as much in 1926 when he requested permission to import a copy of *Ulysses* for use in his course 'Modern Problems in Criticism.' In return Leavis got a call from the Vice Chancellor of Cambridge University, who had been contacted by a Director of Public Prosecution strongly opposed to Leavis's lecturing on *Ulysses*, especially to women. Leavis was not disciplined by the Vice Chancellor; none the less, he never obtained permission to import a copy of *Ulysses*. By the early 1930s government officials in the USA and England had begun to admit exceptions to the general ban if sufficient cause could be established. In the USA, as in England, the first recorded legal importer of *Ulysses* was a physician who wanted the novel for 'scientific' purposes.

The decisive turning point in the fortunes of *Ulysses* came in 1932 when Bennett Cerf of Random House, prompted by the prominent civil liberties lawyer Morris Ernst, decided to engage Ernst to initiate a legal proceeding designed to lift the US ban on Joyce's novel. Ernst promptly arranged for the importation of a copy of the Paris edition of *Ulysses*, ensured that the book was seized by US Customs, and then contested the seizure. So began *The United States of America Against One Book Entitled 'ULYSSES'*. The trials of *Ulysses* had reached epic proportions. And like all good epics, *US* vs. *'Ulysses'* abounded with lively complications and ironic reversals.

Perhaps the greatest irony was that the government officials who ostensibly wanted the ban on *Ulysses* to continue, US Attorney George Medalie's assistants Sam Coleman and Nicholas Atlas, were actually inclined to see it lifted. Their written arguments against *Ulysses*, which were never actually submitted to the Court, read at times like sensitive critical defenses of the novel. Moreover, although Sam Coleman had marked as obscene more than 250 passages in the seized copy of *Ulysses* (which he did submit to the Court), he chose not to read these passages in court, allegedly because of the presence there of a woman, who happened to be Ernst's wife. Ernst's elaborate brief in defense of *Ulysses* was infinitely more methodical and principled than the written arguments of his opponents; and, needless to say, Ernst submitted the brief to the Court. Furthermore, Ernst's courtroom performance was more inspired than that of his opponent, which is hardly surprising, since Ernst believed wholeheartedly in his endeavor.

Having heard the arguments of both sides, Judge John M. Woolsey ruled in Ernst's favour. On 6 December 1933, he declared that *Ulysses* was not legally obscene and could therefore be admitted to the United States. So ended the US ban on Joyce's troublesome sailor; after thirteen years of storm, *Ulysses* finally found a friendly port in the English-speaking world. Once again, other English-speaking countries would soon follow the United States, but not before *Ulysses* had narrowly survived yet another courtroom trial, this time in the New York Court of Appeals.

That trial was initiated by Medalie's successor to the post of US Attorney, Martin Conboy, a former member of the New York Society for the Suppression of Vice who was as passionately opposed to *Ulysses* as Ernst was for it. Conboy, aided by Assistant US Attorney Francis H. Horan, argued his case against *Ulysses* in front of Judges Augustus Hand, Learned Hand, and Martin Manton. Conboy's best efforts notwithstanding, Ernst once again prevailed: in a majority decision Judges Augustus and Learned Hand voted to affirm Woolsey's finding. Judge Manton, however, dissented. Encouraged no doubt by Manton's dissent, Conboy filed for the Attorney General's permission to take the *Ulysses* case to the Supreme Court. This time, however, he was turned down. The formal trials of *Ulysses* were at an end. Conboy withdrew from the field.

Sumner, however, a crusader to the end, fought on. Appropriately, his words are the last in the Department of Justice file pertaining to the *Ulysses* case: 'the good old American fighting spirit is lacking,' he wrote, 'when the Department fails to follow up a hard-won partial victory in a district where "broadmindedness" seems to be considered a judicial virtue.'[10] A number of the English-speaking countries that had shunned *Ulysses* took even longer than Sumner to give up the fight. Ireland lifted its exclusion order regarding *Ulysses* later in 1934. England opened its borders in 1936, thus making way for publication of the Bodley Head edition. Australia lifted the ban on the novel in 1937 – only to lower it again in 1941. The most belated country of all was Canada, where *Ulysses* was not legally available until 1949.

The present work, the first book-length study of the censorship of *Ulysses*, is based on extensive archival research and a number of personal interviews which have led to important discoveries and made possible original insights into the nature and significance of what is surely one of the most important (and poorly understood) censorship cases in modern times. Several discoveries deserve mention here.

Hitherto unexamined US Post Office records reveal that the motives behind the postal suppressions were not only moral but political. The Post Office's 'List of Periodicals, Pamphlets, Circulars, Etc., Held to Be Non-Mailable, January 18, 1918,' for example, identifies *The Little Review* as 'a Publication of Anarchistic tendency.' Other Post Office records indicate that when the magazine was suppressed for publishing Wyndham Lewis's short story 'Cantleman's Spring Mate' in October of 1917, the suppression was carried out under the authority of the Espionage Act of 1917, a piece of legislation drafted and applied for the purpose of eradicating sedition and other forms of political dissent. The presence in the Post Office's file on the October 1917 suppression of *The Little Review* – classed, incidentally, under the rubric of 'Subversive Literature, WWI' – of documents pertaining to the later suppressions of *Ulysses* suggests that government authorities must have read Joyce's novel as a supreme example of literary bolshevism.

Personal interviews with the descendants of US Attorneys Coleman, Atlas, and Horan, records of the US Department of Justice in the National Archives, and pre-conference memoranda in the Learned Hand papers at Harvard reveal the extent to which personal conviction – especially religious – influenced the trials of *Ulysses*. My interview with Judge Jeffrey Atlas, for example, disclosed that Nicholas Atlas was probably largely responsible for the government's sympathetic attitude toward *Ulysses* in the 1932–3 proceeding. As a young man who spent a good deal of time in Greenwich Village, he had encountered *Ulysses* during its serial publication and, like many of his generation, he cherished Joyce's novel as a liberating work of art: he was not inclined to see it suppressed. Conboy's unpublished letter requesting the Attorney General's permission to contest the Woolsey decision confirms that Ernst was not entirely mistaken in suspecting that the government's objections to *Ulysses* included the charge of blasphemy. The pre-trial memorandum written by Judge Martin Manton, also unpublished, betrays similarly religious objections to both *Ulysses* and the Woolsey decision.

One last source deserves mention, in part for the light it sheds on the late trials of *Ulysses* and in part because of the way it has been ignored by legal and literary scholars. The source I have in mind is the copy of *Ulysses* which Ernst arranged to have imported from France, seized, and introduced as the sole piece of evidence in the 1932–3 proceeding in New

York. This book, along with the critical opinions which Ernst had pasted inside its covers, was eventually read by Assistant US Attorney Sam Coleman, who marked in its margins all the passages he deemed obscene by the standards of the day; it thus represents the best record of the nature of the government's case against *Ulysses*. I have drawn on this unique source in various places in my account of the trials; furthermore, I have included all passages marked as objectionable by the Assistant US Attorney in the Appendix. Entitled 'The Censor's *Ulysses*,' it contains a list of all passages censored by the authorities who objected to Joyce's novel between 1918 and 1934, and thus makes possible for the first time a comprehensive understanding of those aspects of the novel responsible for the controversy surrounding its publication.

To my knowledge, the imported copy of *Ulysses* has not been cited by a single legal or literary scholar, although its location in the Rare Books Library at Columbia University has been well known ever since Bennett Cerf deposited it there in 1934. This lack of attention to a crucial historical document suggests that scholars have had some difficulty in taking seriously the US government's objections to *Ulysses*, not to mention the censorship of *Ulysses* in general. Since this difficulty may well constitute an obstacle to appreciation of the arguments developed in the present study, I would like to address its likely cause here before proceeding to outline the arguments themselves.

As far as I have been able to ascertain, difficulty in taking the censorship of *Ulysses* seriously is rooted in scepticism at the idea that parts of *Ulysses* were and are obscene. The grounds for such scepticism would seem to lie in the view that obscenity is a fantasy created by our prudish Victorian forebears, one which we have mercifully moved beyond. Readers inclined to embrace this view would do well to remember that Joyce himself considered parts of *Ulysses* obscene. 'Penelope,' he wrote, is 'probably more obscene than any preceding episode.'[11] This is not to suggest that Joyce accepted the definition of obscenity implied in Queen Victoria's allegedly advising a daughter repulsed at the thought of sexual intercourse with her husband to lie still and think of England. The Victorians and their twentieth-century sympathizers (including, incidentally, Judge Woolsey himself in so far as he defined as obscene anything 'tending to stir the sex impulses') could be excessively prudish; they were inclined to detect obscenity in the most innocent representations of human sexuality, especially where there was any hint of sexual pleasure. Writers like Joyce not only rejected but attacked this Puritanical confusion of the erotic with the obscene. Like him, most moderns have moved beyond the Victorian understanding of obscenity, and have done well to do so. But this does not mean that obscenity, properly defined, is absent from Joyce's novel; nor does it mean that obscenity is a thing of the past.

To the contrary, obscenity is alive and well in our day. In *Working*, Studs Terkel uses the term 'obscenities' to describe the actions of American and European tourists whose manipulative photography of black South African villagers amounts to a *'stealing of the spirit,'* a process whereby human beings are stripped of their dignity and reduced to objects for someone else's gratification.[12] In *The Handmaid's Tale*, Margaret Atwood defines obscenity as language that diminishes the persons to whom it refers. Thus the central character of the novel, the handmaid Offred, writes, 'There is something powerful in the whispering of obscenities, about those in power. ... It deflates them, reduces them to the common denominator where they can be dealt with.'[13] One might add that it also reminds human beings that they are physical creatures, not angels, which helps to explain why satirists like Rabelais, Swift, and Joyce are so fond of it.

Both Terkel's and Atwood's definitions are worth keeping in mind when considering the case of *Ulysses*. So, of course, is Judge Woolsey's. Parts of *Ulysses* are certainly obscene according to Woolsey's Victorian definition; parts are obscene in Atwood's useful and salutary sense; other parts, it seems to me, are obscene according to Terkel's definition, sometimes in ways which reveal Joyce's awareness of the human being's ability to strip others of their dignity, sometimes in ways which suggest that Joyce himself is doing the stripping. The obscenity in *Ulysses* will be discussed further in the course of this book; the point being made here is simply that obscenity is something more than a Victorian fantasy.

In addition to recounting the story of the trials of *Ulysses* with unprecedented attention to the available evidence, the present work develops two original lines of argument regarding the significance and relevance of the trials in the history of law and literature. The first argument may be described provisionally as legal, the second as literary, as iong as it is understood that the two are intimately related and that neither can be extricated from the other. Indeed, as I hope will become abundantly clear in what follows, the importance of the trials of *Ulysses* lies ultimately in their ability to call into question the idea that literature enjoys an autonomy that puts it beyond either the concerns or the influence of the law – or, for that matter, any other aspect of human existence.

The legal argument developed here grew out of my reading of the Woolsey decision, which I encountered in the preface to the Random House edition of *Ulysses*. Woolsey's decision, I realized, was based on a theory of literature radically different from that which had traditionally provided the basis for such decisions. Upon investigating the trial documents, I discovered that the theory underlying the Woolsey decision had been central to Ernst's defense of *Ulysses*. The extent to which Ernst's arguments differed from traditional defenses in such cases can be ascertained most directly by comparing the *Ulysses* case of 1932–3 to the 1857 trial of Flaubert for the writing and publication of *Madame Bovary*.[14]

The prosecution in the Flaubert trial contended that Flaubert, in writing and publishing *Madame Bovary*, had corrupted the morals of the public. More specifically, the prosecution claimed that *Madame Bovary* encouraged vice by celebrating (or at least by refusing to condemn) Emma Bovary's adultery. Flaubert's defense countered the moral arguments of the prosecution with a moral argument of its own: the effect of *Madame Bovary*, the defense attorney claimed, was '*l'excitation à la vertu par l'horreur du vice*' (the encouragement of virtue through the horror of vice).[15] Both prosecution and defense were willing to acknowledge that *Madame Bovary* was a novel of substantial artistry; none the less, they based their arguments for or against Flaubert on moral grounds. Both prosecution and defense believed that *Madame Bovary* influenced its readers morally; for both the question to be answered was whether the moral effect was good or bad.

This common ground prevailed through the Victorian period and into the twentieth century. It forms the basis of the early trials of *Ulysses* in *The Little Review*. Like Flaubert's prosecutor, Sumner and District Attorney Forrester levelled moral charges against the editors of *The Little Review*, claiming that the portion of *Ulysses* they had published was 'obscene, lewd, lascivious' etc.[16] And like Flaubert's legal counsel, Quinn countered with a series of moral arguments, including the idea that the 'strong hard filth' of Joyce would 'brace and deter' rather than corrupt.[17] The evidence indicates, however, that by the 1920s this common moral ground was becoming somewhat unstable. Thus, Margaret Anderson claimed that 'the words "literature" and "obscenity" can not be used in conjunction.'[18] Even Quinn seemed at times inclined to argue the idea that literature, in so far as it was indeed literature, could not in fact corrupt. Quinn, however, did not really believe in the truth of this argument and fell back on the same moral ground as his opponents.

In the 1932–3 *Ulysses* case, this common ground disappeared. Thus, while the government levelled a traditional moral charge against Joyce's novel, claiming that it was obscene and would therefore corrupt its readers, Morris Ernst countered with an argument based substantially on an esthetic theory of art according to which *Ulysses*, in so far as it was a genuine work of art, could not influence its readers for ill. According to the esthetic theory, moral questions simply do not apply to literary works. Oscar Wilde expresses the idea succinctly in the preface to *The Picture of Dorian Gray*: 'There is no such thing as a moral or an immoral book. Books are well written, or badly written. That is all.'[19] In keeping with the logic of the esthetic theory, the real burden of Ernst's defense was not to prove that the moral effect of *Ulysses* was beneficial but rather to establish that *Ulysses* was a genuine work of art. In practical terms, Ernst's case hinged on his ability to get Woolsey to adopt the perspective of literary critics who recognized the artistic merit of *Ulysses* – especially those critics who, like Ernst, were inclined to believe that artistic merit and obscenity could not co-exist. Ernst's awareness of this fact is revealed throughout his written and oral arguments, but is most clearly epitomized in his decision to have a number of critical opinions pasted inside the covers of the copy of *Ulysses* which was to become the sole piece of evidence in the proceeding, a stratagem which ensured that Woolsey could not but accept such opinion as integral to an understanding of the novel.

In his decision Woolsey made it clear that he had indeed accepted the relevance of the critical opinion that Ernst had recommended to his attention and, more importantly, that he had interpreted it in exactly the manner in which Ernst had hoped he would. Woolsey based his finding that *Ulysses* was not legally obscene on a number of what Leslie Fiedler has referred to as 'well-intentioned lies,'[20] four to be precise: first, that there is an absolute and essential difference between literature and obscenity or pornography; second, that the artist's primary intention, the perfection of the work to be made, is his only intention (a view which excludes moral, political, or other intentions); third, that the effect of a work of art as a whole is necessarily the effect of any one of its parts (it follows that because *Ulysses* as a whole is not obscene or aphrodisiac it is nowhere obscene, nowhere aphrodisiac); and fourth, that the effect of works of literature like *Ulysses* on the average reader (Woolsey's *'homme moyen sensuel'*) is always esthetic stasis, never belief or action (implied in this principle is the idea that those who respond to literary works kinetically are simply poor readers).

The presence of these well-intentioned lies in Woolsey's decision in no way undermines his finding that *Ulysses* was not legally obscene by the standards of 1933. As the decision of the Court of Appeals made clear, Woolsey was entirely correct in his finding. Yet the validity of Woolsey's finding does not change the fact that he reached it through well-intentioned lies. The lies were well-intentioned because Woolsey used them to achieve a legitimate and good end, namely, the liberation of one of the greatest literary works of the twentieth century. They were none the less lies because they misrepresented the nature of *Ulysses* and, implicitly, literature in general. And they did so precisely in so far as they gave consummate expression to the esthetic theory of art employed by Ernst and a number of the critics on whom he had relied.

Woolsey's well-intentioned lies thereby point to the importance of the trials of *Ulysses* in legal (and, of course, literary) history, for the Woolsey decision, as far as I have been able to ascertain, represents the first major legal victory of the esthetic theory of art. The theory had been articulated long before Woolsey's time, notably by Théophile Gautier in literature and Immanuel Kant in philosophy, and had been embraced by many writers of the nineteenth century, including Baudelaire, Flaubert, Pater, and Wilde. But not until Woolsey's decision did it succeed in supplanting the traditional moral/esthetic view of art as the law of a Western liberal democracy.

In light of the appeal from the Woolsey decision in 1934, one might be inclined to claim that the victory of the esthetic view of art was short-lived, but the claim would be misleading. It is true that the decision of the majority judges of the Court of Appeals affirms Woolsey's finding (that is, that *Ulysses* is not obscene according to the standards of the day) without embracing fully either Woolsey's esthetic principles or his application thereof to *Ulysses*. It is also true that the Court of Appeals decision is more authoritative than Woolsey's by virtue of its provenance from a higher court. (Moreover, as I contend toward the end of the legal argument I am sketching out here, the Court of Appeals decision is superior to Woolsey's in both its legal reasoning and its literary sensitivity; indeed, its balanced view of *Ulysses* represents a viable middle way between Woolsey's estheticism and Manton's Platonism.) None the less, it is Woolsey's decision that has the higher profile in contemporary culture: when the American Civil Liberties Union cites the *Ulysses* case it refers not to the decision of the higher court but to that of Judge Woolsey. And, like the reputation of the Woolsey decision, the esthetic theory of literature has lived on, not just in the USA but in Western liberal democracies as a whole.

It is precisely the longevity of the esthetic theory of literature that points to the relevance of the Woolsey decision for our day. That relevance lies not in the decision's direct influence on contemporary case law (even the Appeals decision has long been superseded by Supreme Court decisions which place literary censorship more clearly in the context of freedom of speech as protected, for example, by the First Amendment to the US Constitution) or even on the way we think about censorship and freedom of literary speech, but rather in the way it reveals the shortcomings of the esthetic theory as a foundation for commitment to freedom of speech. Collectively, Woolsey's well-intentioned lies imply that a genuine work of literature can have no harmful effect, whether moral, political, or religious, on the beliefs and actions of its readers. And therein rests their misrepresentation of the proper basis for freedom of speech: according to Woolsey and others who would defend artistic freedom by appealing to the esthetic view of art, the proper basis for freedom of speech in the arts is the idea that art affects nothing, subverts nothing, strengthens nothing. That idea not only deprives literature of its

power to influence its readers and thus renders the controversy surrounding the publication of *Ulysses* either nonsensical or incomprehensible, but also fails to provide a lasting foundation for freedom of speech.
We need to be aware of the limitations of the esthetic theory of literature
in this regard, for it continues to figure prominently in contemporary
censorship debates, the controversy surrounding *The Satanic Verses* being
a case in point.

Having sketched the salient features of the legal line of argument
developed in the present work, I turn now to the literary. The literary
argument, like the legal, originated in my reading of the Woolsey decision or, more specifically, my recognition that the Woolsey decision, in
addition to being a legal opinion, is also a literary criticism of *Ulysses* –
and an important one at that. By virtue of its inclusion in both the US
and English editions of Joyce's novel (in 1934 and 1936 respectively),
Woolsey's decision became one of the most widely circulated criticisms
of *Ulysses*. More importantly, it proved – also because of its inclusion in
US and English editions of *Ulysses* – that the censorship had profoundly
influenced the reception of the novel. Realizing that the Woolsey decision was only one of many examples of such influence, I began to inves-
tigate in more general terms the effect of the censorship on the reception
of *Ulysses*.

I was thus led back to the early trials and the talk (later an article) that
'set the key for the critical reception' of *Ulysses*,[21] namely, that which
Valèry Larbaud delivered some months after the definitive suppression
of the serial version of the novel in the United States and shortly before
the publication of the Shakespeare & Company edition in Paris. In examining Larbaud's talk, however, I was surprised to discover that the question of the influence of the censorship on the reception of *Ulysses* could
not be answered adequately before a more fundamental question had
been addressed, namely, What was the effect of censorship on the
writing and revising of *Ulysses*? The bridge between these two major
aspects of the censorship of *Ulysses* is the famous schema of the novel
which Joyce gave to Larbaud for use in his talk.

The function of the schema emerges clearly in light of the primary
rhetorical purpose of Larbaud's talk: to defend *Ulysses* against the
charges of obscenity and anarchy by emphasizing the novel's elaborate
schematic correspondences as proof of its coherence and unity as a work
of art and, at the same time, by shifting attention from the novel's controversial content to its stylistic artifice. In light of Joyce's active involvement in preparations for Larbaud's talk, and his apparent approval of
Larbaud's defensive use of the schema, it is surely significant that while
Larbaud was using the schema to emphasize the schematic correspondences of *Ulysses*, Joyce was using it to guide his writing and revision of

the novel, elaborating the very schematic elements that Larbaud was emphasizing. Given the defensive use to which Joyce encouraged Larbaud to put the schema, I wondered, is it not possible that Joyce elaborated the schematic elements of his novel for similarly defensive reasons? In other words, is it not possible that the censorship of *Ulysses* influenced not only the reception of the novel but also its very shape? To both questions my answer is yes.

Although Joyce's critics are virtually unanimous in emphasizing the fact that Joyce's art was intimately related to his life experience, only Michael Groden has asked similar questions and given a similar answer. Yet Groden's answer, admirably perceptive in suspecting that the censorship may have 'changed the shape of *Ulysses*,'[22] is based only on Groden's surmise that the suppression of *Ulysses* in *The Little Review*, in so far as it freed Joyce from the need to meet deadlines, probably contributed to the inordinate length of the 'Circ,' (Ithaca) and 'Penelope' episodes. Groden's answer, in other words, does not reflect an awareness of the defensive function of the schema; nor, therefore, does it provide an accurate account of the concrete ways the censorship influenced the shape of *Ulysses*.

Given the willingness of Joyce's critics to recognize the close connection between Joyce's art and the vicissitudes of his life, their lack of attention to the influence of censorship on *Ulysses* and on Joyce's art as a whole is remarkable. Joyce's struggle with the censor, after all, cannot be construed as a minor episode in his adventures as an artist. That struggle was a vital part of Joyce's experience long before he attempted to publish *Dubliners*, but even if Grant Richards's rejection of that work – in 1906 – is taken as the beginning of the struggle, it is easy to appreciate its prominence in Joyce's artistic career. In the course of the twenty-seven years following 1906 – during which time Joyce wrote the last stories of *Dubliners*, transformed *Stephen Hero* into *A Portrait of the Artist as a Young Man*, wrote all of *Ulysses* and most of *Finnegans Wake* – Joyce worked with at least one of his major works effectively censored. In the light of his tendency to embody his personal experience in his art, it is difficult to imagine that his prolonged conflict with the censor did not exert a significant influence on the shape of his literary creations.

As the previous paragraph implies, while the question of the effect of the censorship on the writing and revising of *Ulysses* can be approached directly by examining the role of the schema in Joyce's late work on the novel, it cannot be fully answered outside the context of Joyce's journey from the 'nicely polished looking-glass' of *Dubliners* to the obscurity of *Finnegans Wake*.[23] Regarded from its beginning in works of naturalistic prose like *Dubliners*, this journey is towards an increasingly radical style of exile in which naturalism is replaced by symbolism, direct engagement by withdrawal. Regarded from its ending in *Finnegans Wake* (the work in which Joyce finally succeeded in evading the censor once and for all), the journey is Joyce's prolonged attempt at 'making obscenity safe for literature' (see Chapter 3) – without, it should be stressed, abandoning his commitment to complete self-expression. Either view suffices to indicate that the development of Joyce's art was profoundly influenced by the censorship, and from either view *Ulysses* emerges as a decisive turning point in Joyce's artistic journey: as Walton Litz has observed, Joyce travelled from *Dubliners* to *Finnegans Wake* in *Ulysses*.[24]

Having analyzed the effect of censorship on the writing and revising of *Ulysses*, I proceeded from Larbaud's talk to examine the effect of the censorship on the reception of *Ulysses*. As previously mentioned, Larbaud's talk 'set the key for the critical reception' by shifting attention from the provocative content of the novel to its elaborate form, its schematic complexity. It thus occupies a prominent place in what may be loosely called the tradition of critical (as opposed to legal or editorial) censorship of *Ulysses*. That tradition, which actually begins in the essays of Ezra Pound, is characterized by the critic's strategic suppression or avoidance of the controversial elements of Joyce's novel. The extent and influence of this misrepresentation should not be underestimated, especially in light of the fact that the critical reception of *Ulysses* preceded the general availability of the novel by almost thirteen years. By the time *Ulysses* was finally published in the United States in 1934, no less than seven books on the novel were in wide circulation. The most influential of these was undoubtedly Stuart Gilbert's *James Joyce's Ulysses* (1930). Like Larbaud, Gilbert 'leaned backwards to emphasize [the novel's] elaborate form.'[25] He did so by highlighting the schematic elements of the novel while scrupulously avoiding mention of the passages which had figured prominently in the early trials. More than any other critical work on *Ulysses*, Gilbert's book played a crucial role in Ernst's defense of the novel as well as in Woolsey's decision, where its claims regarding the fundamental incompatibility between literature and obscenity are unmistakably echoed.

As the textual history of Stuart Gilbert's book makes clear, the influence of critical books written while *Ulysses* was still under ban did not cease when the ban was lifted in 1934. Books such as Gilbert's are still widely read. Furthermore, the production of critical works written in the tradition of critical censorship continued long after the legal censorship of *Ulysses* came to an end. Richard Ellmann's biography of Joyce is a prime example. In that work Ellmann is sometimes admirably direct in dealing with controversial aspects of Joyce's personal life, but he is remarkably circumspect about the controversial aspects of *Ulysses*. He never troubles to examine the censored portions of the novel, and when he quotes from *Ulysses*, he quotes a bowdlerized version. It is undoubtedly Ellmann who is most responsible for the view that although Joyce's art was profoundly affected by small incidents in his personal life, it was never affected by the censorship.

The effect of the tradition of critical censorship engendered by the legal censorship of *Ulysses* has been to divert attention from the very aspects of the novel that provoked the controversy surrounding its publication and, in doing so, to postpone a truly balanced assessment of *Ulysses*, one that affirms both its insurrectionary, anarchic fire and its ordered, formal complexity; its obscenity and its spirituality. The tradition of critical censorship has also diverted attention from the task of understanding the influence of the legal censorship on the very shape of Joyce's novel. Most importantly, the tradition of critical censorship has obscured the vital relation between *Ulysses* and Joyce's struggle with the authorities who censored it, thereby according to *Ulysses* an autonomy from the complications of life that it does not possess.

The fallacy of the idea of *Ulysses* as an autonomous literary text is evident at every turn in the arguments of the present work, as outlined above, but is most clearly and economically disclosed in the Woolsey decision. By virtue of its presence in the US and English editions of *Ulysses*, the Woolsey decision testifies to the intimate connection between the censorship and the novel. Furthermore, because Woolsey's decision is both a legal opinion that marks a significant turning point in the history of censorship and a literary criticism that encourages a particular reading of Joyce's novel, it points to the connection between the way we read literature and the way we legislate to protect values as fundamental to our culture as freedom of speech. Ultimately, then, the Woolsey decision attests to the value of a sound understanding of the trials of *Ulysses*, for it reminds us of the critical relation between the way we read and the way we live.

1

Ulysses at War

Upon reading the first three episodes of *Ulysses*, Ezra Pound foresaw that Joyce's novel would run afoul of censors on both sides of the Atlantic: 'I suppose we'll be damn well suppressed,' he wrote to Joyce, 'if we print the text as it stands.'[1] Yet the risk of suppression, Pound added, was well worth running because of the brilliance of Joyce's art. As foreign editor of *The Little Review*, Pound conveyed both opinions to Margaret Anderson in New York. According to Anderson, Pound praised Joyce's work highly, but warned that 'it would probably involve [them] in difficulties with the censors.'[2] Anderson agreed on both counts. Upon reading the opening lines of the third episode ('Proteus') – 'Ineluctable modality of the visible: at least that if no more, thought through my eyes. Signatures of all things I am here to read, seaspawn and seawrack, the nearing tide' – she declared, 'This is the most beautiful thing we'll ever have.'[3] In the same breath she implicitly acknowledged that publishing *Ulysses* would involve a struggle with the censors: 'We'll print it if it's the last effort of our lives.'

Anderson was no stranger to such struggles; they had, in fact, inspired the founding of her magazine. The decisive encounter with the censor had occurred in 1912, while Anderson was literary editor at *The Continent*, a Presbyterian magazine in Chicago that expected 'moral rather than literary judgments' from its reviewers.[4] She discovered the strictness of this expectation when she judged Dreiser's *Sister Carrie* to be simply fine work. The magazine's readers (mostly fathers, according to Anderson) sent a storm of letters protesting at her failure to mention that the novel's subject matter was immoral. *Sister Carrie*, they said, was the story of a girl who went astray and was therefore inappropriate reading for the young (especially, of course, young daughters). The editor of *The Continent* agreed. He advised Anderson to avoid the problem in future by stating 'the facts as they were.'[5] Infuriated, she quit *The Continent* and founded *The Little Review*. The year was 1914: as the war to make the world safe for democracy was about to begin in Europe, Anderson and her magazine began their war 'to make the world safe for Art.'[6]

In the first number Anderson predicted, '*The Little Review* ... shall enjoy that untrammelled liberty which is the life of Art.'[7] According to Ben Hecht, *The Little Review* succeeded in becoming a work of art: 'I have met many things in my life that were Art, but they were always Art plus something else – Art plus fame, money, vanity, success, politics, complexes, etc. *The Little Review* was, nakedly and innocently, Art.'[8] But the magazine's suppression by government authorities on five occasions indicates that it never achieved the 'untrammelled liberty' that Anderson took to be art's birthright. The reason is not hard to find: contrary to Hecht's assertion, *The Little Review* was 'Art plus something else,' and that something else was politics. In the broadest sense, the magazine was political because it was opposed to laws which subordinated artistic freedom to moral, political, and religious values. In a more obvious sense, it was political because it supported anarchist leaders like Emma Goldman.

That support reached its height in the December 1915 number of *The Little Review*, where Anderson joined Goldman in a call for revolution. Goldman encouraged readers of the magazine to oppose the military preparedness campaign of men like Theodore Roosevelt and to 'organize the preparedness of the masses for the overthrow of both capitalism and the state.'[9] In 'Toward Revolution,' Anderson reacted to the execution of union activist Joe Hill by asking, 'why didn't someone shoot the governor of Utah before he could shoot Joe Hill? ... Why doesn't some one arrange for the beating-up of the police squad? ... For God's sake, why doesn't some one start the Revolution?'[10] Anderson's editorial caused a scandal in Chicago: the District Attorney there told a Chicago *Tribune* reporter that he would prosecute Anderson and *The Little Review* as soon as the Post Office authorities gave the word.[11]

Over the next two years *The Little Review* would retreat from overt political engagement and concentrate on its war to make the world safe for art. Anderson acknowledged the change of direction in the March 1916 number: 'The Little Review is a magazine of Art and Revolution. If you ask me which it believes in most I shall have to say – Art. Because there is no revolution unless it is born of the same spirit which produces real art.'[12] Even this renunciation of politics, however, acknowledged a connection between politics and art, one which was destined to become stronger – and more vexing – after the USA entered the war in April 1917. The US Post Office's suppression of the October 1917 number of *The Little Review*, mainly because it contained Wyndham Lewis's story 'Cantleman's Spring Mate,' makes this clear.

That suppression occurred on 2 November 1917, the same day that a New York Court of Appeals upheld Postmaster Burleson's decision to suspend the mailing privileges of *The Masses* because its opposition to the war allegedly violated the provisions of the Espionage Act (which provided severe penalties for those who 'wilfully cause ... refusal of duty in the military or naval forces of the United States').[13] The decision of the Court of Appeals overruled Judge Learned Hand's injunction

against the Post Office, issued on the grounds that the magazine's criticism of conscription and the war stopped short of counselling resistance
to the law.[14] The Court of Appeals held that it was not necessary to
demonstrate overt counsel to perform illegal acts.[15] The effect of this
decision 'was to establish the old-time doctrine of remote bad tendency
in the minds of district judges throughout the country.'[16] It is presumably on the basis of that doctrine that *The Little Review* was suppressed
for the first time.

According to the Solicitor of the Post Office, W.H. Lamar, the October
number of Anderson's magazine was declared non-mailable because it
was found to be 'obscene, lewd, or lascivious' within the meaning of
Section 211 of the Criminal Code of the United States (Section 480 of the
Postal Laws and Regulations of 1913).[17] In other words, the Post Office's
motives were allegedly moral. John Quinn, however, suspected political
motives, perhaps because he recognized that Lewis's story about a
German soldier on leave is critical of war. Thus, in the brief he submitted
to the Court in support of Margaret Anderson's motion for an injunction
against the Post Office, Quinn claimed, 'There is nothing under the
Espionage Act involved here. ... I was and am in favor of the prosecution
of The Masses. ... But The Little Review is an entirely different thing.'[18]
Although Judge Augustus Hand's decision in the Cantleman case is
based on ostensibly moral grounds ('there is ground for holding that
portions of the short story in question have a *tendency* to excite lust'),[19]
Post Office records establish that Quinn was not mistaken in suspecting
that political motives played their part. The file pertaining to the case is
catalogued in the Post Office's 'Lists of Subversive Literature, WWI.'
Furthermore, the list that actually mentions the case describes *The Little
Review* as a 'Publication of Anarchistic tendency' and notes that the Post
Office had suppressed the magazine under authority granted by the
Espionage Act.[20]

The suppression of the October 1917 number of *The Little Review*,
which identified the magazine as politically subversive, set the stage for
the Post Office's censorship of *Ulysses*. The Post Office, however, was not
the first censor of *Ulysses*; as incredible as it may seem, that distinction
must be reserved for Ezra Pound.

As foreign editor of *The Little Review*, Ezra Pound had sound practical
reasons for deleting certain passages from the 'Calypso' episode of
Ulysses before relaying it to Margaret Anderson for publication in New
York. For one thing, he wanted to reduce the likelihood that *Ulysses*
would be suppressed by government authorities in the United States. For

another, he wanted to prevent the frankness of *Ulysses* (and the further suppression it would invite) from provoking John Quinn to withdraw financial support crucial to the magazine's welfare. If these practical considerations had been Pound's only reasons for deleting passages from 'Calypso,' then censorship (defined here as the suppression, by a person in a position of authority, of something deemed morally or otherwise objectionable) would be too strong a word to describe the work of his blue pencil.

But Pound had other, more personal, reasons for acting as he did. In his correspondence with Joyce, he presented these reasons as essentially esthetic. This explanation is fair enough as far as it goes, for Pound's esthetic was indeed opposed to Joyce's. Walton Litz's interpretation of the opposition holds that Pound's attachment to realism in the tradition of Flaubert and the Goncourts made him unsympathetic to the 'delight in artifice and design' which found embodiment in the elaborate schematic correspondences of *Ulysses* and which Pound described disparagingly as Joyce's 'medievalism.'[21] Without denying the general validity of Litz's view, I will argue that Pound's objections to *Ulysses* arose from his attachment to a classical, hierarchical esthetic, one which was incompatible with what may be described as Joyce's incarnational, egalitarian tendencies. No purely esthetic explanation, however, can do full justice to Pound's objections to *Ulysses*. Underneath every esthetic lies ethical, political, philosophical, or religious convictions – and Pound's is no exception. Indeed, as previously mentioned, when Pound's esthetic objections to *Ulysses* are examined closely in light of the expurgations they were intended to justify, they appear to be little more than thinly-disguised religious objections to Joyce's tendency to subvert hierarchies cherished by Pound, especially that which separates the erotic and the excremental elements of human sexuality. From this perspective, Pound's expurgation of passages from 'Calypso' deserves to be called censorship.

When Pound first informed John Quinn that he had 'deleted about twenty lines' from the typescript version of 'Calypso,' he noted that he had written to Joyce in order to explain his 'reasons for thinking the said lines excessive.'[22] Not surprisingly, Pound's letter to Joyce cites both his fear of suppression at the hands of the authorities and his reluctance to offend Quinn, but it subordinates these practical factors to esthetic considerations:

Section 4. ['Calypso'] has excellent things in it; but you overdo the matter. Leave the stool to Geo. Robey. He has been doing 'down where the asparagus grows, ['] for some time.[23]

I think certain things simply bad writing, in this section. Bad because you waste the violence. You use a stronger word than you need, and this is bad art, just as any needless superlative is bad art.

The contrast between Bloom[']s interior poetry and his outward surroundings is excellent, but it will come up without such detailed treatment of the dropping feces.... .

Perhaps an unexpurgated text of you can be printed in a greek or bulgarian translation later.

I'm not even sure 'urine' is necessary in the opening page. The idea could be conveyed just as definitely.

In the thing as it stands you will lose effectiveness. The excrements will prevent people from noticing the quality of things contrasted.

At any rate the thing is risk enough without the full details of the morning deposition.[24]

In spite of his doubts about the necessity of 'urine,' Pound refrained from tampering with the celebrated opening of 'Calypso.' Aside from minor changes in spelling and punctuation, he allowed Joyce to introduce his modern-day Ulysses as he had intended to:

MR. LEOPOLD BLOOM ate with relish the inner organs of beasts and fowls. He liked thick giblet soup, nutty gizzards, a stuffed roast heart, liver-slices fried with crust-crumbs, fried cods' roes. Most of all he liked grilled mutton kidneys which gave to his palate a fine tang of faintly scented urine.[25]

Pound did, however, suppress a stronger word from the passage describing Bloom's thoughts as he returns home from Dlugacz's butcher shop carrying the kidney he will eat for breakfast. A newspaper advertisement he has read at Dlugacz's has conjured up images of exotic Eastern Mediterranean life. Then a passing cloud casts a pall on his thoughts:

No, not like that. A barren land, bare waste. Vulcanic lake, the dead sea: no fish, weedless, sunk deep in the earth. No wind could lift those waves, grey metal, poisonous foggy waters. Brimstone they called it raining down: the cities of the plain: Sodom, Gommorah, Edom. All dead names. A dead sea in a dead land, grey and old. Old now. It bore the oldest, the first race. A bent hag crossed from Cassidy's, clutching a naggin bottle by the neck. The oldest people. Wandered far away over all the earth, multiplying, dying, being born everything. It lay there now. Now it could bear no more. Dead: an old woman's: the grey sunken [**cunt**] of the world.

Desolation.

Grey horror seared his flesh. ... Cold oils slid along his veins, chilling his blood: age crusting him with a salt cloak.[26]

Before printing this passage in *The Little Review*, Pound expurgated Joyce's obscene epithet for the Dead Sea and replaced it with 'belly.'[27]

The passage that suffered most extensively from Pound's blue pencil was that which describes Leopold Bloom's early-morning defecation. In the abbreviated version of the jakes passage quoted below, Pound's expurgations have been restored in bracketed bold print. Leopold Bloom has just finished eating (with relish) grilled kidney for breakfast:

He felt heavy, full: then a gentle loosening [**of his bowels**]. He stood up [**, undoing the waistband of his trousers**]. ...

[**A paper. He liked to read at stool.**]

In the table drawer he found an old number of *Titbits*. He folded it under his armpit, went to the door and opened it. ...

He went out [**through the backdoor**] into the garden ... .

He bent down to regard a lean file of spearmint growing by the wall. Want to manure the whole place over, scabby soil. A coat of liver of sulphur. All soil like that without dung. Loam, what is this that is? The hens in the next garden; their droppings are very good I heard. ... Mulch of dung. Reclaim the whole place. ... Always have fresh greens then. ...

[**He kicked open the door of the jakes. Better be careful not to get these trousers dirty for the funeral. He went in, bowing his head under the low lintel. Leaving the door ajar, amid the stench of mouldy limewash and stale cobwebs he undid his braces. Before sitting down he peered through a chink up at the nextdoor window. Nobody.**]

[**Asquat on the cuckstool he folded out his paper, turning its pages over on his bared knees.**] Something new and easy. Our prize titbit. *Matcham's Masterstroke*. Written by Mr. Philip Beaufoy... .

[**He allowed his bowels to ease themselves quietly as he read, reading patiently.**] Life might be so. It did not move or touch him but it was something quick and neat. He read on. Neat certainly. Matcham often thinks of the masterstroke by which he won the laughing witch who now. Hand in hand. Smart. He glanced back through what he had read... .

Might manage a sketch. Time I used to try jotting down on my cuff what she said dressing. Biting her nether lip hooking the placket of her skirt. ... A speck of dust on the patent leather of her boot.

Rubbing smartly in turn each welt against her stockinged calf.
Morning after the bazaar dance when May's band played Ponchielli's
dance of the hours. ... That was the first night. Is that Boylan well off?
...

Evening hours, girls in grey gauze. Night hours then, black with
daggers and eyemasks. Poetical idea; pink, then golden, then grey,
then black. Still, true to life also. Day: then the night.

[**He tore away half the prize story sharply and wiped himself with
it. Then he girded up his trousers, braced and buttoned himself. He
pulled back the shaky door of the jakes and came forth from the
gloom into the air.**]

In the bright light he eyed carefully his black trousers... .[28]

According to Pound, all three of these passages were 'bad art' as Joyce
had written them. Pound's objection to the first two passages – the first
describing Bloom's predilection for kidney, the second his vision of the
Dead Sea – would seem to be that in each Joyce 'waste[s] the violence' by
using a stronger word than he needs. Furthermore, extending Pound's
criticism of the first passage to the second, in each '[t]he idea could be
conveyed just as definitely' in other words. The charge that Joyce
'waste[s] the violence' by using a stronger word than he needs is, in my
opinion, misguided; it is none the less a charge that a critic of Pound's
genius might sustain through careful argument. But the assertion that
'the idea' communicated through Joyce's epithets could be conveyed
'just as definitely' in other words is simply false. If the assertion had been
made by the Solicitor of the Post Office it would remain every bit as
false, but it would not be surprising: the Solicitor, after all, was not hired
to be a literary critic. That Ezra Pound made the assertion is surprising
indeed.

The idea implied in Joyce's use of 'urine' in the first passage quoted
above would seem to be that the tang which the kidneys give to Bloom's
palate derives from the waste they produce, namely, urine, and, furthermore, that this urine can provide culinary pleasure. The idea is admittedly disturbing, and Pound's objection to it is understandable, but to
suggest, as Pound does, that the idea could be equally well expressed in
other words is nonsense. 'Urine' is standard English for the waste
substance secreted by the kidneys. Other terms would introduce un-
welcome meanings. 'Piss' would inject an element of vulgarity at odds
with Bloom's sophisticated delectation. 'Water' or any other genteel
euphemism would reduce the realism of the passage and suggest a
fastidious propriety foreign to Bloom's character.

In the second passage quoted above, the idea of Bloom's vision of the
Dead Sea as 'the grey sunken cunt of the world' (a metaphor evoked by

the 'bent hag' Bloom has just seen crossing the street) would seem to be that the earth, seen through despairing eyes as a barren thing stripped of dignity and goodness, is an obscenity that chills Bloom with a feeling of intense desolation. The obscene, unerotic sexuality of Joyce's image is precisely the source of its power to evoke Bloom's experience of desolation and, of course, to disturb the reader, who has been sharing Bloom's pleasurably erotic association of Molly with lemons, oranges, 'cool waxen fruit,' and the 'heavy sweet, wild perfume' of the Mediterranean.[29] Bloom's vision constitutes a momentary descent into the hell that is properly understood as the absence of love. Bloom's feeling of despair there contrasts sharply with his subsequent thoughts (brought on by the reappearance of the sun) of Molly's 'ample bedwarmed flesh. Ye[s], yes,'[30] thoughts which represent, if not exactly an ascent to heaven, at least a reaffirmation of life's goodness. Pound's substitution of 'belly' retains a hint of the exhausted infertility of Joyce's metaphor, but virtually eliminates its obscene, unerotic sexuality. It thus reduces the image's power to precipitate Bloom's moment of desolation.

Pound's objection to the jakes passage (the third passage quoted above) seems to have arisen not so much from his conviction that Joyce had used a stronger word than he needed (the passage contains no violent epithets – unless 'bowels' fit that description) as from his claim that Joyce had failed to achieve his intended artistic effect. Joyce's intention in the jakes passage, as Pound saw it, was to contrast Bloom's 'interior poetry' with his 'outward surroundings.' Pound believed that this contrast would 'come up without such detailed treatment of the dropping feces' and, furthermore, that 'the excrements'[31] would 'prevent people from noticing the quality of things contrasted.' Assuming for a moment that Joyce intended this simple contrast, it is difficult to see how it is preserved, let alone heightened, by Pound's excisions. Surely Bloom's 'interior poetry' (for example, his thoughts about Ponchielli's poetical dance of the hours) contrasts far more dramatically with 'the stench of mouldy limewash and stale cobwebs' inside the jakes, than with the chicken droppings in the next garden. By deleting entirely Bloom's visit to the jakes, Pound obscured the very contrast he allegedly sought to heighten.

Thus, if we admit provisionally that the passages Pound objected to were 'bad art' as Joyce wrote them, we must also admit (with far less fear of contradiction) that Pound's revisions made (or, in the case of the urine passage, would have made) them worse. Why then did Pound, whose editing of *The Waste Land* inspired T.S. Eliot to honour him in the poem's dedication as '*il miglior fabbro*' (the better craftsman), fail so miserably where Joyce's prose was concerned? It is tempting, of course, to find an answer in the practical necessities of the case, which arguably forced Pound to play the censor. The esthetic objections that Pound elaborates in his letter to Joyce, however, preclude such a simple response. Furthermore, the inadequacy of the objections themselves suggests that they masked Pound's unstated disapproval of Joyce's tendency to undermine rather than preserve hierarchies like that between Bloom's 'interior poetry' and his 'outward surroundings.' In general terms, Joyce's tendency is to subvert a broad range of hierarchies upheld by classical esthetics, including those which separate the high from the low, the heroic from the mundane, the beautiful from the ugly, the pleasing from the disgusting, and ultimately, I would argue, the spiritual from the bodily. More specifically, and more vexatiously from Pound's perspective, Joyce's tendency is to undermine the hierarchy between the erotic and the excremental.

The crucial feature of the jakes passage in this regard is that Bloom enjoys his defecation in a mildly erotic manner. Thus, upon feeling 'a gentle loosening [of his bowels],' Bloom thinks immediately of '[A paper]' because '[He liked to read at stool.]' Having chosen a suitable paper, 'an old number of *Titbits*,' Bloom proceeds into the garden. After stopping to contemplate the virtues of dung as a fertilizer capable of redeeming barren soil, he enters the jakes, sits on the 'cuckstool,' lays the paper on his 'bared knees,' selects for his reading pleasure a story suggestively entitled 'Matcham's Masterstroke' – and proceeds to enjoy himself.

Inside the jakes, Bloom's pleasure in reading what the magazine's editors present as 'Our prize titbit' becomes one with his pleasure in emptying his bowels. The two activities occur simultaneously – Bloom 'allowed his bowels to ease themselves quietly as he read, reading patiently' – and, while they do, Bloom's thoughts refer to both the story he is reading and the feces he is producing: 'Life might be so. It did not move or touch him but it was something quick and neat. He read on. Neat certainly. Matcham often thinks of the masterstroke by which he won the laughing witch who now.' Under the combined influence of his pleasurable defecation and the gentle eroticism of Mr. Beaufoy's story, Bloom contemplates a 'sketch' of his own, which immediately conjures up sensual images of Molly dressing: 'Biting her nether lip hooking the placket of her skirt,' 'Rubbing smartly in turn each welt [of her patent leather boots] against her stockinged calf.'

These sensual images soon give way to Bloom's thoughts of 'Ponchielli's dance of the hours,' the music the band played the night Blazes Boylan's affair with Molly began: 'Evening hours, girls in grey gauze. Night hours then, black with daggers and eyemasks. Poetical idea; pink, then golden, then grey, then black. Still, true to life also. Day:

then the night.' Then, to impress upon his readers that the art of *Ulysses*, even more so than Ponchielli's, is both poetical and true to life as he sees it, Joyce combines the product of Bloom's pleasurable defecation with the eroticism of *Matcham's Masterstroke* in a single, abrupt movement by observing that Bloom 'tore away half the prize story sharply and wiped himself with it.' Bloom's action works in two ways. On one hand it suggests that what Pound refers to as Bloom's 'interior poetry' is, literally, crap. On the other hand it implies that Bloom's excrement is, like *Matcham's Masterstroke* and the sensual thoughts it evokes in Bloom, mildly erotic poetry. Neither possibility can be eliminated in favour of the other in the jakes passage as Joyce has written it; the erotic and the excremental are intermingled.

This intermingling of 'internal poetry' and external squalor, of eroticism and excrement is precisely what Pound's censorship of the jakes passage served to eliminate. By deleting Bloom's visit to the jakes, Pound managed to protect his cherished distinctions. In Pound's version, Bloom experiences a mysterious loosening, picks up the number of *Titbits* and walks out into the garden. The dung he contemplates there is outside of him (the chicken droppings next door) – not within his own bowels. Bloom thus stands aloof from the garden's feast of corruption and regeneration and the contrast between his 'interior poetry' and the squalor of his surroundings remains intact (if attenuated). Furthermore, and more importantly from Pound's perspective, the eroticism of *Matcham's Masterstroke* and the thoughts it stimulates in Bloom are distinguished from the small pleasures of defecation. Thus, in Pound's version, the erotic remains untainted by the excremental.

If we keep in mind the mixing of eroticism and excrement in the jakes passage, we can more easily understand Pound's objections to the other two passages in the 'Calypso' episode. For they, like the jakes passage, function to undermine the conventional distinction between the erotic and the excremental, the pleasurable and the disgusting. By suggesting at the beginning of 'Calypso' that urine can provide culinary pleasure, Joyce challenges the conventional distinction between excrement and food, between a waste product we naturally expel and things we like to chew and swallow. Pound's objection to the Dead Sea passage was probably related to his objections to the other two, with an important difference. In that passage, Joyce's fault was presumably not that he made the disgusting erotic, but rather that he made the erotic disgusting.

Pound's subsequent correspondence with Joyce confirms that his esthetic objections to *Ulysses* owed a great deal to his rejection of Joyce's treatment of things excremental and anal. For example, Pound praised the 'Proteus' episode because it kept excremental matters to a minimum and was therefore: 'Writing, with a large W. and no C.'[32] Even here,

however, Pound was being somewhat less than candid: before printing
the episode in *The Little Review* it seems he had seen fit to suppress the
passage describing a dog pissing on the beach.[33] Later, Pound objected to
'Sirens,' the most musical episode of *Ulysses*, because it culminates in
Bloom's fart: 'Pprrpffrrppfff.'[34] Publicly, Pound had defended Joyce
against H.G. Wells's charge that he was suffering from a 'cloacal obsession,' but where Bloom's fart was concerned he sided with Wells. Pound
did not advocate expurgation – 'I don't arsk you to erase' – but he
expressed his displeasure, warning that *'obsessions* arseore-ial ... shd. be
very carefully considered before being turned loose.... . fahrt yes, but not
as climax of chapter==not really the final resolution of fugue. Classic
detachment wd. suggest Racinian off stage, suppression of last two
lines.'[35] Pound's stated preference for the 'classic detachment' of Racine
would seem to confirm that his objections to *Ulysses* arose from his
attachment to a classical esthetic which insists upon strict hierarchies
between, among other things, the excremental and the erotic.

Further evidence in support of this view can be found in Pound's
poetry. Pound's poetic renderings of the erotic, as Peter Nicholls
has noted, tend to be remarkably 'literary affairs,' unencumbered by
'material or carnal possession.'[36] Sexual intercourse is typically represented metaphorically in terms of fire and light, as in the following
passage from Canto 47 describing the impregnation of the earth goddess
Tellus:

> The light has entered the cave. Io! Io!
>   The light has gone down into the cave,
> Splendour on splendour!
>   By prong I have entered these hills:
> That the grass grow from my body[37]

The same tendency away from the body and toward the spirit, this time
endowed with unmistakable religious significance, is to be found in
Canto 39, in which sexual intercourse involves movement 'from flesh
into light.'[38] Conversely, Pound's depictions of excrement dwell on the
physical and characterize bodily waste as unequivocally vile and disgusting. This tendency is clear in the Hell Cantos which, as Humphrey
Carpenter has observed, 'condemn their victims not to an inferno but to
a stinking mire of human faeces.'[39] In Pound's representations of the
erotic or the excremental, the hierarchy between the spirit and the flesh is
scrupulously maintained; nowhere does one find the slightest hint that,
to quote Yeats, love has pitched his mansion in the place of excrement.

Small wonder then that Pound took exception to Joyce's treatment
of the erotic and the excremental. Unlike Pound's esthetic, Joyce's is

stubbornly incarnational and egalitarian: in Joyce's prose the spiritual is always enfleshed, and the erotic never abandons the humble company of the excremental. Bloom's visit to the jakes makes this abundantly clear. So do Gerty MacDowell's visits to 'that place where she never forgot every fortnight the chlorate of lime' and where she has hung a calendar bearing an image of an aristocratic-looking man offering flowers to his beloved. According to the narrator of 'Nausicaa,' Gerty 'often looked at them dreamily when there for a certain purpose and felt her own arms that were white and soft just like hers.'[40] This same combination of the erotic and the excremental is present in passages that have nothing to do with the jakes. In the description of Leopold's and Molly's lovemaking on Howth Head, the embraces of the lovers occur against the backdrop of a goat that passes, 'walking surefooted, dropping currants.'[41] As Erich Auerbach has argued, prose of this kind entails a mixing of high and low that marks a significant departure from classical decorum of the kind espoused by Pound.[42]

I asserted earlier that Pound's attachment to a classical, hierarchical esthetic rested ultimately on religious foundations. Those foundations, I believe, are to be found in the cult of Eleusis, 'the pagan Greek religion that celebrated ritual coitus,' and which, according to E. Fuller Torrey, Pound believed 'was the true religion.'[43] The crucial aspect of that religion in the context of Pound's esthetic emerges clearly in Humphrey Carpenter's discussion of Pound's lecture 'Psychology and Troubadours.' The Eleusinian mysteries, Carpenter writes, cultivated not a celebration of bodily erotic pleasure but rather 'a sublimation of sexuality into something more refined and intellectual.'[44] It seems, in fact, that this sublimation could occur without physical consummation: Eleusinian practices, in Pound's view, led not to sensual pleasure resulting from 'actual sexual involvement' but rather to 'an intense pleasure derived from the intellectual contemplation of physical beauty.'[45] For Pound, this pleasure was the source of all artistic creativity, whence his unwillingness to see it obscured by the body, let alone desecrated by bodily waste.

Pound's censorship of *Ulysses* reminds us of an important historical fact, namely, that the officials in the United States Post Office and the New York Society for the Suppression of Vice were not the only readers to be wounded by Joyce's pen. And Pound was by no means the only Modernist to be offended by *Ulysses*. D.H. Lawrence condemned the 'Penelope' episode as 'the dirtiest, most indecent, obscene thing ever written.'[46] Virginia Woolf dismissed *Ulysses* as 'merely the scratching of pimples on the body of the bootboy' and described Joyce as a 'virile ... he-goat,' thus articulating objections apparently similar to Pound's.[47] And Amy Lowell lamented to D.H. Lawrence that her fellow Americans could not see 'the difference between envisaging life whole and complete, physical as well as spiritual, and pure obscenities like those perpetrated by James Joyce.'[48]

Pound's censorship of *Ulysses* illuminates another important historical fact as well: that the first censor of the novel was also its first notable champion. The irony of this fact is worth pondering, since it proves that those who were ostensibly defenders of *Ulysses* could also be its opponents. More specifically, as Pound's published defenses of the novel reveal, they could be both at one and the same time. In those defenses, Pound effectively suppressed both his personal objections to *Ulysses* and the passages from which they had arisen, by arguing that Joyce, being the accomplished artist he was, never failed to achieve a legitimately esthetic contrast between beauty and squalor, pleasure and disgust. Thus, Pound defended Joyce against one of *The Little Review*'s disgruntled readers (whose objections to *Ulysses* were actually similar to Pound's) by claiming that 'wherever Joyce has made use of lice, or dung, or other disgusting unpleasantness he has done so with the intention, and with, as a considerable artist, the result of heightening some effect of beauty, or twisting tighter some other intensity.'[49]

In thus denying that Joyce subverts the very distinctions which Pound claims he upholds, Pound initiated a tradition of what may be called the critical censorship of *Ulysses*. As we shall see, notable works in this tradition, especially Stuart Gilbert's *James Joyce's 'Ulysses'*, profoundly affected the reception of *Ulysses*.[50]

Pound's fears that *Ulysses* would provoke further government suppression of *The Little Review* were eventually vindicated in what he called the 'peaceconferentialbolshevikair' of January 1919.[51] That month's number of the magazine, containing the first instalment of 'Lestrygonians,' was denied mailing privileges by the United States Post Office.

The official charge on this and subsequent occasions was the ostensibly moral one of publishing obscenity, but more obviously political objections should not, indeed cannot, be ruled out. The most obvious reason is that the Post Office file on the wartime suppression of *The Little Review* for 'Cantleman's Spring Mate' contains a letter to the Postmaster, New York, from an employee of the Post Office's Translation Bureau, who complains of material in the February–March 1919 number of *The Little Review*:

Most of the passion of this issue of The Little Review is in the cover. There is enough of indecency left over, however, on pages 40–41 and on page 60 to render the issue an offense. The creature who writes this *Ulysses* stuff should be put under a glass jar for examination. He'd make a lovely exhibit![52]

The mere presence of this letter in a file catalogued in the Post Office's 'Lists of Subversive Literature, WWI' establishes that political motives played their part in the suppressions of *Ulysses* in *The Little Review*. Given the provenance of the letter, its location in Post Office files is hardly surprising: the Translation Bureau, after all, had been created to facilitate the Post Office's censorship of 'seditious and treasonable' communications between the United States and foreign nations under the authority of the Trading with the Enemy Act of October 1917.[53]

The question still remains, of course, as to why the US government, however determined it was to suppress politically subversive publications, would bother to trouble with *Ulysses* in *The Little Review*. Readers who have been raised to believe in the strict separation of art and politics (and morality) are naturally inclined to wonder, as did A.R. Orage in 1921, how *The Little Review* could have appeared to be anything other than 'perfectly harmless,' and perhaps to declare with Orage, 'What the giant American can *fear* from Mr. Joyce or from his publication in the "Little Review" passes understanding.'[54] Orage's view notwithstanding, what the 'giant American' feared from *Ulysses* in *The Little Review* is not as incomprehensible as it might appear, especially in light of two historical factors. The first is the fear of a Bolshevik revolution that characterized the post-war years in the United States (and, for that matter, England). The second is the radically revolutionary nature of *Ulysses*, which must have struck its first readers with great force.

Fritz Senn has rightly remarked that 'Few works of literature ... can have appeared more chaotic and less patterned than *Ulysses* did to its first unprepared readers.'[55] Many early reviewers of the novel responded to its apparent chaos in terms which suggest why government authorities in the United States might have been expected to greet its publication with hostility. For example, in rejecting Valèry Larbaud's idea that *Ulysses* marked the 're-entrance [of Ireland] into high European literature,' John Middleton Murray wrote that Joyce

> acknowledges no social morality, and he completely rejects the claim of social morality to determine what he shall, or shall not, write. He is the egocentric rebel *in excelsis*, the arch-esoteric. European! He is the man with the bomb who would blow what remains of Europe into the sky. ... His intention, so far as he has any social intention, is completely anarchic.[56]

S.P.S. Mais likened the anarchic quality of Joyce's novel to the Russian Revolution: 'Reading Mr. Joyce is like making an excursion into Bolshevist Russia: all standards go by the board.'[57] Shane Leslie, a conservative critic who likened *Ulysses* to 'an Odyssey of the sewer,' and feared the effect it would have, described it as 'literary Bolshevism.'[58]

If these literary critics could associate Joyce and *Ulysses* with bomb-throwing anarchists and Bolshevik revolutionaries in 1922, Post Office officials, led by Postmaster Burleson, could surely have done so in 1919. It seems likely that their perspective on the relations between art and politics was aptly expressed by John Sumner (who worked closely with Post Office officials) when he wrote, 'Just as we have the parlor Anarchist and the parlor Bolshevist in political life, so we have the parlor Bolshevists in literary and art circles, and they are just as great a menace.'[59] If another authority is needed in this context, it may be noted that Pound himself assumed that government authorities at the time would see the connection between literary and political revolution. In order to help Joyce in his suit against Henry Carr and Mr Bennett (employees of the British Embassy in Zurich who, Joyce claimed, had threatened to make him suffer unless he would agree to actively support the British war effort), Pound wrote to Sir Horace Rumbold, British Minister in Berne, warning that the continued 'persecution' of Joyce by the officials in Zurich would lead to 'converts to Bolshevism or to the more violent revolutionary factions.'[60]

Further support for the fact that the Post Office's suppressions of *Ulysses* in *The Little Review* were influenced by political considerations can be found in the episodes themselves, as described in the critical reviews quoted above: their radical undermining of traditional literary conventions, their apparent absence of form, their subversion of traditional morality, and their overt attacks on the authority of the state, imperialism, militarism, and so on. Joyce probably had all of these features in mind when he told George Borach, 'As an artist I am against every state. ... The state is concentric, man is eccentric. Thence arises an eternal struggle.'[61] The suppressions of *Ulysses* in *The Little Review* are part of that struggle; they confirm that Joyce's view of the artist as political subversive was something more than just words.

It is thus perhaps not purely by chance that the first instalment of *Ulysses* to fall victim to the Post Office censors, the first part of the 'Lestrygonians' episode, begins with political satire: 'PINEAPPLE rock, lemon platt, butter-scotch. A sugarsticky girl shovelling scoopfuls of creams for a christian brother. ... Lozenge and comfit manufacturer to His Majesty the King. God. Save. Our. Sitting on his throne, sucking jujubes.'[62] This satire of the British Monarch is mild enough, but it could easily have made the Post Office censors see Red in January 1919: the radicals that Burleson and Lamar were determined to silence had often based their opposition to the war on the grounds that it would benefit only the British imperialists. The possibility that the Post Office objected to this and other portions of *Ulysses* because of Joyce's political satire should be taken seriously, especially in light of the coincidence of the suppression of *The Little Review* and the Seattle strike, which began as a limited action of the city's shipyard workers on 21 January 1919, but which by 3 February had developed into a general strike that shook the nation.[63]

The agitated political atmosphere of January–February 1919, of course, is not in itself a sufficient explanation of the initial suppression of *Ulysses* and should not be taken to imply that the Post Office's charges of obscenity were merely masks for political objections. 'Lestrygonians' begins with political satire, but it soon turns to Bloom's thoughts of his courtship of Molly. Bloom's recollections of the pair's amorous encounter on Howth Head, framed by references to a pair of copulating flies, would surely have been considered obscene in 1919: Sam Coleman objected to them fourteen years later.[64] Here, as in many other places in *Ulysses*, Joyce mixes what Pound believed should be kept apart, the culinary, the erotic, and the excremental:

Ravished over her I lay full lips full open kissed her mouth. Yum. Softly she gave me in my mouth the seedcake warm and chewed. ... Pebbles fell. She lay still. A goat. No-one. High on Ben Howth rhododendrons a nannygoat walking surefooted, dropping currants. ... Wildly I lay on her, kissed her: eyes, her lips, her stretched neck beating, woman's breasts full in her blouse of nun's veiling, fat nipples upright.[65]

If the Postmaster in New York had been swayed by the zealous translator who wrote the letter quoted above as the link between the first and subsequent suppressions of *The Little Review*, the February–March 1919 number of *The Little Review* might also have been suppressed. The translator's citation of page 60 indicates that he must have been offended by what Bloom does after he helps a blind man cross a street. His work as a good Samaritan completed, Bloom wonders how the feel of a woman's hair and skin would seem to a blind man. To find out for himself, Bloom feels the hair above his ears, the skin of his cheek, and, after making sure there is no one watching, his belly: 'Walking by Doran's publichouse he slid his hand between waistcoat and trousers and, pulling aside his shirt gently, felt a slack fold of his belly.'[66] Fortunately for Margaret Anderson and her subscribers, the Postmaster was not persuaded that Bloom's actions constituted an actionable offense, so the second part of 'Lestrygonians' passed through the mails unmolested.

In the May 1919 number of *The Little Review*, which contained the second half of the 'Scylla and Charybdis' episode, Margaret Anderson complained of the Post Office's suppression of the January instalment of *Ulysses* and announced, 'To avoid a similar interference this month I have ruined Mr. Joyce's story by cutting certain passages in which he mentions natural facts known to everyone.'[67] Anderson seems to have cut four passages. One of these is a catalogue of illicit sexual relations: 'Sons with mothers, sires with daughters, nephews with grandmothers, queens with prize bulls.'[68] Another passage, the subtitle of a play called *'Everyman His Own Wife,'* deals (as one might expect) with masturbation: *'A Honeymoon in the Hand.'*[69]

Jackson Bryer has written that the passages deleted by Margaret Anderson contained 'what certainly even in 1919 must have been regarded as pretty tame material.'[70] But there are good reasons to believe otherwise. For one thing, the two passages quoted above were deemed obscene by Sam Coleman in 1932–3.[71] If Joyce's references to incest, homosexuality, bestiality and masturbation were found to be objectionable then, it seems reasonable to surmise that they would have appeared all the more so in 1919. The passages mentioning masturbation may have been particularly offensive: even more than free love, which had long been associated in the popular imagination with bomb-throwing anarchists like Emma Goldman, masturbation is anarchic sexuality *par excellence*. In any case, the best reason for believing that the passages Anderson deleted were censorable is that what she left in was enough to bring on the second Post Office suppression of *Ulysses*: the May 1919 number of *The Little Review* was not allowed to pass through the mails.

When Anderson learned that the May 1919 number had been suppressed in spite of her precautions, she contacted Quinn in the hope that he would be able to get the bureaucratic Cyclops to release *Ulysses*. Quinn believed that 'it would be perfectly hopeless to take the matter into Court.'[72] He did, however, think it worth while to prepare a brief in defense of Joyce's novel and its publication in *The Little Review*. Having submitted the brief to the Solicitor of the Post Office, W.H. Lamar, Quinn mailed a copy to Ezra Pound, who described it enthusiastically as 'the best apologia for J[oyce] that has been written,' 'one of the finest defenses not only of J[ames] J[oyce] but of realist literature.'[73] Pound's high opinion of the brief was shared by T.S. Eliot, to whom Pound had sent a copy in the hope that Quinn would agree to have it published in the *Egoist*. In requesting Quinn's permission for its publication, Eliot referred to 'your admirable defense of *Ulysses*.'[74] In spite of this high praise for his work, Quinn declined publication; he had no desire to appear publicly as a defender of 'license' in print.[75]

However brilliant Quinn's brief may have been, Lamar remained convinced that he had been right to deny May's number of *The Little Review* access to the mails, not simply because of *Ulysses*, but because of the contents of the whole number, including '"the cuts contained therein"', Lamar's way of referring to four nude drawings by James Light.[76] Quinn relayed this information to Joyce at the end of June, but Joyce's response reveals that Quinn did not quite manage to make himself understood: 'It is extraordinary that American law allows an employee to penalize a citizen for *not* having committed an offense. I allude to the penalizing of Miss Anderson on account of the suppressed passages.'[77] Anderson had, of course, suppressed passages from the May instalment of *Ulysses*, but it was what remained and not what had been removed that offended the censor.

In November 1919 Margaret Anderson anticipated the Post Office censors once again by cutting yet another passage from *Ulysses*, this one from the beginning of the 'Cyclops' episode. The passage describes a conversation in Barney Kiernan's pub on the deterrent effect of execution by hanging. According to Alf Bergan, 'There's one thing it hasn't a deterrent effect on.' Anderson cut the rest of the conversation:

> — What's that? says Joe.
> — The poor bugger's tool that's being hanged, says Alf.
> — That so? says Joe.
> — God's truth, says Alf. I heard that from the head warder that was in Kilmainham when they hanged Joe Brady, the invincible. He told me when they cut him down after the drop it was standing up in their faces like a poker.
> — Ruling passion strong in death, says Joe.

At this point, Bloom provides the publicans with a scientific explanation, which is parodied with admirable precision.

> The distinguished scientist Herr Professor Luitpold Blumenduft tendered medical evidence to the effect that the instantaneous fracture of the cervical vertebrae and consequent scission of the spinal cord would ... produce in the human subject a violent ganglionic stimulus of the nerve centres of the genital apparatus, thereby causing the elastic pores of the *corpora cavernosa* to rapidly dilate in such a way as to facilitate the flow of blood to that part of the human anatomy known as the penis or male organ resulting in the phenomenon which has been denominated by the faculty a morbid upwards and outwards philoprogenitive erection *in articulo mortis per diminutionem capitis*.[78]

Jackson Bryer's conviction that this passage would have brought on the suppression of the number is probably accurate. Assistant US Attorney Sam Coleman considered portions of the passage to be obscene according to the standards of 1932–3.[79] In any case, Margaret Anderson's anticipation of the Post Office censors proved efficacious this time: the November 1919 number of her magazine sailed through the mails.

In January of 1920, however, the editors of *The Little Review* learned that the Post Office intended to put them out of business if they would not stop printing *Ulysses*.[80] The Post Office authorities backed up their words by denying mailing privileges to January's number of *The Little Review*, which contained the third instalment of 'Cyclops.' Internal evidence would seem to support Jane Heap's contention that the episode was suppressed because of Joyce's 'disrespect for Victoria and Edward' – not to mention their empire.[81] Set in Barney Kiernan's pub, the episode records the conversation of a group of Dubliners who, having condemned the brutality of the British navy and its empire ('on which,' as one patron wittily puts it, 'the sun never rises'), deride Victoria and Edward:

— And as for the Germans, says Joe, haven't we had enough of those sausageeating bastards on the throne from George the elector down to the flatulent old bitch that's dead? ...
— Well! says J.J. We have Edward the peacemaker now.
— Tell that to a fool, says the citizen. There's a bloody sight more pox than pax about that boyo.
— And what do you think, says Joe, of the holy boys, the priests and bishops of Ireland doing up his room in Maynooth in his racing colours and sticking up pictures of all the horses his jockeys rode.
— They ought to have stuck up all the women he rode, says little Alf. And says J.J.:
— Considerations of space influenced their lordships' decision.[82]

January's instalment of the 'Cyclops' episode contained other passages that would undoubtedly have offended the Post Office censors on political grounds. It is worth remembering in this regard that 'The month of January 1920 marked the height of the Great Red Scare.'[83] On the second day of the month, Attorney General Palmer conducted a nation-wide raid against radicals with Communist affiliations rounding up over '4000 suspected radicals ... in thirty-three major cities.'[84] In light of this political climate, neither Burleson nor Lamar could have taken kindly to Bloom's pacifism: 'it's no use... . Force, hatred, history, all that... . everybody knows that it's the very opposite of that that is really life.'[85] Nor could they have approved of the citizen's condemnation of imperialism, particularly its cynical exploitation of Christianity and the Bible:

What about Cromwell that put the women and children of Drogheda to the sword with the bible texts *God is love* pasted round the mouth of his cannon. The bible! Did you read that skit in the *United Irishman* today about that Zulu chief that's visiting England?

— What's that? says Joe.

So the citizen takes up one of his papers and he starts reading out:

— A delegation of the chief cotton magnates of Manchester was presented yesterday to his Majesty the Alaki of Abeakuta by Gold Stick in Waiting, Lord Walkup of Walkup on Eggs, to tender to his majesty the heartfelt thanks of British traders for the facilities afforded them in his dominions. The dusky potentate, in the course of a gracious speech, freely translated by the British chaplain the reverend Ananias Praisegod Barebones, tendered his best thanks to Massa Walkup and emphasized the cordial relations existing between Abeakuta and the British Empire, stating that he treasured as one of his dearest possessions an illuminated bible presented to him by the white chief woman, the great squaw Victoria. ...

— Widow woman, says Ned, I wouldn't doubt her. Wonder did he put that Bible to the same use as I would.

— Same only more so, says Lenehan. And ther[e]after in that fruitful the broadleaved mango flourished exceedingly.[86]

By the standards of January 1920 (which also marked the beginning of Prohibition), the conversation of Joyce's pubgoers was politically subversive.

Joyce may not have appreciated fully that he was sending his wandering hero into such a politically charged atmosphere, but he was certainly aware that *The Little Review* was being censored because of *Ulysses*, as the following letter to Miss Weaver makes clear:

A Mr Heaf or Heap of the *Little Review* wrote to me a very friendly and complimentary letter in which he said that the U.S.A. censor had burned the entire May issue and threatened to cancel their licence if they continue to publish *Ulysses*. This is the second time I have had the pleasure of being burned while on earth so that I hope I shall pass through the fires of purgatory as quickly as my patron S. Aloysius.[87]

Joyce's letter suggests that he had not completely lost his relish for martyrdom, which was just as well, since his suffering at the hands of the censor was far from over.

As Margaret Anderson explained to her readers in March 1920, the February number failed to materialize because of 'The extreme leisure ... on the part of the Obscene Department of the U.S.P.O. in deciding the fate of the January *Little Review*.'[88] Henceforth, the loss of advertising dollars, resulting partly from the publication of *Ulysses* and partly from government suppressions of the magazine, would seriously disrupt the printing of *The Little Review*. Publication of *Ulysses* resumed in March with the appearance of the last part of the 'Cyclops' episode. It continued without further interference from the Post Office authorities through June, the first part of the thirteenth episode ('Nausicaa') appearing in April, the second part two months later. But with the publication of the third instalment of 'Nausicaa' in August 1920, the fortunes of *The Little Review* and Joyce's wandering hero took a sharp turn for the worse.

Ironically, the serious consequences which followed upon the publication of the July–August number of *The Little Review* could perhaps have been averted if the Post Office authorities had been quicker to suspend its mailing privileges. But even the Post Office nods. Not until John Sumner, Secretary of the Society for the Suppression of Vice, had sworn out a warrant against the Washington Square Bookshop for selling him a copy did the Post Office begin to hold up copies of the offending number.[89] By then, as Sumner's warrant makes clear, the damage that would soon bring *Ulysses* to court had already been done. One copy of the July–August number of *The Little Review* mailed by the Post Office had carried *Ulysses* deep into enemy territory.

2

Ulysses and the Young Person

From the beginning of its appearance in *The Little Review*, *Ulysses* had called forth an angry stream of letters protesting at Joyce's disturbing candor. The stream swelled to a flood with the publication of the third and final instalment of 'Nausicaa,' in which Leopold Bloom, aroused by Gerty MacDowell's erotic display of her undergarments, relieves himself by masturbating in his pants.[1] Many of these letters, like that quoted in the introduction, expressed the fear that *Ulysses* might 'reach young minds.'[2] For Margaret Anderson, this fear heralded *The Little Review*'s imminent conflict with the New York Society for the Suppression of Vice, an organization working diligently to protect the 'young minds' in question.[3]

That conflict was precipitated when Anderson, seeking new subscribers for her financially precarious magazine, mailed out unsolicited copies of the July–August number. One recipient of that number was the daughter of a prominent lawyer in New York. As mentioned earlier, the similarity between the lawyer's daughter and Nausicaa is striking: both encounter the storm-tossed hero on the shores of worlds to which the hero is a stranger, the domestic realm and the island of Phaecia respectively. Whether the lawyer's daughter appreciated the parallel or perceived the irony in the fact that the offending portion of *Ulysses* was from Joyce's transformation of Homer's Nausicaa episode is not known. What is known is that she, unlike Homer's heroine, greeted the stranger with hostility. The lawyer's daughter read the July–August instalment of the 'Nausicaa' episode and, offended by the stranger's comportment, handed it over to her father, 'demanding that the magazine be prosecuted.'[4]

The father, as Anderson could have predicted, was only too willing to oblige. He sent the following letter to Edward Swann, District Attorney of New York County:

Dear Sir:
    I enclose a copy under another cover – of a copy of 'The Little Review' which was sent to my daughter unsolicited. Please read the passages marked on pages 43, 45, 50 and 51. If such indecencies don't come within the provisions of the Postal Laws then isn't there some way in which the circulation of such things can be confined among the

people who buy or subscribe to a publication of this kind? Surely there must be some way of keeping such 'literature' out of the homes of people who don't want it even if, in the interests of morality, there is no means of suppressing it.[5]

Swann assigned the complaint to Assistant District Attorney Joseph Forrester, who promptly sought the advice of John Sumner, successor to Anthony Comstock as Secretary of the New York Society for the Suppression of Vice. Their consultation resulted in a decision to prosecute those responsible for the publication and sale of the July–August number of *The Little Review*. Thus, the lawyer's daughter ensured that the editors of *The Little Review* and Joyce's hero would have their day in court.

According to Jackson R. Bryer, the fact that the Vice Society was called into the case by the District Attorney and not vice versa has been 'overlooked in subsequent discussions of the trial.'[6] Quinn, however (as Bryer observes), was well aware of the fact; the conclusion he drew from it was that *The Little Review* case was not one where 'where Sumner or Comstockery, or the Society can be honestly knocked.' Yet it cannot be denied that the District Attorney acted in response to Sumner's advice. Nor can it be denied that the founder of the New York Society for the Suppression of Vice, Anthony Comstock, was largely responsible for the passage and enforcement of the very anti-obscenity legislation that the District Attorney was called upon to uphold. Thus, it makes good sense to see the Vice Society, in its traditional role as the protector of the young person, as the real and active opponent of the editors of *The Little Review*.

From this perspective the conflict between the Vice Society and the editors of *The Little Review* is revealed for what it really was: a clash between the forces of Victorian decorum on the one hand and those of Modern candour on the other. The young person was, after all, a Victorian institution, 'an inconvenient and exacting institution, as requiring everything in the universe to be filed down and fitted to it. The question about everything was, would it bring a blush into the cheek of the young person?'[7] Some twenty years after Dickens's complaint, British writers were still lamenting the young person's power to lord it over writers; critics must, wrote George Moore, stop asking that most silly of all silly questions: 'Can my daughter of eighteen read this book?'[8] As Margaret Anderson's experience at *The Continent* makes clear, critics were still asking the question on the eve of the First World War.

The Little Review was Anderson's answer; the magazine was born to combat the young person's ascendancy. *Ulysses*, from this perspective, was Anderson's ideal warrior. Joyce had long aimed the point of his insurrectionary pen at Victorian decorum, particularly its refusal to countenance realistic literary representations of human sexuality. And in 'Nausicaa' Joyce had taken aim at the institution of the young person herself. The style of the first part of the episode points to Joyce's parodic intent. According to Hugh Kenner the style is that of a 'Victorian lady novelist,' namely, Maria Cummins, author of *The Lamplighters*, a novel whose heroine is also named Gertrude.[9] Francis Russell's view is even more revealing; the episode is written, he claims, in 'the circulating library style of the 'nineties' – which is to say in the style deemed by Victorian lending libraries to be pleasing and instructive to the young person.[10]

Whether or not Sumner detected Joyce's parody of the style implicitly advocated by his Vice Society, he could not have failed to recognize that Joyce's episode constituted a double offense against the values the Society held dear. The first and more obvious occurred when the July–August number of *The Little Review* penetrated the walls of the domestic realm and exposed the young person to the influence of Bloom's perverse sexuality. The second and graver offense had been perpetrated earlier, when Joyce turned Homer's account of the meeting of an innocent Nausicaa and a virtuous Ulysses into a masturbatory encounter between a tainted young person and an unscrupulous man of the world. The gravity of this second offense, it should be stressed, lay not so much in Bloom's defilement of the young person as in the fact that she was not the angelic being of the Victorian imagination. Gerty MacDowell's romantic sentimentality may be that of the archetypal Victorian heroine, but her thoughts and actions are not. As Walter Kendrick puts it, Gerty is 'a classic Young Person, acting as if she had already been debauched by reading *Nausicaa*.'[11] There can be no doubt about Sumner's hostility to this aspect of Joyce's episode. The Secretary of the Vice Society objected explicitly to the passage explaining that Gerty knew about the passion of men like Bloom because her friend Bertha has told her about 'the gentleman lodger that ... had pictures ... of those skirtdancers and ... used to do something not very nice that you could imagine sometimes in the bed.'[12] Likewise he took offence at Bloom's claim that Gerty was aware that Bloom was masturbating as she swung her legs to and fro: 'Did she know what I? Course.'[13] Sumner recognized that Joyce was attacking the very institution he was sworn to protect.

Since, as Noel Riley Fitch has acknowledged, the carnal knowledge evidenced in Gerty's thoughts accounts for a good deal of the Vice Society's hostility toward *Ulysses*, it is worth wondering about the source of those thoughts.[14] Kenner favors 'the Arranger,' the narrator who parodies the Victorian lady novelist in the first part of the 'Nausicaa' episode.[15] But who is the Arranger? The evidence suggests both Bloom and Joyce himself as aspects of that mysterious literary persona.

Gerty's thoughts on the beach, as Sheldon Brivic has noted, are 'at least partly a projection of Bloom.'[16] In the morning, when Bloom reads *Matcham's Masterstroke* in the jakes, he muses that he might try a sketch himself. Gerty's thoughts may well be that sketch. In light of Bloom's mildly erotic musings in the jakes, inspired by Philip Beaufoy's prize titbit and Bloom's own defecation, one wonders whose thoughts lie behind this passage:

> It was Gerty ... who tacked up on the wall of that place where she never forgot every fortnight the chlorate of lime ... the picture of halcyon days where a young gentleman in the costume they used to wear then with a threecornered hat was offering a bunch of flowers to his ladylove with oldtime chivalry through her lattice window. ... She often looked at them dreamily when there for a certain purpose and felt her own arms that were white and soft just like hers.[17]

Gerty, like Bloom, seems aware that love has pitched his mansion in the place of excrement, which suggests that she is thinking what Bloom might like to imagine her thinking.

However persuasive the array of textual evidence that could be mustered in support of the idea that Gerty's thoughts are projected by Bloom, such evidence can never be as compelling as the biographical evidence which suggests that her thoughts are projected by Joyce. As Ellmann has demonstrated convincingly, Gerty MacDowell reflects characteristics of two women Joyce encountered while working on *Ulysses*.

Joyce met the first of the two, a young physician named Gertrude Kaempffer, in Locarno, Switzerland, in 1917. He admired her delicate skin and her fine hands. As Ellmann has pointed out, Gerty MacDowell, in addition to having Miss Kaempffer's name, has her hands: 'Her hands were of finely veined alabaster with tapering fingers and as white as lemon juice and queen of ointments could make them.[18] Joyce made sexual overtures to Gertrude Kaempffer, encouraging her to enter into secret correspondence with him through the mail. Although she refused, Joyce sent her two letters, apparently resembling those which Bloom sends to Martha Clifford in *Ulysses*. In those letters, Joyce attempted to arouse her by recounting the story of his sexual awakening, which had occurred when Joyce, aged fourteen, was asked by the nanny with whom he was walking in the country to look away while she urinated. Joyce, Ellmann writes, 'heard the sound of liquid splashing on the ground. (Joyce used the word "piss," with which the young doctor was unfamiliar.) The sound aroused him: "I jiggled furiously," he wrote.'[19] Earwicker, Ellmann adds, 'was accused of the same offense'; so, of course, was Bloom.

Joyce met the second woman, Marthe Fleischmann, in Zurich in 1918 when he looked out of his window and saw a woman pulling a toilet chain in a neighbouring flat. As Ellmann points out, the act 'had distinct erotic implications' for Joyce.[20] Marthe Fleischmann walked with a limp and spent her days 'reading romantic novels'; so does Gerty MacDowell. Marthe Fleischmann permitted the sort of correspondence Joyce had desired to have with Gertrude Kaempffer, and when she met with Joyce a good deal of their conversation turned on 'the congenial subject of women's drawers, always a titillating topic for him.'[21] Gerty MacDowell is also interested in underwear:

As for undies they were Gerty's chief care and who that knows the fluttering hopes and fears of sweet seventeen … can find it in his heart to blame her? She had four dinky sets, with awfully pretty stitchery, three garments and nighties extra, and each set slotted with different coloured ribbons … . She was wearing the blue for luck.[22]

Leopold Bloom, of course, shares Joyce's interest in women's drawers; the sight of Gerty's excites him just as the sight of Marthe's had excited Joyce. Whether the provocatively erotic display of Gerty's drawers excited Joyce is a more difficult question to answer, but in light of the biographical details mentioned above it seems plausible that it did. In any case, it seems fair to say that Gerty MacDowell's physical and psychological attributes, not to mention her response to Bloom on the beach, are the expression of Joyce's own perverse sexual fantasies. If this is indeed the case, then it also seems fair to say that the 'Nausicaa' episode contains obscenity not only according to the prudish Victorian definition of the term but also according to Studs Terkel's definition, for in that episode Joyce treats the central female character reductively as an object for his own gratification.

From John Sumner's point of view, of course, the question of whether Bloom or Joyce was responsible for debauching Gerty's mind was unimportant. He recognized that her mind *was* debauched, and he believed that other young minds would meet the same fate if the editors of *The Little Review* were not prevented from circulating more copies of their July–August 1920 number. So he wasted no time in bringing the editors of the magazine to court. On 29 September 1920 Sumner obtained several copies of the July–August issue from Josephine Bell Arens, co-owner of the Washington Square Book Shop ('New York's most vigorous purveyor of [*The*] *Little Review*,'[23] and submitted these copies, along with a written complaint, to Jefferson Market Police Court. The Magistrate, believing that Sumner's complaint was justified, issued a summons requiring Mrs Arens to appear before him.

Three days later Anderson and Heap informed John Quinn that *The Little Review* had been apprehended. Quinn told them that he 'didn't give a damn' for *The Little Review* and that 'it would serve them damnably right if it was permanently excluded from the mails.' He contemptuously dismissed their aim of 'broadening the public' along with their conviction that 'they were doing a fine thing to publish Joyce unexpurgated.' When they responded that both Pound and Joyce favoured unexpurgated publication, Quinn countered, 'Pound and Joyce – hell! Joyce is in Zurich. ... Pound is in London. ... They don't know the general effect. They are artists.' Although Quinn did not care about *The Little Review*, he recognized that suppression of the July–August instalment of *Ulysses* would 'damn the book as a whole.' In order to save Joyce's novel, and for no other reason, Quinn called Sumner on the telephone ('Tactful talk. Nothing got by spitting in public official's eye, even though it's a small eye') and arranged to have Anderson and Heap substituted for Josephine Arens as the defendants in the case.

The substitution occurred at Jefferson Market Police Court on 4 October 1920. Anderson took advantage of the occasion to tangle with Sumner. Ignoring Quinn's advice to avoid confrontation, she and Heap informed Sumner that they 'gloried'[24] in the July–August number and that they 'would do it again.' Furthermore, they said they welcomed the prosecution, claiming it would be 'the making of *The Little Review*.' Anderson maintained her attitude of defiance the next time she met Sumner, this time in front of the Washington Square Bookshop where the two crusaders argued passionately. Anderson considered Sumner the ideal enemy ('I won every point and he seemed to like it'), one who, she believed, could be persuaded to change his mind:

> If I had had time I would have invited him to tea every day for a month, so that we might have got down seriously to an abstract discussion of ideas. I am willing to wager that at the end of the month he would have become as fanatical about a new set of ideas as he still is about his present set.[25]

Anderson was an incorrigible optimist.

Quinn was much too practical to sympathize with Anderson's optimism, yet he too hoped to change Sumner's mind. To that end, he met the Vice Society Secretary for lunch on 15 October. In the course of that meeting, Sumner drew Quinn's attention to those passages in the 'Nausicaa' instalment which he found particularly offensive.[26] Quinn '[f]rankly admitted there were parts [in the July–August episode of 'Nausicca'] that should not have been published in [a] magazine,' especially one claiming the privileges of cheap mailing, but he argued that it would be unfair to suppress *The Little Review* on the basis of parts of *Ulysses*. Successful prosecution of the magazine, he explained, would wrongfully exclude the publication in book form of a fine literary work by a serious writer. To persuade Sumner to drop the case, Quinn appealed to expert testimony, supplying Sumner with a copy of the October number of the *Dial* containing Evelyn Scott's article on Joyce as a 'Contemporary of the Future.' Quinn also said that he would urge Joyce to publish no more of *Ulysses* in *The Little Review*. Sumner considered this a 'novel suggestion,' but added that he could not agree to it without the approval of District Attorney Swann. If Sumner ever presented Quinn's proposal to the District Attorney it must have fallen on deaf ears, for the government proceeded with its case against the editors of *The Little Review*. On 21 October, Anderson, Heap, Quinn and Sumner met again in Jefferson Market Police Court, this time for the preliminary hearing.

Quinn had not planned to attend the preliminary hearing at all, convinced as he was that the Magistrate, Joseph E. Corrigan, would hold Anderson and Heap for trial in the Court of Special Sessions. When Quinn's assistant informed him that Corrigan was unwilling to hold the editors on the basis of Sumner's affidavit and would therefore read the July–August number for himself, Quinn rushed to court. Upon arrival he beheld an amusing scene:

> There was Heep [sic] plus Anderson, and plus heaps of other Heeps and Andersons. Some goodlooking and some indifferent. The two rows of them looking as though a fashionable whorehouse had been pinched and all its inmates haled into court, with Heep in the part of the brazen madame. The stage was filled with police officers in blue uniforms with glaring stars and buttons, women and men by twos and threes awaiting arraignment or sentence, niggers in the offing, chauffeurs awaiting hearings; pimps, prostitutes, hangers-on and reporters – also whores, on the theory of 'Once a journalist always a whore.'

This was precisely the sort of spectacle that Quinn had hoped to avoid, for he disliked Joyce's work being associated with Greenwich Village bohemia, and he did not want the connection bandied about in the press, whence, presumably, his low opinion of the journalist (Quinn's racism is not so easily explained).

By the time Quinn arrived, Sumner had read his complaint against Anderson and Heap, claiming that the July–August number of *The Little Review*, particularly upon pages 42, 43, 44, 45, 46, 47, 48, 50, 51, 53, 55, 57, 59, 60, ... is so obscene, lewd, lascivious, filthy, indecent and disgusting, that a minute description of the same would be offensive to the Court and improper to be placed upon the record thereof.[27]

Anderson and Heap, Sumner added, had admitted to being the publishers of the said magazine and stated that 'they gloried in it.'[28] Corrigan, having listened to Sumner's complaint, had retired, as Quinn put it, to his 'legal chambers'; he was still reading the object of Sumner's compliant when Quinn arrived in the courtroom. Quinn, demonstrating that he had the Joycean ear for scatological puns, conveyed his observations on the subject to Pound: 'I don't know whether the judicial urinal or judicial water closet abutted on his chambers but I supposed it did. At any rate, chambers struck me as the right place for him to read the July–August number.'

When Magistrate Corrigan emerged from his chambers, he greeted Quinn with a smile and took his seat. Then Quinn stood up to speak. So, apparently, did Anderson and Heap, both of whom were eager to play their part in the courtroom drama. When Quinn discovered them standing next to him he dismissed them brusquely: '"What are you doing here? You don't belong here. Go back to your seats."' Once his clients had withdrawn, Quinn began his performance – of which he thought highly: 'I hit out from the shoulder and I don't think that there has ever been quite the same kind of speech delivered in a New York court in my time.'

As he had done when he met with Sumner over lunch, Quinn began by reminding Corrigan that Joyce was a serious writer of high reputation in the world of letters. He then 'got right down to the discussion of whether the July–August number was filthy in the meaning of the law.' Quinn's argument in this regard commenced with the admission that 'there was filth in literature and art, but that it was not filth that would corrupt, but rather that would brace and deter.' In other words, filth in literature and art has a healthy moral effect since it discourages vice by making it disgusting, whereas filth within the meaning of the law has an immoral effect since it encourages vice by making it attractive. In making this admission, Quinn left himself a choice between two lines of argument, one theoretical, the other pragmatic.

According to the theoretical line of argument, the literary work, precisely in so far as it is a literary work, cannot be obscene, for even its filth, which is disgusting rather than alluring, is morally beneficial. If Quinn had desired to pursue this tack, his task would have been to build on what he had said regarding Joyce's reputation as a serious writer and thus to establish the July–August instalment of *Ulysses* as a work of literature which, by virtue of that fact, could not be deemed legally obscene.

Quinn, however, does not seem to have been comfortable enough with this approach to argue it convincingly. He remained on safe ground when he compared Joyce's filth with that of Swift and Rabelais, authors whose status as serious artists was beyond question. But he bogged down in contradiction when he contrasted 'the strong hard filth of a man like Joyce with the devotion to art of a fort [sic] flabby man like Wilde,' claiming in the process that whereas Wilde's work corrupted, Joyce's did not. In reasoning thus, Quinn undermined his own argument: few, after all, would assert that Wilde's work is not literature, and if it can corrupt so can other literary works. Quinn's unfortunate illustration established that literary obscenity and legal obscenity are not necessarily mutually exclusive.

In light of Quinn's logical difficulties with the theoretical line of argument he could have pursued, it is not surprising that he adopted a more pragmatic approach, according to which the question of 'whether a thing was filthy should be tested by its effect.'[29] On the basis of this standard, Quinn then argued that 'Joyce's treatment of sex would not drive men to whore houses or into the arms of lewd women but would drive them away from them.'[30] In order to illustrate his contention that the July–August portion of 'Nausicaa' would discourage rather than encourage lewd acts – and in order to give his audience a dose of what he assumed they had come for – Quinn laid out the following hypothetical situation:

'If a young man is in love with a woman and his mother should write to him saying: "My boy, the woman you are infatuated with is not a beautiful woman. ... She sweats, she stinks, she is flatulent. Her flesh is discolored, her breath is bad. She makes ugly noises when she eats and discharges other natural functions ...," those remarks might be considered by some refined person as filthy, but they are not filthy within [the] meaning of the law. They would not send the aforementioned son to the arms of that fairy, but would be more likely to turn him from her in disgust.'

Then, without troubling to show Magistrate Corrigan how 'Nausicaa' resembled the mother's words to her son, Quinn proceeded to define the sort of reader on whom the effect of the episode was to be tested.

The proper test of the episode, he argued, would be 'its effect upon the average man or woman, not its effect upon a degenerate on one side, or a convent bred saphead on the other.' Quinn was aware, of course, that the July–August number of *The Little Review* had fallen into the hands of a young woman, but he rejected her as the standard by which the 'Nausicaa' episode should be judged. In so doing, he repudiated the

Hicklin rule, which defined the proper legal test of obscenity as 'whether the tendency of the matter charged as obscenity is to deprave and corrupt those whose minds are open to such immoral influences, and into whose hands a publication of this sort may fall.'[31] In this respect, and in this respect only, Quinn attempted to make new law, for the Hicklin rule prevailed as the standard test of obscenity in Quinn's day.

Quinn was far too practical to assume that Corrigan would be willing to throw out Hicklin. He therefore concluded his argument by claiming that neither the average person nor the young person was endangered by 'Nausicaa': 'an innocent person would not understand the sex allusions and therefore could not be corrupted by them; and for the same reason, a person who could understand them had already been "educated" and therefore could not be corrupted by them.'[32] Corrigan listened patiently to Quinn's argument, but his ruling indicates that he felt obliged to uphold the Hicklin rule: '[T]here was one episode in the book that *anyone could understand*...: "That was the episode where the man went off in his pants, which *no one could misunderstand*, and that I think is smutty, filthy within the meaning of the statute"' (emphasis mine). What 'anyone could understand,' what 'no one could misunderstand,' could be understood by the innocent young person.

All Quinn could do now was score one final debating point, and he did so by turning his logic against Corrigan, accusing the judge of having 'a corrupt and depraved mind, for only a corrupt and depraved mind would understand the meaning of the passage.'[33] Corrigan was amused, but not converted: he held Anderson and Heap over for trial in the Court of Special Sessions and fixed the bail at $25 for each of the defendants.[34] Quinn had predicted from the outset that his clients would be held over for trial in the Court of Special Sessions, but he took about as much pleasure in being an accurate prophet of doom as Cassandra, especially since his failure to capitalize on the promise of dismissal which had unexpectedly arisen made him doubly convinced that conviction was certain. Corrigan, according to Quinn, would have discharged Anderson and Heap 'if he felt he possibly could.' With these bitter thoughts in mind, Quinn departed from the court, refusing, of course, to speak with journalists.

The outcome of the preliminary hearing left Quinn with two options to pursue. The first was to try once again to convince the District Attorney to drop the prosecution in exchange for a promise that publication of *Ulysses* would be discontinued. Quinn held out little hope, however, that this approach would succeed, and rightly so, for the District Attorney refused to bargain. Quinn was therefore obliged to pursue his second option, namely, to postpone the trial as long as possible in the hope that Joyce could finish *Ulysses* and have it published in a single volume before the conviction could be handed down. To this end Quinn arranged for a couple of postponements. Recognizing, however, that this tactic would not provide him with the delay he desired, Quinn applied to have the case transferred from the Court of Special Sessions, 'where a trial is had before three judges,' to the Court of General Sessions, 'where a trial is before a judge *and jury*.'[35] Quinn's stated justification for this request was that a jury was better able than three judges to determine whether a book was obscene, but this claim was purely tactical. Quinn believed conviction was certain in either court; his only goal in requesting a trial by jury was to delay that conviction for as long as possible.

Quinn's tactic bore immediate, though short-lived, fruit, for while the motion for transfer was pending Quinn was able to have the Special Sessions trial adjourned once more, to 4 February 1921. When Quinn appeared in the Court of General Sessions and argued his motion for transfer before Judge Crain, a personal friend, he stressed that suppression of the July–August number of *The Little Review* would result in serious financial loss to both the editors of the magazine and James Joyce, who might lose his copyright to *Ulysses* in the USA. Ironically, Judge Crain was 'so impressed' by Quinn's argument that he denied the motion; 'there were,' he said, 'important literary and property rights at stake' and Quinn could have these resolved much sooner in the Court of Special Sessions.[36] A jury trial, the judge added, 'would hold the case up for a year or a year and a half.'[37] Quinn was thus hoist by his own petard and forced to take his chances before the Court of Special Sessions. He did succeed in obtaining one more adjournment, but could do no more; the trial would take place on 14 February 1921.

Believing that conviction was 'absolutely certain,' Quinn was initially resolved to make no changes in his courtroom strategy: 'All I can do is to make the argument along the lines that I did before the magistrate.'[38] If he had been able, he would have presented expert testimony and offered in evidence passages of comparative literature. But Quinn was aware, as his 'Affidavit and Motion for Transfer' makes clear, that such practices were not allowed in cases of this kind. Some six days before the trial, however, Quinn altered his strategy. He asked Anderson, first, to arrange to have on hand two or more 'character witnesses' who could testify as to the reputation and motives of *The Little Review* and, second, to suggest at least two people who could testify to both the 'the serious nature of Joyce's work' and the tendency of the 'Nausicaa' episode.[39] Quinn knew, of course, that such evidence was inadmissible, but he hoped that the Court might receive it 'in mitigation of sentence.'[40] Having made this one alteration to his previous strategy, Quinn was ready to play his role in the new trial: 'People of the State of New York against Margaret C. Anderson and Jane Heap.'

Everyone stood up as Chief Justice Frederic Kernochan and Associate Justices James McInerney and Joseph Moss entered the courtroom. Margaret Anderson wondered, 'Why must I stand up as a tribute to three men who wouldn't understand my simplest remark?' but she stood up none the less, perhaps as a concession to Quinn's desire that she and Jane Heap remain 'inconspicuous, meek and silent' throughout the trial.[41] The proceedings began much as they had done in Jefferson Market Police Court some four months earlier. Sumner repeated his complaint against the editors of *The Little Review*. And Quinn (after questioning the competence of the three judges – as opposed to a jury – to judge the case) began to explain who James Joyce was, what he had written, and the extent of his reputation as a man of letters.[42] The judges swiftly confirmed Quinn's prediction that they would be less receptive than Corrigan had been by informing him that they could not see 'what bearing those facts [had] on the subject,' and that their only function was to decide 'whether certain passages of "Ulysses"' violated the statute.[43]

The unwillingness of the judges to consider Joyce's literary reputation may have induced Quinn to abandon the theoretical argument he had attempted before Judge Corrigan. Whatever the reason, abandon it he most certainly did. He made no mention of his previous distinction between filth in literature and filth within the meaning of the law, nor did he claim that the two were mutually exclusive. Instead, he pursued the pragmatic argument that 'Ulysses could not and would not corrupt people.'[44] Before Magistrate Corrigan, Quinn had pursued this line of argument by claiming that the effect of *Ulysses* was to disgust rather than corrupt. Before the Special Sessions judges, however, Quinn's emphasis fell not on the tendency of *Ulysses* to disgust but rather on the sheer incomprehensibility of Joyce's work: 'I argued there that nobody could understand what Ulysses was about and therefore it could not corrupt any one.'[45] As he put it to Joyce later, this was 'the only tack that could be taken with the three stupid judges.'[46]

To further these arguments, Quinn asked the Court to allow expert witnesses to assess the probable effect of the 'Nausicaa' instalment on the readers of *The Little Review*. Surprisingly, the request was granted, so Quinn called upon his first witness, John Cowper Powys. In his opinion, and very much in keeping with Quinn's argument, *Ulysses* was 'too obscure and philosophical a work to be in any sense corrupting'; it was 'a beautiful piece of work in no way capable of corrupting the minds of young girls.'[47] Quinn's second witness, Phillip Moeller of the Theater Guild, eventually arrived at a similar conclusion. He began, however, by describing the 'Nausicaa' episode as 'an unveiling of the subconscious mind, in the Freudian manner,' assuring the judges that he saw 'no possibility of these revelations being aphrodisiac in their influence.'[48] '"Here, here,"' one of the judges remonstrated, '"you might as well talk Russian. Speak plain English if you want us to understand what you're saying."' Pressed for a less erudite explanation of the effect of the 'Nausicca' episode on the average reader, Moeller replied: '"I think it would mystify him."' But even this plain talk seems to have left the judges dissatisfied. '"Yes,"' one of them replied, '"but what would be the effect?"'

Powys and Moeller had corroborated Quinn's claim that the average reader would not understand *Ulysses* and could therefore not be corrupted by it, but the response of the judges to Moeller's testimony must have made Quinn wish for more supporting testimony, whence his announcement that he had three more witnesses to call: Scofield Thayer, editor of the *Dial*; the Reverend Percy Stickney Grant, an Episcopal priest and author; and Ernest Boyd, a literary critic who had written on *Ulysses*.[49] The judges, however, had heard enough. They denied Quinn's request for more witnesses, announced their intention to read the July–August number for themselves, and adjourned the trial for a week until 21 February.[50]

When the trial reconvened Quinn made what, according to him, 'many people in court called a brilliant argument.'[51] First, he re-emphasized the incomprehensibility of *Ulysses* by likening it to 'cubistic painting, experimental, tentative, revolutionary, if you like, but certainly not depraving or corrupting.'[52] This time, however, he drove home his point by arguing that the inscrutability of Joyce's work was due not only to its artistic innovation but also its artistic failure. Thus, he argued that the obscurity of the 'Nausicaa' instalment was due to the absence of adequate punctuation, itself the result of Joyce's failing eyesight.[53] Going a step further, Quinn employed what Margaret Anderson considered 'a final bit of suave psychology (nauseating and diabolical)' and admitted: '"I myself do not understand "Ulysses" – I think Joyce has carried his method too far in this experiment."'[54] Second, ever unwilling to risk everything on a single line of argument, Quinn claimed that if anyone *could* understand the episode of *Ulysses* in question he would be disgusted rather than attracted by its treatment of sex. Thus, he admitted that *Ulysses* was '"disgusting in portions, perhaps, but no more so than Swift, Rabelais, Shakespeare, the Bible."'[55] As he had done before, Quinn insisted that the reader on whom the effect of the July–August number of *The Little Review* should be tested was the average person: *Ulysses*, he said, was '"neither written for nor read by school girls."'[56]

Once Quinn had completed his arguments, Forrester announced his intention of reading the offending passages aloud. Apparently Sumner and he had decided that they were not too obscene to be placed on the record of the Court after all.[57] One of the judges was therefore obliged to come gallantly to Margaret Anderson's rescue. Regarding her with paternal concern, he was inclined to refuse Forrester permission to read the obscenity in her presence. '"But she is the publisher," said John Quinn, smiling. "I am sure she didn't know the significance of what she was publishing," responded the judge.'[58] In the end, the judge relented and Forrester was allowed to proceed.

No accurate record of the passages he read to the Court has survived, but in light of Forrester's circuitous claim that 'some of the chief objections had to do with a too frank expression concerning a woman's dress when the woman was in the clothes described,'[59] it seems likely that the Assistant District Attorney read the passage leading to the episode's (not to mention Bloom's) climax:

The eyes that were fastened upon her set her pulses tingling. She looked at him a moment, meeting his glance, and a light broke in upon her. Whitehot passion was in that face, passion silent as the grave, and it had made her his. At last they were left alone without the others to pry and pass remarks, and she knew he could be trusted to the death, steadfast, a man of honour to his fingertips. She leaned back far to look up where the fireworks were and she caught her knee in her hands so as not to fall back looking up and there was no one to see only him and her when she revealed all her graceful beautifully shaped legs like that, supply soft and delicately rounded, and she seemed to hear the panting of his heart his hoarse breathing, because she knew about the passion of men like that, hotblooded, because Bertha Supple told her once in secret about the gentleman lodger that was staying with them out of the record office that had pictures cut out of papers of those skirtdancers and she said he used to do something not very nice that you could imagine sometimes in the bed. But this was different from a thing like that because there was all the difference because she could almost feel him draw her face to his and the first quick hot touch of his handsome lips. Besides there was absolution so long as you didn't do the other thing before being married and there ought to be woman priests that would understand without telling out and Cissy Caffrey too sometimes had that dreamy kind of dreamy look in her eyes so that she too, my dear, and besides it was on account of that other thing coming on the way it did.

And Jackey Caffrey shouted to look, there was another and she leaned back and the garters were blue to match on account of the transparent and they all saw it and shouted to look, look there it was and she leaned back ever so far to see the fireworks and something queer was flying about through the air, a soft thing to and fro, dark. And she saw a long Roman candle going up over the trees up, up, and they were all breathless with excitement as it went higher and higher and she had to lean back more and more to look up after it, high, high, almost out of sight, and her face was suffused with a divine, an entrancing blush from straining back and he could see her other things too, nainsook knickers, four and eleven, on account of being white and she let him and she saw that he saw and the it went so high it went out of sight a moment and she was trembling in every limb from being bent so far back that he could see high up above her knee where no-one ever and she wasn't ashamed and he wasn't either to look in that immodest way like that because he couldn't resist the sight like those skirtdancers behaving so immodest before gentlemen looking and he kept on looking, looking. She would fain have cried to him chokingly, held out her snowy slender arms to him to come, to feel his lips laid on her white brow. And then a rocket sprang and bang shot blind blank and O! then the Roman candle burst and it was like a sigh of O! and everyone cried O! O! and it gushed out of it a stream of rain gold hair threads and they shed and ah! they were all greeny dewy stars falling with golden, O so lovely! O so soft, sweet, soft![60]

Furthermore, in light of Sumner's objections to particular passages on the pages cited in his affidavit, it seems likely that Forrester would also have read those passages which reveal that Bloom, as Magistrate Corrigan put it, 'went off in his pants.' Thus, he might have read the following:

Mr. Bloom with careful hand recomposed his shirt. O Lord, that little limping devil. Begins to feel cold and clammy. After effect not pleasant. ... Still I feel. The strength it gives a man.[61]

There she is with them down there for the fireworks. My fireworks. Up like a rocket, down like a stick.[62]

Still she was game. Lord, I am wet. Devil you are. Swell of her calf. Transparent stockings, stretched to breaking point.[63]

Did me good all the same. Off colour after Kiernan's, Dignam's. For this relief much thanks. In *Hamlet*, that is. Lord! It was all things combined. Excitement. When she leaned back felt an ache at the butt of my tongue.[64]

Perhaps they get a man smell off us. What though? Cigary gloves Long John had on his desk the other. Breath? What you eat and drink gives that. No. Mansmell, I mean. Must be connected with that because priests that are supposed to be are different. Women buzz round it like flies round treacle. O father, will you? Let me be the first to. That diffuses itself all through the body, permeates. Source of life. And it's extremely curious the smell. Celery sauce. Let me.

Mr. Bloom inserted his nose. Hm. Into the. Hm. Opening of his waistcoat. Almonds or. No. Lemons it is. And no, that's the soap.[65]

Having read these or similar passages, Forrester launched into a bitter denunciation of *Ulysses*, the editors of *The Little Review*, and even Quinn himself. In so doing, Forrester unwittingly inspired Quinn to argumentative brilliance:

'If your Honors please, *I offer Mr. Forrester in evidence as the defendants' chief exhibit.* Just look at him, still gasping for breath at the conclusion of his denunciation, his face distorted with rage, his whole aspect apoplectic. Is he filled with lewd desires? Does a reading of that chapter want to send him to the arms of a whore? Is he filled with sexual desire? Not at all. He wants to murder somebody. He wants to send Joyce to jail. He wants to send those two women to prison. He would like to disbar me. He is full of hatred, venom, anger and uncharitableness. But lust? There is not a drop of lust or an ounce of sex passion in his whole body. He is filled with anger and hate. He is my chief exhibit as to the effect of Ulysses.'[66]

According to Quinn, this performance made the judges laugh, which gave him reason to believe that he would win the case. The evidence suggests that he came close to doing so. Two of the judges (presumably the two Quinn later described as 'more interested in eating and smoking and perhaps drinking and poker-playing probably or church-going ... than they were in reading *The Little Review*') admitted that they could not understand Joyce's work.[67] '"I think that this novel is unintelligible,"' said Justice McInerney.[68] But Chief Justice Frederic Kernochan (whom Quinn described as 'an ass without the slightest glimmer of culture' who none the less 'knows the meaning of words') 'admitted that he understood what the chapter meant and swung the two other ignora-muses to his view.'[69]

Thus, the editors of *The Little Review* were found guilty of publishing obscenity, fined $50 each, and enjoined from publishing further instal-ments of *Ulysses*. They were then led off to be fingerprinted for their crime.[70] *The Little Review's* war to make the world safe for art had ended in defeat for the forces of art, for the magazine had failed to print the work that Anderson described as 'the prose masterpiece of my generation.'[71]

Anderson and Heap attributed their defeat to the limitations of both US culture and Quinn's defense. Their dissatisfaction was undoubtedly accentuated by Quinn's stooping to argue before the Court of Special Sessions that the incomprehensibility of Joyce's work was due to artistic failure. But it was rooted firmly in their rejection of the theoretical grounds on which Quinn had based his defense of *Ulysses*, particularly his admission that a literary work could be obscene.

In opposition to Quinn, Anderson believed that 'the words "literature" and "obscenity" can not be used in conjunction any more than the words "science" and "immorality" can.'[72] Her defense of Joyce, as she explained before the case was heard in the Court of Special Sessions, would have differed radically from Quinn's:

> I should begin my (quite unnecessary!) defense of James Joyce with this statement: I know practically everything that will be said in court, both by the prosecution and the defense. I disagree with practically everything that will be said by both.
> *I do not admit that the issue is debatable.*
> *I state clearly that the (quite unnecessary!) defense of beauty is the only issue involved.*
> *...So that we come to the question of beauty in the Art sense,* – that is, to the science of aesthetics, ... which establishes whether any given piece of writing, painting, music, sculpture, is a work of Art.[73]

Heap summed up Anderson's position succinctly when she wrote, 'The only question relevant at all to "Ulysses" is – Is it a work of Art?'[74]

This question, according to Anderson, can be answered only by one familiar with the fundamentals of esthetics:

> *First, that to a work of Art you must bring aesthetic judgment, not moral, personal, nor even technical judgment.* It is not the *human feelings* that produce this kind of judgment. *It is a capacity for art emotion, as distin-guished from human emotion, that produces it.*

> *Second, that only certain kinds of people are capable of art emotion (aes-
> thetic emotion). They are the artist himself and the critic whose capacity for
> appreciation proves itself by an equal capacity to create.*[75]

Thus, Anderson dismissed the idea that art can be judged by ordinary
moral standards, just as she rejected the idea that art can be understood
by ordinary persons relying on ordinary perception. Small wonder, then,
that she was frustrated with Quinn's defense of *Ulysses*.

Quinn's arguments, as we have seen, differed in virtually every
important respect from those which Anderson would have made. Quinn
had argued that Joyce was a genuine artist and that *Ulysses* was a work
of literature, but he admitted (in spite of an attempt to do otherwise) that
the words *literature* and *obscenity* could indeed be used in conjunction.
Thus, instead of denying that *Ulysses*, as a serious literary work, could be
obscene, he had tried to show that the obscenity in *Ulysses* would deter
rather than corrupt. In other words, Quinn's arguments in defense of
Ulysses, like the arguments of the prosecution, acknowledged the validity of the moral judgement of art; he attempted to convince the Court
that the effect of 'Nausicaa' on the average person was not morally
harmful. Furthermore, while he had argued that those who could be corrupted by 'Nausicaa' would not be able to understand it, he did not
attempt to argue, as Anderson would have, that anyone who believed
that a work of art like *Ulysses* could have any adverse moral effect whatsoever betrayed a serious lack of understanding of art.

In evaluating Anderson's criticisms of Quinn's defense, then, it should
be kept in mind that they arise from a fundamental disagreement about
the nature of literature. Quinn, as we have seen, had tried to adopt
Anderson's radical distinction between literature and obscenity. His
failure to develop a sustained argument in defense of that distinction can
be attributed to several factors, the most important of which is probably
simply that Quinn did not believe in it. As the possessor of a collection of
highly literary obscenities by Pascin and others, he was aware that literature and obscenity could sometimes stand on very friendly terms.
Furthermore, as his courtroom arguments made clear, he believed that
certain works of literature (Oscar Wilde's, for example) are capable of
corrupting. Another factor in Quinn's rejection of Anderson's view of
art, of course, is that Quinn did not believe it capable of convincing the
judges. The evidence would seem to vindicate Quinn in this regard.
Quinn had tried, after all, to convince the judges that Joyce was an artist
and that 'Nausicaa' was a serious work of literature, but they deemed
such considerations irrelevant, inadmissible. How, then, could he have
argued the judges lacked the knowledge of the science of esthetics that
would have allowed them to understand Joyce's art?

Given the limitations imposed upon him by his own view of literature and the unwillingness of the judges to place much value on literary merit, Quinn made the best argument he could. If his best was not good enough, the fault was not entirely his. Given his commonsensical idea of what it means to understand a work of literature – a view undoubtedly shared by the judges – it was virtually impossible for him to persuade the Court that 'Nausicaa' was incomprehensible to the average person. Furthermore, the portion of *Ulysses* that Quinn was obliged to defend, one of the most erotic sections of the novel, made it extremely difficult to convince the Court that its effect was to deter rather than to incite lust. Quinn's disadvantage in this regard points to a difficulty inherent in the circumstances of the case which no defender of *Ulysses* could have overcome.

Without being aware of it implications, Ernest Boyd touched on this difficulty in an article published shortly after the Court of Special Sessions had decided against *The Little Review* and *Ulysses*. Boyd complained that the US court lacked the civilized view of art expressed in the French decision which had exonerated Flaubert of corrupting public morals through *Madame Bovary* in 1857. Having asserted that the arguments of the prosecution in the Flaubert case differed little from those used against the editors of *The Little Review*, Boyd adds that the prosecutor in the French case had had the 'elementary honesty to confess at the start that isolated passages are hardly a fair test of a whole work.'[76] Boyd thus raises a crucial question about the prosecution of 'Nausicaa' in *The Little Review*, namely, to what whole was Quinn (let alone the prosecutor) to appeal?

Several commentators on *The Little Review* prosecution have claimed that Quinn's arguments anticipated those that would be made by Morris Ernst in 1932–3. As Jackson Bryer puts it, 'Morris Ernst's arguments in defense of Joyce's novel were not very different from those of John Quinn.'[77] As we shall see, this view is misleading in several respects. The most important of these in the present context lies in the fact that, unlike Quinn, Ernst was able to base his argument on the principle that a work of art is to be judged as a whole. Quinn was well aware of the importance of this principle, which explains why he urged Joyce (via Ezra Pound) to withdraw *Ulysses* from serial publication:

> It is a very unique work of art, but it is not a work of art to published in a magazine, for the background as well as the frame and lighting are important in showing a piece of art. ... there are things in *Ulysses* that would be alright in a book, but which it was stupid to think could be got away with in a monthly magazine.

From this point of view it can be seen that Joyce's refusal to withdraw *Ulysses* from serial publication put Quinn at a tremendous disadvantage, since it denied him the possibility of defending part of *Ulysses* by appealing to the whole. Quinn was not even defending a complete episode of the novel; he was trying to protect a part of a part of *Ulysses*. As late as 1934, one of the judges who affirmed the Woolsey decision in the Court of Appeals admitted privately that he would condemn *Ulysses* 'if the obscene passages were strung together as they were in the abstract condemned by the Court of Special Sessions.'[78] In light of this fact, Quinn can hardly be blamed for failing to prevent the suppression of *Ulysses* in 1921.

Some weeks after Margaret Anderson's and Jane Heap's conviction, the consequences of the suppression of *Ulysses* began to make themselves felt. Early in April, B.W. Huebsch wrote to Quinn in order to decline Joyce's novel:

> A New York court having held that the publication of a part of [*Ulysses*] in The Little Review was a violation of the law, I am unwilling to publish the book unless some changes are made in the manuscript as submitted to me by Miss H.[S]. Weaver who represents Joyce in London.
>
>   In view of your statement that Joyce declines absolutely to make any alterations, I must decline to publish it.[79]

As Quinn had predicted, other publishers followed, in spite of Quinn's considerable efforts on Joyce's behalf. By April, Joyce was in despair: '"My book will never come out now,"' he told Sylvia Beach, proprietor of Shakespeare & Company in Paris; Miss Beach's response is well known: '"Would you let Shakespeare and Company have the honor of bringing out your *Ulysses*?"'[80] Joyce's response to that offer, of course, is also common knowledge.

What is less well known, or perhaps more generally forgotten, is that the suppression of *Ulysses* in *The Little Review* meant that '[a]ll hope of publication in the English-speaking countries, at least for a long time to come, was gone.'[81] Furthermore, the time it would take to bring the English-speaking countries around to allowing Joyce's world-disturbing sailor to cross their borders depended upon the reception of the Paris edition. These considerations were surely on Joyce's mind as he worked to prepare the reading public for *Ulysses* and *Ulysses* for the reading public, which accounts for the fact that the censorship of *Ulysses* in *The Little Review* affected not only the critical reception of the novel, but its very shape.

3

Making Obscenity Safe for Literature

As previously mentioned, the effect of censorship on the writing and revising of *Ulysses* can be appreciated fully only in light of the role of censorship in Joyce's journey from what he referred to as the 'nicely polished looking-glass' of *Dubliners* to the obscurity of *Finnegans Wake*.[1] An important clue to the nature of that role is to be found in the 'Letter of Protest' published in *Our Exagmination Round his Factification for Incamination of Work in Progress*, the first book of criticism on *Finnegans Wake*. In that letter, an exasperated reader by the name of G.V.L. Slingsby asks, 'Is Mr. Joyce's hog Latin making obscenity safe for literature?'[2] According to Stuart Gilbert, who was working closely with Joyce at the time, Slingsby was actually Joyce himself under the guise of his *alter ego*, and Slingsby's question was Joyce's mischievous way of suggesting that the ribald language of *Finnegans Wake* was indeed making obscenity safe for literature.[3]

If making obscenity safe for literature meant getting works containing obscenity past the censor, then Gilbert (not to mention Joyce) was right. Joyce's search for a publisher for *Dubliners* had lasted eight years. His efforts to see *Portrait* into print were more successful; thanks in large part to the assistance of Ezra Pound and Miss Weaver, they lasted only two years. The serial publication of *Ulysses* in *The Little Review*, however, was thwarted on four occasions by the US Post Office before being snuffed out definitively by the New York courts in 1921. Attempts at serial publication of the novel in England failed because of the refusal of the printers to set the type. And although *Ulysses* was successfully published in Paris in 1922, it would remain banned throughout most of the English-speaking world until it was admitted to the United States in 1933. In sharp contrast to these earlier works, *Finnegans Wake*, which began to appear serially in 1924 in the Paris periodical *transition*, managed to evade all confrontation with the censor.

A plausible explanation of this development might seem to be that Joyce had reacted to the censorship of his earlier works by shying away from obscenity in *Finnegans Wake*. Gilbert assures us, however, that this was not the case. The 'ribaldry of *the Wake*,' he writes, is the culmination of the 'mild audacities' of *Dubliners* and *A Portrait of the Artist as a Young Man* and the 'larger freedom' of *Ulysses*.[4] Indeed, in *Finnegans Wake* Joyce deals candidly with moral taboos – notably the incestuous desire of father for daughter – which he only hints at in *Ulysses*. In other words, while Joyce's confrontations with the censor undoubtedly influenced his development as an artist, they never made him abandon his holy office of mentioning the unmentionables.

Another plausible explanation for the censorship-free publication of *Finnegans Wake* might seem to be that a change in social mores had made the unmentionables mentionable after all. This explanation presents a real temptation for us chronolotrous moderns, but in the present case chronology itself makes it unpersuasive. *Ulysses*, of course, was definitively suppressed by the New York courts in 1921, some three years before the initial appearance of *Finnegans Wake*, but *Ulysses* remained banned throughout most of the English-speaking world until 1933. And during those thirteen years *Ulysses* was actively, not merely nominally, banned. As will be made clear later in this chapter, US and British Customs authorities regularly confiscated copies of *Ulysses* seized at ports and border crossings throughout those countries until the early 1930s. Furthermore, as late as 1928 the New York Society for the Suppression of Vice, led by John Sumner, raided the Gotham Book Mart and seized not only a smuggled copy of *Ulysses* but also forty copies of Paul Jordan Smith's *A Key to the ULYSSES of James Joyce*.[5] Sumner watched the Gotham Book Mart, the main purveyor of *transition* in New York, like a hawk. He was certainly aware that 'Work in Progress,' as *Finnegans Wake* was then entitled, was by the author of *Ulysses*. Why then did he not attempt to suppress it?

This question cannot be answered with certitude, but it is surely significant that the celebrated difficulty of *Finnegans Wake* makes its obscenity virtually impossible to recognize. In *Finnegans Wake*, Joyce's journey from the 'nicely polished looking-glass' of *Dubliners* culminates in the obscurity of the nocturnal dream world. Strictly speaking, the sub-conscious world of dreams cannot be articulated in language (a fact which points to the artifice of a good deal of *Ulysses* and *Finnegans Wake*), but if it could, the language would certainly be a foreign tongue, radically unlike that which we use during our waking hours. To this extent, *Finnegans Wake* is realistic, for it is written in what is essentially a foreign language, Joyce's idiolect, a language in which readers of the novel may acquire proficiency, but only after a great expense of time and effort.

Joyce's recourse to this foreign tongue has been accounted for in a variety of ways, none of which acknowledges the role of censorship in his development as an artist. Yet the connection between censorship and Joyce's recourse to a foreign language in *Finnegans Wake* is implied repeatedly in Joyce's correspondence, as when Pound, complaining of Bloom's visit to the jakes in 'Calypso,' expressed the hope that an unexpurgated edition of *Ulysses* could be printed 'in a greek or bulgarian translation later.'[6] The same connection is implied again when Joyce, discussing the 'eventual publication' of *Ulysses*, informs Miss Weaver that the novel is 'to be printed, possibly, in Africa.'[7] The connection is implied yet again when Joyce laments to Stanislaus the expurgation of passages from 'Cyclops' and predicts that the unexpurgated version of his novel will have to be published in Japan.[8]

As these letters suggest, Joyce had at his disposal two ways of preventing the censorship of his books. One was to publish them in foreign countries where English – and therefore Joyce's writing – would not be understood by the authorities. This was the way Joyce was forced to pursue in the case of *Ulysses*. The second way was to continue publishing in English-speaking countries, but in a language foreign enough to baffle any authorities inclined to ascertain whether they should be banned as obscene. This was the way, it seems to me, that Joyce chose to follow in the case of *Finnegans Wake*. Both ways of evading the censor, both ways of making obscenity safe for literature, involve exile of one kind or another, a fact which points to the decisive influence of Joyce's early confrontations with the censor, for it was under the pressure of those confrontations that Joyce first chose the path of exile that culminated in *Finnegans Wake*.

Before examining Joyce's early struggles with the censors, we should note that the James Joyce/Paul Léon Papers recently made available to the public at the National Library of Ireland lend credence to the idea that Joyce's experiences with the censors affected his writing of *Finnegans Wake*. They certainly call into question the prevailing view that Joyce was unconcerned with and unaffected by the censorship of his works. The papers make it clear that Joyce was indeed preoccupied with the adventures of *Ulysses* in the US courts, and that he played an active role in ensuring that the US legal decisions would be appended to the English edition of the novel in order to fend off further censorship there (according to Paul Léon, Joyce attached 'primordial importance' to the matter).[9] The papers also reveal that Joyce's fear of censorship affected his presentation of *Finnegans Wake* to the reading public. Most telling in this regard is Léon's letter to Richard de la Mare, which explains that the censorship of *Ulysses* in the USA 'confirmed Mr. Joyce in his original reluctance to make known the title of his new book.'[10] Joyce's withholding of the title of *Finnegans Wake* surely provides grounds for believing that Joyce's experiences with the censors affected his writing in other ways.

The first of these experiences occurred during Joyce's second year (1899–1900) at University College, Dublin, when the college's president attempted to suppress Joyce's essay 'Drama and Life,' presumably because he disagreed with its rejection of the idea that the drama should be morally edifying. The second happened almost two years later (in October 1901), when Joyce's essay attacking Dublin's Irish Literary Theatre for producing mediocre but moral Irish plays, 'The Day of the Rabblement,' was rejected by *St. Stephen's*, the University College magazine, apparently because it contained a reference to d'Annunzio, a writer whose name appeared on the Index.[11] Forced to resort to private publication, Joyce introduced his essay (along with another essay that had been rejected by *St. Stephen's*) by announcing, '"These two Essays were commissioned by the Editor of St. Stephen's for that paper, but were subsequently refused insertion by the Censor."'[12]

These early conflicts with the censor were largely responsible for Joyce's growing sense that he was being persecuted by the religious authorities for his revolutionary ideas. And this sense of persecution, as his letter to Lady Gregory makes abundantly clear, was in turn the primary motivation for his decision to leave Ireland for Paris in 1902:

> I want to achieve myself – little or great as I may be – for I know that there is no heresy or no philosophy which is so abhorrent to my church as a human being, and accordingly I am going to Paris. ... And though I seem to have been driven out of my country here as a misbeliever I have found no man yet with a faith like mine.[13]

Ellmann has rightly observed that 'Joyce needed exile as a reproach to others and a justification of himself,' and that 'like other revolutionaries, he fattened on opposition,'[14] but it should not be forgotten that censorship – and not any need on Joyce's part – was directly responsible for Joyce's growing sense of exile. As Richard Brown puts it, 'exile and censorship were closely tied' in Joyce's mind.[15]

The movement from censorship to exile repeated itself when Joyce returned to Ireland early in 1903 because of the illness of his mother. His second departure for Paris (in 1904) was preceded by two more conflicts with the censor, the first involving the autobiographical essay 'A Portrait of the Artist,' in which Joyce presents himself as an artist rebel who will look to the heresiarchs, not the Church, for guidance.[16] The magazine to which Joyce submitted this work rejected it, according to Joyce's brother, 'because of the sexual experiences narrated in it.'[17] This, incidentally, was the first instance of censorship to give an indication of just how fruitful Joyce's struggle with the censor would be, for it provoked Joyce to begin work on *Stephen Hero*.[18] The next work to fall prey to the censor was 'The Holy Office,' a broadside in which Joyce attacks his Irish contemporaries for their hypocritical prudery, and declares that his will be the holy office of exposing what they fear to discuss. The broadside was submitted to and swiftly rejected by *St. Stephen's*, the same magazine that had previously rejected 'The Day of the Rabblement.'[19]

In Joyce's mind, the forces of censorship behind these rejections found expression in the incident that encouraged his second journey into exile, namely, his violent ejection from his residence in the Martello tower at the hands of Oliver St John Gogarty in mid-September. According to Ellmann,

> The incident solidified Joyce's intention of leaving the 'trolls', as he
> continued to call the forces that threatened his integrity. ... There was
> little hope that ... he could continue his work in his own country. He
> wished to be a writer, not a scapegoat, and foresaw a less irritated life
> on the continent.[20]

It is worth noting in this regard that in *Ulysses*, where Gogarty becomes Buck Mulligan, Stephen believes that Mulligan's hostility towards him belies fear of his art: 'He fears the lancet of my art as I fear that of his. The cold steelpen.'[21] The night after his eviction from the Martello tower, Joyce (accompanied by Nora, with whom he had fallen in love) became an exile once again.

Given the close connection between Joyce's art and life, his exile was bound to have literary consequences. Joyce acknowledged one such consequence early in 1905:

> I have come to accept my present situation as a voluntary exile – is it
> not so? This seems to me important both because I am likely to gener-
> ate out of it a sufficiently personal future ... and also because it sup-
> plies me with the note on which I propose to bring my novel to a
> close.[22]

The novel referred to was *Stephen Hero*, which Joyce never completed, but the ending he had in mind would eventually figure in the closing pages of *A Portrait of the Artist as a Young Man*:

> I will not serve [says Stephen Dedalus] that in which I no longer
> believe whether it call itself my home, my fatherland or my church:
> and I will try to express myself in some mode of life or art as freely as I
> can and as wholly as I can, using for my defence the only arms I allow
> myself to use – silence, exile, and cunning.[23]

The effects of exile – and thus of the censorship which provoked and sustained it – on Joyce's art would not be confined to the resolution of the plot of *Portrait*; Joyce's early conflicts with the censor would affect the content of *Stephen Hero* as well. In Chapters 17 and 18 of that novel (both of which were written during February 1905), Joyce represents the controversy surrounding his presentation of his essay 'Drama and Life' at University College. In doing so, Joyce reveals not only that censorship affected his art in diverse ways, but also that he was well aware of the defensive value of the esthetic theories he had formulated during the early stages of his exile in Paris and Pola, theories which had not figured in the version of 'Drama and Life' which Joyce actually presented at University College.

In *Stephen Hero*, Stephen uses his esthetic theories, which he describes as '"applied Aquinas,"' in a paper designed to refute 'the antique principle that the end of art is to instruct, to elevate, and to amuse':

> 'I am unable to find even a trace of this Puritanic conception of the esthetic purpose in the definition which Aquinas has given of beauty … . The qualifications he expects for beauty are in fact of so abstract and common a character that it is quite impossible for even the most violent partizan to use the Aquinatian theory with the object of attacking any work of art that we possess from the hand of any artist whatsoever.'[24]

The defensive value of Aquinas's theory of beauty is dramatized after Stephen learns that the President of the College, whom the Auditor of the Literary and Historical Society describes as 'the Censor,' will not allow him to read his paper. The President's fundamental objection to the paper is that Stephen's theory, 'if pushed to its logical conclusion – would emancipate the poet from all moral laws.'[25] Without denying the truth of the President's insight, Stephen justifies his position by appealing to Aquinas: 'I have only pushed to its logical conclusion the definition Aquinas has given of the beautiful. … Aquinas is certainly on the side of the capable artist. I hear no mention of instruction or elevation.'[26] Disarmed by this theorizing, the President allows Stephen to present his paper without further interference.

In addition to influencing the plot of *Portrait* and the content of *Stephen Hero*, Joyce's early conflicts with the censor engendered what may be described as the style of exile that Joyce began to develop early in 1907, shortly after Grant Richards refused to publish *Dubliners* (on 26 October 1906). The story of that refusal has been too well recounted elsewhere to need retelling here. What does need emphasis is that Joyce's frustration with the publisher was intense, and that Richards's rejection of *Dubliners* coincides with three major events in Joyce's career: the writing of 'The Dead,' the transformation of *Stephen Hero* into *A Portrait of the Artist as a Young Man*, and the conception of *Ulysses*. A letter Joyce wrote to

Stanislaus at the time indicates that these developments were related to his struggles with the forces of censorship. Joyce's frustration with Richards had made further work on *Stephen Hero* impossible and made Trieste unbearable.[27] Even after Joyce had left Trieste and settled in Rome, however, he remained unable to proceed with *Stephen Hero*. When Stanislaus urged him to get on with the novel, Joyce responded, 'I have written quite enough and before I do any more in that line I must see some reason why – I am not a literary Jesus Christ.'[28] Given the close relation between censorship and exile in Joyce's mind, it is hardly surprising that 'The Dead,' as Ellmann puts it, was Joyce's 'first song of exile.'[29]

Ellmann has in mind the apparent fondness with which Dublin is presented in 'The Dead,' a fondness which the other stories in *Dubliners* lack, and which one might expect to find in the works of an artist aware that a return to his country was becoming increasingly unlikely. But this is not the only sense in which 'The Dead' is a song of exile, for Joyce's new fondness for Dublin is accompanied by a new style involving both elaborate symbolism and pronounced inwardness. Anthony Burgess detects the appearance of this new style in Gretta Conroy's revelation to her husband Gabriel of the passionate love she has known as a young woman:

> The complex of emotions which takes possession of Gabriel's soul on this disclosure and on Gretta's transport of re-lived grief needs something more than a naturalistic technique for its expression. We see the emergence of a new Joyce, the deployment of the cunning of the author of *Ulysses*, and experience a visitation of terrible magic.[30]

The new Joyce Burgess has in mind is the one who transforms the snow that falls on the night of Gretta's revelation from 'the sublunary snow that drops on a winter city' to a symbol of supernatural resonance that 'unites the living and the dead.'[31] Thus, in adopting the style of exile Joyce moves from naturalism to symbolism.

The other remarkable stylistic development at the end of 'The Dead,' one which in a sense necessitates Joyce's recourse to symbolism, is the turn from the external drama that has played itself out at the social gathering Gretta and Gabriel have attended to the internal distress of Gabriel after the shock of Gretta's revelation. Once again, this development points to the future course of Joyce's work. As Herbert Gorman has argued, the subjectivity that creeps into the ending of 'The Dead' (Gabriel's intensely private and inexpressible response to Gretta's revelation) looks forward to 'that hidden subconscious territory' that Joyce would explore in *Portrait* and *Ulysses*[32] – not to mention *Finnegans Wake*.

These two developments, the reliance on symbolism rather than naturalism, and on internal rather than external drama, appearing as they do hard upon the rejection of *Dubliners* and the consequent heightening of Joyce's awareness of himself as an exile, mark the beginning of the style of exile.

That style becomes even more pronounced in Joyce's transformation of *Stephen Hero* into *A Portrait of the Artist as a Young Man,* his second song of exile, perhaps because Joyce did not complete it until after his most traumatic – and decisive – encounter with the censor. That encounter occurred in 1912 in Dublin, where Joyce had gone in a last ditch attempt to salvage his contract with Maunsel & Co for the publication of *Dubliners.* In the course of this visit, Maunsel's representative George Roberts informed Joyce that he had come to realize that 'the book's implications were anti-Irish and therefore out of keeping with his aims as an Irish publisher.'[33] Joyce's efforts to change his mind were all in vain, as they had been since 1909: Roberts refused to publish *Dubliners.* He did, however, offer to sell Joyce the sheets to his work. Unfortunately, these were in the possession of the printer George Falconer, who unexpectedly announced that he would not permit the distribution of such an unpatriotic work. On 11 September 1912, he destroyed what Joyce had hoped for three years would be the first edition of *Dubliners.* Devastated, Joyce left Ireland that night; he would never set foot there again.

Until Roberts's and Falconer's rejection of *Dubliners* Joyce's exile had been tentative, open to the possibility of return. But the Joyce that Mary and Padraic Colum saw on the day the sheets of *Dubliners* were burned was 'a Joyce now going into exile in earnest':

> It is from the time of this departure from Dublin in 1912 that the word 'exile' in the sense of 'banishment,' 'proscription' comes to be used by Joyce as something that evokes all one's spiritual powers and by doing so leads to creativeness. 'I go to encounter for the millionth time the reality of experience and to forge in the smithy of my soul the uncreated conscience of my race.' That was not said by the Stephen Hero whose book was written in Dublin, but by the Stephen Dedalus who after his final departure from Ireland transformed that book.[34]

It is impossible to say exactly how much of the transformation of *Stephen Hero* into *Portrait* occurred after Joyce's final departure from Ireland and how much before. Joyce scholars disagree. The distinction between the pre-1912 and post-1912 transformation of *Stephen Hero* into *Portrait,* however, is far less important than the fact that *Portrait* is Joyce's second censorship-induced song of exile.

In transforming *Stephen Hero* into *Portrait* Joyce travelled further along the path he had begun to follow in 'The Dead.' First, he abandoned the simple naturalism of *Stephen Hero* and adopted an elaborate symbolism. Second, he dropped the dramatic objectivity of *Stephen Hero* and turned inward to Stephen's consciousness, which became 'the theatre of whatever drama the book attempts to present.'[35] As Harry Levin has put it, in *Portrait* '[d]rama has retired before soliloquy'; thus, what is 'explicitly stated' in the naturalistic prose of *Stephen Hero* tends to be 'obliquely implied' in the symbolism of *Portrait*.[36] This shift from the dramatic to the psychological and from the naturalistic to the symbolic can be seen clearly in Joyce's transformation of Stephen's esthetics. In *Stephen Hero*, as we have seen, Stephen's theories about art are presented dramatically as 'applied Aquinas' and, as such, they have a clear rhetorical purpose: to protect Stephen's liberty as an artist from the power of the censor. In *Portrait*, however, the drama gives way to soliloquy, or something very closely resembling it.

In *Portrait*, the controversy regarding 'Drama and Life' virtually disappears, and the original defensive function of Stephen's applied Aquinas can only be inferred from Stephen's confrontations with McCann, the political propagandist who wants Stephen to sign a testimonial in support of universal peace, and with Davin, the Irish patriot who would have Stephen join the nationalist cause by learning Irish.[37] In the latter case, Stephen refuses to enlist in the nationalist cause by implying a connection between Davin's unwillingness to hear about his private life and the nationalist movement's intolerance of art that does not serve its purposes: 'This race and this country and this life produced me, he said. I shall express myself as I am.'[38] Only after these exchanges does Stephen expound his esthetic theories. He does so in the presence of Lynch and for no obvious reason. He begins, as Joyce did in his Paris notebook, by defining the tragic emotions of pity and terror. He then defines improper art:

> The feelings excited by improper art are kinetic, desire or loathing. Desire urges us to possess, to go to something; loathing urges us to abandon, to go from something. These are kinetic emotions. The arts which excite them, pornographical or didactic, are therefore improper arts. The esthetic emotion (I use the general term) is therefore static. The mind is arrested and raised above desire and loathing.[39]

The original defensive function of Stephen's theories is further disguised by virtue of the fact that Joyce presents them in a context which is, as W.T. Noon has observed, at once comic and symbolic.[40] For example, in the following passage Stephen's theories seem less important than the comically symbolic contrast they make possible between Lynch's crude animality and Stephen's cerebral speculation:

> —You say that art must not excite desire, said Lynch. I told you that one day I wrote my name in pencil on the backside of the Venus of Praxiteles in the Museum. Was that not desire?
> —I speak of normal natures, said Stephen. You also told me that when you were a boy in that charming carmelite school you ate pieces of dried cowdung.
> Lynch broke again into a whinny of laughter and again rubbed both his hands over his groins but without taking them from his pockets.[41]

In addition to disguising the defensive function of Stephen's esthetic theories, a function clearly evident in *Stephen Hero*, such symbolic statement serves to conceal the defensive function of the theories in Joyce's own struggle with the censor. As Noon recognized,

> The painstaking elaboration and interweaving into the finished work of the three principal symbols – the Daedalus myth; the poet as God-creator, redeemer, and priest; and the betrayal-crucifixion theme – counterpoints the presentation of Stephen's aesthetic arguments and enables Joyce to stand apart from them in a way which is not possible in [*Stephen Hero*].[42]

By integrating Stephen's presentation of his esthetic theory into the symbolic structure of *Portrait* in this manner, Joyce makes it 'an illustration of the theory itself' in so far as it does not seem to aim at encouraging belief or action in the reader.[43] He also achieves the impersonality of dramatic art which Stephen himself describes as an integral part of his theories: 'The artist, like the God of the creation, remains within or behind or beyond or above his handiwork, invisible, refined out of existence, indifferent, paring his fingernails.'[44] Thus, without appearing to do so, Joyce defends the literary artist's work against the charge of immorality and rejects the demand that art instruct and edify.

Lest this idea seem far-fetched, it should be noted that John Yeats had urged Quinn to employ Stephen's theories in his defense of *Ulysses* in the New York courts:

> In *A Portrait of an Artist as a Young Man* ... I came on these words – 'the feelings excited by improper arts are kinetic desire or loathing. Desire urges us to possess, to go to something; loathing urges us to abandon, to go from something. The arts which excite them [,] pornographic or didactic are therefore improper arts. The esthetic emotion (I use the

general term) is therefore static[.] The mind is arrested [and] raised above desire [and] loathing–'

I can't but think that this quotation is most important[.] Joyce is, *as you know*, a very serious artist working out his problems with the most intense diligence – and in this paragraph he defines for us his purpose. [And] that it is to lift the mind above both desire and loathing – [and] it expresses his very strong disapproval of the art that incites desire – what he calls pornographic art – In all his art his object is to get rid of desire [and] loathing [and] bring about a perfect tranquillity of the mind [and] soul – what he calls a *static* state as opposed to the *kinetic*[.] If therefore anything he writes awakens bad or libidinous desire it is not his fault.[45]

As we have seen, the passage from *Portrait* that Yeats senior quotes above did not figure directly in Quinn's defense of *Ulysses*, but it is featured prominently in Stuart Gilbert's *James Joyce's 'Ulysses'* (1930), a critical work that exerted a profound influence on Judge Woolsey's decision to lift the ban on Joyce's novel in 1933.

Stephen's esthetic theory, it should be emphasized, is the theory of an artist in exile. This is the case not just because Joyce formulated it during his exile, but because the theory effectively removes the artist from the political realm in a double sense. In one sense, Stephen's theory of stasis exiles the artist by arguing that the state has no reason to constrain the artist's freedom; in another sense, the theory exiles the artist by arguing that his art cannot affect the beliefs or actions of his contemporaries.

In addition to being the theory of an artist in exile, Stephen's theory points to the defensive value of the style of exile in which it is presented. As Stephen explains to Lynch, the stasis on which his defense of artistic freedom rests is 'called forth, prolonged and at last dissolved by what I call the rhythm of beauty.'[46] For Joyce, such rhythm was associated with liberation. Thus he defined the lyric as the '"simple liberation of a rhythm."'[47] The liberation, as Robert Scholes has shown in his discussion of the poem that Stephen Dedalus makes up in reaction to the threat he receives in the first chapter of *Portrait*, is of the poet as well as the rhythm. The threat in question is that, to punish Stephen for something he has said, 'the eagles will come and pull out his eyes.'[48] The poem Stephen composes mentally in reaction is, in part,

> *Pull out his eyes,*
> *Apologise,*
> *Apologise,*
> *Pull out his eyes.*[49]

As Scholes points out, the poem (a rhythmic repetition of words and phrases) 'offers the child a refuge' from the threat.[50] When this view of the liberating quality of rhythm is combined with Stephen's definition of the word – 'the first formal esthetic relation of part to part in any esthetic whole or of an esthetic whole to its part or parts or of any part to the esthetic whole of which it is a part'[51] – it seems plausible that Joyce's turn from direct naturalistic statement in *Stephen Hero* to an increasingly elaborate use of symbolic motifs in *Portrait* was intended, among other things, to free his art from the threat of the censor.

In considering whether Joyce really believed in Stephen's esthetic theory, his comment on the Viconian theories of *Finnegans Wake* is instructive: 'I would not pay overmuch attention to these theories beyond using them for all they are worth, but they have gradually forced themselves on me through the circumstances of my life.'[52] Both points are useful: Stephen's esthetic theories did force themselves on Joyce through the actions of those who would constrain his freedom as an artist; and Joyce did use them for all they were worth to defend himself against those enemies.

Joyce's need to defend himself against the censor was far from over when he wrote the last chapter of *Portrait* in the months following his final departure from Ireland in 1912. By the end of 1913, however, during which he wrote *Exiles* and continued to work on *Portrait*, Joyce's publication prospects began to brighten. In November Grant Richards requested a second look at the manuscript of *Dubliners*. And in December, Ezra Pound contacted Joyce for the first time, asking permission to publish a poem in his Imagist anthology and requesting a look at any other publishable material. The beginning of 1914 brought more good news. Pound informed Joyce that he would send *Portrait* off for serial publication in the *Egoist* and three stories from *Dubliners* to New York for publication in H.L. Mencken's magazine, the *Smart Set*. Then, at the end of January, Grant Richards, who had rejected *Dubliners* in 1906, agreed to publish it after all. Three days later, on Joyce's birthday (2 February), the *Egoist* commenced serial publication of *Portrait*. Joyce must have felt it was all a dream; for the first time in nine years he had flown free of the nets of the censor.

It was at this time, in March 1914, that Joyce began to write *Ulysses*. Ellmann has argued that the publication of *Dubliners* and *Portrait* (along with other factors, such as the emotional and financial support Joyce began to receive through Ezra Pound, and Joyce's move from Trieste to the neutral city of Zurich) led to a less insurrectionary vision in *Ulysses* than in *Portrait*.[53] For Ellmann, this development is embodied most clearly in the transfer of Joyce's affections from Stephen Dedalus the rebel artist to Leopold Bloom the complacent husband, the real hero of

Ulysses. This view of Joyce's novel, however, neglects several important facts, including the brevity of Joyce's respite from the censor in 1914–15, the circumstances surrounding the conception of *Ulysses*, and the controversy provoked by its serial publication.

Joyce's respite from the interference of the censor lasted only eleven months. As early as January, 1915, by which time Joyce had written only the first episode of *Ulysses*, the printers who set type for the *Egoist* had begun to suppress passages of *Portrait*. Joyce would not be aware of this fact until July, but he learned in May that Grant Richards, who had published *Dubliners* in June 1914, was declining his option to publish *Portrait*. Richards's explicit reason was the war and the related general depression, but as Ann Catherine McCullough has pointed out, he 'hinted at censorable content as his underlying reason'[54]: 'I am afraid of the book. It demands a public of intelligent readers. There are such readers but they are difficult to get at; and they are peculiarly difficult to get at now.'[55]

By the end of May 1915, before he had completed the second episode of *Ulysses*, Joyce had every reason to believe that his troubles with the censor were far from over. By July, after Joyce had left Trieste for Zurich and completed the second episode of *Ulysses*, there could have been no doubt in his mind, for it was then that he discovered that the January instalment of *Portrait* had been expurgated by the printers. In the same month, publisher Martin Secker rejected *Portrait*, after Joyce's agent, James Pinker, had insisted that the novel be published unexpurgated. Joyce was perfectly aware that other publishers would follow, especially after the suppression of D.H. Lawrence's *The Rainbow* early in November. In other words, the relative freedom from censorship that Joyce enjoyed in 1914 15 was altogether too brief to bring about a change in the direction of Joyce's artistic development.[56]

Ellmann's view of *Ulysses* as less insurrectionary than *Portrait* is also called into question by the fact that Joyce conceived of the novel long before 1914. Like 'The Dead' and *Portrait*, the first two songs of Joyce's exile, *Ulysses* was born in the wake of Grant Richards's rejection of *Dubliners*. About a week after Richards had first rejected *Dubliners* in 1906, Joyce informed Stanislaus, 'I have a new story for Dubliners in my head. It deals with Mr Hunter' (a Dubliner rumoured to be Jewish and to have an unfaithful wife).[57] By 13 November, about two weeks after Grant Richards had confirmed his rejection of *Dubliners* for the last time, Joyce had also arrived at a name for his story: 'Ulysses.'

According to Giorgio Melchiori, Joyce's recollection of Hunter is to be found in his Roman experience: the 'memory of Mr Hunter came back to him ... because he recognized in that unremarkable figure ... his own present condition as a friendless expatriate in a city whose very architecture celebrated the triumph of a religion he had rejected.'[58] Joyce's reading in Rome, according to Melchiori, also illuminates his choice of Hunter. In Guglielmo Ferrero's *Young Europe*, Joyce found a sympathetic identification of the Jews with the 'missionary conscience.'[59] And in the anti-clerical newspaper *L'Asino*, which described the Socialist Party Congress then in progress in Rome as taking place under the scrutiny of two '"colossal gendarmes, the Quirinal and the Vatican,"' Joyce found an expression of the 'basic implications' of the title of his story, an image of his own attempt to navigate between Church and State in *Ulysses*.[60]

Melchiori's analysis is certainly plausible, but it should be noted that Joyce did not need the works of Ferrero or the political commentary of *L'Asino* to remind him that he was an exile with a mission (or 'holy office') who was forced to navigate between the perilous obstacles of Church and State. What forces, if not those of Church and State, were ultimately responsible for Joyce's early encounters with the censor and Richards's rejection of *Dubliners*? From the beginning, Joyce conceived of his exile as a strategy in his struggle with Church and State, as his letter to Lady Gregory makes clear. And from the beginning, the opposition of Church and State manifested itself most forcefully in the censorship of his work. Richards's rejection of *Dubliners*, more than Joyce's Roman experience, strengthened Joyce's sense of himself as an exile.

It is first and foremost from this perspective that the 'basic implications' of Joyce's title should be seen. If, as Melchiori asserts, the political message of *Ulysses* is the attempt to find a liberating passage between the Scylla and Charybdis of Church and State, then the title of the novel should be understood to refer not just to its hero, Leopold Bloom, but to the novel itself. Joyce's experiences with the censor could not have helped but drive home the fact that books, like artists, are citizens of republics, where they are liable to be suppressed as subversive. Thus, it may well be that *Ulysses* was conceived and written as a book that would evade the censorship of Church and State without compromising Joyce's holy office of pursuing candour. If this view is correct, Joyce could hardly have chosen a better name for his novel. Ulysses was the cunning warrior who devised the Trojan Horse, who navigated the perilous waters between Scylla and Charybdis, who blinded the Cyclops, and then escaped his wrath by hiding in the fleece of a ram. As the history of the novel's reception makes clear, Joyce's *Ulysses* would do likewise.

The controversial nature of that reception also calls into question Ellmann's view of *Ulysses* as less insurrectionary than *Portrait*. As previously mentioned, the reception of *Ulysses* included four suppressions of *The Little Review* by the United States Post Office and two courtroom battles in New York in 1920–1; the subsequent banning of the novel throughout most of the English-speaking world; a major court battle in

New York, which culminated in a decision lifting the ban on the novel in 1933; the appeal from that decision in 1934, which resulted in a split opinion affirming the 1933 decision; and, finally, the failed attempt to make a further appeal to the US Supreme Court. Far from suggesting that *Ulysses* was less insurrectionary than *Portrait*, this controversy tends rather to confirm that *Ulysses* far surpasses both *Dubliners* and *Portrait* in the daring of its forays into forbidden terrain.

In December 1917, as we have seen, Pound warned Joyce that *Ulysses* would be censored if published without expurgation. Serialization of the novel in *The Little Review* began in March 1918. By July (shortly after he had completed the 'Hades' episode), Joyce knew that Pound had suppressed passages from the 'Calypso' episode. Thus, on 29 July, Joyce asked Miss Weaver to inform B.W. Huebsch that 'the fourth episode of *Ulysses* as published in the June issue of the *Little Review* is not my full text and that the excised paragraphs must be reinstated and the altered words restored in any proof he may set up.'[61] It is more difficult to say when he learned of the Post Office suppressions. Since the suppression of the January 1919 *Little Review* would have prevented him from obtaining a copy, he may have suspected government intervention as early as March or April. The censorship of *Ulysses* was certainly on his mind in mid-May, when he informed James Pinker that 'neither [Grant Richards] nor any other publisher in London would ever publish it or find anyone to print it or to buy it, if printed.'[62]

Quinn wrote to inform him of the Post Office's suppression of the May *Little Review* at the end of June, so Joyce certainly knew of it by sometime in July.[63] It seems unlikely that Quinn's letter could have reached him in less than a week; none the less, the censorship of *Ulysses* was clearly on Joyce's mind on 2 July, when he informed Harriet Shaw Weaver that the writing of *Ulysses* would take longer than expected:

> As regards my book *Ulysses* it will not be finished, I suppose, for a year or so and when it is finished (if it is finished) I do not believe that Mr Richards or any of his colleagues in the United Kingdom will publish it or even find printers to print it. Some personal worries have also retarded its progress ... . [Huebsch] intends to call on you with regard to an eventual publication of the book – to be printed, possibly, in Africa.[64]

On 18 May 1918, Joyce had informed Miss Weaver that *Ulysses* would be finished by the summer of 1919.[65] Now that the summer of 1919 had arrived, however, Joyce was estimating that it would take at least another year and a half to finish the job.

One reason that *Ulysses* was taking longer than anticipated was that Joyce's artistic goals were changing. Michael Groden has argued that Joyce passed through three distinct stages in the course of his work on *Ulysses*. The first stage, including the first nine episodes from 'Telemachus' to 'Wandering Rocks,' is characterized by Joyce's use of the interior monologue and his interest in character. The final stage, including the last four episodes from 'Circe' to 'Penelope,' are distinguished by the appearance of new styles and an interest in schematic correspondences. In the middle stage, covering the episodes from 'Wandering Rocks' to 'Oxen of the Sun,' Joyce begins to experiment with the monologue technique and to adopt a series of 'parody styles' while maintaining a balance between the 'stylistic surface' and the 'human story.'[66]

Although the middle stage begins with 'Wandering Rocks' (in which Joyce uses the monologue technique to represent the minds of characters other than Stephen and Bloom) and 'Sirens' (in which he distorts the original style radically), it is not until 'Cyclops' that Joyce definitively abandons the novel's initial style. Groden stresses that the 'Cyclops' episode represents a crucial turning point:

> [Joyce's] earliest work on 'Cyclops' in mid-June 1919 may ... represent the precise chronological point at which he stopped writing one kind of book, basically concerned with Stephen and Bloom, and began to write another, in which a succession of parody styles, and eventually a group of schematic correspondences, began to take over.[67]

According to Groden, this change in Joyce's artistic goals was not planned in advance.[68] In considering its cause, Groden suggests simply that Joyce's previous technique had become confining, inadequate for Joyce's expanding vision, perhaps even tiresome;[69] he does not suspect that the change in Joyce's style might have been related to the censorship of *Ulysses* in New York. Yet the possibility is enticing, because Joyce's writing of 'Cyclops' (mid-June to October 1919) coincides roughly with his discovery that the May 1919 *Little Review* had been suppressed on account of the second half of 'Scylla & Charybdis,' a discovery which undoubtedly reminded him that the trials of *Ulysses* were far from over.[70] In light of Joyce's earlier responses to the censorship of his works, and of the fact that the shift in 'Cyclops' from character to style, from story to structure, effects a transfer of the reader's attention away from the controversial action of the story to its artifice, just as the turn from naturalism to symbolism in *Portrait* diverted attention from the dramatic action of *Stephen Hero* – in light of all this, it seems reasonable to suspect the change of style in 'Cyclops' was motivated at least in part by the censorship of *Ulysses* in New York. Groden insists that the 'translation' of the story of Stephen and Bloom which occurs in 'Cyclops' 'does not mean that the style represents an impediment to our understanding of some real action,'[71] but the style certainly makes the 'real action' of the episode more difficult to determine and, in doing so, makes possible a more effective defense against the censor.

In the months following his discovery that *Ulysses* had been suppressed by government authorities in the United States, Joyce remained aware of and vexed by the censor's attacks on his novel. '*The Sirens* has not yet been printed,' he wrote Stanislaus in September. 'I am now writing *The Cyclops*. Here and there passages have been cut, ruining my text. They will however be put back when the book is published. It will be printed, I expect, in Japan.'[72] In December Joyce lamented his publication difficulties to Carlo Linati, linking the fate of *Ulysses* with that of his earlier works:

> The story of my books is very strange. For the publication of Dubliners I had to struggle for ten years. The whole first edition of 1000 copies was burned at Dublin by fraud; some say it was the doing of priests, some of enemies, others of the then Viceroy or his consort, Countess Aberdeen. Altogether it is a mystery. ... As for the *Portrait*, it was refused by nearly all the publishers in London. ... My new book *Ulysses* was to appear in the *Egoist* of London. The same old story. From the very beginning the printers refused again. It appeared in fragments in the New York *Little Review*. Several times it was taken out of circulation through the post, by the action of the American Government. Now legal action is being taken against it.[73]

And early in January 1920, by which time he was working on 'Nausicaa,' Joyce complained to Frank Budgen that the first part of 'Cyclops' had appeared 'with excision of the erection allusion.'[74]

The best approach to defining the way in which these suppressions of *Ulysses* affected Joyce's late writing and revision of the novel is through the strategies Joyce used to prepare the public to receive the Paris edition of his novel. As previously mentioned, Joyce was acutely aware of the importance of that reception, and, having become by that time a 'shrewd publicist'[75] for his own works, he would not forgo any opportunity to smooth the waves for his embattled hero. Just as Athena intervened on behalf of her beloved *Ulysses*, so Joyce would do what he could for his novel.

Joyce found his opportunity in Valèry Larbaud, a French writer of note whom he had met through the good offices of Sylvia Beach and Shakespeare & Company. Crazy about *Ulysses* and eager to promote Joyce's work, Larbaud offered to write an article for *La Nouvelle Revue Française* to be based on a talk on Joyce and *Ulysses* he would deliver at Adrienne Monnier's bookshop, La Maison des Amis des Livres. Joyce readily accepted these offers and, as Litz has observed, 'took an active part in the preparations' that ensued.[76] Joyce chose the passage to be read in English at Larbaud's talk (from 'Sirens') and, in the intervening months, met with Larbaud regularly and 'discussed the novel in detail.' Finally, when the talk was imminent, Joyce sent Larbaud the celebrated 'schema' or plan of *Ulysses*.

We will have occasion to discuss the details of the schema later. For the time being it will suffice to note that Joyce seems to have attached considerable importance to it. He first mentioned his intention of sending it to Larbaud in a letter dated 6 November 1920. Then, nine days later, after he had sent the schema as intended, Joyce wrote to Larbaud requesting its return: 'Can you let me have that little plan I gave you of *Ulysses*. I shall amplify it and send it back next day. Please let me have it tomorrow.'[77] Eleven days later, Joyce wrote to Larbaud once again, asking if they could dine together that night: 'I hope so as I want to show you and comment on the new plan and discuss this matter which is rather delicate, I think, and important.'[78]

Why was this schema important to Joyce? The question is perhaps most effectively answered if it is subsumed under the question of how Larbaud's talk was intended to smooth the waters for *Ulysses*. The text of Larbaud's talk, delivered in December 1921 and later published as 'James Joyce' in *La Nouvelle Revue Française*, provides the answer. In that text, Larbaud reveals his purpose at once. The reputation of Joyce in the literary world, he says, is analogous to that of Einstein or Freud among scientists. For some, Joyce is the greatest living writer in English, the equal of writers like Swift, Sterne, Fielding. None the less, to the New York Society for the Suppression of Vice, Joyce is only 'an Irishman who has written a pornographic work entitled *Ulysses*.'[79] Larbaud then makes his own position abundantly clear:

> We cannot hesitate one instant between the judgments of the members of the Vice Society and the opinion of men of letters who know the work of James Joyce. It is implausible that people cultivated enough to savour a writer this difficult mistake a work of pornography for a work of literature.[80]

Having posited a clear (though questionable) distinction between pornography and literature, Larbaud proceeds (via cursory treatments of Joyce's biography and early works) to *Ulysses*. The literate reader of *Ulysses*, Larbaud argues, one who is equipped to persevere beyond the confusion of the first few pages, will come to realize that the novel is made up of eighteen parts dealing with different aspects of life in the Irish capital. In this respect *Ulysses* is like *Dubliners*, but a crucial difference distinguishes these two books. *Dubliners* 'has no unity; each story is isolated'; by contrast, the episodes of *Ulysses* form a unified whole: 'We must acknowledge it: although each of these eighteen parts differs from all the others in form and language, they form nonetheless an organized whole, a book.'[81]

At this point, when he is desirous of establishing the unity of *Ulysses* as a whole, Larbaud introduces the contents of the schema:

And at the same time that we arrive at this conclusion, all sorts of concordances, analogies and correspondences between these different parts appear to us, as when one regards the night sky for a little while, the number of visible stars appears to grow. We begin to discover and divine symbols, a sketch, a plan … .[82]

Later, Larbaud elaborates:

Thus each episode will deal with a particular science or art, contain a particular symbol, represent a given organ of the human body, have its particular colour (as in the Catholic liturgy), have its proper technique, and in terms of the episode's time, correspond to one of the hours of the day.

This is not all, and in each of the panels thus divided, the author will inscribe new symbols even more particular, the correspondences.

In order to be more clear, let us take an example: episode IV of the adventures. Its title is Aeolus: the setting in which it takes place is a newspaper office; the time at which it takes place is noon; the organ to which it corresponds: the lung; the art of which it treats: rhetoric; its colour: red; its symbolic figure: the editor-in-chief; its technique: the enthymeme; its correspondences: a person who corresponds to Homer's Aeolus; incest compared to journalism; the floating island of Aeolus: the press; the person named Dignam, who died suddenly three days before and to whose funeral Bloom went (which constitutes the episode of the descent to Hades): Elpenor.[83]

Having taken the trouble to describe in great detail and with great emphasis the elaborate design of *Ulysses* in order to convince the reader that Joyce's novel is a coherent, unified whole – which therefore cannot, according to the terms of Larbaud's argument, be obscene – Larbaud proceeds to make the remarkable assertion that the elaborate structure which Joyce describes in the schema is 'for himself, not for the reader; no title or subtitle reveals it to us. It's up to us, if we want to take the trouble, to discover it.'[84] Larbaud's logic is here clearly at odds with his rhetoric, for if the analogies and correspondences described by the schema are not for the reader, why has Larbaud emphasized them for the reader's benefit? The obvious answer is the censorship of *Ulysses*: Larbaud, encouraged by Joyce, emphasized the schematic elements of *Ulysses* in order to defend the novel against the attacks of the censor.

The fact that Larbaud (and after him Stuart Gilbert and others) used the schema to defend *Ulysses* against the censor does not necessarily prove that Joyce wrote the symbols, analogies, and correspondences which the schema describes into *Ulysses* for the same defensive purposes. However, in light of Joyce's earlier literary responses to the censorship of his works, the possibility should not be dismissed out of hand, for several reasons. For one, circumstances surrounding the initial appearance of the schemata suggest that their importance may always have been associated in Joyce's mind with the need to defend his novel against the censor. For another, the schema plays a crucial role in Joyce's late writing and revision of *Ulysses*, especially after Joyce learned that the novel had been definitively suppressed by the New York courts: while Joyce was encouraging Larbaud to emphasize the schematic elements of *Ulysses*, Joyce was actively writing them into the novel. Finally, Joyce's schema-inspired late work on *Ulysses* really did make for a more effective defense of the novel than the one Quinn had been able to mount in 1920–1.

Joyce first began to talk about the 'schematic structurings' of his novel in September 1920 while he was working on 'Circe.' In a letter to John Quinn, Joyce referred to the 'scheme' of his novel, and in a letter to Carlo Linati he included 'a sort of summary – key – skeleton – scheme (for your personal use only).'[85] Why does the schema appear at this time? In light of Joyce's reasons for producing the Larbaud schema in 1921, it seems reasonable to suspect that censorship might have had something to do with it.

The subject could not have been far from Joyce's mind in September 1920. By that time he was well aware that the serial version of *Ulysses* had been suppressed three times in the United States. In August, Joyce had received a foreboding letter from John Quinn proposing a private edition of *Ulysses*, the implication clearly being that a public edition was becoming increasingly unlikely. In the same month he had received word that Harriet Shaw Weaver, because of difficulties with printers, had decided to abandon her long-cherished plans to publish *Ulysses* in England. Joyce's letter to Linati strongly suggests that these developments were related to the appearance of the schemata: after introducing the schemata Joyce proceeds to discuss the censorship of *Ulysses*:

> For seven years I have been working at this book – blast it! ... No English printer wanted to print a word of it. In America the review was suppressed four times.[86] Now, as I hear, a great movement is being prepared against the publication, initiated by Puritans, English Imperialists, Irish Republicans, Catholics – what an alliance! Gosh, I ought to be given the Nobel prize for peace![87]

In light of the rough coincidence of Joyce's interest in the schema and his growing conviction that a movement was afoot to prevent publication of *Ulysses* (a conviction confirmed early in November when Joyce learned that the 'Nausicaa' episode had been suppressed),[88] it would seem significant that Joyce's artistic goals took a second remarkable turn at the same time. That turn first manifested itself in Joyce's work on 'Circe,' which he had begun writing in May–June 1920. At that time, he seems to have planned an episode similar in scope and length to 'Cyclops,' 'Nausicaa,' and 'Oxen of the Sun,' each of which had taken about three months to write.[89] But by the end of September, shortly after he had sent Linati a copy of the schema, Joyce informed Frank Budgen that 'Circe,' instead of moving smoothly toward completion, was getting 'wilder and worse and more involved.'[90] In the same letter, Joyce expressed his confidence that it would 'all work out,' but it would take him almost three more months to complete the episode. In December, Joyce finally announced that 'Circe' was finished. The episode had required an unprecedented eight drafts, stretched to about twice the length and taken about twice the time of any previous episode.

In considering why 'Circe' took so long, Groden shrewdly looks to the censorship of *Ulysses* in *The Little Review*. Noting that the suppression of the July–August 1920 instalment of 'Nausicaa' had made the publication of 'Circe' improbable, thus eliminating all submission deadlines, Groden suspects that the US censorship influenced Joyce's composition of 'Circe,' allowing Joyce to develop the episode far beyond 'the proportions originally devised.'[91] In 1921, Groden notes, this process of expansion would repeat itself with the 'Ithaca' and 'Penelope' episodes. Thus, with the February 1921 ruling of the New York Court of Special Sessions in mind, Groden writes, 'The judges in the *Little Review* case may have provided another of the accidents that changed the shape of *Ulysses*.'[92] Groden is right to link the censorship of *The Little Review* to the composition of *Ulysses*, but he does not fully grasp the nature of the connection. For him, the censorship of *The Little Review* accounts for only the remarkable length of 'Circe' and 'Ithaca' and 'Penelope': no previous episodes, he notes, had developed so far beyond the proportions originally devised.

Groden's analysis of the link between the censorship and the shape of *Ulysses* goes no further because he perceives no connection between the censorship and the schema. And the schema, as Groden himself emphasizes, plays a crucial role in the final stage of Joyce's work on *Ulysses*, a stage which begins as 'Circe' gets 'wilder and worse and more involved':

> Both in new work and in revision, his last stage of work is marked by his goals of expansion and elaboration. ... His well-known revision of earlier episodes occurred almost exclusively during this stage – he added many new Homeric and other correspondences to the earlier episodes, and he 'recast,' 'amplified,' or 'retouched' them to resemble the later ones more closely. The schemata he prepared during this stage and offered to selected friends as guides to his book serve as emblems of his last period of work on *Ulysses*.[93]

As Walton Litz has observed, the last stage of writing and revision accounts for the striking difference between the text of the Paris edition of *Ulysses* and the version that appeared serially in *The Little Review*:

> When one reads the versions of the early episodes published between 1918 and 1920 in the *Egoist* and *Little Review* one is struck immediately by the absence of many of those elaborate 'correspondences' documented by Stuart Gilbert and outlined by Joyce on a chart he circulated among his friends. The familiar *schema* of the novel – the correspondence of each episode to a particular organ, colour, symbol, and art, and the casting of each episode in a distinctive style – is absent from the earlier versions. One of Joyce's major aims in revising the earlier episodes of *Ulysses* was to impose this elaborate pattern of correspondences upon them.[94]

In other words, the elements of *Ulysses* first described in the Linati schema, and later elaborated in the schema Larbaud used to defend *Ulysses* against the accusations of the censors in December 1921, were written into *Ulysses* between September 1920 and February 1922.

According to Groden, Joyce's mining of earlier episodes for the expansion and elaboration of 'Circe' was so extensive that, by the time the episode was finished, *Ulysses* itself had become 'one great "character."'[95] Groden's choice of words is telling, for it underlines the fact that 'Circe,' by beginning the transformation of *Ulysses* into 'a vast scheme of references and correspondences that could be linked in new juxtapositions,'[96] increased the unity of the novel and shifted attention from the thoughts and actions of its characters to its elaborate artifice as a text.

The same can be said of the so-called 'great revision' of *Ulysses* which Joyce undertook in the summer of 1921, a revision that completed the transformation of the novel into the spectacularly elaborate web of symbols, motifs, and correspondences envisioned by the schemata. In the course of this late revision,

> Joyce added over eighty 'alimentary allusions' to 'Lestrygonians' after he sent the typescript to Darantiere; all are extensions of the schema entries for the episode's 'organ' and 'correspondences' – the esophagus, and hunger, food, and teeth. Similarly, he added numerous references to the heart in 'Hades' and new musical puns in 'Sirens.' In another extension of the schema, he revised several episodes to achieve a greater 'expressive form'; examples of this are the flower imagery in 'Lotus Eaters' and the newspaper subheads in 'Aeolus.'[97]

The following passage from 'Lotus-Eaters,' quoted by Litz, provides a good indication of Joyce's preoccupation with schematic concerns in his late revisions (the relevant additions appear in italics):

> He tore the flower gravely from its pinhold smelt its almost no smell and placed it in his heart pocket. *Language of flowers. They like it because no-one can hear. Or a poison bouquet to strike him down.* Then, walking slowly forward, he read the letter again, murmuring here and there a word. *Angry tulips with you darling manflower punish your cactus if you don't please poor forgetmenot how I long violets to dear roses when we soon anemone meet all naughty nightstalk wife Martha's perfume.* Having read it all he took it from the newspaper and put it back in his sidepocket.[98]

Although Joyce's late revision continues the transformation he had initiated in 'Circe,' it 'does not seem to have occurred to him before the summer of 1921,' some two months after he discovered that *Ulysses* had been definitively suppressed by the Court of Special Sessions in New York.[99] But by mid-June 1921, Joyce was combining the writing of 'Ithaca' and 'Penelope' with the radical revising of earlier episodes which would increase the length of some of them by more than one-third. His work received a setback at the beginning of July, when he suffered an eye attack which would incapacitate him for five weeks, but from the time of his recovery in August 1921 until the publication of *Ulysses* on 2 February 1922, Joyce would proceed with his revisions.

The timing of the great revision thus increases the likelihood that it was provoked in part by Joyce's growing awareness of the vulnerability of his novel to the attacks of the censor and motivated by his desire to defend his work.[100] So does the coincidence of Joyce's use of the schema in the late writing and revising of *Ulysses* with his use of the schema in the preparations for Larbaud's talk. Finally, so does the letter Joyce sent to Harriet Shaw Weaver in June. In the course of discussing a number of the many rumours about himself, Joyce wrote:

> There is a further opinion that I am a crafty simulating and dissimulating Ulysses-like type, a 'jejeune jesuit', selfish and cynical. There is some truth in this, I suppose: but it is by no means all of me (nor was it of Ulysses) and it has been my habit to apply this alleged quality to safeguard my poor creations. ... [ellipses Joyce's][101]

If Joyce's late elaboration of the schematic elements of *Ulysses* is, in part at least, an attempt to safeguard his poor creation, then we would do well to ponder once again the implications of the novel's title in relation to the work it names. If the book proper rather than (or in addition to) Leopold Bloom is the counterpart of Homer's hero, then the schematic elaborations of the novel may be thought of as analogous to the disguise that Ulysses adopts at the advice of Athena, and which makes possible his victorious homecoming. The analogy holds good in so far as Joyce's elaboration of the schematic elements of *Ulysses* eventually facilitated the novel's homecoming to the United States in 1933 by providing Morris Ernst with the means whereby he could mount a brilliant defense of the novel.

The schematic structurings which Joyce emphasized in his late work on *Ulysses* helped Ernst to defend the novel from the attacks of the censor in several ways. First, they increased the apparent unity of the novel by emphasizing what Joseph Frank has called its 'spatial form.' Frank's discussion of the concept in relation to *Ulysses* helps to clarify both the importance of the whole as a defense of the parts and the need to emphasize those elements which would make an apprehension of the whole possible:

> A knowledge of the whole is essential to an understanding of any part; but unless one is a Dubliner, such knowledge can be obtained only after the book has been read and all the references fitted into their proper place and grasped as a unity. Although the burdens placed on the reader by this method of composition may seem insuperable, the fact remains that Joyce, in his unbelievably laborious fragmentation of narrative structure, proceeded on the assumption that a unified spatial apprehension of his work would ultimately be possible.[102]

In light of Larbaud's use of the schema, one might explain Joyce's use of the schema in the writing and reception of *Ulysses* as the product of his desire to hasten a 'unified spatial apprehension' in order to prove, among other things, that his novel was a coherent work of art.

The second way in which Joyce's late revisions to *Ulysses* facilitated an effective defense of the novel is related to the first, for by facilitating the apprehension of the spatial form of *Ulysses*, they made it possible for the reader of the novel to 'feel the rhythm of its structure,' as Stephen Dedalus says.[103] As previously mentioned in relation to *Portrait*, apprehension of the rhythm of a work is what calls forth the stasis which ensures (in theory at least) that the work cannot be deemed obscene, pornographic, or otherwise morally harmful:

> Beauty expressed by the artist cannot awaken in us an emotion which is kinetic or a sensation which is purely physical. It awakens, or ought to awaken, or induces, or ought to induce, an esthetic stasis, ... a stasis called forth, prolonged and at last dissolved by what I call the rhythm of beauty.[104]

The third way in which Joyce's late revisions served to protect the novel is closely related to the first two, for in emphasizing its elaborate formal unity, its intricate web of symbolic correspondences, its Homeric parallels, they shifted attention, or at least permitted the shift of attention, from the thoughts and actions of the characters to the artifice of the novel as a whole. In so doing they distracted attention from the controversial parts of the novel. Although he does not suspect that this was one of Joyce's aims in revising *Ulysses*, Litz has noted the same shift in emphasis in discussing Joyce's late revisions of 'Aeolus':

> Joyce, in revising *Ulysses*, ran the danger of placing disproportionate emphasis on the *schema* of the novel. The analogy between Bloom's adventures in the newspaper office and Ulysses' at the isle of Aeolus is a secondary aspect of the episode, and the various correspondences (Colour, Art, Organ) are less important than the dissection of Irish public life or the development of Bloom's character. However, Joyce's revisions placed these secondary qualities in a prominent position, and although they do not obscure the episode's major themes there is a significant shift in emphasis between the 1918 and 1922 versions.[105]

These observations lead Litz to conclude that 'The *schema* upon which Joyce relied during his revisions was overemphasized,'[106] but this view reflects Litz's belief that the important action in *Ulysses* occurs at the level of the characters and their experiences. From the point of view of

Joyce's defensive use of the schema, however, what happens on the level of the schematic correspondences is also important. Or, to put it another way, if the schematic correspondences were over-emphasized, they were over-emphasized for a very practical reason. Interestingly, Litz's reflections implicitly support the idea that in *Ulysses*, under the pressure of censorship, Joyce was making important steps toward the safe obscurity of *Finnegans Wake*: 'Fortunately the human forces of Bloom and Stephen … kept the revisions of *Ulysses* from completely overshadowing the *données* of each episode. But in *Finnegans Wake*, … one often finds crucial elements in the first drafts which have been totally obscured by the time the final version is reached.'[107]

This brings us to the fourth and final way in which Joyce's revisions helped to save *Ulysses* from the censor: by emphasizing the novel's complex formal unity, its intricate web of symbolic correspondences, and its elaborate artifice, Joyce's late revisions emphasize that the language of art is not the same as the language of the marketplace, but rather a foreign language that must be diligently studied before it can be understood. In other words, Joyce's late revisions provide grounds for arguing that to understand *Ulysses* is not to appreciate its action at the level of the human characters but rather to appreciate the novel itself as a character in its own right, a character with an intricate language all of its own. In this regard in particular, Joyce's late transformation of *Ulysses* should be seen as anticipating the linguistic idiosyncrasy of *Finnegans Wake* which, as previously mentioned, finally allowed Joyce to complete the task of making obscenity safe for literature and thus fly free of the nets of the censor.

The need to defend *Ulysses* against the charge of obscenity, however, would continue for many years after the publication of the Paris edition. By the end of 1922, the US authorities were regularly confiscating copies of the Paris edition – even those Sylvia Beach had disguised with dust jackets bearing titles like *Shakespeare's Works* and (better yet) *Merry Tales for Little Folks*.[108] Harriet Shaw Weaver's Egoist Press edition, also published in Paris (October 1922) so as to avoid trouble with English printers, fared no better. Before the end of the year, Miss Weaver's representative in Paris, John Rodker, informed her that 400 copies for US subscribers had been confiscated by US Customs.[109] The second Egoist edition of 500 copies of *Ulysses*, published in January 1923 to replace those destroyed by Customs authorities in the USA, met with a similar fate, this time at the hands of the English Customs authorities, who confiscated 499 copies in Folkestone harbour. After Miss Weaver declined to contest the forfeiture, the confiscated copies were destroyed.[110] The situation was similar in Canada and Ireland, where *Ulysses* was confiscated and burned by

Customs officials as early as 1922.[111] Thus, by 1923 *Ulysses* was largely banned from the English-speaking world.

In the USA 'condemnation of the work was so strong that both the Post Office and the Bureau [of Customs] pressed hard for the prosecution of anyone who used the mails to introduce Americans to the "stream of consciousness" of Joyce's people in Dublin.'[112] Small wonder then that attempts to publish *Ulysses* there, even in expurgated form, failed. The first such attempt came in 1925–7 when Samuel Roth, the much-prosecuted publisher of literary erotica and pornography, attempted to serialize Joyce's novel in his *Two Worlds Monthly*, a magazine 'Devoted to the Increase of the Gaiety of Nations.' Roth's serialization was unauthorized and, to add insult to injury, bowdlerized. When Joyce complained of both facts (in the 'Letter of Protest' he wrote in order to obtain a court injunction against Roth), he provided Roth with what must have been one of very few opportunities to take the moral high ground:

> They say I harmed him by publishing his work without his permission and by not including those parts which caused editions of *Ulysses* to be burned on both shores of [the] Atlantic. Why, Lord, does a whole world become indignant when an American publisher refuses to permit an Irish writer to disport on the pages of his journals as if he were in the privacy of his own lavatory?[113]

Whereas Joyce had objected to Roth's expurgations from *Ulysses*, government authorities in New York took offense at what he had left in. On 10 March 1927 a *New York Times* headline announced that Roth would be tried for the publication of *Ulysses* in *Two Worlds Monthly*.[114] The spokesman for the plaintiff, the Clean Books Committee of the Federation of Hungarian Jews in America, alleged that Roth's magazines, notably *Two Worlds Monthly*, were poisoning the minds of their readers.[115] Roth's trial took place, appropriately enough, in the Jefferson Market Police Court, where Anderson and Heap had been tried eight years earlier. The outcome of the trial is not known, but if Roth's record in cases brought against him by the New York Society for the Suppression of Vice is any indication, it probably ended in conviction.[116]

Roth's second attempt to publish *Ulysses* in the USA, this time in the form of a single volume disguised as the authorized ninth printing of the Paris edition,[117] occurred in 1929; it was no more successful than the first. According to Slocum and Cahoon, a major police raid on the premises of Roth's Golden Hind Press in 1929 led to the confiscation of many copies of *Ulysses*.[118] Roth's second attempt to publish the novel confirms that *Ulysses* could not be imported to or distributed in the United States during the 1920s without serious risk of criminal prosecution.

F.R. Leavis's experience in England in 1926 suggests that similar conditions prevailed across the Atlantic. Leavis's troubles began when he asked Galloway & Porter, booksellers, to request permission to import a copy of *Ulysses* 'for purposes of illustration and comment in his course "Modern Problems in Criticism."'[119] As a result of that request, the Chief Constable of the Cambridge Police, who suspected that the booksellers might be 'the victims of a hoax,' arranged for discreet inquiries into 'who and what Dr. F.R. Leavis of Emmanuel College is.'[120] Leavis learned of these inquiries when the Vice Chancellor of Cambridge University invited him to call. In the course of their meeting, the Vice Chancellor presented Leavis with a typescript prepared by the Public Prosecutor which referred to *Ulysses* as '"indescribably filthy"' and requested that Leavis be 'suitably and firmly dealt with.'[121] Leavis explained that he had no intention of prescribing *Ulysses* for study, adding that he saw no reason why an interested student should not be free to read it – 'or to try.'[122] The Vice Chancellor passed this information (minus the addition) on to the Director of Public Prosecutions, who was apparently satisfied, for he pursued the matter no further. Leavis, none the less, was never granted a licence to import *Ulysses*, and he claimed that the incident had caused him harm at the hands of those in power at Cambridge who did not like the kind of book he loaned to undergraduates.[123]

In both England and the United States, it was not until the early 1930s that government authorities began to admit individual exceptions to the general ban on *Ulysses*. Such exceptions were generally granted to importers with credentials capable of convincing customs authorities that they required the novel for scientific purposes. For example, in the spring of 1931 Smiley Blanton, MD, Professor of Child Study at Vassar, applied for and was granted permission to import both *Ulysses* and *Lady Chatterley's Lover* because he was interested in the former's revelation of 'mental abnormalities and disease' and the latter's depiction of 'morbid mental conditions.'[124] The first British citizen to obtain legally a copy of *Ulysses* seems to have been a medical doctor who in December of 1930 wanted it 'for special psychological study.'[125] Aside from such individual cases, *Ulysses* would not be legally available to US and English readers until 1934 and 1936 respectively. The one exception to this pattern is significant in light of what I have said about Joyce's journey toward *Finnegans Wake* as part of his attempt to make obscenity safe for literature: by 1931, almost three years before the English version could be circulated, the French translation of *Ulysses* was being 'sold openly' in New York.[126]

In pondering the significance of the adventures of *Ulysses* from the time of its publication in Paris until the early 1930s, it is worth noting that the novel's association with Samuel Roth could only have confirmed government authorities in their conviction that Joyce's novel was obscene. It is also worth noting that Sylvia Beach and Harriet Shaw Weaver, being fully aware of the compromising nature of such association, had done their best to prevent it. When Harriet Shaw Weaver had first informed Sylvia Beach that Roth was actively pursuing *Ulysses* for serial publication in New York, Miss Beach did not hesitate to recommend refusal.[127] Likewise, and for the same reasons, Miss Beach had resisted the overtures of Jack Kahane of Obelisk Press in Paris, who had confessed his admiration of Miss Beach for her discovery of a book as obscene as *Ulysses*, 'and never relinquished the hope of persuading [her] one day to let the Obelisk Press take it over.'[128] And, again for the same reasons, shortly after the publication of *Ulysses* in Paris, Miss Beach declined D.H. Lawrence's offer of *Lady Chatterley's Lover*: she had been saddened at seeing *Ulysses* listed in catalogues of erotica, alongside works ranging from Cleland's *Fanny Hill* to *Raped on the Rail*, and she had no intention of encouraging that sort of thing by publishing Lawrence's novel.[129]

Roth's attempts to publish *Ulysses* indicate, of course, that these well-intentioned attempts to keep *Ulysses* out of compromising company were unsuccessful. So do US Customs records, which indicate that in 1928 *Ulysses* was apprehended in Minneapolis in the company of books such as *The Strangest Voluptuousness*, *Draped Virginity*, and *Aphrodite*, by Pierre Louys (see Chapter 4). The importer of these works, A. Heymoolen, claimed that all possessed literary merit, but Customs officials did not buy the argument: they denied entry to all of the publications on the grounds of obscenity. The US Customs records also indicate that *Ulysses* spent a good deal of time in the company of Lawrence's *Lady Chatterley's Lover* (with which *Ulysses* vied for the notoriety of being the most scandalous novel of the 1920s). In spite of Sylvia Beach's best efforts, *Ulysses* and *Lady Chatterley* found each other out.

The association of *Ulysses* with the world of erotica and pornography points to the central challenge faced by those critics who joined Joyce in his struggle to make obscenity safe for literature, namely, to establish that *Ulysses* was not to be known by the company it had been keeping in the suitcases of dubious men of letters like Heymoolen of Minneapolis. Once *Ulysses* had been published in Paris, Joyce's efforts to make obscenity safe for literature focused on the writing of *Finnegans Wake*, but Joyce also participated in the ongoing critical effort to defend *Ulysses* against the charge of obscenity. That effort, which constitutes one of the unique features of the reception of *Ulysses*, was considerable: by the time *Ulysses* made its first legal appearance in the English-speaking world, it had been preceded by seven book-length studies, including Herbert Gorman's *James Joyce: His First Forty Years* (1924), Paul Jordan Smith's *A*

Key to the Ulysses of James Joyce (1927), and Stuart Gilbert's *James Joyce's 'Ulysses'* (1930).[130] In addition, *Ulysses* was the subject of numerous critical articles, such as T.S. Eliot's '*Ulysses*, Order and Myth' and Edmund Wilson's 'James Joyce.'

Since the books and articles were written and distributed before *Ulysses* was generally available, many, especially the books, were intended as substitutes rather than companions for *Ulysses*. Thus their introductions contained apologies for lengthy quotations, extensive plot summaries and the like. Not surprisingly, the censorship of *Ulysses* could never be far from their authors's minds. Many of them were written with the rhetorical purpose, sometimes openly stated but more often unobtrusively present, of defending *Ulysses* against the attacks of the censor. This was attempted in a variety of ways. Some critics denied that *Ulysses* was anywhere obscene. Others, like Larbaud, acknowledged that the novel was obscene in places but not corrupting. Others chose to divert attention from the controversial passages of the novel by discussing its Homeric parallels, its elaborate form, its style, and so on. In one way or another, many of these critics wrote in what I have called the tradition of the critical censorship of *Ulysses*, as initiated by Ezra Pound's essays.

Not all of these books and articles figured directly in the defense of *Ulysses* in the forthcoming legal proceedings in New York. Some, however, figured prominently indeed.

4

The United States against *Ulysses*

By 1931 Joyce and his agents were once again seeking a publisher for *Ulysses* in the United States. Thus, in August, Sylvia Beach's sister, Mrs Beach Denis, informed Alexander Lindey, an attorney at the law firm of Wolff, Greenbaum, and Ernst, that Sylvia Beach was 'tremendously interested in the legalization of *Ulysses*.'[1] So was Lindey. In conveying his report of his conversation with Mrs Denis to Ernst, he wrote, 'I still feel very keenly that this would be the grandest obscenity case in the history of law and literature, and I am ready to do anything in the world to get it started.'[2] Ernst, who was apparently of the same mind, attempted to get the case started by offering his services to Ben Huebsch, the US publisher of *Dubliners* and *Portrait* who hoped also to publish *Ulysses*. Huebsch, however, proved unable to reach an agreement with Sylvia Beach, who then controlled the US rights to the novel, and so withdrew from the field at the end of 1931. As Huebsch himself informed Bennett Cerf in December, this left the way open for Random House.[3] At about the same time, Cerf received a call from Robert N. Kastor, a New York stockbroker who was the brother of Joyce's daughter-in-law Helen.[4] Kastor would soon be going to Europe; he wondered if Cerf would like him to tell Joyce that Random House was ready to attempt to publish *Ulysses*. Cerf leapt at the offer. Knowing that Ernst was interested in waging a fight to lift the ban on the novel, Cerf met with the lawyer to discuss the terms of the contract to be offered to Joyce and to make plans for the legal battle that would have to be fought if Joyce accepted.

Cerf believed that Ernst would manage the case 'better than anybody else in the country.'[5] Ernst's credentials were certainly impressive. He had co-authored *To the Pure* (1928), a 'flamboyant attack on literary censorship.'[6] Soon thereafter, he had successfully defended *The Well of Loneliness*, a controversial novel about female homosexuality by Radclyffe Hall. In 1930, Ernst had won his client the right to publish and distribute Mary Ware Dennett's sex education pamphlet *The Sex Side of Life: An Explanation for Young People*. He had also obtained freedom for Dr Marie Stopes's *Married Love*, and Arthur Schnitzler's *Casanova's Homecoming*. By the time Cerf offered him the *Ulysses* case, Ernst could indeed be expected to deliver a formidable defense of *Ulysses*.[7] Cerf therefore had good reason to be pleased when Ernst agreed to take the case on agreeable terms (modest fees up front and a 5 percent royalty on sales).

All Cerf needed now was for Joyce to sign the contract he had sent with Kastor, which offered Joyce $1,000 upon signing as an advance on royalties of 15 percent, with the understanding that Joyce could keep the money whether or not Cerf succeeded in publishing *Ulysses*. Kastor delivered the contract to Joyce in February; in March Joyce accepted the Random House offer.

Once Cerf received a copy of the contract bearing Joyce's signature, the battle to publish *Ulysses* began in earnest. Ernst advised Cerf to have a copy of *Ulysses* shipped from France to the Port of New York and confiscated by US Customs officials. Random House would then initiate legal proceedings to contest the confiscation. There were two reasons for proceeding in this manner. First, it would allow Cerf to minimize his financial risk.[8] Second, it would enable Ernst to introduce critical opinion as evidence in the subsequent proceedings, as Cerf's instructions to Paul Léon (Joyce's friend and assistant in Paris) make clear:

> Please buy for us a copy of the latest edition of *Ulysses*. If there has been printed in French any circular containing opinions of prominent men or critics on this book, paste a copy of this circular into the front of the book. It is important that this circular be actually pasted into the book, as if it is separate we may not be able to use it as evidence when the trial comes up, but if these opinions of respected people are actually pasted in the book, they become, for legal purposes, a part of the book, and can be introduced as evidence.[9]

The importance of this stratagem cannot be overemphasized. By virtue of the fact that the imported copy of *Ulysses* was destined to be the sole piece of evidence in the upcoming proceedings, Ernst's decision to have the opinions of literary critics pasted therein was clearly motivated by his desire to ensure that the opinions of literary critics would be the fundamental standard by which *Ulysses* would be judged.

Léon responded promptly to Cerf's request, specifying that *Ulysses* would sail from France on the SS *Bremen* and arrive in New York with the following critical material pasted inside its covers:

(1) the protest against Roth's piracy of *Ulysses* signed by 167 writers, and the injunction against Roth issued by the US courts;
(2) a circular on the German translation of *Ulysses*, and a circular with opinions on the French translation;
(3) *Extracts from Press Notices* of the English (Paris) edition of *Ulysses*;[10] and

(4)   four critical articles, as follows:

   (i)   Marcel Brion, 'Ulysse,' *La Revue Hebdomadaire*, 4 (20 Apr. 1929) pp. 365–7

   (ii)   Louis Cazamian, 'L'Oeuvre de James Joyce,' *Revue Anglo-Américaine*, 2 (Dec 1924), pp. 97–113

   (iii) Stuart Gilbert, 'Irish Ulysses: Hades Episode,' *Fortnightly Review*, 126 (Jul. 1929), pp. 46–58

   (iv) Valèry Larbaud, 'James Joyce,' *La Nouvelle Revue Française*, 18 (Apr. 1922), pp. 385–409.[11]

Once the criticism-laden copy of *Ulysses* had set sail for the USA, Cerf arranged for its confiscation by Customs authorities in New York by sending an agent to receive the novel upon its arrival in port.[12] The agent had to work for his pay. The day of arrival was terrifically hot, and the customs officers were more desirous of going home than of confiscating anything. The agent therefore had to insist on inspection of the suitcase containing *Ulysses*. Even after the customs officer had discovered the novel, he was not eager to confiscate: '"Oh, for God's sake, everybody brings that in. We don't pay any attention to it."'[13] Only after Cerf's agent insisted that *Ulysses* was legally contraband did the customs officer do his duty and seize the novel.

Soon thereafter, Lindey received notification from Assistant Collector H.C. Stewart that *Ulysses* had been 'detained as in violation of Section 305 of the Tariff Act as obscene.'[14] In the same letter, Stewart drew Lindey's attention to the 1928 Customs Court decision in which *Ulysses*, along with a number of other works – including *The Law Concerning Draped Virginity* by A. Beverland, *The Strangest Voluptuousness* by L.R. Dupuy, and *Aphrodite* by Pierre Louys – had been denied entry to the United States by virtue of its obscenity.[15] Lindey responded that *Ulysses* had not come up for separate consideration or comment in the Customs decision; furthermore, he claimed that 'all the items (insofar as one may judge by the titles) were, unlike *Ulysses*, technical works dealing with unnatural passion.'[16] In fact, as the presence of *Aphrodite* makes clear, *Ulysses* was not the only literary work to be mentioned in the Customs decision. In any case, Stewart was not persuaded by Lindey's argument that *Ulysses* was fundamentally unlike the rest of the books with which it was seized in 1928, and he forwarded the imported copy of *Ulysses* to the office of the US Attorney, Southern District of New York.

The novel ended up in the hands of Samuel Coleman, Chief Assistant US Attorney, who dutifully undertook the daunting labour of reading it. When he had traversed the first three hundred pages, he received an offer from Lindey to supply him with books (notably Paul Jordan

Smith's *A Key to James Joyce's Ulysses*) to help him in his reading. Coleman, however, informed Lindey that he preferred to 'plough through the book without external aid the first time.'[17] Thus guided by his own lights, Coleman reached the opinion that *Ulysses* was a 'literary masterpiece' but none the less 'obscene within the meaning of the federal law.'[18] Unwilling to take upon himself the responsibility of initiating proceedings, however, Coleman sought the opinion of his superior, US Attorney George Medalie. Persuaded of the importance of *Ulysses*, Medalie was reluctant to proceed, but his reading of the novel, notably 'the latter part of the book, particularly as to the musings of the wife,' eventually convinced him that he would have to do so.[19]

Thus, on 9 December 1932 Medalie initiated libel proceedings against *Ulysses* in a deposition which claimed that the novel had been imported in violation of the Tariff Act of 1930 and moved the Court to condemn and destroy the book according to the law.[20] In response, Ernst filed the 'Claimant's Answer,' which denied that *Ulysses* had been imported in violation of the Tariff Act and moved the Court to admit the novel into the United States.[21] So began one of the most celebrated obscenity trials in US history – *The United States of America Against One Book Entitled 'Ulysses.'*

From the outset, the government proved remarkably co-operative. Medalie was eager to read any documents that Ernst and Lindey could produce in defense of *Ulysses*. Furthermore, he was receptive to the claimant's desire to have the case heard by a sympathetic judge. Together, Ernst and Medalie worked out a procedure according to which both parties waived their right to a trial by jury. Ernst, who for obvious reasons had been eager to avoid a trial by jury (the jurors, after all, would not have been literary critics like those whose opinions were pasted inside the imported copy of *Ulysses*), considered the US Attorney's decision to forgo trial by jury as a preliminary victory.

After the procedure was agreed upon, the problem of obtaining the most favorable judge remained unsolved. Judge Woolsey, the obvious choice, was unavailable, so Coleman decided to file the libellant's motion for confiscation before Judge Cox, whom both parties had always regarded as the best alternative. Thus, on 23 May 1933, both parties filed motions for judgment on the proceedings. Judge Cox, however, refused to entertain the motions and adjourned the hearing until 16 June – also known as Bloomsday, the day on which Leopold Bloom wanders through Dublin in *Ulysses*.

While both parties were waiting anxiously to find out which judge would be sitting on the sixteenth, Lindey applied to have *Ulysses* declared a 'classic' by the government of the United States. Like the initial stratagem of pasting critical opinions inside the imported copy of

Ulysses, this second stratagem had been devised by Ernst, who had advised Senator Bronson Cutting to propose the inclusion of the 'classic' provision during the US Customs censorship fight of 1929–30.[22] Aware of this provision, Ernst recognized in it an opportunity of getting the government to drop its case against *Ulysses*. To this end, he arranged to have another copy of Joyce's novel sent from Europe, this time directly to him. When the book arrived, he wrote to US Customs, asking if they had changed their attitude towards *Ulysses*. If not, Ernst wrote, he intended to surrender the book and then contest the seizure under the relevant provision of the Tariff Act of 1930. When the Customs authorities informed him that they had not changed their mind about *Ulysses*, Ernst had Lindey prepare his 'Petition for the Release and Admission of *Ulysses* into the United States on the Grounds that It Is A Classic.'

Well aware that 'unsupported statements or allegations'[23] to the effect that a book is a classic would not be considered, Lindey backed up his petition with an impressive array of critical opinion attesting to the eminence of *Ulysses* in the world of letters. In so doing, Lindey confirmed the importance of the initial stratagem of pasting critical opinion inside the copy of *Ulysses* imported for the legal proceedings, attempting to ensure once again that the opinions of literary critics would be the standard by which Joyce's novel would be judged. According to Lindey, such opinions proved that *Ulysses* 'is a modern classic in every sense of the word. It has endured the test of time.'[24] Apparently aware that Samuel Johnson (whose test of time was a century) might have found this judgment premature, Lindey elaborates: 'We have long ago repudiated the theory that a literary work must be hundreds or thousands of years old in order to be a classic. We have come to realize that there can be *modern* classics as well as ancient ones.'[25]

Lindey's petition is remarkable for its tendency to underplay the novel's controversial aspects. Thus, while its first exhibit ('Statements Made by Representative Men Concerning *Ulysses*') contains statements acknowledging that parts of the novel are obscene or pornographic, its other exhibits are more reticent. The second exhibit ('Excerpts from Critical Reviews of *Ulysses*'), for example, allegedly presents a 'a cross-section of critical opinion.'[26] But when its excerpts are compared to those selected by Joyce for inclusion in *Extracts from Press Notices of 'Ulysses'* (pasted inside the imported copy of the novel) it becomes clear that they do not present a full cross-section of critical opinion. They do not, for example, include James Douglas's view that *Ulysses* is 'the most infamously obscene book in ancient or modern literature.'[27] Nor do they include Arnold Bennett's view that *Ulysses* 'is not pornographic, but it is more indecent, obscene, scatological, and licentious than the majority of professedly pornographical books.'[28] Lindey's version quotes Bennett as saying simply, 'The book is not pornographic.'[29] This same tendency is apparent in the other exhibits in Lindey's petition. 'Comments of Librarians on *Ulysses*' contains only favourable responses, excluding responses which 'demonstrated that acceptance of *Ulysses* was significantly more subdued outside literary circles' than within.[30] Such responses included one from a public librarian in Riverside, California, who reported that interest in *Ulysses* came mostly from 'army officers and men of leisure,' and another from a librarian at Johns Hopkins University, who wrote that while *Ulysses* was interesting it was 'not a classic.'[31]

While the Commissioner of Customs was considering Lindey's petition, it became apparent that Judge Coleman, a 'strait-laced Catholic' whom both claimant and libellant believed was 'about the worst man on the bench' for the case, would be sitting on Bloomsday.[32] Lindey therefore proposed another adjournment. Assistant US Attorney Nicholas Atlas, who was looking after the *Ulysses* case in the absence of Samuel Coleman, approved. Using Coleman's absence as their excuse, Lindey and Atlas arranged to have the motions put over until 11 July 1933. Their success in this regard prepared the way for a happier Bloomsday.

When 16 June finally arrived, Lindey received word from the Commissioner of Customs that his petition for the release of *Ulysses* had been granted. He and Ernst must have been delighted; even so, the language of the Commissioner must have jarred their ears: in giving his permission he referred to Lindey's petition for the release of a copy of *Ulysses* under the discretionary authority granted the Secretary of the Treasury under section 305 of the Tariff Act of 1930 'to admit obscene books.'[33] The unstated assumption of the government's admission, of course, is that a work of outstanding literary merit can also be obscene.[34] Thus, in admitting *Ulysses* as a classic, the Commissioner of Customs agreed roughly with Coleman's view of the novel as a literary masterpiece that was none the less obscene. It is precisely this view that Lindey and Ernst were at pains to deny.

Lindey's success in getting the government to admit *Ulysses* as a classic had immediate repercussions. Shortly thereafter, Coleman and Atlas announced that the US Attorney's Office wanted yet another adjournment. They claimed they needed time to prepare their brief, but the truth was that Lindey's victory at Customs, combined with the advent of a new Federal administration, a new Secretary of the Treasury, and a new Postmaster, had led the government to consider dropping the libel proceedings.[35] Sensing an opportunity for an early victory, Ernst sent Coleman and Atlas a copy of Lindey's petition, hoping that it would sway the government's decision.[36]

While the US Attorney's Office was digesting Lindey's petition, the motions for judgment on the proceedings filed in May came up before the Court (25 July 1933) – with unhoped-for results. Since the unacceptable Judge Coleman was sitting again, Atlas requested adjournment to 8 August. This request was denied by Judge Coleman on the grounds that Judge Cox, who would then be sitting, did not want the case. Atlas then requested 15 August, but Judge Patterson, who would be sitting on that day, also refused to hear the case. As a result, the motions were set over until 22 August when the judge sitting would be none other than John Woolsey.

This stroke of good fortune notwithstanding, Ernst and Lindey continued their efforts to convince the US Attorney's Office to drop the proceedings. They met with Coleman and Atlas on 7 August and, the next day, sent a package containing material which Coleman and Atlas had requested in the course of the meeting, including nine books which had been the objects of previous obscenity cases, two briefs prepared by Ernst and Lindey, a leaflet containing critical comments on the French translation of *Ulysses*, a map of the United States indicating libraries which had or were interested in getting a copy of *Ulysses* and, finally, a copy of 'James Joyce: A Critical Study,' by Peter A. Pertzoff.[37] By 15 August, however, it was clear that Coleman and Atlas would not drop the proceedings and that the decision as to whether or not *Ulysses* would be allowed to enter the United States would be left up to Judge Woolsey.

Shortly after the US Attorney's office had made clear its intention to proceed against Joyce's novel, Woolsey announced that he would hear argument without briefs and that briefs should not be submitted unless he called for them. This arrangement accorded with the wishes of the government, but not with those of Random House and its legal counsel. Cerf was convinced that all material gathered in defense of *Ulysses* should be turned over to Woolsey 'before he has a chance to complete his reading of the book.'[38] Lindey and Ernst were of the same mind. Thus, early in September, Lindey ignored Woolsey's directive, sending him a copy of the 'Claimant's Preliminary Memorandum' (containing the material presented in Lindey's petition) and two critical books on *Ulysses*. Lindey would have sent a third book, but he had learned from Sam Coleman that Woolsey already had a copy of Stuart Gilbert's *James Joyce's 'Ulysses'*; he therefore contented himself with sending Paul Jordan Smith's *The Key to the Ulysses of James Joyce* and Herbert S. Gorman's *James Joyce: His First Forty Years*. One month later, Ernst and Lindey would supplement this material with a copy of the 'Claimant's Memorandum.' Due to a number of delays, Woolsey would not hear argument until 25 November 1933. He would have plenty of time to familiarize himself with the material of which Ernst and Lindey hoped he would take 'judicial notice.'[39]

The introductory section of the 'Claimant's Memorandum,' like the criticism-laden imported copy of *Ulysses* and the petition to have another copy of the novel admitted as a classic, reveals that the opinion of literary critics pertaining to *Ulysses* would play a crucial role in Ernst's defense of *Ulysses*.[40] More specifically, it establishes that such critical opinion would be used to oppose the view (adopted by both the US Attorney's office and the Secretary of the Treasury) that a work of literary merit can also be obscene. Thus, Ernst supports his assessment of Joyce as 'the most important figure in world literature today' by appealing to the opinion of nine literary critics, including Stuart Gilbert, Rebecca West, Arnold Bennett, and Edmund Wilson.[41] It follows, Ernst continues, that *Ulysses* cannot possibly be obscene: 'It is monstrous to suppose that a man of the stature of Joyce would or could produce a work of obscenity.'[42]

Ernst's contention that literature and obscenity are mutually exclusive or, as Margaret Anderson had put it, that 'the words "literature" and "obscenity" can not be used in conjunction,'[43] identifies his theoretical perspective as essentially esthetic. Those who adhere to the esthetic theory reject the idea that the work of art has moral implications and consequences and may therefore be judged by moral standards, especially when these standards deem the work to be morally harmful. In their desire to protect art from the ignorant hands of the philistine, as Malcolm Cowley has wryly observed, they sometimes brand those who *do* apply moral judgements to art as, well, immoral. Seen in this light, Ernst's choice of 'monstrous' as an epithet for those who think that *Ulysses* is obscene suggests that his commitment to the esthetic view of art – be it heartfelt or strategic – is substantial.

Ernst's epithet, in addition to revealing his adherence to an esthetic view of art, also suggests the way in which that theory, which is intended, after all, to affirm the value of art, ironically tends to reduce the artist and his or her works to upholders of the existing social order. This point emerges clearly if more traditional forms of libel are inserted into Ernst's statement regarding the 'monstrous' supposition that Joyce could produce a work of obscenity according to the standards of the 1930s: 'It is monstrous to suppose that James Joyce could produce a work of sedition'; or, 'It is monstrous to suppose that James Joyce could produce a work of blasphemy.' Is it really so monstrous to believe that a writer like Joyce could produce a work that undermined the moral or political or religious order of his day? If so, it is presumably equally monstrous to believe that an artist could influence the culture of his or her day in any way whatsoever.

Ernst's reliance on an esthetic theory of art accounts for the most important difference between his argument and the one made by John Quinn in 1920–1. Quinn, as we have seen, responded to the charge that

Ulysses (at least the portion of 'Nausicaa' contained in the July–August number of *The Little Review*) was morally corrupting with a moral argument of his own, namely, that the novel was 'bracing' rather than corrupting. Ernst's conviction that literature and obscenity are mutually exclusive led him to take a different approach. Thus, instead of responding to the government's claim that *Ulysses* was obscene (and therefore corrupting) by arguing that the novel's moral effect was healthy, Ernst chose instead to argue that *Ulysses* was indeed a work of substantial literary artistry which could not, by definition, be deemed obscene.

From this perspective, the heart of Ernst's six-point argument in defense of *Ulysses*, the place where the mutual exclusivity of obscenity and literature is most emphatically pressed, is the third point. The esthetic view of art manifest there, however, informs Ernst's argument as a whole. The six points of the argument are as follows:

I.   The test of obscenity is a living standard, and *Ulysses* must be judged by the *mores* of the day.

II.   *Ulysses* is not obscene as a matter of law.

III.   *Ulysses* is a modern classic. The United States Government has officially acknowledged it as such. It cannot therefore be deemed obscene.

IV.   The intrinsic features of *Ulysses*, as well as certain extrinsic facts, negate any implication of obscenity.

V.   *Ulysses* has been generally accepted by the community, and hence cannot be held to be violative of the statute.

VI.   *Ulysses* must be judged as a whole, and its general purpose and effect determined. On that basis it must be cleared.[44]

Ernst supports the first point – 'The test of obscenity is a living standard, and *Ulysses* must be judged by the *mores* of the day' – by appealing convincingly to experience. He points out that whereas a woman who bared her arms and legs on a beach in 1900 would have been arrested, the bathing suits of the 1930s 'leave very little of the human form concealed.'[45] These changing moral standards, Ernst observes, have been reflected in the reception of literary works: Charlotte Brönte's *Jane Eyre*, George Eliot's *Adam Bede*, Whitman's *Leaves of Grass*, and Hardy's *Tess of the d'Urbervilles* were decried as obscene, lewd, and indecent in their day, yet they are now acknowledged as great literary works. The changing moral standards of society are also manifested, according to Ernst, in the subject matter of many recent books – including Radclyffe Hall's *The Well of Loneliness*, Dr Marie Stopes's *Married Love*, and Thomas Mann's *Death in Venice* – which deal 'more and more boldly with sex.'[46] In light of these facts, Ernst concludes, '*Ulysses* clearly does not violate our obscenity statute.'[47]

On the surface of it, the first part of Ernst's argument would seem to be almost entirely moral, but in a note to the concluding statement quoted above, Ernst draws Judge Woolsey's attention to Stuart Gilbert's 'scholarly analysis of "indecency" in *Ulysses: James Joyce's "Ulysses,"* pp. 19–22,'[48] a move which effectively shifts his argument from moral to esthetic grounds. In the course of that analysis, Gilbert asserts that there is 'nothing "indecent"' in *Ulysses*, if indecency is defined as 'anything calculated to excite sexual passion.'[49] In support of this assertion, Gilbert emphasizes that in *Ulysses* Joyce's object was to present 'an *aesthetic* image of the world.'[50] 'Aesthetic emotion,' he adds 'is *static*.' Gilbert then quotes from *Portrait*:

> 'The mind is arrested and raised above desire and loathing.' 'The feelings excited by improper art are kinetic, desire and loathing. Desire urges us to possess, to go to something; loathing urges us to abandon, to go from something. The arts which excite them, pornographical or didactic, are therefore improper arts.'[51]

Gilbert is willing to acknowledge that in places *Ulysses* does not fully realize the ideal of esthetic stasis, but he insists that stasis *is* achieved where the excitation of sexual passion is concerned, which is to say where obscenity, as it is defined by the US courts, is a possibility: 'The feeling of desire, which urges us to possess, is absent; there is not the least pornographical appeal; but the loathing, which urges us to abandon ... is, one can but feel, active in certain passages.'[52]

According to Gilbert, in *Ulysses* Joyce manages to 'ban kinetic feelings from his readers' minds'[53] where such kinetic feelings would provide grounds for accusing the novel of obscenity. Furthermore, Gilbert argues, Joyce manages to do so precisely because he succeeds in creating a work of literary art that brings about an esthetic stasis in his readers. Ernst's approving reference to Gilbert's analysis of indecency, one which upholds Ernst's introductory distinction between literature and obscenity, thus confirms that the primary burden of his argument in defense of *Ulysses* will be to convince Woolsey that *Ulysses* is indeed a work of literary merit. Once that is proved, the fact that 'the test of obscenity is a living standard' assumes a place of minor importance.

Before proceeding to establish that *Ulysses* is unquestionably a work of literary merit, Ernst argues his second point – that '*Ulysses* is not obscene as a matter of law.' Ernst's goal here is to show that legal definitions of obscenity, like social mores, have changed with time and that Victorian definitions – as enshrined in the Hicklin rule – are no longer valid. Thus, Ernst points out that whereas the Victorian test of obscenity (as laid down in 1968 in *Regina* v. *Hicklin* (LR 3 QB 360)) defined the term broadly, considering it synonymous with epithets like 'lewd,' 'licentious,' 'indecent,' the modern practice is to define the term more narrowly as that which tends *'"to excite lustful and lecherous desire"'* (emphasis Ernst's).[54] Likewise, whereas the Victorian test used the young person to determine whether a work would corrupt, modern decisions use the *'normal* person' (emphasis Ernst's).[55] Furthermore, whereas the Victorian test deemed the motive or intention of the author to be irrelevant, the modern practice acknowledges that the intention of the author must be taken into account, and that before a work can be deemed obscene under the statute it must be shown that the excitation of lustful desire or impure thought is the author's *'main purpose'* (emphasis Ernst's).[56] Finally, whereas the Victorian test justified the suppression of an entire book on the basis of obscene portions therein without reference to the whole, modern practice holds that the court must 'consider the book as a whole even though some paragraphs standing by themselves might be objectionable.'[57]

Since much of this second part of Ernst's argument, like his first, addresses moral questions and might therefore seem to contradict my claim that Ernst's argument as a whole is esthetic rather than moral, I draw the reader's attention to Ernst's conclusion of his discussion of legal definitions of obscenity: 'One can no more say that *Ulysses* is obscene than that life or thought is obscene.'[58] Is it, one wonders, really impossible to say that life is obscene at times? Pound certainly did not think so. According to him, *Ulysses* is 'obscene, as life itself is obscene in places.'[59] Ernst, however, determined to avoid any moral criticism of *Ulysses*, insists that the thing is unthinkable. Another, more practical point is worth making in the present context, namely, that the question of whether or not *Ulysses* is obscene according to the definitions of obscenity accepted by the courts becomes largely irrelevant if it can be established, first, that a work of literature simply cannot be obscene and, second, that *Ulysses* is indeed a work of literature. Once the literary merit of *Ulysses* is established, the breadth or narrowness of the definition of obscenity is no longer crucial, nor is the identity of the person upon whom such obscenity would be tested. Nor, for that matter, are questions relating to authorial intention or the relation of part of whole.

To establish that *Ulysses* is a work of literary art which cannot, by definition, be obscene is the primary objective of Ernst's third – and crucial – point: '*Ulysses* is a modern classic. The United States Government has officially acknowledged it as such. It cannot therefore be deemed obscene.' In arguing this point, the fruit of the strategy that led to the insertion of critical opinion in the copy of *Ulysses* imported for the purpose of initiating the legal proceedings in the first place and to Lindey's petition to have *Ulysses* admitted as a classic, Ernst is not content merely to remind the Court that the Commissioner of Customs has declared *Ulysses* to be a classic, a work of outstanding literary merit. Instead, he is at pains to assert the incompatibility of obscenity and literary excellence:

> *Webster's Collegiate Dictionary* ... defines a classic as a 'a work, especially in literature or art, of the highest class and of acknowledged excellence.'
>
> The words 'classic' and 'obscenity' represent polar extremes. They are mutually antagonistic and exclusive. That which is obscene, corrupts and depraves – it cannot be 'of the highest class and of acknowledged excellence.'[60]

This distinction, Ernst goes on to claim, has been upheld by the courts: 'The courts have time and again reaffirmed this, emphasizing the principle that the law of obscenity cannot be invoked to suppress works which have stood the test of time, and have won lasting recognition and acclaim.'[61] Ernst's claim notwithstanding, this was precisely the principle being contested. As we have seen, Sam Coleman had conceded that *Ulysses* was a 'literary masterpiece,' but none the less insisted that it was obscene within the meaning of Federal law. And the Commissioner of Customs had admitted a copy of *Ulysses* under the authority of a provision of the Tariff Act of 1930 which allowed him 'to admit obscene books.' As these examples indicate, the government admitted the principle that a work could be both a classic by virtue of its literary merit and obscene.

Ernst's interpretation of the principle that works of outstanding literary merit cannot be suppressed under the statute is that such merit is simply incompatible with obscenity. Thus, when he cites approvingly an article from the *London Law Journal* according to which *'a classical work is not obscene* unless the circumstances of its sale or exhibition are such as to draw attention to those parts of the work which, if considered out of their historical and literary context, would have a depraving effect' (emphasis Ernst's), he does so with the understanding that the potentially depraving effect of parts of classical works is effectively eliminated by virtue of their inclusion in the literary work as a whole.[62] Here again, however, Ernst's is not the only possible explanation of why classic status confers immunity from the obscenity statute. In upholding the Post Office's decision to deny mailing privileges to the 'Cantleman's Spring Mate' number of *The Little Review* (October 1917), Judge Augustus N. Hand articulated another view, according to which the '"classics" ... are ordinarily immune from interference, because they have the sanction of age and fame and usually appeal to a comparatively limited number of readers.'[63] In other words, the classics are immune from the obscenity statute not because their parts are without power to harm but because they have been esteemed over time and, to paraphrase Mark Twain, they have been more esteemed than read.[64]

As the foregoing paragraph makes clear, Ernst's insistence that literary excellence and obscenity are 'mutually antagonistic and exclusive' influenced his interpretation of various intrinsic characteristics of the literary work, notably the relation between part and whole. That insistence, not surprisingly, can be detected in Ernst's articulation of his fourth point: 'The intrinsic features of *Ulysses*, as well as certain extrinsic facts negate *any implication* of obscenity' (emphasis mine). Ernst was far too good a lawyer to rely exclusively on Woolsey's willingness to accept his distinction between literature and obscenity. Thus, in discussing the intrinsic features of *Ulysses*, he emphasizes not only the integrity of the novel as a work of art but also the daunting difficulty which renders the novel inaccessible to all but the most capable and assiduous readers. In so doing, Ernst delivers an argument capable of satisfying a judge who might be inclined to follow Augustus Hand's reasoning to the effect that the classics are generally exempt from the obscenity statute by virtue of their acknowledged literary merit and their limited readership. More importantly, at least from the point of view argued in Chapter 3, Ernst establishes beyond reasonable doubt the defensive value of both the schema that had guided the late writing and revision of *Ulysses* and the style of exile which Joyce had begun to develop in response to Grant Richards's rejection of *Dubliners* and which was leading him steadily toward the obscurity of *Finnegans Wake*.

Ernst's initial discussion of the intrinsic features of *Ulysses* is commonsensical and straightforward. Having noted that illustrations 'may tend to enhance the potency of [a] work for good or ill,' he reminds the Court that Joyce's novel has none.[65] He also observes that *Ulysses* was published openly by Shakespeare & Company and that the book has always borne Joyce's name; thus, 'The element of concealment – almost invariably present in a work of pornography – is wholly absent here.'[66] Furthermore, he points out, the title of *Ulysses* 'does not challenge the curiosity of the lascivious.'[67] Moreover, *Ulysses* is 'far too tedious and labyrinthine and bewildering for the untutored and the impressionable who might conceivably be affected by it. Such people would not get beyond the first dozen pages.'[68]

At this point, Ernst proceeds to discuss the intrinsic features of *Ulysses* in more sophisticated literary terms:

> *more important than any of the foregoing are style and method.* The very definition of obscenity calls for something which will corrupt and deprave. It is axiomatic that only what is understandable can corrupt.

The worst Chinese obscenity is innocuous to anyone not acquainted with the language. If an author's style is incomprehensible to all but a comparatively few who are concededly immune to what the censor calls the suggestive power of words, the work cannot be said to be obscene. (emphasis mine)[69]

The language and emphasis of Ernst's argument have shifted; it is no longer merely what has traditionally been called the content of a work that is to be understood, or the author's representation of the thought and action of his or her characters, but rather the author's 'style' and 'method.' On one hand, Ernst's assertion here is every bit as common-sensical as the first part of his discussion of the intrinsic features of *Ulysses*: style and method, after all, may well constitute formidable barriers to understanding, and as Ernst goes on to establish convincingly, they do where *Ulysses* is concerned. On the other hand, however, Ernst's discussion of style and method opens the way to a very different notion of what it means to understand a literary work, one much more in keeping with Ernst's conviction that to establish literary integrity is to dismiss any implication of obscenity.

Ernst introduces this new idea of what it means to understand *Ulysses* when he explains the novel's 'Gargantuan complexity':

It is not only the language that is baffling; the construction is almost unbelievably involved. As Stuart Gilbert has pointed out, each episode of *Ulysses* has its Scene and Hour of the Day, is associated with a given Organ of the human body, relates to a certain Art, has its appropriate symbol and a specific Technic, and has a title corresponding to a character or episode in the *Odyssey*. Certain episodes also have their appropriate Colour.[70] For instance the episode in the office of the *Freeman's Journal and National Press* is entitled Aeolus; its Hour is 12 noon; its Organ the lungs; its Art rhetoric; its Color red; its Symbol editor; its Technic enthymemic.[71]

In presenting this idea of what it means to understand *Ulysses*, Ernst covers ground inaccessible to Quinn. Quinn argued that the objectionable instalment of 'Nausicaa' was incomprehensible to innocent and susceptible readers in so far as they were unfamiliar with the realities represented in Joyce's prose. He also argued that Joyce's prose was simply impenetrable as Chinese is impenetrable to those unfamiliar with Chinese. But he could only throw up his hands in defeat when Magistrate Corrigan said he understood perfectly well the passage in which Bloom 'went off in his pants.' Ernst, however, had another option. As the above passage indicates, he could argue that to understand

Ulysses is to grasp fully the remarkable complexity of the novel as a whole.

In so arguing, Ernst is not merely claiming that *Ulysses* is incomprehensible to all but the most sophisticated of readers. It is true, of course, that if understanding *Ulysses* requires detailed knowledge of its schematic complexity, as defined by Stuart Gilbert, then very few readers, and certainly no reader approaching the novel for the first time (without, that is, the aid of Gilbert's book), can be said truly to understand *Ulysses*. As Edmund Wilson confessed in 1930, a good deal of the schematic complexity of *Ulysses* would have evaded everyone – including the most discerning of literary critics – if Gilbert had not emphasized the schema in *James Joyce's 'Ulysses'*.[72] In appealing to the schematic complexity of *Ulysses*, then, Ernst is claiming that the novel is inaccessible to the average reader. But he is also claiming that *Ulysses* is indeed a coherent artistic whole. More important, he is implying that those who do not apprehend fully the schematic complexity of the novel as a whole simply do not understand *Ulysses* and are therefore not competent to judge it. Admittedly, Ernst does not develop this implication at length, but it follows naturally enough from his oft-repeated conviction that literature and obscenity are mutually exclusive, a conviction which implies that those who consider *Ulysses* obscene do not know what literary integrity is.

Before proceeding to the rest of Ernst's discussion of the intrinsic features of *Ulysses*, I would like to pause briefly here to make two points regarding Ernst's use of Gilbert to emphasize the 'Gargantuan complexity' of *Ulysses*. The first is that it proves beyond any reasonable doubt the defensive value of the schema and, of course, the schematic elements of *Ulysses*. In other words, it demonstrates that Joyce was not wasting his time when he participated in the critical effort at 'making obscenity safe for literature,' notably by ensuring that Gilbert, like Larbaud before him, would make appropriate use of the schema. The second point to be made regarding Ernst's use of Gilbert is simply that Gilbert's discussion of the elaborate schematic complexity of *Ulysses* provided Ernst with an economical means of putting Judge Woolsey in mind of the elaborate coherence of the novel as a whole.

Having asserted that to understand *Ulysses* is to apprehend the complex construction of the novel as a whole, Ernst proceeds to claim that it is also to overcome the formidable barriers of its style. Thus, to understand *Ulysses*, the reader must be able to overcome 'such forbidding polysyllabic barriers as *contransmagnificandjewbangtantiality* ..., and *mahamanvantara* ..., and *weggebobbles* ..., and *theolololologicphilological*'.[73] Furthermore, the reader must be able to fathom 'such incomprehensible paragraphs' as that which stands at the beginning of 'Proteus,' which so impressed Margaret Anderson: '"Ineluctable modality of the visible: at least that if no more, thought through my eyes. ..."'[74] Such excerpts, according to Ernst, are typical of the novel as a whole: 'There is no reason to multiply illustrations. If one opens *Ulysses* at random almost anywhere, one will confront passages meaningless on the surface, and decipherable only after concentrated study.'[75] Ernst's point, of course, is that *Ulysses* is a classic by virtue of not only its literary quality but also its limited readership: 'The book is a treasure-trove, to be sure; but its riches are so well hid in grottoes of recondite learning, of classical allusions, of literary and scientific profundities, that the average seeker – blindly groping about in the surrounding maze – soon tires of the venture and turns back.'[76]

The significance of Ernst's point from the perspective of the style of exile which Joyce developed in the course of his journey from the 'nicely polished looking-glass' of *Dubliners* to the obscurity of *Finnegans Wake* emerges clearly when Ernst seeks critical confirmation of it in Paul Jordan Smith's *A Key to James Joyce's Ulysses*. According to Smith, before the language of *Ulysses* can be understood it '"has to be translated."'[77] Ernst himself, of course, has implicitly likened the language of *Ulysses* to Chinese; furthermore, he has claimed that it has to be 'deciphered.' Thus, Ernst argues that *Ulysses* is incomprehensible to the average reader because it is effectively written in a foreign language. In doing so he confirms, first, that Joyce's style of exile, which culminates in the foreign language of *Finnegans Wake*, was an effective defense against the censor and, second, that in this key respect at least Joyce does indeed travel from *Dubliners* to *Finnegans Wake* in *Ulysses*.

Before moving on to the rest of Ernst's argument, it should be noted that his discussion of the intrinsic features of *Ulysses* scrupulously avoids engagement with the controversial episodes like Bloom's masturbation on the beach in 'Nausicaa.' These, presumably, were too comprehensible for Ernst's purposes. We touch here on yet another important difference between Ernst's and Quinn's defenses of *Ulysses*. Quinn's defense of such episodes ultimately took the form of a moral argument according to which they repelled rather than allured the reader. Ernst, by contrast, appeals to the novel's style and method, arguing that these, rather than the content, do the repelling:

> There is no need in this memorandum to analyze the stream-of-consciousness method which Joyce brought to such a high degree of perfection in *Ulysses*. It will suffice to say that the nature of this method in itself is such as would discourage and repel rather than attract the average reader.[78] The latter is interested in action, not in cerebration.[79]

Ernst's point, of course, is familiar by now: the style of *Ulysses* renders it incomprehensible to all but the most sophisticated readers. This particular formulation of the idea is none the less striking for its curious consonance with the esthetic basis of Ernst's argument as a whole, for it registers the distance Ernst has travelled from the moral concerns that figured so prominently in Quinn's defense of *Ulysses* in 1920–1.

Having dealt at length with the intrinsic features of *Ulysses*, Ernst proceeds to the extrinsic circumstances which should be taken into account in judging its alleged obscenity, including 'the author's literary reputation, the opinions of critics, the attitude of librarians, the acceptance of the book in representative libraries and institutions of learning, and the mode of distribution.'[80] Throughout his discussion of these circumstances, Ernst reiterates his conviction that Joyce's stature as 'a supreme literary artist' is simply incompatible with the charge of obscenity.[81] For example, in acknowledging that libraries like the Library of Congress, the New York Public Library, and the Widener Library at Harvard have copies of *Ulysses*, Ernst contends, 'It goes without saying that pornography finds no place on the shelves of reputable libraries.'[82] In the same vein, before pointing out that *Ulysses* has been taught in English courses at Harvard and elsewhere, Ernst claims, 'It would be absurd to assume that an obscene work would appear as assigned reading in our leading institutions of learning.'[83]

Ernst's next (fifth) point – that '*Ulysses* has been generally accepted by the community and hence, cannot be held to be violative of the statute' – was supported by the material appended to Lindey's Petition for the admission of *Ulysses* as a classic, which was submitted to Woolsey as part of the claimant's 'Preliminary Memorandum.' As previously mentioned, that material included statements made by '[r]epresentative [m]en concerning *Ulysses*.' According to Ernst, such men – 'college professors, critics, educators, authors, librarians, clergymen and publishers' who 'speak for the body social' – provide the only means of measuring public opinion, which 'furnishes the only true test of obscenity.'[84] Ernst's view of the way in which community values are to be ascertained reflects an attachment to representative rather than direct democracy. The opinion of the man in the street is not to be taken directly but filtered through the 'responsible men' mentioned above. The same view, incidentally, is implicit in Ernst's preference for trial by judge rather than jury, which is itself a reflection of Ernst's conviction that the judgement of *Ulysses* should be left to expert literary critics.

Ernst's sixth and final point – that '*Ulysses* must be judged as a whole, and its general purpose and effect determined' – has been present, explicitly and implicitly throughout his argument. In treating it at the end of his argument, Ernst reiterates that the test for obscenity is 'to be applied to the *whole* book, and not to excerpts which may be singled out.'[85] Here, as earlier, the decisions Ernst quotes in support of this point leave open the question of whether books of literary merit can contain parts that are obscene according to the legal definition of the word. For example, in the *Peabody* decision the Court said, 'There are passages in the books in question which, published separately and alone, would be considered indecent and their distribution or importation prohibited but a literary work cannot be called obscene, if, here and there may be found some expression which is obscene.'[86] On one hand, the Court provides some justification for thinking that literary merit negates the charge of obscenity, not only on the level of the whole but on the level of the parts. The reference to 'passages in the books … which, published separately and alone, would be considered indecent' implies, or at least leaves room for inferring, that these passages cannot be construed as obscene when published as integral parts of a literary whole. On the other hand, the claim that a literary work cannot be deemed obscene 'if, here and there may be found some expression which is obscene' suggests that the parts of a literary work may legitimately be deemed obscene even if the work as a whole may not.

Ernst's treatment of the relation between part and whole in his sixth point shares in this ambiguity:

> *Ulysses* should not and cannot be judged on the basis of isolated passages. Granting that it contains occasional episodes of doubtful taste, the fact remains that obscenity is not a question of words nor of specific instances, nor even of whole chapters. It is a question of entirety. To justify the condemnation of *Ulysses* it must be deemed to violate the law as a whole.
>
> The Court has read the book and knows that such portions of it as may conceivably be challenged are a negligible fraction of the whole.[87]

In admitting that *Ulysses* contains 'episodes of doubtful taste' which 'may conceivably be challenged,' Ernst does not admit (though he may seem to imply) that parts of *Ulysses* are obscene. Nor does he do so anywhere else in his argument. In light of his oft-repeated conviction that a work of literary merit cannot be obscene (expressed, for example, when he claims that the status of *Ulysses* as a literary classic negates *'any implication* of obscenity,' it seems legitimate to suspect that Ernst's unwillingness to acknowledge that parts of *Ulysses* are obscene reflects not just strategic rhetorical prudence but also his conviction that they could not possibly be so. As I have indicated earlier, this interpretation of Ernst's sixth point is certainly compatible with the esthetic view of art which underlies his defense of *Ulysses*, particularly in so far as that view provides warrant for Stuart Gilbert's belief that a genuine work of literature achieves a stasis that effectively precludes the possibility of any harmful moral effect whatsoever.

Ernst's concluding remarks, although they sometimes seem to acknowledge the validity of the traditional moral defense of literature, confirm that his defense of *Ulysses* is essentially esthetic. Ernst reiterates his conviction that the obscene and the literary are incompatible: 'The notion of pornography is wholly inconsistent with an artist's serious effort to mirror and perpetuate truth in literature.'[88] In support of this idea, Ernst cites Herbert Gorman, who paraphrases the esthetic view of literature that Stephen articulates in *Portrait*: 'pornography is as abhorrent to the writer as didacticism.'[89] This view can obviously be used to argue that literature is incapable of influencing readers for ill. The corollary of this notion is the idea that the true work of literary art can have only a beneficial effect. Ernst's claim that Joyce, by shedding light on the 'murky chambers of the human mind,' helps us to 'banish darkness and taint' would seem to imply acceptance of that idea.[90] Strictly speaking, however, the esthetic view of literature, by virtue of the stasis it posits in the reader, implies that the work of art is incapable of influencing for either evil *or* good. And it is precisely on this point that Ernst confirms that he embraces an esthetic view of literature: '*It is doubtful*,' he writes, '*if people are influenced by what they read*' (emphasis mine).[91]

The government's case against *Ulysses* was never laid out with the precision of Ernst's arguments in its defense. Unlike Ernst, the US Attorney's Office followed Woolsey's directive and did not submit a written brief. The government's arguments must therefore be pieced together from two internal memoranda, from Sam Coleman's enumeration of allegedly obscene passages in *Ulysses* (as recorded in the copy of the novel confiscated by US Customs, forwarded to the US Attorney's Office, and eventually submitted to Judge Woolsey), and from newspaper and other accounts of the oral arguments before Judge Woolsey, which took place on 25 November 1933.[92] One of the government memoranda, entitled '*United States* v. "*Ulysses*,"' can be confidently attributed to the hand of Nicholas Atlas, since its discussion of *Ulysses* is virtually identical to that which Atlas later published as 'James Joyce' in *Scraps*, the newsletter of the US Attorney's Office, Southern District of New York.[93] The other memorandum, 'Analysis of Books Submitted to Us by the Claimant in the *Ulysses* Case for Comparison,' seems to have been prepared largely by someone else, probably Sam Coleman, though Atlas's participation cannot be completely ruled out.

Before examining Atlas's memorandum, we do well to recall that Ernst and Lindey, hoping to convince the government to drop its case against *Ulysses*, had supplied Coleman and Atlas with material they had gathered for the defense of *Ulysses*, including Lindey's 'Petition.' Although Ernst's and Lindey's dealings with Coleman and Atlas were generally amicable, those dealings were strained by the latter's tardiness in returning this material, which caused Lindey to suspect them of trying to prevent him and Ernst from turning it over to Woolsey before the oral argument.[94] Lindey's suspicions arose when he discussed the return of the documents with Atlas and found the US Attorney 'quite evasive.' Atlas explained the delay by saying that he 'wanted to keep the material as he needed it in the preparation of his brief.' Lindey, however, was of the opinion that Atlas 'could not have any conceivable use for any of the stuff.' Lindey was assuming, of course, that Atlas's interest in the documents was motivated by a desire to win the government's case against *Ulysses*. Atlas's memorandum invites another interpretation, namely that Atlas's reluctance to relinquish the documents was motivated by his desire to argue the government's case against *Ulysses* in a manner that would make it clear that the government was not whole-hearted in its ostensible desire to censor Joyce's novel.

Atlas's memorandum certainly makes it clear that he made ample use of the critical material that Ernst and Lindey had gathered in defense of *Ulysses*. It begins by quoting Larbaud's opinion that Joyce was as well known among writers as Freud or Einstein among scientists.[95] Following Larbaud, Atlas provides a brief biographical sketch of Joyce, then proceeds to discuss *Chamber Music*, *Dubliners* and *Portrait*. With Joyce's earlier work out of the way, Atlas broaches the subject of *Ulysses*, being careful to communicate the government's unprejudiced attitude toward the novel:

> ... we approach the book with great respect. We realize that the substance of the book is a microcosm, depicted and represented in a most literary, most sensitive, and very scientific way. We admit that the book is to be praised for its style, which is new and startling. ... We distinguish its method and realize that this is a new method in the creation of the novel. ... Finally, we realize that this is literature and poetry.[96]

Having made it clear that the government was not prejudiced against *Ulysses*, Atlas might have been expected to address the government's objections to the novel; instead, he proceeds to describe the happenings of *Ulysses* in a manner which, by avoiding mention of the objectionable passages, gives the impression that the government's libel has little or no basis. Atlas's summary of the action of the novel is a consummate example of the tradition of critical censorship initiated by Ezra Pound:

Bloom, too, has his troubles. He is married to an Irishwoman of whom he has reason to believe – and, before the day is done, of whom he is sure – that she commits adultery. He has had a personal grief in that he has lost one of his children, a son. And he moves about Dublin, doing all the things that people do, going to business, preparing his own breakfast in his dissatisfied household, going to funerals, going to the beach … .[97]

Atlas does not even hint at Bloom's masturbation at the beach, let alone mention that it caused the suppression of *Ulysses* in 1920–1.

When Atlas quotes from *Ulysses* it is not to provide an example of the novel's alleged obscenity but rather to illustrate its 'rare poetry,' as in the following beautiful passage from 'Telemachus': 'Woodshadows floated silently by through the morning peace from the stairhead seaward where he gazed. Inshore and farther out the mirror of water whitened, spurned by lightshod hurrying feet. White breast of the dim sea.'[98] As the above makes clear, Atlas's memorandum is a literary evaluation of *Ulysses* which does not concern itself with the moral effect of the novel at all. As such, it is clearly *not* intended to convince anyone that *Ulysses* should be suppressed. In fact, by stressing that *Ulysses* is an impressive work of art, it implicitly argues that the government's motion to confiscate and destroy the novel should be denied.

Atlas's admiration for *Ulysses* can be traced back to 1918 when, a fifteen-year-old with an interest in languages, literature and the arts, he began to spend time with artists in Greenwich village, often accompanied by Joseph T. Shipley, President of the Drama Critics Guild of New York and a teacher at Atlas's highschool.[99] Thus he was familiar with *The Little Review* and was probably aware of the prosecution of the magazine because of its serial publication of *Ulysses*. During the 1920s, Atlas lived in the Village, on Gay street, some two blocks from the office of *The Little Review*. After graduating from Fordham's law school in 1924, Atlas practised occasional law, taught English at City College, and worked as a literary critic at the *Brooklyn Daily Eagle*, where he met De Hirsch Margulies. It was through the good offices of Margulies, who travelled to Paris and brought back copies of the Shakespeare & Company edition of *Ulysses*, that Atlas obtained his first copy of Joyce's wandering hero. By the time he became involved in the government's case against *Ulysses*, Atlas had developed a strong admiration for Joyce's works. *Ulysses* had come to him, as it had come to many of his generation, with the force of a liberating revelation; he could hardly be expected seriously to move the Court to confiscate and destroy it.

The second government memorandum – 'Analysis of Books Submitted to Us By the Claimant in the *Ulysses* Case for Comparison' – takes a less sympathetic, though by no means hostile, attitude toward *Ulysses*, which suggests that Coleman and not Atlas was its primary author. Unlike Atlas's memorandum, Coleman's admits the validity of moral arguments where literature is concerned. For example, in discussing *Madeleine* (purportedly the autobiography of a prostitute) Coleman writes that it 'would be a deterrent from vice to those who read it.'[100] And in evaluating the Court's decision in the case of Erskine Caldwell's *God's Little Acre*, he states that a work adjudged not obscene as a whole could none the less contain obscene parts: 'Apparently the Court felt that the book as a whole was not obscene and could not by reason of certain obscene passages be held so to be.'[101] More important, Coleman asserts that parts of *Ulysses* are in fact obscene. Thus in discussing Gautier's *Mademoiselle de Maupin*, he writes, 'Certainly the book contains no such obscenities as *Ulysses*, there being no bawdy words, no bawdy scenes.'[102] Coleman's conclusion refers to these 'obscenities' euphemistically as things unmentionable in 'polite society':

> In *Ulysses* we have to deal with a book highly serious in its purpose but permeated throughout with expressions, allusions, clichés, and situations which even in this day and age could not be mentioned in any society pretending to call itself polite, and certainly not in mixed company, no matter how free that mixed company may be.[103]

Atlas's and Coleman's memoranda – not to mention the fact that neither were submitted to the Çourt – suggest strongly that the government was not eager to suppress *Ulysses*, a suggestion confirmed by Coleman's subsequent response to Judge Woolsey's decision: '"I feel just as Judge Woolsey does about the book. ... The result is, I think, a wholesome one. I welcome the decision and am satisfied with it."'[104] Why, then, had the government refused to drop its libel against the novel? According to Coleman, '"The reason for the action was that there had been so much adverse criticism of the book and such adulation of it, on the other hand, that the government felt that there should be an authoritative ruling at this time as to whether or not the book was 'obscene.'"'[105] These comments help to explain why the US Attorney's Office had not bothered to formulate anything in the way of a coherent argument in favor of the suppression of *Ulysses* and been content instead to let its case rest almost entirely on the offending passages mentioned in Coleman's memorandum and annotated in the confiscated copy of the novel submitted to Woolsey.

The confiscated copy of *Ulysses* reveals that the US Attorney's Office deemed a total of 260 passages to be obscene by the standards of 1932–3. The 260 offending passages are distributed over 198 separate pages, roughly 25 per cent of the pages that make up the 1922 Paris edition of the novel. The substantial majority of these are to be found in the latter episodes of the novel:

Episode		Offending passages
1.	Telemachus	0
2.	Nestor	0
3.	Proteus	0
4.	Calypso	0
5.	Lotus-Eaters	1
6.	Hades	0
7.	Aeolus	0
8.	Lestrygonians	5
9.	Scylla and Charybdis	7
10.	Wandering Rocks	0
11.	Sirens	0
12.	Cyclops	25
13.	Nausicaa	17
14.	Oxen of the Sun	29
15.	Circe	89
16.	Eumaeus	12
17.	Ithaca	19
18.	Penelope	56
Total		*260*

Since these passages constitute the foundation of the government's case against *Ulysses* – and therefore constitute the best means of assessing the nature of that case – they are reproduced in their entirety in the Appendix.

If the number of objectionable passages implies that the government's case against *Ulysses* was built on a solid (if not reasoned) foundation, Coleman's memorandum indicates that the foundation was precarious: given Coleman's conviction that the offending passages could under no circumstances be read in mixed company, the presence of one woman in the courtroom could effectively undermine the government's case altogether. According to Ernst, this is exactly what transpired. Before the hearing began, Coleman confided to Ernst his belief that the government could not win the case. When Ernst asked for an explanation, Coleman replied, '"The only way to win the case is to refer to the great number of vulgar four-letter words used by Joyce. This will shock the judge and he will suppress the book. But I can't do it."'[106] '"Why?"' asked Ernst. '"Because there is a lady in the courtroom,"' Coleman replied. Ernst, upon discovering that the woman in question was his wife, assured Coleman that she was '"a former newspapergal and a present schoolteacher. She's seen all these words on toilet walls or scribbled on sidewalks by kids who enjoy them because of their being taboo."' In spite of Ernst's assurances, Coleman insisted that he could not utter these words in mixed company.

The hearing, held on 25 November 1933 in a small, crowded courtroom, was informal.[107] Woolsey smoked and 'talked freely from the bench and from time to time told of his extremely difficult position in being required to pass on a book that for ten years had evoked the most violent denunciations and praise from all manner of learned men and women.'[108] His listeners, in addition to Ernst's wife Margaret, included Random House editors Bennett Cerf, Donald Klopfer, and Saxe Commins, as well as Whit Burnett, the editor of *Story*. An old enemy was also present, the man responsible for the long-standing ban on *Ulysses*: John S. Summer, still Secretary of the New York Society for the Suppression of Vice.

As the representative of the libellant, Sam Coleman spoke first, asking the Court 'not to think of him personally as "a puritanical censor" because he contended that *Ulysses* was "obscene" and accordingly should not be permitted to be sold in [the United States].'[109] The details of Coleman's opening remarks have not survived, but he presumably proceeded to articulate the 'publicly avowed basis' of the government's case against *Ulysses*, namely, 'The sexual titillation of episodes, more particularly the dreams at the end of the book, and the use of unparlorish words.'[110] Woolsey admitted that he, too, was troubled by parts of the novel, especially Molly's monologue:

> 'This isn't an easy case to decide. ... I think things ought to take their chances in the market place. My own feeling is against censorship. I know that as soon as you suppress anything the bootlegger goes to work. The people see about as much of the prohibited article as they otherwise would and the profits go into illegal channels. Still. ... Still there is that soliloquy in the last chapter. I don't know about that. But, go on with the case.[111]

Since Coleman refused to read passages from *Ulysses*, he did not have much of a case to go on with. He did, however, argue that *Ulysses* was obscene. The general lines of his oral argument, none of which seems to have been developed at length, can be inferred from his response to Judge's Woolsey's request for a definition of obscenity. Before Coleman could answer, Woolsey suggested that '"a thing may be said to be obscene where its primary purpose is to excite sexual feeling."' Coleman was not satisfied with this definition:

'I do not think that obscenity necessarily should be limited to exciting sexual feeling. I can understand people reading something that does not excite them in such a manner but which they might still pass on as being obscene. I should say a thing is obscene by the ordinary language used and by what it does to the average reader. It need not necessarily be what the author intended. On these grounds, I think there are ample reasons to consider *Ulysses* to be an obscene book.'[112]

If this newspaper account of Coleman's oral arguments is accurate, then the main principles of his case against *Ulysses* were as follows: first, obscenity should be defined broadly as in *Regina* v. *Hicklin*; second, authorial intention (literary or otherwise) should not preclude the possibility of obscenity; third, the literary value of the whole of *Ulysses* should not preclude the obscenity of its parts: 'No one would dare attack the literary value of the book. ... But there is obscenity in it.'[113] Thus, Coleman apparently disagreed with several of Ernst's arguments. He did not, however, question the validity of expert literary opinion, although he intimated that it was perhaps more equivocal than Ernst had indicated. Nor did he deny that the proper test of obscenity was the average person, as opposed to the vulnerable young person. The evidence suggests, however, that Coleman did not press his arguments with much conviction.

Since Coleman refused to read from *Ulysses*, the way was open for Ernst to take the initiative. His first step was to take up one by one the four-letter Anglo-Saxon words used in *Ulysses*:

> When I got to the word 'fuck' I explained how one of the possible derivations was 'to plant' an Anglo-Saxon agricultural usage. The farmer used to fuck the seed into the soil. I told the Judge I liked the word. I didn't use it in parlors because it made me unpopular, but the word had strength and integrity.
>
> 'In fact, your Honor, it's got more honesty than phrases that modern authors use to connote the same experience.'
>
> 'For example, Mr. Ernst' asked the Court.
>
> 'Oh – "they slept together." It means the same thing.'
>
> The Judge smiled. 'That isn't even usually the truth.'[114]

At that moment Ernst knew 'the case was half won.'[115]

Significantly, Ernst's treatment of the word 'fuck' does not depend upon its literary context; instead, it implies that the word, taken in itself, is not obscene. Thus Ernst attempts to defend *Ulysses* against the charge of obscenity by purifying, or rendering unproblematic, the language of sex and, by implication, human sexuality itself. Thomas Merton recognized a

similar desire behind D.H. Lawrence's attempt to make a religion of sex.
Merton's remarks shed considerable light on both Ernst's argument and
Joyce's novel:

> There is all the difference in the world between a conscience that seeks
> security in rigid and puritanical repression of sex and a civilized expe-
> rience of ambivalence in sex, in a society where ideals are one thing
> and realities another. Joyce accepted that ambivalence and lived with
> it. One wonders if Lawrence, who insisted on breaking through it alto-
> gether and making a religion of sex, was not in some sense the greater
> idealist and the greater puritan. As to those who imagine that sex can
> exist in modern life without any ambivalence at all – as if there were
> no inner tension between *eros* and *thanatos* – one wonders if they are
> happier than the rest or just more thick-skinned.[116]

Whether Ernst belongs to the 'happier' or the 'thick-skinned' is not at
issue here, but his argument betrays remarkable insensitivity toward the
English language.

Ernst's assertion to the contrary notwithstanding, 'to fuck' does not
mean the same as 'to sleep together.' The latter expression is undoubtedly euphemistic, but its meaning can none the less be situated between
'to fuck' and 'to make love,' as the following passage from Margaret
Atwood's *The Handmaid's Tale* makes clear. The narrator, a woman
forced by the Republic of Gilead to produce children for the political
elite, is describing her sexual intercourse with a military commander:

> My red skirt is hitched up to my waist, though no higher. Below it the
> Commander is fucking. What he is fucking is the lower part of my
> body. I do not say making love because this is not what he's doing.
> Copulating too would be inaccurate, because it would imply two
> people and only one is involved.[117]

According to Atwood, the word 'fuck' is obscene precisely because,
like the activity it describes, it strips the act of sex of its peculiar human
dignity. Ernst might have countered that the word attempts to restore to
human sexuality the wholesome (and unambivalent) meaning it has in
the animal kingdom. But human beings do not enjoy the innocence of the
animal kingdom. As Merton has argued, Joyce's treatment of sexuality in
Ulysses suggests that he was acutely aware of the profound ambivalence
of human sexuality; he recognized the connection between *eros* and
thanatos, as his tendency to mix eroticism and excrement makes clear.

The second main line of Ernst's oral arguments emerged in response
to Woolsey's repeated desire to know if Ernst had read *Ulysses* in its

entirety. Ernst feared that the question implied a willingness 'to condemn on the theory that it would do society no harm to suppress a book so long, so dull and so dreary.'[118] Ernst's fear seems curious in light of his previous use of the difficulty of *Ulysses* as an argument *against* suppression of the book. In any case, a far more disturbing implication of Woolsey's questioning is surely that if it could be shown that *Ulysses* was rarely read in its entirety, Ernst's argument that the novel should be judged as a whole could conceivably lose a good deal of its force. Ernst answered Woolsey's 'potential state of mind' as follows:

'Yes, Judge – ten years ago I tried to get through *Ulysses* but couldn't. This year in preparation for the trial, I *had* to read it. And while reading it I was invited, in August, to speak at the Unitarian Church in Nantucket on the New Banking Act and the reopening of the banks after the Holiday.'

'What's that got to do with my question?' said Judge Woolsey.

'Well, I addressed about four hundred people. I was intent on what I was saying. And still, when I finished, I realized that while I was talking about banking, I was also thinking at the same time about the long ceiling-high windows on the sides, the clock and eagle in the rear, the painted dome above, the gray old lady in the front row, the baby in the sixth row, and innumerable other tidbits.

'Judge,' I said, 'that's *Ulysses*. I went back to my reading with a new appreciation of Joyce's technique, the stream of consciousness put into words. And now, your Honor, while arguing to win this case I thought I was intent only on this book, but frankly, while pleading before you, I've also been thinking about that ring around your tie, how your gown does not fit too well on your shoulders, and the picture of George Washington back of your bench.'

The Judge smiled. 'I've been worried about the last part of the book but now I understand many parts about which I've been in doubt. I have listened as intently as I know how but I must confess that while listening to you I've also been thinking about the Heppelwhite chair behind you.'

'Judge,' I said, 'that's the book.'[119]

Thus, Ernst shrewdly responded to Woolsey's question about the readability of *Ulysses* by recapitulating an important part of his written argument, namely, the idea that to understand the novel was to understand Joyce's use of the stream-of-consciousness technique. Woolsey's response to Ernst's explanation of that technique suggests that the judge was largely in agreement.

After hearing the arguments of both sides, Woolsey apologized for having taken so long in bringing the case to a hearing. He recognized that the claimant was anxious for a decision; none the less, needing more time to make up his mind, he reserved decision. While he was formulating his opinion, Ernst supplied him with yet another memorandum, which contained material Woolsey had requested in the course of the hearing.[120] In that memorandum Ernst dramatically underlined a crucial implication of the legal procedure being followed:

> The Court is sitting herein as judge and jury. The sole evidence presented is *Ulysses*....
> It is no abuse of analogy to say that this proceeding is something like a capital case. *Ulysses* stands before the Court as defendant. Charged with being a menace to public morals, it is fighting for its life. If condemned, it faces destruction by a means (i.e., confiscation) no less complete than that of hanging or electrocution.[121]

Having made a last plea on behalf of Joyce's novel, Ernst rested his case. The fate of *Ulysses* was now in Judge Woolsey's hands.

5

The Well-intentioned Lies of
the Woolsey Decision

On 6 December 1933 Judge Woolsey announced his decision: *Ulysses*, he wrote, was not legally obscene and could therefore be admitted to the United States. Woolsey's decision bestowed upon the United States the distinction of being the first English-speaking country to lift its ban on *Ulysses*; it thus made some amends for that country's lead in suppressing the novel many years before. In according protection of the law to *Ulysses*, the Woolsey decision dried up the stream of continental editions of the novel that adventurous travellers had been smuggling through US Customs since 1922 and freed *Ulysses* from the 'restricted' holdings of libraries across the country. More importantly, by quelling the storm of controversy which had tossed *Ulysses* from the time of its appearance in *The Little Review*, it set Joyce's world-disturbing novel off on a new journey toward respectability.

Woolsey's decision, widely circulated for many years in the Random House and Bodley Head editions of Joyce's novel, is undoubtedly the most celebrated document of the trials of *Ulysses*. Joyce scholars, legal historians, and cultural historians alike habitually refer to it as a 'landmark' or 'monumental' or 'historic' or 'famous' decision. Yet in spite of this renown, the nature and significance of the decision have yet to be appreciated. The explanation of this lack of appreciation, I believe, lies in a failure to recognize that the Woolsey decision embraces and elaborates the esthetic theory of literature which underlay Ernst's defense of the novel.

The Woolsey decision lays down four principles for determining whether a work is obscene, 'as legally defined by the Courts ...: tending to stir the sex impulses or to lead to sexually impure and lustful thoughts.'[1] This definition, it should be noted, branded as obscene anything tending to arouse sexual desire, anything erotic; it thus permitted Woolsey to equate the obscene with the pornographic ('designed to cause sexual excitement') and the aphrodisiac ('provocative of or heightening sexual desire').[2] Gloria Steinem and others have argued convincingly that these terms are by no means synonymous.[3] None the less, Woolsey's definition of obscenity treated them as such, and the major principles of his decision, not to mention his application thereof, must be understood accordingly.

In applying these four principles to *Ulysses*, Judge Woolsey articulated
a number of what Leslie Fiedler has called 'well-intentioned lies.'[4]
According to my count, Woolsey's decision contains four such lies. Their
presence in Woolsey's decision, it should be stressed, in no way undermines his finding that *Ulysses* was not legally obscene by the standards
of 1933. As the 1934 decision of the Court of Appeals made clear,
Woolsey was entirely correct in his finding. Woolsey's well-intentioned
lies, however, remain well-intentioned lies for all that. I adopt Fiedler's
provocative phrase because, like Fiedler, I consider Woolsey's decision
to be 'palpably false as criticism' of *Ulysses*.[5] My purpose here is to establish that in applying his cardinal principles to *Ulysses*, Woolsey misrepresented or falsified Joyce's novel in four distinct ways. These
misrepresentations or falsehoods were well-intentioned because
Woolsey used them to achieve a legitimate and good end: the liberation
of one of the greatest literary works of the twentieth century. They were
none the less lies (or falsehoods) because they misrepresented the nature
of *Ulysses* and, implicitly, literature in general. They did so, I will argue,
precisely because they gave consummate expression to the esthetic
theory of art employed by Ernst and embraced by Woolsey.

The first principle of Woolsey's decision was that the judge should
consult the criticism written about the book he must decide upon. The
same principle, as we have seen, was the cornerstone of Ernst's arguments. Early in the decision Woolsey explicitly acknowledges his debt to
the critical works on *Ulysses* which Ernst had encouraged him to read:

> I have read 'Ulysses' once in its entirety and I have read those pas-
> sages of which the government particularly complains several times.
> In fact, for many weeks, my spare time has been devoted to the consid-
> eration of the decision which my duty would require me to make in
> this matter.
> 'Ulysses' is not an easy book to read or to understand. But there has
> been much written about it, and in order properly to approach the
> consideration of it it is advisable to read a number of other books
> which have now become its satellites.[6]

These were not idle words: during his vacation Woolsey had 'ploughed
through *Ulysses* … reading the eleven "satellite" books he said were necessary to give him completer [sic] understanding of that erudite Joyce's
classic and mythological allusions.'[7]

Woolsey's reading of these texts (which include virtually every book
written on *Ulysses* at the time) greatly influenced the interpretation he
cast on the other three principles that provide the framework of his

NON-MAILABLE LIST   January 18, 1918.

File No.	Name & Location	Description	Issues excluded	Remarks.
49537	Little Review, The Chicago, Ill	Publication of Anarchistic tendency	October, 1917	Esp.
47441	Log Cabin, The Chicago, Ill		8/8/17	"
47756	Libro Blanco Aleman, Mexico City	Pamphlet		"
47755	LaDictadura Mundial, Mexico City	"		"
46602	Leader, The San Francisco, Cal	Supposedly Anarchistic	4/7/17	Sec. 211, Pen.Code.

THE LITTLE REVIEW
A MAGAZINE OF THE ARTS
MAKING NO COMPROMISE WITH THE PUBLIC TASTE

"ULYSSES"
by
JAMES JOYCE

1. (above) US Post Office 'List of Periodicals, Pamphlets, Circulars, etc.' Held to Be Non-Mailable, 18 January 1918', page 5.

2. (left) Cover, *The Little Review*, March 1918.

3. James Joyce, as he appeared in *The Little Review*,
   July - August 1920.

4. Margaret
Anderson

5. John Quinn

Names and Record of Persons Arrested on Complaint of the New York

No.	Date of Arrest	NAME & RESIDENCE OF PRISONER	Age	ALIASES	Nationality	Religion	Education	Married No. of Child/dau.	Occupation	Warrant Issued by	OFFENCE	Committed	Discharged
133.	Sep. 5.	Harry Davis, Mills Hotel No. 7.			U.S.			8.	Waiter	N.Y. Ct.	Dis.Cond.Dof		
134.	" "	Michael W. Craven 52 1088. 123 St.			Ireland Cath			M	Salesman	"	"		
135.	" 9	Robert Turner 33 193 W. 139		Colored	U.S. Prot.			M.	Porter	28 Print.	"		
136.	" 14	Jos. Goldstein 31 160 R'd Ave. B'klyn			Russia Jew.			S.	Sailor	N.Y. Ct.	"		
137.	" "	Jas. P. Wheeler 37 Charlotte, Pa.			U.S. Prot.			8.	Salesman	"	"		
138.	" 15	Herbert Rexford 34 47 Ten Broeck St. Albany			U.S. Prot.			M.	Chauffeur U.S. Commr. 4 Photos. O'Neill, Albany, pictures	Mailing obscene pictures	yes.	
139.	" 16	Jacob Jacobson 63 151 E. 84 St.			Denmark Prot.			S.	Kitchen man	N.Y.P.D.	Dis.Cond.Dof (2nd)		
140.	" 17	Geo. P. Farr 63 161 W. 36.			U.S. Prot.			S.	Det. Police Dept.	N.Y. Ct.	"		
141.	" "	Louis Forgno 22 ... St.			Spain Cath.			S.	Clerk	"	"		

6. 'Names and Record of Persons Arrested on Complaint of the New York Society for the Suppression of Vice, during the Year 1920', page 8.

7. John Sumner (in the middle) at work c.1935.

8. Sylvia Beach and James Joyce at Shakespeare and Company, Paris.

9. Report of Seizure,
US Customs Service,
23 October 1931.

10. Morris L. Ernst

11. Judge John M. Woolsey

12. Nicholas Atlas

13. Samuel Coleman

relaxation of the thing done : the fallaciously inferred debility of the female the muscularity of the male : the variations of ethical codes : the natural grammatical transition by inversion involving no alteration of sense of an aorist preterite proposition (parsed as masculine subject, monosyllabic onomatopœic transitive verb with direct feminine object) from the active voice into its correlative aorist preterite proposition (parsed as feminine subject, auxiliary verb and quasimonosyllabic onomatopœic past participle with complementary masculine agent) in the passive voice : the continued product of seminators by generation : the continual production of semen by distillation : the futility of triumph or protest or vindication : the inanity of extolled virtue : the lethargy of nescient matter : the apathy of the stars.

In what final satisfaction did these antagonistic sentiments and reflections reduced to their simplest forms, converge ?

Satisfaction at the ubiquity in eastern and western terrestrial hemispheres, in all habitable lands and islands explored or unexplored (the land of the midnight sun, the islands of the blessed, the isles of Greece, the land of promise) of adipose posterior female hemispheres, redolent of milk and honey and of excretory sanguine and seminal warmth, reminiscent of secular families of curves of amplitude, insusceptible of moods of impression or of contrarieties of expression, expressive of mute immutable mature animality.

The visible signs of antesatisfaction ?

An approximate erection : a solicitous adversion : a gradual elevation : a tentative revelation ; a silent contemplation.

Then ?

He kissed the plump mellow yellow smellow melons of her rump, on each plump melonous hemisphere, in their mellow yellow furrow, with obscure prolonged provocative melonsmellonous osculation.

The visible signs of postsatisfaction ?

A silent contemplation : a tentative velation : a gradual abasement : a solicitous aversion : a proximate erection.

What followed this silent action ?

Somnolent invocation, less somnolent recognition, incipient excitation catechetical interrogation.

14. Page 690, confiscated copy of *Ulysses* (Paris: Shakespeare and Company, 1930), as annotated by US Attorney's Office, 1932-3.

15. Martin Conboy

16. Judge Martin Manton

17. Judge Learned Hand

18. Judge Augustus Hand

decision. In order to appreciate the nature of that influence, we should note that the critical satellites of *Ulysses* Woolsey read encouraged him to evaluate the novel in light of another, even more celestial, group of works. For the authors of the critical satellites, more or less united in their desire to dispel the charges of obscenity that had been levelled against *Ulysses*, had shifted the emphasis of debate from the controversial subject matter of the novel to 'questions of literary form and to analogies with past literary greatness.'[8] In the opinion of Valèry Larbaud, for example, Joyce's work was to be compared with that of Swift, Sterne, Fielding and Homer. According to T.S. Eliot, the crucial analogy was with Homer's *Odyssey*. Stuart Gilbert identified Pater, Flaubert and Tolstoy as important influences on Joyce, and placed *Ulysses* in the context of works by writers such as Ovid, Shakespeare, Ibsen and Proust.

Works by these great writers – which may be described as creative satellites of *Ulysses* – unquestionably illuminate Joyce's novel, but they are not the only creative works that do so. Joyce also derived inspiration from popular literary forms like the newspaper, the sentimental romance and, more significantly, pornography. According to Leslie Fiedler, 'of all the popular modes porn is most central to *Ulysses*':

> We must therefore read that novel not only in the Modernist context of Proust and Mann, Eliot and Pound – along with those mythographic source books from which Joyce drew the references and allusions he tabulated for Linati [and Gilbert]; but also side by side with the volumes we find Bloom turning over at a bookstall in the episode of the 'Wandering Rocks': *The Awful Disclosures of Maria Monk*, *Aristotle's Masterpiece*, *Tales of the Ghetto* by Leopold von Sacher-Masoch, *Fair Tyrants*, by James Lovebirch, *Ruby, the Pride of the Ring*, and especially *Sweets of Sin*, by Paul de Kock, whose name in a world of Hibernian punsters evokes much hilarity.[9]

This expanded view of the satellites of *Ulysses*, which calls into question any strict distinction between literature and pornography, has the virtue of agreeing with historical fact in two important respects.

First, as Richard Brown has observed, Joyce himself had a 'lively interest' in pornographic writing.[10] Thus, of the works that Fiedler mentions above, Joyce read Maria Monk's *The Awful Disclosures of Maria Monk*, 'Aristotle's' *Aristotle's Masterpiece*, and Leopold Sacher Masoch's *Tales of the Ghetto*.[11] Likewise, he read John Cleland's *Fanny Hill*, and an English translation of the Comte de Mirabeau's *Le Rideau Levé*, which, according to Brown, 'parades its erotic intentions under the outrageous publisher's imprint "Putitin, Rogers & Co. Nineinch Street."'[12] (Joyce also read more obscure but none the less suggestive works like *History of Excess* and

Lustful Acts. Another title deserves mention as well in the present context, for Joyce's pornographic reading included Adrian Beverland's *The Law Concerning Draped Virginity,* one of the books apprehended with *Ulysses* by US Customs officials in Minneapolis in 1928 (see Chapter 4).

Pornographic works such as these made their presence felt in *Ulysses.* As Brown has observed, Joyce used 'erotic or mildly erotic magazines which he knew' to characterize Stephen Dedalus, who brings home from Paris the '"rich booty" of "*Le Tutu*" and "*Pantalon Blanc et Culotte Rouge*."'[13] In similar fashion, Joyce sheds light on Molly's character through the books she likes to read: works like *Ruby, Pride of the Ring* (illustrated, as Bloom notes, with the image of a man with a whip who stands over a woman who lies naked on the floor), and novels like *Sweets of Sin* by Paul de Kock (if Bloom is right to think that she would prefer it to the other titles he peruses on the bookstand in 'Wandering Rocks').[14] According to Fiedler, Molly is also characterized by the kind of pornographic works she does *not* like, as when she objects in the 'Penelope' episode to the brutality of *Aristotle's Masterpiece*.[15]

Joyce's characterization of Bloom relies even more heavily on such works. As Brown has noted, Joyce revealed an aspect of Bloom's character by attributing to him an interest in the 'suggestive, sometimes masochistic flavour' of the magazine *Photo Bits,* the Easter number of which is the source of the '*Bath of the Nymph*' picture that hangs above the conjugal bed.[16] Even more revealing is Bloom's attraction to the books he peruses in the 'Wandering Rocks' episode, especially *Sweets of Sin.* Bloom's enjoyment of such books is confirmed in 'Ithaca' when he imagines his utopian 'Bloom Cottage' as a place where there will be room for the 'lecture of unexpurgated exotic erotic masterpieces.'[17] Bloom's pornographic inclinations are also revealed, as Brown has noted, in the photographs he owns. These include

> 2 erotic photocards showing: a) buccal coition between nude señorita (rere presentation, superior position) and nude torero (fore presentation, inferior position): b) anal violation by male religious (fully clothed, eyes abject) of female religious (partly clothed, eyes direct).[18]

Bloom also has photographs of his wife, which he shows to Stephen in the 'Eumaeus' episode. Brown is surely right to claim that a connection is established between these two groups of photographs in the 'Circe' episode when Mrs Mervyn Talboys levels the following accusation against Bloom:

> This plebeian Don Juan ... sent me in double envelopes an obscene photograph ... . I have it still. It represents a partially nude señorita,

frail and lovely (his wife as he solemnly assured me, taken by him from nature), practising illicit intercourse with a muscular torero, evidently a blackguard.[19]

Both Fiedler and Brown have recognized the significance of such passages in any attempt to appreciate the pornographic dimension of *Ulysses*. For Fiedler they suggest that Joyce

> seems sometimes to have suspected himself of being the peddlar of his own most shameful erotic fantasies, a writer of dirty letters to the world, in short, ... a pornographer. Of this charge, Judge Woolsey may have acquitted him in a New York courtroom; but at the continuing trial in the depths of his inner mind (the trial recorded in the text of *Ulysses* itself, at its Nighttown center), he was constantly being found guilty.[20]

For Brown, they confirm that the pornographic inclinations of the Blooms flavour their life together: 'Bloom and Molly' he writes, 'see their relationship through the eyes of "a volume of peccaminous pornographical tendency": *Sweets of Sin*.'[21]

The same claim can be made, it seems to me, about Bloom's relations with other women. Bloom's correspondence with Martha Clifford is a case in point. So is his encounter with Gerty MacDowell. As a passage near the end of the 'Nausicaa' episode makes clear, Bloom's voyeurism on the beach is inextricably intertwined with his pornographic photographs (featuring a 'nude' or 'partially nude señorita') and *Sweets of Sin* (in which 'frillies' and 'Raoul' figure prominently):

> O sweety all your little girlwhite up I saw dirty bracegirdle made me do love sticky we two naughty Grace darling she him half past the bed met him pike hoses frillies for Raoul to perfume your wife black hair heave under embon *señorita* young eyes Mulvey plump years dreams return tail end Agendath swoony lovey showed me her next year in drawers return next in her next her next.[22]

The pornographic dimension of *Ulysses* is not restricted to passages dealing explicitly with sexual encounters.

As Brown has pointed out, Joyce incorporated into his novel the 'distinctive linguistic flavour' of pornography.[23] By way of example, Brown mentions a title from a list of '*the World's Twelve Worst Books*' in 'Circe': '*Love-letters of Mother Assistant (erotic)*,' but the linguistic flavour of pornography is also to be found in Joyce's frequent use of the pun. The following example, which describes Bloom's thoughts while he is eating his lunch in Davy Byrne's pub, is one of many:

Dignam's potted meat. Cannibals would with lemon and rice. White missionary too salty. Like pickled pork. Expect the chief consumes the parts of honour. Ought to be tough from exercise. His wives in a row to watch the effect. **There was a right royal old nigger. Who ate or something the somethings of the reverend Mr MacTrigger.**[24]...

—Wife well?

—Quite well, thanks....

—Doing any singing those times?...

—She's engaged for a big tour end of this month....

— ... Who's getting it up?...

Mr Bloom cut his sandwich into slender strips. *Mr MacTrigger. Easier than the dreamy creamy stuff. His five hundred wives. Had the time of their lives.*

—Mustard, sir?

—Thank you.

He studded under each lifted strip yellow blobs. *Their* lives. I have it. *It grew bigger and bigger and bigger.*

—Getting it up? he said. Well, it's like a company idea, you see. Part shares and part profits.

—Ay, now I remember, Nosey Flynn said, putting his hand in his pocket to scratch his groin. Who is this was telling me? Isn't Blazes Boylan mixed up in it?[25]

As this and the passages quoted above indicate, the inclusion of pornographic works among the satellites that illuminate *Ulysses* is warranted not only because Joyce read them but also because he embodied their vision in his novel.

So much for the first respect in which an expanded view of the satellites of *Ulysses* agrees with historical fact. The second has to do with events subsequent to the writing and initial publication of the novel. As we have seen, publishers of erotica, including Samuel Roth, were interested in adding *Ulysses* to their list. And when *Ulysses* was apprehended by US Customs in Minneapolis in 1928, its travelling companions included *The Law Concerning Draped Virginity, The Strangest Voluptuousness,*[26] *The Vice of Women,* and *Aphrodite.* Lest one be inclined to dismiss this occurrence as an isolated historical accident, it should be noted that when Collector's Publications of California published an edition of *Ulysses* in 1967,[27] the titles advertised at the end of the book included *Skirts, San Francisco Babylon, Cruel Lips,* and *The Ups and Downs of Super Dick.* Here, as in Minneapolis in 1928, the works of Homer, Shakespeare and Swift were conspicuously absent.

Lindey, as we have seen, emphatically denied that there existed any similarity between *Ulysses* and the other works confiscated in

Minneapolis; they were, 'unlike *Ulysses*, technical works dealing with unnatural passion.' Ernst, as we have also seen, made a similar distinction in his written argument, emphasizing again and again that literature and obscenity are mutually exclusive. Ernst's and Lindey's insistence on this strict distinction may have been more strategic than heartfelt, but the distinction is no less false for that. As the examples of *Aphrodite* and *Fanny Hill* make clear, obscenity (or erotica, or pornography) can be highly literary. Conversely, as the Collector's edition of *Ulysses* indicates, literary works of great stature can be attractive to pornographers.

Judge Woolsey, however, favored Ernst's view that there was a strict distinction to be made between literature and pornography (or erotica, or obscenity); thus, a crucial well-intentioned lie finds its way into his decision, emerging most clearly in his statements on Joyce's intention. First, Woolsey denies that Joyce wrote *Ulysses* with pornographic intent: 'in "Ulysses," in spite of its unusual frankness, I do not detect anywhere the leer of the sensualist. I hold, therefore, that it is not pornographic.'[28] Second, he asserts that Joyce wrote *Ulysses* with artistic intent: 'In writing "Ulysses," Joyce sought to make a serious experiment in a new ... literary genre.'[29] Woolsey does not explicitly state, as Margaret Anderson did, that the words *literature* and *obscenity* cannot be used in conjunction; none the less, Leslie Fiedler is right to observe that the assumptions behind Woolsey's view of Joyce's intention 'reflect a key dogma of Literary Modernism: that whatever is truly literature (and especially "new" or "experimental" or "serious" literature) cannot be pornography, and conversely, whatever is porn cannot be "serious" literature.'[30]

As the foregoing paragraph indicates, Woolsey's well-intentioned lie regarding the distinction between literature and pornography underlies his treatment of his second major principle, namely, that in determining whether a given work is legally obscene, the judge should ascertain the intent with which it was written: 'in any case where a book is claimed to be obscene it must first be determined, whether the intent with which it was written was what is called, according to the usual phrase, pornographic, – that is, written for the purpose of exploiting obscenity.'[31] Woolsey makes it clear that this principle is potentially of great importance: 'If the conclusion is that the book is pornographic, that is the end of the inquiry and forfeiture must follow.'[32] He also confirms the importance of the preceding principle by asserting that the determination of authorial intent should be informed by a reading of the criticism the allegedly obscene book has engendered. Thus, directly after he observes that the reading of the satellites of *Ulysses* makes 'the study of "Ulysses" ... a heavy task,' Woolsey writes: 'The reputation of "Ulysses" in the literary world, however, warranted my taking such time as was necessary to enable me to satisfy myself as to the intent with which the book was written.'[33]

The length of Woolsey's discussion of Joyce's intention – almost two pages of a five-page decision – indicates that this was the crucial critical principle of his decision. It also suggests that it was in coming to grips with what the satellites of *Ulysses* had to say on the subject that he expended most of the 'great deal of work' it took 'to come to a decision in the case on grounds which [he] thought properly supported it'[34] As we have seen, Woolsey found the grounds he sought in an interpretation of authorial intention involving a strict distinction between literature and pornography (or, to put it more generally, between literature and harmful writing).

Based as it is on a well-intentioned lie about the difference between literature and pornography, Woolsey's treatment of authorial intention contains a well-intentioned lie of its own, namely, that the intention of the artist is always and everywhere a tautology. Woolsey recognized that Joyce was 'undoubtedly' a 'real artist'; it followed for him that Joyce's intention in writing *Ulysses* could be adequately described as the intention to create a work of art, a new literary genre.[35] Northrop Frye explains the tautology in a way that illustrates how it tends to exclude moral considerations from discussions of literature: 'A poet's primary concern is to produce a work of art, and hence his intention can only be expressed by some kind of tautology.'[36] Significantly, Frye's argument equates the artist's 'primary concern,' with his 'intention,' not with his 'primary intention' as one might expect. It follows, for both Frye and Woolsey, that the artist's primary intention is his/her only intention (at least the only one relevant to the critical judgment of his/her work), and that that intention is exclusively artistic – not moral (or immoral), political (or seditious), or religious (or blasphemous).

A great deal can be said, of course, for the idea that the primary intention of the artist *qua* artist is to produce a work of art. But the artist's primary intention is not necessarily his/her only intention. To the contrary, the artistic or esthetic motive can exist in union with others, be they moral, political or otherwise. Orwell makes the point succinctly: 'When I sit down to write a book, I do not say to myself, "I am going to produce a work of art." I write it because there is some lie that I want to expose. ... But I could not do the work of writing a book ... if it were not also an esthetic experience.'[37] On those rare occasions when Joyce discussed his own intentions as an artist, he identified himself more closely with Orwell's position than with either Woolsey's or Frye's. Like Orwell, Joyce had some lies that he wanted to expose.

Arthur Power acknowledged as much when he described Joyce as 'a literary conspirator, who was determined to destroy the oppressive and respectable cultural structures under which we had been reared.'[38] One cultural standard that Joyce particularly disliked was that which dictated that candour in sexual matters would not be tolerated; he therefore resolved to be a prophet of what he described as 'the new realism,' which takes as its theme 'the subterranean forces, those hidden tides which govern everything and run humanity counter to the apparent flood: those poisonous subtleties which envelop the soul, the ascending fumes of sex.'[39]

It was surely in his capacity as a literary conspirator who wished to destroy conventional standards of respectability that Joyce chose to incorporate elements of pornography into *Ulysses*. In doing so, as Brown has argued, Joyce 'deliberately disrupt [ed] any kind of esthetic designed to exclude sexual subjects, eroticism, or even vulgarly pornographic art.'[40] In other words, Joyce's esthetic points to the falsehood in Woolsey's view that literary intent necessarily precludes pornographic intent or, to put the point in more general terms, that literary intention necessarily excludes moral (or immoral) intentions.

It may be objected that in places Woolsey seems to admit that artistic intention has a moral component. Thus, he acknowledges 'Joyce's sincerity and his honest effort to show exactly how the minds of his characters operate.'[41] But, as Woolsey defines it, Joyce's honesty is an esthetic rather than a moral virtue. The artist, according to Woolsey, is moral or immoral only in so far as he is faithful or unfaithful to his chosen technique: 'If Joyce did not attempt to be honest in developing the technique which he has adopted in "Ulysses," the result would be psychologically misleading and thus unfaithful to his chosen technique. Such an attitude would be artistically inexcusable.'[42] As far as Woolsey is concerned, an artist who remains faithful to his technique can do no wrong.

It may also be objected that Woolsey's definition of Joyce's intention, although it involves a strict opposition between pornographic and artistic *intent*, does not necessarily preclude the possibility that an artistically intended work could have an adverse moral *effect*. In fact, at the end of his discussion of Joyce's intention, Woolsey distinctly appears to admit the possibility of a work's being both artistic in intent and obscene in its effect: 'it is not sufficient merely to find … that Joyce did not write "Ulysses" with what is commonly called pornographic intent, I must endeavor to apply a more objective standard to his book in order to determine its effect in the result, irrespective of the intent with which it was written.'[43] But, given Woolsey's contention that the intent with which a work was written cannot be both artistic and pornographic (that is, morally offensive in the eyes of the law), and his opinion that *Ulysses* was written with artistic intent, it is difficult to imagine how he could find the novel's *effect* to be anything but innocuously esthetic.

In fact, Woolsey's firm distinction between pornographic and artistic intent effectively precludes the possibility that *Ulysses,* or any other work written with genuine artistic intent, could have a morally harmful effect. Woolsey acknowledges as much when he asserts that an artistic technique can only be judged by its own standards:

> Whether or not one enjoys such a technique as Joyce uses is a matter of taste on which disagreement or argument is futile, but to subject that technique to the standards of some other technique seems to me to be little short of absurd.
>
> Accordingly, I hold that 'Ulysses' is a sincere and honest book, and I think that the criticisms of it are entirely disposed of by its rationale.[44]

In making this assertion, Woolsey effectively dismisses the possibility of judging *Ulysses,* or any other work of art, by moral standards.

Thus, Woolsey's application of his third principle – that the effect of the libelled work must be tested on *'l'homme moyen sensuel'*: 'a person with average sex instincts' – leads to a forgone conclusion. Having defined *obscene* as 'tending to stir the sex impulses or to lead to sexually impure and lustful thoughts,' Woolsey introduces his objective test:

> Whether a particular book would tend to excite such impulses and thoughts must be tested by the court's opinion as to its effect on a person with average sex instincts – what the French would call *l'homme moyen sensuel* – who plays, in this branch of legal inquiry, the same role of hypothetical reagent as does the 'reasonable man' in the law of torts and 'the man learned in the art' on questions of invention in patent law.[45]

We do well to note here that *l' homme moyen sensuel* had become an object of ridicule in the course of the nineteenth century. Matthew Arnold called him the philistine, the man of crude sensibilities incapable of appreciating esthetic sweetness and light. Oscar Wilde located his appreciation of art on the level of the American who ordered a reproduction of the Venus de Milo only to return it when he discovered it was missing its arms. And, as Ezra Pound's satirical poem *'L'Homme Moyen Sensuel'* makes clear, Arnold's and Wilde's views persisted in the early twentieth century.[46] In Woolsey's hands, however, *l'homme moyen sensuel* undergoes a remarkable transformation. An obvious reason for this is that, by virtue of the fact that Woolsey presides as both judge and jury, *l'homme moyen sensuel* in the *Ulysses* case is Woolsey himself. If the judge's sex instincts were average, little else about him was. According to Ernst, he was 'one of those rare jurists who was a rounded, physically as well as spiritually, human being who, unlike many members of the bench and bar, read widely in fields remote from his professional interests.'[47] More to the point, he had read the critical satellites of *Ulysses*, a feat to which few men of letters – let alone *les hommes moyen sensuels* – could lay claim. We touch here on the third of Woolsey's well-intentioned lies, one pertaining to the character of *l'homme moyen sensuel*. Since Woolsey's assessment of that character is most apparent in his response to *Ulysses* as a whole, we will turn to Woolsey's interpretation of his fourth principle now, returning to *l'homme moyen sensuel* later.

Woolsey's fourth and final major principle is that the effect of the libelled work must be construed as the dominant effect of the work in its entirety. In order to make the 'objective standard' against which the dominant effect of the whole of *Ulysses* would be measured even more objective, Woolsey consulted two unidentified friends: 'These literary assessors – as I might properly describe them – were called on separately, and neither knew that I was consulting the other. They are men whose opinion on literature and on life I value most highly. They had both read "Ulysses," and, of course, were wholly unconnected with this cause.'[48] The literary assessors, whom we now know were Henry Seidel Canby and Charles E. Merrill, Jr,[49] agreed with his opinion that 'reading "Ulysses" in its entirety, as a book must be read on such a test as this, did not tend to excite sexual impulses or lustful thoughts.'[50] Considered as the basis for judging that *Ulysses*, taken as a whole, was not legally obscene, Woolsey's opinion here is sound. If he had gone no further, his decision would have contained one less well-intentioned lie.

Instead of stopping with the idea that *Ulysses* as a whole is not obscene, however, Woolsey proceeds to assert that the novel is *nowhere* obscene:

> I am quite aware that owing to some of its scenes 'Ulysses' is a rather strong draught to ask some sensitive, though normal, persons to take. But my considered opinion, after long reflection, is that, whilst in many places the effect of 'Ulysses' on the reader undoubtedly is somewhat emetic, nowhere does it tend to be an aphrodisiac.[51]

Woolsey repeats this understanding of the relation between the whole and the parts of *Ulysses* on several occasions in the course of his decision. Thus, after declaring his conviction that *Ulysses* is not pornographic, he declares, 'I do not detect anywhere the leer of the sensualist.'[52] Likewise, although he acknowledges that *Ulysses* is sometimes disgusting, Woolsey insists, 'I have not found anything that I consider to be dirt for dirt's sake.'[53]

In making such statements, Woolsey formulates his fourth well-intentioned lie regarding *Ulysses*, for parts of the novel *are* obscene according to Woolsey's definition. Joyce himself acknowledged as much. Thus, he informed Frank Budgen that the 'Penelope' episode was 'probably more obscene than any preceding episode.'[54] And, according to Sylvia Beach, he considered parts of his novel erotic:

> Many fine writers have produced erotica, and a few of them, Baudelaire and Verlaine, for instance, have even succeeded in making the subject interesting. ... Joyce, needless to say, had no such purpose in writing *Ulysses*. He was no specialist, but a general practitioner – all the parts of the body came into *Ulysses*. As he himself said plaintively, 'There is less than 10 percent of *that* in my book.'[55]

Joyce's appraisal of the amount of eroticism and/or obscenity in *Ulysses* may or may not be accurate, but it seems safe to assume that less than 10 per cent is more than nothing. Thus, Joyce himself authorizes the view that parts of *Ulysses* do in fact 'exploit obscenity,' that parts of *Ulysses* do in fact reveal the 'leer of the sensualist.'

As to whether or not such parts constitute 'dirt for dirt's sake,' the question depends upon one's view of authorial intention in literature. If one follows Woolsey in asserting that Joyce's primary intention – that is, to make a work of literature which by definition has nothing in common with pornography – was his only intention, it follows that every part of *Ulysses* was exclusively intended to further that end; it also follows, of course, that no part of the novel contains dirt for dirt's sake. If on the other hand, one adopts the view that a writer's primary intention may go hand in hand with other intentions, it follows that parts of *Ulysses* may exist to further both the ends of the work as a whole and other less obviously esthetic ends, such as the celebration of dirt for dirt's sake. The problem with the former view where Joyce's novel is concerned is that it suppresses the very qualities of *Ulysses* that provoked the controversy surrounding the novel's publication and denies that Joyce, by incorporating elements of pornography into his art, was determined to undermine the very moral and literary standards which the Woolsey decision implicitly upholds.

In any case, it most certainly is untrue that *Ulysses* is *nowhere* aphrodisiac (and therefore nowhere obscene in the eyes of the law of 1933) because its dominant effect is not aphrodisiac. As Leslie Fiedler, Richard Brown, Margot Norris, Jules David Law, and others have noted,[56] Joyce's novel contains many erotic or pornographic passages, the most obvious and celebrated of which are perhaps those describing Bloom's encounter with Gerty MacDowell.[57] Others include Bloom's ogling of the woman in

Dlugacz's, his conversation with Molly in 'Calypso' (in which soiled undergarments, chamber pots, and the works of Paul de Kock all figure prominently), and his delectation of the silk stockings of the proud, rich woman he sees in front of the Grosvenor hotel, to mention just a few in the first part of the book.[58] The passages from 'Ithaca' and 'Circe' quoted earlier in this chapter could also be mentioned in this context, as could many of the passages that figure in the Appendix. In many of these, the reader of *Ulysses* – along with Molly, and Bloom, and Joyce himself – sees through eyes that share the pornographical tendency of books like *Sweets of Sin*. After the 1933 trial, when he was free to be more candid than he had been during the trial, Morris Ernst himself acknowledged that parts of *Ulysses* were aphrodisiac: 'No great work of fiction has survived unless it has provided some sexual stimulation.'[59] Leslie Fiedler puts it more emphatically: 'To read *Ulysses* … without being titillated represents as inadequate a response as reading it without laughing or weeping.'[60]

We are now in a position to appreciate the third well-intentioned lie of Woolsey's decision, namely, that *l'homme moyen sensuel* as Woolsey has defined him is really the man in the street. As previously mentioned, Woolsey's *homme moyen sensuel* is really a projection of Woolsey himself, a man distinguished from the man in the street by, among other qualities, a high degree of literary sophistication. It is precisely that sophistication, not any deficiency in sex instincts, which ensures that Woolsey's *homme moyen sensuel* is never sexually aroused by *Ulysses*. Thanks to Stuart Gilbert (who is himself indebted to Stephen Dedalus), he knows that 'Aesthetic emotion is *static*.'[61] Knowing that, and knowing also that Joyce's novel is a brilliant work of art, Woolsey's *homme moyen sensuel* is not to be sexually aroused by anything in *Ulysses*. By the same token, however, he is not to be mistaken for the man in the street, whose reaction to literature tends to be more kinetic. Ironically, a far more truthful representation of *l'homme moyen sensuel* is to be found in *Ulysses* in the person of Leopold Bloom, whose response to the eroticism of *Sweets of Sin* is, as S.L. Goldberg has observed, 'completely kinetic':[62]

'Warmth showered gently over him, cowing his flesh. Flesh yielded amid rumpled clothes. Whites of eyes swooning up. His nostrils arched themselves for prey. Melting breast ointments (*for him! For Raoul!*). Armpits' oniony sweat. Fishgluey slime (*her heaving embonpoint!*). Feel! Press! Crushed! Sulphur dung of lions!'[63]

As indicated above, Woolsey's literary sophistication (and therefore his reading of *Ulysses*) was indebted to the critical satellites he had read in preparation for the hearing, particularly to Stuart Gilbert's *James Joyce's 'Ulysses.'* Ernst, of course, hoped that Gilbert's book would influence Woolsey. Thus, as previously mentioned, he not only offered to send the judge a copy of the book, but he also used his brief to draw the judge's attention to 'Stuart Gilbert's scholarly analysis of "indecency" in *Ulysses: James Joyce's "Ulysses,"* pp. 19–22.'[64] This section of Gilbert's book, which is explicitly designed to defend *Ulysses* against the charge of obscenity, contains the passage on esthetic stasis quoted above. There can be no doubt that Woolsey read this section of Gilbert's book, and read it carefully, for it contains other critical observations which find expression in Woolsey's decision.

For example, Gilbert writes of *Ulysses*, 'there is nothing "indecent" in it, if the framers of the Irish Censorship Bill correctly construed indecency as "anything calculated to excite sexual passion." These passages are, in fact, cathartic and calculated rather to allay rather than to excite the sexual instincts.'[65] Woolsey seems to echo this view when he writes, 'whilst in many places the effect of "Ulysses" on the reader undoubtedly is somewhat emetic, nowhere does it tend to be an aphrodisiac.' Woolsey makes his debt to Gilbert even more explicit when he writes, 'I do not detect *anywhere* the leer of the sensualist': in discussing Swift's influence on *Ulysses*, Gilbert cites one of Swift's biographers to the effect that '"The sensualist's leer is foreign to [Swift's] work."'[66]

Woolsey's use of Gilbert's book confirms that his reading of the critical satellites of *Ulysses* exerted a decisive influence on his well-intentioned lies about the novel. More specifically, it suggests that Woolsey may well have derived the esthetic theory which finds expression in these lies, albeit indirectly, from James Joyce himself, who put the theory into Stephen Dedalus's mouth in *Portrait*. I have argued in Chapter 3 that, given the close connection between Joyce's life and art, Stephen's theory of esthetic stasis should be understood not only as Stephen's attempt to defend his autonomy as an artist but also as Joyce's attempt to do the same. In Woolsey's decision that attempt bore fruit.

A number of contemporary commentators on the Woolsey decision were aware that, in addition to being an important legal decision, it was a literary criticism of *Ulysses*. One writer observed that Woolsey's decision contained 'canons of intelligent literary criticism.'[67] Another wrote that the decision 'read like an exceptionally intelligent and enthusiastic book review.'[68] Yet another characterized Woolsey as 'the most eminently-placed of book critics; a reviewer whose word quite literally is law.'[69] Some legal scholars were of the same opinion: a contributor to the *George Washington Law Review* wrote, 'Aside from the legal value of the opinion, it is recommended as an excellent book review.'[70]

Virtually all of these commentators, however, failed to recognize that Woolsey's criticism of *Ulysses* contained a number of well-intentioned lies. One notable exception was a writer in *The Nation* who praised Woolsey's decision, adding the wish that it had included an admission that

> Only a legal fiction makes it necessary to pretend that the real question at issue is whether or not *Ulysses* is likely to 'stir the sex impulses.' At least half the recognized diversions of civilized mankind are intended to do that to a greater or less extent, and society recognizes the process as not only permissible but necessary to its welfare.[71]

Such intelligent criticism of Woolsey's decision was rare, for two good reasons. First, the well-deserved stature of *Ulysses* as a major work of art made it clear that Woolsey was right in his crucial finding of fact, namely, that the novel was not legally obscene and could therefore be admitted to the United States. Second, by the time Woolsey handed down his decision, the fascist attack on literary freedom in Germany had become a factor in US censorship cases. As Paul Boyer has observed,

> the *Ulysses* decision ... was widely seen as America's answer to Hitler's repressions. Judge Woolsey and Morris Ernst made the point explicit a few days after the clearing of *Ulysses* when they made a joint speaking appearance at the inauguration of a Manhattan exhibit of the titles destroyed in the German book burnings.[72]

In light of these facts, searching criticism of the well-intentioned lies in Woolsey's decision was hardly to be expected.

Even less to be expected was an understanding of the significance of the Woolsey decision in legal history. As previously mentioned, that significance resides in the fact that the Woolsey decision marks the first major legal victory of the esthetic theory that informs Woolsey's well-intentioned lies, the first time that the esthetic theory of art supplants the traditional moral–esthetic theory of art (which prevailed in the 1857 trial of Flaubert and the early trials of *Ulysses*) as the law of a Western liberal democracy.

The majority of legal thinkers, poets, novelists, critics, publishers, and other commentators who wrote on the Woolsey decision in 1933–4 did not appreciate its real significance. They tended to believe, however, that the decision would prove to be important. Ernst, for example, wrote that it promised to become 'a major event in the history of the struggle for free expression,' adding that it would be difficult to overestimate its importance.[73] As if to prove his own point, he asserted that Woolsey's 'repeal of the sex taboo in letters' might prove to be more important than the repeal of prohibition. Manley O. Hudson, a distinguished professor of International Law at Harvard, praised the decision and said that Woolsey had 'produced a vista which ought to last.'[74] Lewis Gannett, literary editor and critic, wrote that Woolsey's 'great decision' was 'sure to prove a monument.'[75] Heywood Broun, columnist and critic, questioned whether the Woolsey decision was as important as Ernst had suggested, but agreed that it marked 'a new high in judicial liberalism.'[76] Bennett Cerf of Random House believed that Woolsey's 'monumental decision' would make the judge 'famous for all time.'[77] With few exceptions, those who commented on the Woolsey decision praised it as a work of enlightened jurisprudence that would have significant and lasting consequences.

Joyce himself was pleased with Woolsey's decision, although his reasons for being so, aside from the obvious fact that the decision meant a substantial increase in royalty income, are not easily discernible. Joyce's initial response, announced by Paul Léon, was enticingly cryptic: 'Mr. Joyce finds the judge to be not devoid of a sense of humour.'[78] Whatever Joyce may have had in mind in making this utterance, it seems safe to assume that he was less concerned with the quality of Woolsey's criticism of *Ulysses* than with the significance of his decision in Joyce's long struggle to make obscenity safe for literature.[79] This concern is evident in a letter Joyce wrote on 20 December 1933: 'Thus one half of the English speaking world surrenders. The other half will follow.'[80]

The US Attorney's Office was also content with the decision. According to Alexander Lindey, Nicholas Atlas 'seemed delighted.' Sam Coleman, as previously noted, welcomed Woolsey's decision. US Attorney George Medalie does not seem to have made any public statements, but he must have agreed with his assistants, for he did not initiate an appeal from the Woolsey decision. If the matter had remained in Medalie's hands, the formal trials of *Ulysses* would have come to an end in 1933. But just as the reception of Joyce's novel had been influenced initially by the Great Red Scare, so it would be affected once again by political developments. While Judge Woolsey was deciding the fate of *Ulysses*, F.D. Roosevelt had been elected as President of the United States and it would not take him long to replace the Republicans in the US Attorney's office with Democrats of his own choosing. Probably seeing the writing on the wall, Medalie submitted his letter of resignation in November 1933; he was soon replaced by Martin Conboy.

As a former officer of the New York Society for the Suppression of Vice, Conboy could hardly be expected to look upon the Woolsey decision with equanimity.[81] On the contrary, he was likely to interpret that decision as thwarting the Vice Society's hitherto successful attempt to suppress a notorious work of obscenity; furthermore, he may well have regarded his timely appointment as US Attorney as providing him with an opportunity to vindicate the Society's view of *Ulysses*. In any case, Conboy wasted no time in seeking to reverse Judge Woolsey's decision. Early in February 1934, he informed US Attorney General Homer S. Cummings that he was considering an appeal, and within two weeks he had made up his mind: 'I recommend strongly,' he wrote to the US Attorney General, 'that an appeal be taken to the Circuit Court of Appeals.'[82] That appeal, however misguided its intention, had the virtue of bringing about the vindication of *Ulysses* on saner grounds than those of the Woolsey decision, and of thereby reaffirming the strengths of the moral–esthetic view of art as a viable middle way between a narrowly moral view of art on the one hand and a narrowly esthetic view on the other.

6

Late Encounters with the Enemy

In requesting permission to contest Woolsey's decision to admit *Ulysses* to the USA, Conboy acknowledged, 'there may be a legitimate difference of opinion as to the nature of the book within the meaning of the provisions of the Tariff Act'; none the less, he believed that the book was obscene and hoped that the Court of Appeals would find that Woolsey had erred in finding otherwise. Conboy probably also believed that his predecessors in the US Attorney's Office had failed to present a convincing case against *Ulysses*. He was aware, of course, that Medalie and his assistants had not submitted a formal memorandum outlining the government's objections to the novel. He may also have been aware that the government's position in 1933, at least as he understood it, was characterized by remarkably weak logic. According to Conboy, 'It was the Government's position was that ULYSSES is in no sense comparable to any book, of literary merit or no, heretofore passed on by the courts and that it must be treated as in a class by itself, and that as such it was obscene.'[1] Surely Conboy recognized that such an argument lends itself more readily to a defense of the novel than to an attack upon it: if you want to prove that a work is obscene, it is difficult to see how you further your case by arguing that the work in question is unlike any work hitherto deemed obscene by the courts.

In support of his contention that *Ulysses* should be deemed legally obscene, Conboy drew the Attorney General's attention to pages '12, 13, 14, 17, 21, 349, 350, 331–335, 357, 367, 382, 383, 385, 386, 408, 684, and from 690 on.'[2] He thus made it clear that the grounds for the government's case against *Ulysses* had shifted: Coleman had not objected to anything on pages 12, 13, 14, 17, or 21; nor had he objected to every page of 'Penelope.' Examination of the first five pages cited by Conboy indicates that he was more perturbed than Coleman had been by the blasphemous passages in the novel. The pages in question contain no flagrant obscenities, but they do include a liberal smattering Buck Mulligan's mockery of religion. At one point, for example, Mulligan responds to the milkwoman's 'Glory be to God' by explaining to Haines, 'The islanders ... speak frequently of the collector of prepuces.'[3] Conboy's disapproval of such passages supports Ernst's contention that the government's objections to *Ulysses* were to its blasphemy as well as its obscenity;[4] at the same time it indicates that Conboy's Catholicism was not without bearing on his case against the novel.

On 6 March 1934, Assistant US Attorney General Joseph B. Keenan gave Conboy permission to proceed with the appeal. Keenan laid out the grounds for his decision in detail. He concedes that *Ulysses* is 'difficult to understand' and 'hard to read'; however, whereas in the Woolsey decision this fact tends to negate the charge of obscenity (as Ernst had argued it should), in Keenan's opinion it proves that the novel 'depends for its success, if it may be deemed to be successful, upon the filthy, obscene, and coarse matter contained within its pages, which appears to make it popular with certain elements of the American public.'[5] In the same vein, Keenan concedes Woolsey's point that *Ulysses* is a frank and truthful portrayal of the actions and thoughts of certain Dubliners, but whereas in Woolsey's decision this fact negates the charge of obscenity, for Keenan it does not. According to him, 'without doubt, some of the language used and the thoughts portrayed are filthy, "obscene" and "immoral" if taken by themselves. (See, among others, pages 685–689, 704, 705, 711, 725).'[6]

Having acknowledged that parts of *Ulysses* are obscene within the meaning of the statute, Keenan demonstrates a shrewd understanding of the grounds on which Woolsey had based his decision:

It is thought that Judge Woolsey, in holding that this book is not 'obscene' and 'immoral' within the meaning of the statute has looked upon it from an artistic and literary sense, and from his own point of view, which would be far from that of a man of ordinary intelligence and of an ordinary appreciation of literature and art. Should not the book be looked upon, not from the standpoint of one of unusual attainments in the field of learning, but from the standpoint of what is commonly known as the man on the street?[7]

These observations indicate that Keenan was aware not only of the extent to which Woolsey's decision is based on literary rather than moral criteria but also of the fact that Woolsey's *l'homme moyen sensuel* was emphatically not the man in the street.

For Keenan, the crux of the matter hinges ultimately on the proper definition of obscenity. Here again, the Assistant US Attorney General rejects a crucial aspect of Woolsey's decision. Instead of agreeing with the definition of 'obscene' which Woolsey adopted in the *Ulysses* case ('tending to stir the sex impulses or to lead to sexually impure thoughts'), Keenan (like Coleman) adopts the broader definition which, he notes, Woolsey himself had laid down in *U.S.* v. *Contraception* (51 F. (2d) 821). In that case, Woolsey had adopted the Oxford English Dictionary's definition of 'obscene' and 'immoral':

> Obscene – 1. Offensive to the senses, or to taste or refinement; disgusting, repulsive, filthy foul, abominable, loathsome. Now somewhat archaic. 2. Offensive to modesty or decency; expressing or suggesting unchaste or lustful ideas; impure; indecent, lewd.
>   Immoral – The opposite of moral; not moral. 1. Not consistent with, or not conforming to moral law or requirement; opposed to or violating morality; morally evil or impure; unprincipled, invidious, dissolute. (Of persons, things, actions, etc.) 2. Not having a moral nature or character; non-moral.

In Keenan's opinion, 'If the language used in "Ulysses" is to be judged by these definitions, there is no argument needed to convince one that the book is "obscene" and "immoral" *unless it is lifted out of such class by its artistic attainments*' (emphasis mine).[8]

In other words, if Keenan had believed that *Ulysses* was a 'modern classic,' he might have recommended against appeal. He was not, however, willing to regard *Ulysses* as an outstanding work of literature: 'The book is not one which would appeal to the man of ordinary intelligence because of its attainments in the field of literature.'[9] Thus, Keenan argued that *Ulysses* had not obtained a 'position in the field of literature' capable of lifting it out of the class of the legally obscene.[10] Keenan's ignorance of the stature of *Ulysses* in the world of letters suggests that he was unfamiliar with Ernst's and Lindey's written arguments. At the same time, it proves beyond a doubt that the critical opinion gathered together in those documents was of crucial importance in defending *Ulysses* against the charge of obscenity.

In summary, the decision of the Attorney General's Office to authorize Conboy's appeal from the Woolsey decision was based on Keenan's rejection of its definition of obscenity as well as several of its key features, including:

1.   the need to read the critical satellites of *Ulysses* which, among other things, established beyond any reasonable doubt the reputation of *Ulysses* as an outstanding work of literature;
2.   the relevance of the author's intention (whether this be construed as 'artistic creation' or 'scientific truth'), at least in so far as this is taken to negate the possibility of obscenity;
3.   the importance of judging the work of art as a whole rather than on the basis of its parts, at least in so far this is taken to preclude the

possibility that the obscenity of the parts may justify condemning the work as a whole; and

4. the importance of judging the effect of *Ulysses* on *l'homme moyen sensuel*, at least as Woolsey had defined him.

Soon after his request for appeal was approved by the Attorney General (7 March 1934), Conboy filed his 'Brief for the Claimant-Libellant,' wherein he rejected every principle of the Woolsey decision. To begin with, Conboy claims that the proper test of obscenity is the Hicklin rule, namely, 'whether the tendency of the matter is to deprave and corrupt the morals of those whose minds are open to such influence and into whose hands a publication of this sort may fall.'[11] According to Conboy, 'It does not require lengthy argument to establish that *Ulysses* is obscene under this test. It is sufficient to read pages 173, 213, 214, 231–233, 318, 359–364, 398–399, 423–424, 434, 443, 458, 467–468, 489–491, 500, 508, 522–525, 527, 552–553, 555–556, 718–720, 724–727, 731, 738–739, 744–755, 754–755, 761–762, 765.'[12] By insisting on the Hicklin rule as the proper test for obscenity, Conboy rejects not only Woolsey's definition of 'obscene' but, more importantly, his fourth principle, namely, that the person on whom the effect of a given work should be tested is *l'homme moyen sensuel*. Unlike Woolsey, Conboy believes that the proper test should be the young person into whose hands *Ulysses* might fall.

Having rejected Woolsey's fourth principle, Conboy proceeds to do the same to his first – regarding the relevance of critical opinion – and his second – regarding the relevance of authorial intention: 'No argument may be based upon the purpose of the author, his literary importance or unimportance or psychological truthfulness or falsity. ... A book that is obscene is not rendered less so by reason of the fact that the matter complained of is in fact truthful.'[13] Likewise, Conboy rejects Woolsey's third principle – that the work should be judged as a whole – at least in so far as Woolsey interprets this to preclude the possibility that the obscenity of the parts could condemn the whole. In Conboy's opinion, a sufficient number of obscene passages could and in fact did render *Ulysses* obscene as a whole:

The fact that some portions of the book are unobjectionable under the statute is immaterial. It is not necessary that every incident and every experience described in it shall be obscene to justify a conviction of obscenity. Taking the test of obscenity which has been established in the Federal Courts and applying it to the numerous passages of grossly obscene matter with which this book fairly reeks, there can be no doubt that the District Court erred in its determination that *Ulysses* is not obscene.[14]

Shortly after Conboy had filed his brief on behalf of the government, Ernst submitted his 'Brief for Claimant-Appellee,' which was essentially the same as the memorandum he had submitted to Woolsey, except that it incorporated the material which had been appended to Lindey's petition (and submitted to Woolsey independently). The three judges who would hear the appeal would therefore have before them all the information that Woolsey had, with two notable exceptions. First, the copy of *Ulysses* with which they would be supplied would not be the imported, criticism-laden copy which had been given to Woolsey; instead, they would read Joyce's text in the 1934 Random House edition. Second, Ernst and Lindey would not take the liberty, as they had done with Woolsey, of ensuring that the judges had copies of the books by Herbert Gorman, Paul Jordan Smith, and Stuart Gilbert: this time *Ulysses* would not enjoy the same degree of protection from its critical satellites as it had when Woolsey sat on the bench.

The appeal would be heard beginning 16 May by Judges Martin T. Manton (presiding), Learned Hand, and Augustus N. Hand. Of these three judges the one most likely to rule against Conboy was Learned Hand. In *United States* v. *Kennerley* (1913) (a case involving the novel *Hagar Revelly*), he had respected the authority of the jury to determine whether a novel could be banned from the mails, but in doing so he had forcefully articulated both his dissatisfaction with the Hicklin rule and his commitment to freedom of expression. Augustus N. Hand's inclination is more difficult to ascertain. In 1917, he had upheld the Post Office's decision to exclude the 'Cantleman's Spring Mate' number of *The Little Review* from the mails. By contrast, in 1930 he had written the unanimous Appellate Court decision which overturned an obscenity decision against Mary W. Dennett's *The Sex Side of Life*, a sex education pamphlet for children. That decision did not explicitly reject the *Hicklin* rule but was 'generous' enough to lend itself in support of that rejection.[15] Martin Manton was certainly more inclined than either of the Hands to sympathize with Conboy's objections to *Ulysses*; as a conservative Roman Catholic, he undoubtedly shared many of them.

According to newspaper accounts of the trial, Conboy began the proceedings by reading various definitions of *obscene* from standard dictionaries, observing that these reference works were in substantial agreement that the word meant 'offensive to modesty, chastity, delicacy, purity and decency.'[16] He then attempted to show that Random House had admitted *Ulysses* was all of these things by publishing *Ulysses* with a dust jacket featuring James Douglas's violent denunciation of the novel, as published in the *Sunday Express*. Significantly, the excerpt in question was the same one that Joyce had included in his *Excerpts of Press Notices* –

and that Ernst and Lindey chose not to include in their defense. Douglas wrote,

> I say deliberately that it is the most infamously obscene book in ancient or modern literature. The obscenity of Rabelais is innocent compared with its leprous and scabrous horrors. All the secret sewers of vice are canalized in its flood of unimaginable thoughts, images and pornographic words. And its unclean lunacies are larded with appalling and revolting blasphemies directed against the Christian religion and against the name of Christ.[17]

Ernst's and Lindey's exclusion of this excerpt from their defense of *Ulysses*, combined with Random House's decision to display it prominently (after the Woolsey decision had confirmed the success of Ernst's and Lindey's strategy), indicates that there is a world of difference between protecting a book from the attacks of the censor and selling that book to the public.

Having drawn the Court's attention to Random House's use of Douglas's review, Conboy summarized the action of *Ulysses*, commencing with the surprising assertion that it had 'nothing to do with that Ulysses who was the hero of the *Odyssey* but [was] rather "a setting forth of what purports to take place in one day in the life of a Hungarian Jew in Dublin, together with his thoughts and ruminations and those of his wife."'[18] Conboy apparently continued as follows:

> All vices and all licentious thoughts are set forth without restraint and without attempt to palliate or minimize their offensiveness. … Sexual practices, normal and abnormal, arc dealt with, as is the use of contraceptives. A large part of the book is taken up with minute descriptions of performances and conversations in a brothel, where the supposed hero spends a lot of time.[19]

Conboy's denial of the parallel with the *Odyssey* should perhaps be interpreted as his refusal to accept the 'supposed hero' of Joyce's novel as a genuine hero. Homer's Ulysses, after all, is courageous and dignified in speech, not to mention gentlemanly and modest in the presence of the princess Nausicaa – all things which Bloom is not.

After these introductory arguments, Conboy read out passages from *Ulysses* in order to prove that the book was in fact obscene. As he read, '[b]lushing, stammering, rocking nervously on his heels,' the judges sat solemnly on the bench, yellow pencils in hand, listening and reading along in their own copies of the novel.[20] After Conboy had read for about ten minutes, one of the two women attending the trial left the courtroom. Her departure inspired one reporter to poetry:

> Two little girlies
>   Went to court for fun;
> The lawyers read *Ulysses* –
>   Then there was one.[21]

The woman in question was not the only one to show signs of impatience. At one point, Learned Hand interrupted Conboy: '"Are you going to read the whole book?"' Conboy earnestly responded: '"I'll give you a generous sampling."'[22] (Another report of the proceedings indicates that Learned Hand asked Conboy if he believed the Court should read *Ulysses*, to which Conboy is said to have responded: '"No," ... "I will read a generous sampling from this product of the gutter. I do not believe it will be necessary for your honors to read the entire book."'[23]) Conboy was true to his word: he read until the Court adjourned for lunch; when it reconvened he read until another adjournment was announced; and when the Court reconvened the following day, Conboy read some more.[24]

One journalist reported that Conboy read a total of twenty-five passages.[25] Another observed that the passages read had 'particular reference to the stream-of-thought soliloquizing of Mrs. Molly Bloom.'[26] It seems safe to assume, then, that Conboy read virtually all of the passages mentioned in his brief, including the following excerpts from 'Penelope':

> ... he must have come 3 or 4 times with that tremendous big red brute of a thing he has I thought the vein or whatever the dickens they call it was going to burst though his nose is not so big after I took off all my things ...[27]

> ... I never in all my life felt anyone had one the size of that to make you feel full up he must have eaten a whole sheep after whats the idea making us like that with a big hole in the middle of us like a Stallion driving it up into you because thats all they want out of you with that determined vicious look in his eye I had to halfshut my eyes still he hasn't such a tremendous amount of spunk in him when I made him pull it out and do it on me considering how big it is ...[28]

> ... hes heavy too with his hairy chest for this heat always having to lie down for them better for him put it into me from behind the way Mrs Mastiansky told me her husband made her like the dogs do it and stick out her tongue as far as ever she could ...[29]

… I wished he was here or somebody to let myself go with and come again like that I feel all fire inside me or if I could dream it when he made me spend the 2nd time tickling me behind with his finger I was coming for about 5 minutes with my legs round him I had to hug him after O Lord I wanted to shout out all sorts of things fuck or shit or anything at all …[30]

… I tried with the Banana but I was afraid it might break and get lost up in me somewhere yes because they once took something down out of a woman that was up there for years covered with limesalts theyre all mad to get in there where they come out of youd think they could never get far enough up and then theyre done with you in a way till the next time yes because theres a wonderful feeling there all the time so tender how did we finish if off yes O yes I pulled him off into my handkerchief pretending not to be excited but I opened my legs I wouldnt let him touch me inside my petticoat I had a skirt opening up the side I tortured the life out of him first tickling him I loved rousing that dog in the hotel rrrsssst awokwokawok his eyes shut and a bird flying below us he was shy all the same I liked him like that morning I made him blush a little when I got over him that way when I unbuttoned him and took his out and drew back the skin it had a kind of eye in it theyre all Buttons men down the middle on the wrong side of them Molly darling he called me what was his name Jack Joe Harry Mulvey was it yes …[31]

… yes Ill sing Winds that blow from the south that he gave after the choirstairs performance Ill change that lace on my black dress to show off my bubs and Ill yes by God Ill get that big fan mended make them burst with envy my hole is itching me always when I think of him I feel I want to …[32]

… Ill put on my best shift and drawers let him have a good eyeful out of that to make his micky stand for him Ill let him know if thats what he wanted that his wife is fucked yes and damn well fucked too up to my neck nearly not by him 5 or 6 times handrunning theres the mark of his spunk on the clean sheet I wouldnt bother to even iron it out that ought to satisfy him if you dont believe me feel my belly unless I made him stand there and put him into me Ive a mind to tell him every scrap and make him do it in front of me serve him right its all his own fault if I am an adulteress …[33]

… thats what a woman is supposed to be there for or He wouldnt have made us the way He did so attractive to men then if he wants to kiss my bottom Ill drag open my drawers and bulge it right out in his face as large as life he can stick his tongue 7 miles up my hole as hes there my brown part then Ill tell him I want £1 or perhaps 30/– Ill tell him I want to buy underclothes then if he gives me that well he wont be too bad I dont want to soak it all out of him like other women do I could often have written out a fine cheque for myself and write his name on it for a couple of pounds a few times he forgot to lock it up besides he wont spend it Ill let him do it off on me behind provided he doesnt smear all my good drawers O I suppose that cant be helped Ill do the indifferent 1 or 2 questions Ill know by the answers when hes like that he cant keep a thing back I know every turn in him Ill tighten my bottom well and let out a few smutty words smellrump or lick my shit or the first mad thing comes into my head then Ill suggest about yes O wait now sonny my turn is coming Ill be quite gay and friendly over it ...[34]

When his reading marathon was ended, Conboy wrapped up his case against *Ulysses* in a manner which makes it clear that his objections to the novel envisaged its blasphemy as well as its obscenity: '"This is an obscene book. ... It begins with blasphemy, runs the whole gamut of sexual perversion, and ends in unspeakable filth and obscenity."'[35]

It was now Ernst's turn to speak. He praised *Ulysses* as "'a great work of fiction'" and Joyce as a "'majestic genius.'"[36] He dismissed Conboy's use of James Douglas's attack on *Ulysses*, arguing that while the government had been able to produce only one critic who was shocked by the book, fifty or more famous critics had commended it. He reminded the Court that *Ulysses* was taught in English courses at Harvard and sought by many libraries in the United States. He objected to Conboy's use of excerpts of *Ulysses* and insisted that the entire book must be taken into account. He also discussed the changing standards of the day, and mentioned that the novel had been published openly, bearing the name of the author. Finally, he insisted that authorial intention was relevant and that *Ulysses* was written to present a study of the human mind.

Ernst's oral arguments before the Court of Appeals differed from those he presented to Woolsey in two respects. First, he seemed more willing to use conventional moral arguments in defense of *Ulysses*. For example, he suggested that because parts of *Ulysses* make the reader blush, they act to repel rather than to corrupt. For another, Ernst agreed with Learned Hand's suggestion that writings like *Ulysses* could be disgusting rather than lustful (another version of Woolsey's contrast between emetic and aphrodisiac). Second, Ernst seemed more willing to acknowledge that parts of *Ulysses* were aphrodisiac. For example, he made the remarkable declaration that 'No great work of fiction that has survived is without sexual stimulation.'[37] In speaking of *Ulysses* in this way, Ernst himself calls into question one of the well-intentioned lies of the Woolsey decision, one which Ernst's own arguments had undoubtedly encouraged.

After Ernst completed his arguments, the judges announced that they would take their time in formulating their decision. Before conferring about the nature of that judgement, each judge wrote a memorandum in which he voted either to affirm or reverse Woolsey's decision. These pre-conference memoranda, as Gerald Gunther has observed, 'reveal three distinctive minds at work, with the Hands on one side and Manton clearly on the other.'[38]

Learned Hand voted to affirm. He believed that Woolsey was right in finding that *Ulysses* was not legally obscene. He did not, however, accept Woolsey's contention that *Ulysses* was 'nowhere aphrodisiac.' To the contrary, he believed that parts of the novel 'could incite lustful feelings not only in the mind of a youthful person, but of a normal adult.'[39] According to Hand, such passages must be judged on the basis of their relevance to the whole of the work of which they are a part:

> If a man writes a book which is all libidinous, he has and should have no immunity. But there are themes whose truthful and complete expression involves what taken alone ought to have no immunity; the whole portrayal does not excite libidinous feelings. The conflicting interests are the freedom of authors to express themselves fully and as they wish as against the debauching of their readers' minds. I do not say that a theme, harmless in itself, may not be so treated as to condemn it; it would be dangerous to lay down as an absolute principle that anything relevant to the development of a story or a theme innocent as a whole, must escape, may not condemn the whole. But it is clear that without taking the work as a whole we cannot decide. ... Personally, I would be disposed to make relevance the test almost always.[40]

Applying this test to *Ulysses*, Learned Hand concludes that Woolsey's finding should be upheld, since 'the offending passages are clearly necessary to the epic of the soul as Joyce conceived it, and the parts which might be the occasion for lubricity in the reader are to my thinking not sufficient to condemn a very notable contribution to literature.'[41]

Like his cousin, Augustus Hand believed that parts of *Ulysses* were erotic:

> Perhaps the monologue of Mrs. Bloom in its immediate effect is erotic but on the whole it is pitiful and tragic and much of the book is so. The

comedy in it is mixed up with tragedy. I think it is less light than such passages as that where Rabelais describes the bridegroom who went to bed with a mallet. Such humor is simply coarse and not erotic at all, whereas some of *Ulysses* certainly is.[42]

And, again like his cousin, Augustus Hand acknowledged that the proper test of the obscenity of *Ulysses* could only be the novel as a whole: 'Much standard literature will be excluded if we do not hold that a book is to be judged as a whole in respect to general effect and objective purpose.' Augustus Hand did not, however, accept Learned Hand's emphasis on relevance as a test for obscenity ('I do not think it possible to generalize or to adopt the test of mere relevancy of obscene passages to the author's design'); instead, he affirmed the importance of judging the work's effect: 'So far as I can find any test it is of the effect of the book as a whole.'

In considering the question of where the government should draw the line between works containing acceptable amounts of obscenity and those exceeding those amounts, Augustus Hand wrote: 'I would have no hesitation in drawing the line right here if the obscene passages were strung together as they were in the abstract condemned by the Court of Special Sessions.'[43] This is a remarkable contention indeed, not only because it reveals the judge's familiarity with the 1920–1 prosecution of the editors of *The Little Review*, but because it indicates that he would have suppressed once again the section of 'Nausicaa' which had appeared in the July–August 1920 *Little Review* if it were to be published without the protection of the novel as a whole. The trials of *Ulysses* offer no clearer vindication of Pound's contention that the best defense of the parts of *Ulysses* was the whole of *Ulysses*. For in the context of the novel as a whole, it could not be said that the offending passages were 'strung together' as they were in the portion of 'Nausicaa' condemned by the Court of Special Sessions. Thus, Augustus Hand did not deem his differences with Woolsey sufficient to call into question his finding of fact: 'I am not prepared to say that Woolsey's finding of fact ... is without substantial basis.'[44] In other words, Augustus Hand, like Learned Hand, disagreed with Woolsey's contention that *Ulysses* is 'nowhere aphrodisiac,' while agreeing with Woolsey's finding that the novel taken as a whole is not aphrodisiac.

Judge Manton disagreed; he voted to reverse Woolsey's decision. His memorandum makes it clear that, like Conboy, he objected to all of Woolsey's major principles, not to mention Woolsey's finding of fact. More importantly, Manton's memorandum reveals that he took offense at Woolsey's hint that Joyce's treatment of sex was typically Irish. This is surely the implication to be drawn from Manton's closing statement: 'It is not necessary to say, as [Judge Woolsey] did, that "it must be remembered that his (Joyce) [sic] locale was Celtic and his season Spring." I vote to reverse.'[45] Manton's objection to Woolsey's reference to Celtic culture appears similar to G.K. Chesterton's objection to Cecil Maitland's claim that Joyce's allegedly unhealthy sexuality was the result of the influence of the Roman Catholic Church.[46] The idea that Joyce's preoccupation with sex was to be explained in terms of his Celtic (and therefore Catholic) locale, especially coming from a Protestant judge, could easily have contributed to Manton's objections to Woolsey's decision.[47]

When the Court of Appeals announced its decision on 7 August 1934, it confirmed that the three judges had maintained their pre-conference positions: Learned and Augustus Hand voted to affirm the Woolsey decision; Manton, dissenting, voted to reverse. The majority opinion upholds Woolsey's finding of fact and affirms his critical principles. It does not, however, subscribe to either the well-intentioned lies that Woolsey told in applying these principles to *Ulysses* or the esthetic view of art which they expressed. The majority appellate opinion is therefore substantially superior to Woolsey's both as a legal opinion and a literary criticism. The author of the opinion was Augustus Hand, whose pre-conference opinions figure prominently, but as Gerald Gunther has claimed, the most influential thinking was Learned Hand's.[48]

Augustus Hand begins the majority opinion by accepting Woolsey's first principle – that the critical satellites of *Ulysses* should be taken into account: '*Ulysses* is rated as a book of considerable power by persons whose opinions are entitled to weight. Indeed it has become a sort of contemporary classic.'[49] He then proceeds to affirm Woolsey's second principle – that authorial intention should be take into account. According to Hand, Joyce's intention, like Milton's, was to deal with 'things unattempted yet in prose or rime.' It may well be, he continues, that Joyce chose to deal 'with things that very likely might better have remained "unattempted"'; none the less, 'his book shows originality and is a work of symmetry and excellent craftsmanship of a sort.'[50] In other words, Hand acknowledges that Joyce's intention was to create an original work of literature.

For Woolsey, as we have seen, these two principles effectively precluded the possibility that any part of *Ulysses* could be deemed obscene; for the majority appellate judges, however, they do no such thing. Thus, while the majority judges accept Woolsey's third principle – that the proper test of obscenity must take account of the work as a whole and not just the offending parts – they do not follow Woolsey in asserting that because *Ulysses* is not obscene or aphrodisiac as a whole it is *nowhere* obscene or aphrodisiac. To the contrary, as they did in their pre-conference memoranda, the majority judges admit that 'numerous long passages in *Ulysses* contain matter that is obscene under any fair definition of the word.'[51] For the majority judges, the question of whether the obscene parts of *Ulysses* condemn the work as a whole is to be answered in the context of the work as a whole.

In articulating exactly what it means to judge the work as a whole, the majority opinion combines Learned Hand's emphasis on the test of relevance with Augustus Hand's preference for the test of the dominant effect. Thus, the majority opinion finds that the obscene passages in *Ulysses* are

> relevant to the purpose of depicting the thoughts of the characters and are introduced to give meaning to the whole, rather than to promote lust or portray filth for its own sake. The net effect even of portions most open to attack, such as the closing monologue of the wife of Leopold Bloom, is pitiful and tragic, rather than lustful. ... The book as a whole is not pornographic, and while in not a few spots it is coarse, blasphemous and obscene, it does not, in our opinion, tend to promote lust. The erotic passages are submerged in the book as a whole and have little resultant effect.[52]

In rejecting the Hicklin rule as the proper test of obscenity, the majority opinion adopts Woolsey's fourth principle – that the effect of *Ulysses* is to be measured on *l'homme moyen sensuel* (the average man) – but without subscribing to Woolsey's characterization of him as a sophisticated reader who experiences only esthetic emotion when reading literary works and upon whom *Ulysses* can have no kinetic effect whatsoever. Thus, the majority opinion acknowledges that books like *Ulysses* may well produce adverse effects in some persons. Having said that, however, the majority judges insist, 'confiscation for such a reason would destroy much that is precious in order to benefit a few.'[53] If *Ulysses* were to be suppressed on the basis of these passages, the majority judges go on to say, Shakespeare's *Venus and Adonis*, *Hamlet*, and *Romeo and Juliet*, and perhaps even Homer's *Odyssey* would have to be suppressed as well.[54] The fact that the law has not suppressed them indicates that works of literature should not be banned merely because they contain *some* obscene passages.[55]

In concluding, the majority judges emphasize that their responsibility in cases of this kind is to weigh the benefits of a given artistic work against its adverse effects. Thus, they find that the benefits of 'a book of artistic merit and scientific insight' like *Ulysses* outweigh its shortcomings, or, to put it in more general terms, that the benefits of artistic freedom generally outweigh the harm that such freedom may cause:

Art certainly cannot advance under compulsion to traditional forms and nothing in such a field is more stifling to progress than limitation of the right to experiment with a new technique. ... We think that *Ulysses* is a book of originality and sincerity of treatment and that it has not the effect of promoting lust. Accordingly it does not fall within the statute, even though it may justly offend many.[56]

Manton undoubtedly agreed with his fellow judges that *Ulysses* 'may justly offend many,' but he dissented strongly from the majority opinion that the Woolsey decision should be affirmed in its crucial finding of fact – if not in every detail of its theoretical basis or its interpretation of Joyce's novel. In voting to reverse the Woolsey decision, Manton rejected every one of its major principles, just as he had done in his pre-conference memorandum.

If Woolsey's opinion represents the esthetic view of art, according to which a work of art can have no adverse effect whatsoever, Manton's represents a narrowly moral view that may be described as Platonic.[57] According to the former view, a work of art should never be suppressed; according to the latter, a work of art that adversely affects its readers, *should* be suppressed, regardless of its literary merit. In so far as Manton's opinion stands at the opposite extreme from Woolsey's it emphasizes the extent to which the opinion of the majority appellate judges represents a middle way between the two, a way which is saner than either.

In Manton's opinion, there could be no reasonable doubt about the obscenity of *Ulysses*: 'Who can doubt the obscenity of this book after a reading of the pages referred to, which are too indecent to add as a footnote to this opinion? Its characterization as obscene should be quite unanimous by all who read it.'[58] In making this assertion, the test of obscenity Manton has in mind is not that adopted by Woolsey and the appellate judges but rather the Hicklin rule: 'whether the tendency of the matter charged as obscenity is to deprave and corrupt those whose minds are open to such immoral influences, and into whose hands a publication of this sort may fall.'[59] Armed with the Hicklin rule, Manton dismisses the idea that critical opinion should be taken into account in judging a book like *Ulysses*: 'No matter what may be said on the side of letters, the effect on the community can and must be the sole determining factor.'[60]

Manton also dismisses Woolsey's contention that authorial intention should be taken into account. Thus, he cites approvingly a decision in which the court held that 'the object of the use of the obscene words was not a subject for consideration.' For Manton the test of obscenity is independent of the question of whether the author of a work intended to amuse or edify:

Ulysses is a work of fiction. It may not be compared with books involving medical subjects or description of certain physical or biological facts. It is written for alleged amusement of the reader only. The characters described in the thoughts of the author may in some instances be true, but, be it truthful or otherwise, a book that is obscene is not rendered less so by the statement of truthful fact.[61]

Manton's Platonic leanings are unmistakable. The poet or writer of fiction is concerned not with truth but with amusing an audience. Furthermore, the truth of a work is no justification for its existence: some truths, according to Plato, should never be spoken.

Having thus disposed of Woolsey's second principle, Manton rejects his third, namely, that the work of art should be judged as a whole. According to Manton, 'the decision to be made is dependent entirely upon the reading matter found on the objectionable pages of the book (pages 173, 213, 214, 359, 361, 423, 424, 434, 467, 488, 498, 500, 509, 522, 526, 528, 551, 719, 724–727, 731, 738, 739, 745, 746, 754–756, 761, 762, 765, Random House Edition).' Manton clarifies his contention that *Ulysses* is to be judged on the basis of these passages by asserting that previous federal court decisions do not oblige him to accept the principle that 'the book is to be judged as a whole': a book 'may be obscene because portions thereof are so.'[62] And since Manton has rejected the idea that the literary merit of *Ulysses* has any bearing on the case, he is unwilling to accept the whole of *Ulysses* as justification for its objectionable parts.

Manton's rejection of Woolsey's fourth principle – that the effect of the work is to be measured on *l'homme moyen sensuel* – is implicit in his adoption of the Hicklin test, but he makes the point explicit in stressing that the law against obscenity is designed to serve the interests of society as a whole, including the young:

> If we disregard the protection of the morals of the susceptible, are we to consider merely the benefits and pleasures derived from letters by those who pose as the more highly developed and intelligent? To do so would show an utter disregard for the standards of decency of the community as a whole and an utter disregard for the effect of the book upon the average, less sophisticated member of society – not to mention the adolescent. The court cannot indulge any instinct it may have to foster letters. The statute is designed to protect society at large – of that there can be no dispute – notwithstanding the deprivation of benefits to a few, a work must be condemned if it has a depraving influence.[63]

Manton's claim that '[t]he court cannot indulge in any instinct it may have to foster letters' reveals his opposition to Woolsey's willingness to undermine (or, in the case of the appellate judges, to qualify) the traditional subordination of art to morality. His opposition is essentially Platonic, as the conclusion of his opinion makes clear:

Congress passed this statute against obscenity for the protection of the great mass of our people. ... The people do not exist for the sake of literature; to give the author fame, the publisher wealth, and the book a market. On the contrary, literature exists for the sake of the people; to refresh the weary, to console the sad, to hearten the dull and downcast, to increase man's interest in the world, his joy of living and his sympathy in all sorts and conditions of men. Art for art's sake is heartless and soon grows artless; art for the public market is art not at all, but commerce; art for the people's service is a noble, vital and permanent element of human life.

...The people need and deserve a moral standard; it should be a point of honor with men of letters to maintain it. Masterpieces have never been produced by m[e]n given to obscenity or lustful thoughts – men who have no Master. Reverence for good work is the foundation of literary character. A refusal to imitate obscenity or to load a book with it, is an author's professional chastity.

Good work in literature has its permanent mark – it is like all good work, noble and lasting. It requires a human aim – to cheer, console, purify or ennoble the life of people. Without this aim, literature has never sent an arrow close to the mark. It is by good work only that men of letters can justify their right to a place in the world.[64]

A good deal can undoubtedly be said for Manton's view of the function of art and the responsibility of the artist, but little can be said in defense of the narrowness of his definition of 'good work.' For Manton, as for Plato, the poet's place in the republic is assured only if he morally edifies its citizens. In his opinion Joyce did not do so in *Ulysses*; *Ulysses*, therefore, should not be admitted to the United States. The appellate judges showed more wisdom in recognizing that the literary merit of Joyce's novel far outweighed any adverse effects its obscenity might have.

Martin Conboy was of a different mind. Soon after he learned of the Court of Appeals decision, he wrote to the Attorney General requesting that an application for a writ of *certiori* be made to the Supreme Court. In that letter, Conboy pointed out that Manton had dissented from the majority opinion, and that the appellate court had overruled the Hicklin test of obscenity in allowing the Woolsey decision to stand. Conboy's explanation of the way in which the appellate court had allegedly erred in upholding the Woolsey decision confirms that the honesty of the majority judges regarding the obscenity of parts of *Ulysses* was not without risk:

> it is submitted that the Court erred in holding that 'Ulysses' as a whole is not obscene, while conceding that many of its passages undoubtedly fall within the meaning of that term. Indeed, even if the Court is correct in its position that the book is to be judged as a whole, rather than by particular passages which it contains, it nevertheless seems clear that the objectionable passages in 'Ulysses' are so numerous and so lengthy that they permeate and color the whole book to such an extent that they render the entire book obscene.[65]

In light of these considerations, Conboy expressed his confidence that if a writ of *certiori* were granted by the Supreme Court the decisions of the lower courts would be reversed.

This time, however, Conboy's confidence would not be put to the test: the Attorney General, following the recommendation of Harry S. Ridgely, refused the US Attorney's request for further appeal. Ridgely supplied several grounds for this decision. First, at dispute in the *Ulysses* case was only 'a question of fact or of the weight of evidence,' and the Supreme Court had made it clear that it would not review such cases.[66] Second, the question of fact presented by the *Ulysses* case was not important enough to justify further appeal:

> Whether one agrees or disagrees with the conclusion of the two courts below, it seems clear that the question presented cannot be characterized as one of gravity or general importance. A decision holding the book here involved to be obscene would furnish no standard or test in future cases involving different publications.[67]

After quoting passages from the majority opinion which reveal its grounds for affirming Woolsey's decision, Ridgely states a third reason for denying Conboy's request.

In Ridgely's opinion, only twenty-one of the twenty-seven passages in *Ulysses* objected to by the US Attorney fall 'within the accepted test of obscenity.' Furthermore, 'Some of the passages are exceedingly brief, but in any event, they are taken from a book of 767 pages, and thus form an exceedingly small portion of the book.'[68] A fourth factor in Ridgely's recommendation against appeal is the persuasive nature of the claimant's brief: 'One reading the carefully prepared and exhaustive brief of the claimant is not surprised at the holding of the Circuit Court of Appeals.'[69] In addition to these substantive grounds for refusing Conboy's request for permission to apply for a writ of *certiori*, Ridgely cites two practical reasons for his recommendation. First, the Supreme Court would be unlikely to grant such a writ. Second, 'unless the Government is prepared to insist that the obscenity of a book or publication is to be determined by the obscenity of any particular passage of such a book or publication, ... we could not succeed in reversing the judgement below even though we could obtain the writ.'[70]

Martin Conboy responded to the Attorney General's decision by accepting defeat; he put an end to his campaign against *Ulysses*. John Sumner, however, remained unwilling to concede victory to his long-time enemy. Department of Justice records indicate, fittingly, that Sumner's was the last voice to encourage the US government to maintain its ban on Joyce's novel. Several months after the appellate court decision was announced, Sumner wrote to the Attorney General to object to rumours that there would be no further appeal:

> We are sorry if this is the case. ... Certainly if the decision of the Circuit Court of Appeals stands it is difficult to know what book may be successfully prosecuted under the Federal law for obscenity. The language in Ulysses and the incidents described occurring throughout the book, and particularly near the end thereof are such as in our opinion would bring about the condemnation of this book by any court not influenced by extraneous matters such as were introduced into this case.[71]

When the Attorney General's Office responded to this letter (which attests, by the way, to the crucial importance of literary opinion in both the Woolsey decision and the appellate decision which upheld it) by repeating its refusal to appeal to the Supreme Court, Sumner could not resist one last word: 'It seems to me that the good old American fighting spirit is lacking,' he wrote, 'when the Department fails to follow up a hard-won partial victory in a district where "broadmindedness" seems to be considered a judicial virtue.'[72] In 1921 Margaret Anderson had predicted that, given a couple of hours in which to argue, she could convince Sumner to switch sides in the war to make the world safe for art. Her hope was wildly optimistic. The Vice Society's Secretary fought against the forces of art to the bitter end.

Conclusion

When the US Attorney General refused to allow Conboy to take the appeal from the Woolsey decision to the Supreme Court, the formal trials of *Ulysses* came to an end, but the consequences of those trials have continued to make themselves felt up to the present day. The consequences are literary and legal, cultural and political, for the trials of *Ulysses* (or, more accurately, the defensive strategies which they engendered) have influenced not only the way we read Joyce's novel and other works of literature, but also our understanding of the proper basis for freedom of speech.

The literary consequences of the trials, as I have argued, are twofold. The first is the text of *Ulysses* itself, in so far as Joyce's elaboration of its schematic elements was motivated by a desire to protect his creation from the attacks of the censor. The second is the reception of *Ulysses*, in so far as this was affected by the efforts of critics like Pound, Larbaud, Gilbert and others to defend the novel against the charge of obscenity by diverting attention from its controversial content to its formal, schematic structure. We have already examined the reception of *Ulysses* from the time of its publication up to the 1932–3 trial; we turn now to the influence of the censorship on the critical reception of the novel since then.

That influence has been substantial, for several reasons. One is that many of the early critical works which were used to defend *Ulysses* against the charge of obscenity, especially Stuart Gilbert's *James Joyce's 'Ulysses'*, have continued to be widely read. Another is that some prominent later critics of *Ulysses*, notably Richard Ellmann, have adopted defensive strategies similar to those used by Gilbert and other early critics. Yet another is that the Woolsey decision was appended to both the British and US editions of *Ulysses*, where it remained until 1960 and 1986 respectively.[1]

The inclusion of the Woolsey decision in both editions was motivated by the very defensive strategies it embodied, since it was designed to protect Joyce's novel from further censorship (and censure). Provision for its inclusion in the first US edition was stipulated in the contract between Random House and Joyce, according to which the publisher reserved the right to include a foreword written by an author other than Joyce (a provision made by Bennett Cerf at the suggestion of Morris Ernst). In a letter to Robert N. Kastor, Joyce's American representative at the time, Cerf clarified the nature and intent of this clause:

> Referring to the sentence about the possible inclusion of a foreword by another author in our edition, let me point out that *this foreword will be*

in no sense a criticism of Ulysses. It may prove advisable, however, to put in a brief note by a prominent attorney embodying the decision of the judge who legalizes the book. The inclusion of this decision in our volume will protect us in any future court action that may arise in connection with the publication. If the decision is not included, it is possible that on any succeeding action the court would not allow us to introduce previous decisions as evidence (emphasis mine).[2]

As Cerf's assurance that the foreword would not be a criticism of *Ulysses* implies, Joyce objected to the inclusion of any such criticism in the Random House or any other edition of his novel, and he made his objection clear when Cerf sought his permission to incorporate the schema that Larbaud, Gilbert, and others had used in defending the novel against the charge of obscenity. Cerf believed that in publishing the schema Random House would be 'rendering a tremendous service to the reading public.'[3] Paul Léon's prompt response stated, 'Mr. Joyce is definitely opposed to the inclusion of the chart,' and explained, '*Ulysses* is a piece of belles lettres, i.e. pure literature; if it needs explanations these belong to the class of critical and historical writings, not to the book itself.'[4]

Joyce's reluctance to incorporate such criticism into the US edition of *Ulysses* may well have reflected his conviction that, as he told Beckett, he had 'oversystematized *Ulysses*.'[5] But, his reluctance, whatever its cause, came too late. Furthermore, it was inconsistent with his previous actions, not only in terms of his elaboration of the schematic elements in his writing and revising of *Ulysses*, but also in terms of his encouragement of Larbaud and Gilbert to emphasize these same schematic elements to defend the novel against the censor. In fact, Joyce had already consented to incorporation of criticism in *Ulysses* by approving of Ernst's strategy of pasting critical opinion inside the covers of the copy of the Paris edition imported to the USA for the 1932–3 trial. In any case, the criticism to which Joyce objected would find a home in *Ulysses* in a form that partially disguised its presence there, namely, the Woolsey decision.

Joyce never seemed to regard Woolsey's decision as a criticism of *Ulysses*. Cerf, however, must have recognized it as precisely that: a stylish and authoritative criticism that would teach the public how to read Joyce's novel. A letter from Alexander Lindey to Woolsey indicates that Woolsey thought so as well:

With respect to the form in which your opinion is to be incorporated in the forthcoming American edition of *Ulysses*, I am passing your thought on to Random House. I believe, as you do, that the intelligent reader will find the entire opinion, excepting only the practice part and the citations, of much interest and enlightenment.[6]

If Lindey and Woolsey were right in their estimation of the decision's power to enlighten readers of *Ulysses*, then it has enlightened many: by virtue of its inclusion in both the US and British editions of *Ulysses*, Woolsey's decision became the most widely circulated criticism of the novel.

The Woolsey decision, of course, was by no means the only work of criticism to disseminate the defensive strategies used to protect *Ulysses* in the course of the trials. Many of the critical works which were written during the ban on *Ulysses* – and which influenced Woolsey's decision – have continued to circulate widely. The most influential of these is undoubtedly Stuart Gilbert's *James Joyce's 'Ulysses,'* which went into its second edition in 1955.

The preface of the first edition of Gilbert's book had openly warned, 'this study necessarily presents a bowdlerized and imperfect image of the original,' encouraging serious readers to 'buy, borrow or purloin a copy of the complete book.'[7] The new preface, still in circulation today, is not as candid. It acknowledges that the 'pedantic tone' of the book was motivated in part by the desire to protect *Ulysses* against the censor, and it suggests Gilbert's preference for the formal qualities of the novel over its controversial content, but it does not mention that the book presents a bowdlerized version of the original:

I have not tried to alleviate the rather pedantic tone of much of the writing in this Study. For one thing, Joyce approved of it; and, for another, we who admired *Ulysses* for its structural, enduring qualities and not for the occasional presence in it of words and descriptive passages which shocked our elders, were on the defensive, and the pedant's cloak is often a convenient protection against the cold blasts of propriety.[8]

Although Gilbert neglected to mention that his extensive quotations from *Ulysses* were bowdlerized in the first edition of his book, he did not trouble to eliminate or even reduce such bowdlerization in the new edition. Thus, instead of quoting Joyce's full description of Bloom's despair in 'Calypso' – 'The oldest people. Wandered far away over all the earth, captivity to captivity, multiplying, dying, being born everywhere. It lay there now. Now it could bear no more. Dead: an old woman's: the grey sunken cunt of the world'[9] – Gilbert prefers, '"The oldest people. Wandered far away over all the earth, captivity to captivity, multiplying, dying, being born everywhere. It lay there now. Now it could bear no more. Dead. …"'[10]

Likewise, Gilbert does not quote fully Bloom's thoughts at the end of the 'Lotus-Eaters' episode:

He foresaw his pale body reclined in it at full, naked, in a womb of warmth, oiled by scented melting soap, softly leaved. He saw his trunk and limbs riprippled over and sustained, buoyed lightly upward, lemonyellow: his navel, bud of flesh: and saw the dark tangled curls of his bush floating, floating hair of the stream around the limp father of thousands, a languid floating flower.[11]

Gilbert prefers the following:

He foresaw his pale body reclined in it at full, naked, in a womb of warmth, oiled by scented melting soap, softly laved. He saw his trunk and limbs riprippled over and sustained, buoyed lightly upward, lemonyellow … a languid floating flower (ellipsis Gilbert's).[12]

Thus, Gilbert's book, which contains countless examples of this type of bowdlerization, has continued to censor *Ulysses*, giving readers a distorted picture of the novel by making it seem more polite and 'respectable' than it is. In the process, Gilbert's book has made it more difficult to understand what the controversy surrounding the publication of *Ulysses* was all about.

Gilbert's book has impeded understanding of that controversy not merely by bowdlerizing *Ulysses*, but also by emphasizing its elaborate form and schematic structure. Here again, Gilbert's motives in proceeding in this manner are made much clearer in the original preface than they are in the 1955 version. In 1930, Gilbert wrote,

if the structure and true import of *Ulysses* be misapprehended, its influence is apt to be misleading, not to say pernicious. For it seems at first sight a mere fantasia of the subconscious, the manifesto of those forces of disorder which riot in the back of the mind, a demonstration that indiscipline and anarchy can subserve creative achievement. One of the objects of this study is to assert the falsity of such a view.[13]

The language of this passage, words and expressions like 'manifesto,' 'forces of disorder,' 'riot,' and 'anarchy,' effectively implies that the controversy surrounding the publication of *Ulysses* was inherently political. By contrast, the language of the new preface describes the initial perception of *Ulysses* in terms which underplay the novel's ability to provoke such controversy: 'in those early days most readers and many eminent critics regarded *Ulysses* as a violently romantic work, an uncontrolled outpouring of the subconscious mind, powerful but formless. Thus it was necessary to emphasize the "classical" and formal elements.'[14]

My equation above of readers of *Ulysses* with readers of Gilbert's book, incidently, is not made without reflection. Indeed, the book's influence cannot be adequately appreciated without recognizing that, especially at the universities, Gilbert's book has accompanied many readers on their first excursion into the territory of *Ulysses*. In many cases, the reading of Gilbert's book has actually preceded the reading of Joyce's novel. At times it has undoubtedly served as a substitute for *Ulysses*, just as it did while the novel was under ban. The dust jacket of the first edition described Gilbert's book as 'the only substitute for the original,' which in light of the existing ban was at least understandable. The same cannot be said for the message on the back cover of the current edition of the book, which informs the would-be reader, 'Most serious Joyce readers owe to Stuart Gilbert their first introduction to the richness and complexity of ULYSSES. His monumental pioneer analysis remains an essential Baedeker.'[15]

This view of the value of Gilbert's book does not provide a flattering picture of 'serious' readers of Joyce, who, one would hope, would owe their first introduction to the richness and complexity of *Ulysses* to the novel itself, but it may well indicate the way in which Gilbert's book is often used. That a guide like Gilbert's is necessary in order properly to approach *Ulysses* seems to be generally accepted. Even Clifton Fadiman singles out Joyce's novel as the one book on his list of lifetime reading which requires a guide: 'In this one case, read a good commentary *first*. The best short one is by Edmund Wilson, the best long ones by Stuart Gilbert and Anthony Burgess.'[16]

Gilbert's book was undoubtedly one the most influential of the early critical works on *Ulysses* written in the tradition of critical censorship initiated by Pound, but it was certainly not the last. Miles A. Hanley's *Word Index to James Joyce's Ulysses* contains an interesting (and humorous) example of the way in which a lively interest in the form of Joyce's novel has often gone hand in hand with a remarkable unwillingness to discuss its controversial content. In a short essay at the end of the book designed to show how the index can be used to trace structural patterns of 'image-words,' Martin Joos chooses the word *prize*.[17]

The word first occurs, according to Joos, when Bloom is 'reading his morning paper.'[18] In quoting the relevant passage, Joos omits the portions in brackets:

'[Asquat on the cuckstool] he folded out his paper turning its pages over on his bared knees. Something new and easy. [No great hurry. Keep it a bit.] Our prize titbit. *Matcham's Masterstroke*. Written by

Mr Philip Beaufoy, Playgoer's club, London. Payment at the rate of one guinea a column has been made to the writer. Three and a half. Three pounds three. Three pounds thirteen and six.'[19]

For the next occurrence of *prize*, Joos provides a page number, but he does not quote the relevant passage, which reads as follows: 'He tore away half the prize story sharply and wiped himself with it.'[20] Joos is evidently determined not to mention that Bloom is defecating while reading Beaufoy's prize titbit. He is thus following in the footsteps of Ezra Pound, perhaps for similar reasons, even though the US ban on *Ulysses* has been lifted.

Joos's search for occurrences of *prize* eventually leads him to the passage describing Bloom's thoughts on the beach in 'Nausicaa':

> Bloom is idling on a beach and wondering what the onlookers may be thinking about him: 'See ourselves as others see us. So long as women don't mock, what matter? That's the way to find out. Ask yourself who he is now. *The Mystery Man on the Beach*, prize titbit story by Mr Leopold Bloom. Payment at the rate of one guinea per column.'[21]

So concerned is Joos to show that these recurrences reveal Bloom to be a man interested in money and literary pursuits, that he neglects to mention what Bloom is doing on the beach or, more specifically, the extent to which Bloom's musings in the jakes are linked to his masturbation on the beach. He thus follows in the footsteps of Assistant US Attorney Nicholas Atlas, who wrote that Bloom goes to the beach as people do and who said nothing about what Bloom does there (see Chapter 4).

Writers like Joos may have written of *Ulysses* in this evasive manner because, although the ban on the novel had been lifted in New York in 1933, the general atmosphere throughout the 1930s, 1940s and even 1950s still required discretion. Historical circumstances lend some credence to this view. As late as 1959 *Ulysses* was seized with other allegedly indecent literature in a morality squad raid in St Louis, Missouri.[22] The Woolsey decision, incidentally, was not binding on states other than New York; obscenity proceedings could therefore have been initiated in Missouri.

It is worth noting in this context that the Woolsey decision made the United States the *first* English-speaking country to open its borders to *Ulysses*; the others followed, as Joyce predicted they would, but slowly. Surprisingly, Ireland led the pack by lifting its exclusion order regarding *Ulysses* around 1934.[23] In England, the ban on the novel was not lifted until 1936. In Australia, the novel was first banned in 1927, and although this ban was lifted in 1937, it was lowered again in 1941; thereafter,

Ulysses was (technically at least) available to only '"*bona fide* applicants"' (scientists, students, and so on).[24] In Canada, through which copies of *Ulysses* had once been smuggled into the United States, the novel could not be legally obtained until 1949, although it seems to have been generally available long before then.[25]

A far more influential example of the critical censorship of *Ulysses* practiced by Joos is provided by the work of Richard Ellmann, a critic whose evasions cannot be excused by an appeal to such historical circumstances. As surprising as it may seem in light of Ellmann's candour regarding Joyce's life in *James Joyce*, Ellmann was inclined to align himself with the schematizers when it came to *Ulysses*. The clearest (though by no means the most influential) example of Ellmann's inclinations in this regard is perhaps his *Encyclopedia Americana* article on Joyce.[26] The notable feature of the article is that, while it highlights the importance of the schema to an understanding of *Ulysses* by providing a photoreproduction of a condensed version of the schema itself, it neglects to mention that *Ulysses* was the object of censorship. Coming as it does from a critic who professedly recognizes the intimate connection between Joyce's life and his art, this omission is curious, too curious to be without significance.

Not surprisingly, this same tendency to highlight the formal aspects of *Ulysses* while underplaying its controversial content is evident throughout Ellmann's major book on the novel, *Ulysses on the Liffey*, as the preface makes clear:

> The book's total meaning depends so heavily upon a perception of its form that any hints by the author demand attention. At first, Joyce chose to insist upon his book's Odyssean parallels, but after inserting them into the serial publication of some chapters, he removed them, evidently confident that the book might be taken on its own terms. Yet he was not comfortable at the thought that his art might too successfully conceal his art, and made sure that Stuart Gilbert revived the Homeric titles for his book, *James Joyce's 'Ulysses,'* in 1934.[27]

Perhaps because he mistakes the publication date of Gilbert's book as 1934, thus placing it after Woolsey's lifting of the ban on *Ulysses* rather than before (actual publication was 1930), Ellmann seems unaware that Gilbert's emphasis on the Homeric parallels was motivated by the desire to defend Joyce's novel against the attacks of the censor. Thus, instead of de-emphasizing the schematic elements of *Ulysses*, Ellmann proceeds to out-Gilbert Gilbert. Hugh Kenner saw this clearly and wrote that Ellmann had aligned himself with the old tradition that general ideas will do, and that the meaning of *Ulysses* is to be sought on some plane where large generalities intersect. That approach was understandable in 1930. Stuart Gilbert for one was constrained not only to demonstrate that the Blue Book of Eccles was something more than a cloud of verbal gas with dirty words in it, but also to conduct this demonstration on behalf of a public which couldn't be presumed to have access to a copy of the book. That was one reason for the prominence he gave the famous Schema. For Mr. Ellmann, on the contrary, exposition doesn't start from schemata, it converages on them.[28]

Kenner's awareness of the defensive value of the schema makes him sensitive to Ellmann's tendency throughout *Ulysses on the Liffey* to de-emphasize the 'natural substrate, real people in a real city,' in favour of 'the schematic need to turn the people instantly into terms in a massive allegory.'[29] For example, Kenner notes that Ellmann delights in mythologizing Molly Bloom as the earth-goddess, 'Gea-Tellus, then, by bringing her down with a thump onto the orange-keyed chamberpot at 7 Eccles street, in demythologizing her into an old shoe.' Kenner responds to Ellmann's criticism by asking a pointed rhetorical question: 'Alas, that old shoe; surely what Joyce demythologizes her into is Marion Tweedy Bloom?'

A similar tendency to emphasize the formal aspects of *Ulysses* at the expense of its controversial content can be detected in Ellmann's biography of Joyce. For example, although Ellmann cursorily mentions the first three suppressions of *Ulysses* at the hands of the US Post Office authorities, he never bothers to quote the passages that provoked them. Not even when he discusses at some length the suppression of 'Nausicaa' and the ensuing trials in the New York courts does he trouble to quote from the offending passages.[30] He does state that the 'obscene passages' culled by Sumner were read, but the closest he comes to actually describing the contents of the suppressed section of the episode is to refer to 'Gerty MacDowell's exhibition of her drawers.'[31] In his introduction, Ellmann acknowledges Joyce's radical mixing of the lovely and the filthy by asking, 'What other hero defecates or masturbates like Bloom before our eyes?'[32] Yet his treatment of the prosecution of the 'Nausicaa' episode fails to indicate that Bloom's masturbation takes place on the beach before Gerty MacDowell's eyes as well as our own.

This is not the only occasion on which Ellmann deftly avoids discussing the details of Bloom's encounter with Gerty MacDowell. He writes, for example, that Arthur Power 'labored at the *Nausicaa* episode, but, being unaccustomed to the technique, misunderstood parts of it as actual events. Joyce was irritated: '"That didn't take place at all," he said, "only in Bloom's imagination."'[33] In recounting this exchange, Ellmann neglects to mention that Power was 'enquiring into the details of what actually occurred during Bloom's encounter with Gerty MacDowell on the beach.'[34] In other words, Ellmann neglects to point out that Joyce's response was evasive, an expression of the author's unwillingness to discuss Bloom's masturbation. Instead of questioning this evasiveness on Joyce's part, Ellmann imitates it by shifting attention from the controversial content of 'Nausicaa' to its technique.

Such decorous evasions on Ellmann's part are not confined to the 'Nausicaa' episode. His treatment of Pound's response to 'Sirens' reveals the same tactics:

> In London his friends had received an earlier episode, the *Sirens*, with some disquiet. Joyce was elated when he finished it, but on June 18 he received a letter from Pound, 'disapproving of the *Sirens* [as Joyce informed Budgen], then modifying his disapproval and protesting against the close and against 'obsession' and wanting to know whether Bloom (prolonged cheers from all parts of the house) could not be relegated to the background and Stephen Telemachus brought forward.'[35]

Ellmann avoids coming to grips with either the contents of 'Sirens' or Pound's objections thereto. He does not mention that 'the close' of the episode consists of Bloom's fart, his anal music. Nor does Ellmann specify that Pound's objection was to Joyce's 'arsoreal, cloacal' obsession (See Chapter 1).

Even on those relatively rare occasions when Ellmann does quote from *Ulysses*, he takes care to avoid inclusion of controversial passages. For instance, in order to illustrate his contention that 'Bloom's monologue is a continuous poetry, full of phrases of extraordinary intensity,' Ellmann quotes the Dead Sea passage as follows (omitting the section in brackets):

> A barren land, bare waste. Vulcanic lake, the dead sea: no fish, weedless, sunk deep in the earth. No wind would lift those waves, grey metal, poisonous foggy waters. Brimstone they called it raining down: the cities of the plain: Sodom, Gomorrah, Edom. All dead names. A dead sea in a dead land, grey and old. Old now. It bore the oldest, the first race. A bent hag crossed from Cassidy's clutching a noggin bottle by the neck. The oldest people. Wandered far away over all the earth, captivity to captivity, multiplying, dying, being born everywhere. [It lay there now. Now it could bear no more. Dead: an old woman's: the grey sunken cunt of the world.][36]

Although Ellmann is not obliged to quote the passage in its entirety, his omission of the last lines is dubious, especially in light of his desire to establish that Bloom's monologue is 'full of phrases of extraordinary intensity.' Ellmann's treatment of this passage indicates clearly that he is writing in the tradition of critical censorship initiated by Pound and popularized by Gilbert.

Ellmann's biography is full of similar evasions, and their cumulative effect on his readers's appreciation of *Ulysses* is not trivial. In the case of the 'Nausicaa' episode they hinder, among other things, an understanding of the extent to which Bloom's encounter with Gerty MacDowell struck at the Vice Society's very *raison d'être*. In the case of Pound's response to 'Sirens,' they underplay the extent to which Joyce's art was capable of offending not only the philistines but also the Modernists of his day. Where the Dead Sea passage is concerned, they misrepresent the nature of Bloom's thoughts and thus fail to convey a sense of the extent to which the poetry of *Ulysses* undermines literary decorum. Taken together, Ellmann's evasions discourage appreciation of those elements of Joyce's art which caused the storm of controversy at the time of its publication.[37]

What is true of Ellmann's work in this regard is true of the whole tradition of critical censorship inspired by the desire to defend *Ulysses* against the attacks of the censor. As Richard Brown has recently observed, the net effect of that tradition has been to postpone critical study of those aspects of the novel which provoked the censor's attacks in the first place, including, not surprisingly, the whole question of Joyce's treatment of sexuality.[38] Study of the closely related question of Joyce's representation of excrement has also been delayed, making it possible for Vincent Cheng to remark recently, 'I have been surprised to find, given the fecal fecundity of the topic in Joyce's works, how little scholarly work has been done on this topic.'[39] By postponing discussion of these elements of *Ulysses*, the tradition of critical censorship has made it difficult to arrive at a balanced view of *Ulysses*, one which does justice to both its beauty and its obscenity, one which acknowledges the novel's turbulent past as a living aspect of the novel we read in our day.

Along with critical works by Gilbert, Joos, and Ellmann, Woolsey's decision has misrepresented *Ulysses* by making it seem far more 'respectable' and less insurrectionary than it really is; it has thus contributed to the difficulty in arriving at a balanced view of the novel. However, as long as the decision was included in the Random House and Bodley Head editions, it possessed one virtue that the other critical works did not. For one thing, it reminded readers of *Ulysses* that the novel had provoked great controversy at the time of its publication. For another, it attested to the fact that the censorship had affected not only the critical reception but the very form in which *Ulysses* was presented to the reading public. Thus, it served to alert readers to the intimate relation between the legal and literary aspects of the *Ulysses* case and, more importantly, to call into question the idea of the autonomy of literature from the complications of life. I should add that the Woolsey decision also invited further investigation into the censorship trials themselves. This book, as I have made clear in the Introduction, is the result of my response to that invitation.

In this context, Random House's recent decision to drop Woolsey's opinion from the US edition of *Ulysses* deserves consideration. Random House editor Anne Freedgood explained the decision as follows:

> The reason the trial-related documents were omitted from the 1986 Random House and Vintage editions of ULYSSES is simple: we felt that with the complete list of ULYSSES editions, the Richard Ellmann preface and the Hans Walter Gabler afterword, the book had enough additional material, and that since it is now recognized primarily as a literary masterpiece, there ·was no need to emphasize its symbolic position as a challenge to the obscenity laws and make the volume longer than it already was, although the trial is certainly mentioned in the jacket copy.[40]

Freedgood's letter reveals, among other things, that the strict distinction between the literary and the non-literary (a distinction implicit in the Woolsey decision and many other works intended to defend *Ulysses* against the censor) is no longer confined to a small group of literary critics. Because *Ulysses* is recognized 'primarily as a literary masterpiece,' according to Freedgood, there is no need 'to emphasize its symbolic position as a challenge to the obscenity laws.' In addition to suggesting a curious reversal of literary and historical value (*Ulysses* is a real literary masterpiece; its position in the history of censorship is 'symbolic') this formulation betrays a tendency to establish the autonomy of art by cutting the literary work off from its historical roots. The implication of this move is clearly that an understanding of the censorship of *Ulysses* is not essential to an understanding of the novel, that the censorship is of (symbolic) historical interest only. The 1986 Random House edition (the Gabler edition) of *Ulysses*, in which the censorship of the novel is relegated to a brief mention on the rear jacket, gives the same message.

These developments are to be regretted, not only because an understanding of the censorship of *Ulysses* is necessary for a balanced appreciation of the novel itself, but also because they obscure the fact that the trials of *Ulysses*, or more accurately the defensive strategies which the censorship engendered, have figured prominently in the history of censorship and have thus affected not only the reading of *Ulysses* but also understanding of the proper basis for freedom of speech, especially in United States, of course, but in other Western liberal democracies as well. Of the legal decisions produced in the course of the trials, the most influential, at least in the cultural (as opposed here to the legal) realm, is undoubtedly the Woolsey decision. By virtue of its inclusion in both the US and British editions of *Ulysses*, as Gerald Gunther has claimed, it has become 'one of the most widely read judicial opinions in history.'[41]

Morris Ernst and other early commentators therefore had grounds for predicting that the influence of decision would be great, and subsequent evaluation has tended to prove them right. Legal historian Edward de Grazia identifies the Woolsey decision as a landmark in the history of censorship.[42] Theologian Harold C. Gardiner, SJ writes that the Woolsey decision 'laid down the modern test, which has since been recognized as the keystone of modern American legislation, of obscenity.'[43] Cultural historian Ann Ilan Alter is more emphatic. She states that the Woolsey decision was 'the first in a series of decisions, climaxing with *Lady Chatterley's Lover* in 1958, that opened the way for the virtual end of moral censorship in the United States.'[44]

Even critics who doubt that the Woolsey decision is truly a judicial landmark acknowledge its importance. One such critic, social and intellectual historian Paul S. Boyer, argues that the Woolsey decision is significant, 'both for the immediate effect it had upon the circulation of an important work of literature and for the emblematic role it has come to play in twentieth-century censorship history.'[45] Literary scholars, well aware of the importance of *Ulysses* in modern literature and generally uninterested in extraneous legal entanglements, have tended to restrict the significance of the Woolsey decision to the effect it had on the circulation of *Ulysses* in the United States. Along with Richard Ellmann, they habitually refer to the Woolsey decision as 'famous,' a 'landmark,' and so on.

Subsequent evidence indicates that these assessments of the place of the trials of *Ulysses* and the Woolsey decision in the history of censorship are warranted. For example, when the Canadian Parliament passed new obscenity legislation in 1959, one critic evaluated it by warning: 'It would be much simpler for a book like *Ulysses* to be banned under the new definition than the old.'[46] For another example, when the American Civil Liberties Union recently warned that the US Justice Department had begun to use laws passed to combat organized crime in order to prosecute pornographers, it noted: 'When you first read *Ulysses*, your edition probably contained the landmark decision permitting Joyce's classic to be imported legally into the United States. That was in the 1930s, so you thought the issue of explicit sex in literature was settled and was "history."'[47] For a final example, when The Pacifica Foundation recently decided to test the US Federal Communications Commission's new censorship guidelines it did so by requesting advance clearing for its annual Bloomsday (16 June) broadcast of the 'Penelope' episode of *Ulysses*.[48] In particular, it wanted to know if it could broadcast words and phrases including, '"come three or four times with that tremendous big red brute of a thing,"' '"put it into me from behind ... like the dogs do it,"' '"fucked yes and damn well fucked too,"' and '"stick his tongue 7 miles up my hole."'[49] Pacifica's aim was presumably to use the prestige of the Woolsey decision to ensure a favourable ruling. The FCC's response declined to give a ruling one way or the other, but it confirmed the success of Pacifica's strategy by quoting Woolsey's decision, thus confirming its authority and influence in US culture.

The significance of the Woolsey decision, however, is not to be measured in terms of the number of times it is mentioned in contemporary debates regarding censorship, but rather in terms of the light that its well-intentioned lies can throw on the esthetic theory of art as a basis for freedom of speech. Recent censorship controversies like the case of Salman Rushdie and *The Satanic Verses* reveal that the esthetic theory which informs Woolsey's decision continues to be proposed as a basis for freedom of speech. Witness, for example, the recent 'DECLARATION OF IRANIAN INTELLECTUALS AND ARTISTS IN DEFENSE OF SALMAN RUSHDIE,' signed by 'about fifty prominent Iranians living in exile':

> The signers of this declaration, who have shown in many different ways their support for Salman Rushdie now and in the past, believe that freedom of speech is one of the greatest achievements of mankind, and point out, as Voltaire once did, that this freedom would be meaningless unless human beings had the liberty to blaspheme. No one and no group has the right to hamper or hinder this freedom in the name of this or that sanctity.
>
> We emphasize the fact that Khomeini's death sentence is intolerable, and stress that in judging a creative work of art no considerations are valid other than aesthetic ones.[50]

In light of the currency of such appeals to the esthetic theory of art, we do well to wonder if the well-intentioned lies of the Woolsey decision regarding the nature of *Ulysses* might not have their counterpart where freedom of speech is concerned. The lies can be summarized as follows: first, that literary works like *Ulysses* have nothing in common with works of pornography like *Fanny Hill*; second, that artistic intention precludes other intentions – moral, political, or religious – that might oppose or undermine values which the law (rightly or wrongly) upholds; third, that a literary work like *Ulysses* which, judged as a whole, is not legally obscene, is nowhere aphrodisiac, nowhere pornographic, nowhere obscene; and fourth, that *l'homme moyen sensuel*, the average person, responds to art in a resolutely static (or esthetic) manner.

In so far as these criticisms of *Ulysses* articulate an esthetic theory of art according to which a work of genuine literary art cannot, *ipso facto*, be obscene, they contribute to the corollary idea that works like *Ulysses* can have no serious adverse effect whatsoever, be it moral, political, religious or otherwise. This view makes it seem dubious to regard literature as a sword, but if the metaphor has any validity at all, it is surely a sword of the two-edged variety. Thus, if the Woolsey decision denies the power of literary works to harm those who read them it also denies their power to influence for the good. In other words, if a theory of literature denies literature the power to subvert things which are good, it also denies it the power to subvert those which are evil. Literature either has the ability to influence readers morally, politically, philosophically or religiously or it has not.

It is not a question here of moralizing about what literature should or should not do, but rather of acknowledging what it does do, or seems to do, in reality as we know it. The theory of literature behind the Woolsey decision emphasizes what literature *should be* rather than what it *is*. As Stephen Dedalus expresses it in *Portrait*, the theory holds that art 'awakens, or ought to awaken, or induces, or ought to induce, an esthetic stasis' rather than a kinesis or action.[51] Significantly, when Stephen's listener confesses that he sometimes responds to art kinetically, Stephen reminds him, 'we are just now in a mental world,'[52] a response which confirms the theory's idealistic thrust.

The theory is not without value in making broad distinctions between literature (writing which aims primarily at an esthetic end) and rhetoric (writing which aims primarily at inducing belief or action).[53] But it should also be admitted that its value is limited, and nowhere are its limitations more obvious than where it is a question of accounting for the reception of controversial works. More specifically, the limitations of the esthetic theory articulated in the Woolsey decision are revealed in its inability to account for the controversy surrounding the publication of *Ulysses* itself, and by the same token, the more recent examples of Václav Havel's plays and Salman Rushdie's *Satanic Verses*. The reception of these works proves unequivocally that the effect of literary works is sometimes remarkably kinetic, that such works may at times affect the way in which individuals – not to mention governments – think and act.

Furthermore, the reception of the works of all three writers confirms the power of literature to undermine or subvert the existing moral, political, or religious order. There is no question, of course, of denying that the works of Joyce, Havel, and Rushdie are works of literature of the first order. And while one might argue that people ought not to have responded as they did, the fact is that they did so and that any theory of art worth its salt should be able to account for this fact. Before examining the implications for literary theory of the reception of these works, however, we should stop for a moment to anticipate an unwarranted assumption that the examples of Joyce, Havel, and Rushdie may encourage.

Although the theory behind the Woolsey decision cannot, strictly speaking, account for any kinetic effect of literature whatsoever, harmful or otherwise, the assumption implicit in the theory is that genuinely literary works necessarily have a *good* effect (thus Woolsey's view that *Ulysses* may disgust or repel the reader from what is distasteful but not allure or corrupt). In other words, the assumption is that literary works subvert only that which deserves to be subverted, whether it be bourgeois materialism, religious dogmatism, or hypocritical sexuality. Those who regard literature from this perspective might be inclined to see confirmation of their theory in the examples cited above. After all, did not *Ulysses* play a role in undermining unhealthy Victorian attitudes about human sexuality? Is it not the case that Václav Havel's plays helped undermine one of the most corrupt and oppressive political regimes in history? And is it not true, as a contributor to the *New York Times Book Review* put it, that although Rushdie may have been '"insensitive to treat so playfully a subject that for millions of people is deadly serious[,] ... coming to tolerate such playfulness is a necessary step for Muslims on the road to enlightenment and freedom"'?[54]

I suspect that the majority of those whose inhabit modern liberal democracies would answer 'yes' to these questions, and it might seem to follow from this that literature does in fact only undermine that which is deserving of subversion. The falsity of this view appears when it is a question of the effect of literary works on values which citizens of modern liberal democracies hold dear – and rightly hold dear – such as respect for women and racial minorities. How many of those who would be quite comfortable with the idea that literature subverts only that which is deserving of subversion, such as Victorian sexual morality, Soviet communism, or Muslim fundamentalism, would be as comfortable with the idea where it was a question of the subversion of respect for Jews or women? How many, for example, would seriously deny that the representations of Shylock in *The Merchant of Venice* and Fagin in *Oliver Twist* are subversive of respect for Jews? How many would earnestly refuse to accept that the representation of women in a good deal of 'canonical' literature serves to denigrate them and perpetuate the myth that they are inferior to men?

The point I am making here is simply that behind the idea that the effect of literature is always good, or that literature only subverts what is corrupt and nefarious, is often complacency arising from the assurance that one's own values are not in jeopardy. Thus, behind the idea that a genuinely literary work cannot undermine sexual morality is often the view that sexual morality is hardly worth worrying about. Behind the idea that literary works cannot undermine religious faith is often the belief that religious faith is not really important. And behind the idea that denigrating literary representations of Jews and women do not undermine respect for them is the conviction that such respect is not crucial to the welfare of the human community.

The evidence suggests, however, that literature does have the power to subvert or strengthen both false values which we would be better off without and true values which we would do well to nurture. It follows that a good theory of literature should be able to explain this power. As previously mentioned, the esthetic theory behind the Woolsey decision is singularly unable to do so, which explains why it serves to make the controversy surrounding the publication of *Ulysses*, as well as works like Václav Havel's plays, and Salman Rushdie's *Satanic Verses*, seem only absurd, a mere reflection of the ignorance of those who read and react to them kinetically.

Since each one of Woolsey's well-intentioned lies contributes to the esthetic theory's inability to account for the kinetic effects of literature, each is worth examining in its own right. The principle that the judge/critic of a work should consult its critical satellites is sound, but by defining these satellites narrowly as works of literary criticism like Stuart Gilbert's *James Joyce's 'Ulysses'* and classic literary creations like Dante's *Inferno*, Woolsey's decision denies the real connections between literary works like *Ulysses* and other, less obviously literary productions. In the case of *Ulysses* the relevant connection is with the pornographic works which Joyce drew upon in writing his novel. In the cases of Havel and Rushdie, the relevant connections are with political manifestos and religious texts respectively. In all three cases, the connection is with works generally assumed to be more rhetorical, more kinetic, than literature as conventionally understood (at least since Kant).

The principle that the judge/critic should take into account the author's intention is also sound, but by insisting that such intention be interpreted tautologically as artistic intention which admits of no other intentions, the Woolsey decision denies that authors of literary works have others intentions as well. In the case of Joyce and *Ulysses* these intentions were those of 'a literary conspirator, who was determined to destroy the oppressive and respectable cultural structures under which we had been reared.'[55] Havel's and Rushdie's intentions can only be conjectured, but one would surely not be far off the mark to suggest the collapse of Soviet totalitarianism and the subversion of Muslim absolutism respectively. In any case, the point is that while all genuine literary artists share the intention of producing a work of art, this intention does not preclude other, less narrowly artistic, intentions.

The principle that the judge/critic should take into account the work as a whole is perhaps the most compelling of Woolsey's four principles, but Woolsey interprets it in such a way as to preclude any autonomy of the parts relative to the whole. He thereby misrepresents the power of the parts of a literary work to influence its readers, perhaps, but not necessarily, by epitomizing tendencies of the whole. This power is most acute in the early stages of the reception of a given work, as the works of Joyce, Havel, and Rushdie make abundantly clear. The recent controversy surrounding the publication of Rushdie's *Satanic Verses*, for example, has had far less to do with the work as a whole than with the parts which portray Mohammed as a lying hypocrite, which indicates that the parts of a literary work are far more powerful and independent than Judge Woolsey's theory allows.

Finally, the principle that the judge/critic should take into account the effect of the work in question on the average person is eminently sane. But Woolsey's 'l'homme moyen sensuel' has little in common with the average person. According to the logic of Woolsey's decision, the average man is one who subscribes to his sophisticated definitions of the three principles discussed above, and therefore knows that genuine literature does not induce to action of any kind. Nothing could be further from the truth. Students of literature and literary critics may respond to literary works as Woolsey's theory suggests they should, but the average person most certainly does not.

Thus, the esthetic theory of art that is articulated in Woolsey's well-intentioned lies about *Ulysses* produces a well-intentioned lie about the proper basis for freedom of speech. According to the logic of Woolsey's decision, that basis is the one expressed by Morris Ernst in the concluding section of his defense of *Ulysses*, namely, the idea that people are not influenced by what they read. To call this view into question by drawing attention to the extent to which Woolsey's key principles are well-intentioned lies is, of course, to highlight the need for a literary theory which does justice to the ethical and political elements of literature as well as the esthetic element. As Wayne Booth has observed, talk of a 'revived ethical and political criticism of art' often raises fears of renewed censorship, and '"political suppression of artists."'[56] These fears help to explain why the esthetic view of art is attractive to those looking for a defense against censorship.

However attractive this method of avoiding censorship may seem in the short term, however, it will not serve in the long run. As the examples of *Ulysses*, Vaclav Havel's plays, and *The Satanic Verses* make clear, people *are* influenced by what they read, and the truth in this regard should not be sacrificed for the sake of expedience. Furthermore, in light of the experiences of Havel and Rushdie, one has to wonder about the effectiveness of the esthetic theory as a way of defending writers against censorship. Is it not the case that the theory is little more than a reassuring fiction that is believed only in Western liberal democracies and even there rejected as a falsehood during times of crisis? And is it not the case that the theory, while it fails to provide a sound defense against censorship when it really counts, encourages a dangerous indifferentism? After all, if the books we read do not affect the way we think and act, why should we exert the effort required really to understand them?

Ultimately, a lasting commitment to freedom of speech can be based only on respect for the individual's need to express himself or herself freely and recognition that such respect is essential to the common good. Far from denying that people are influenced by what they read, such respect must openly acknowledge that even works which we refuse to censor may be harmful in certain respects. Rooted as it is in respect for the dignity of the human person and recognition of the common good, this view affirms that our commitment to freedom of speech will necessarily require suffering on our part, but that it is better to let the weeds grow with the wheat than to destroy the wheat to get rid of the weeds.

The great advantage of this view of the proper basis for freedom of speech is that it keeps alive the idea that reading is a dangerous activity, one which can bring about personal and political transformation. Simone Weil once wrote, 'By the power of words we always mean their power of illusion and error,'[57] but the idea of reading as a dangerous activity should be broad enough to include the danger of illusion and error as well as the danger of enlightening revelation. Canadian novelist Mordecai Richler expresses this view when he describes *All Quiet on the Western Front* as 'a time bomb' capable of undermining some of the reader's most cherished preconceptions and prejudices: 'I never expected that a mere novel, a stranger's tale, could actually be dangerous, creating such turbulence in my life, obliging me to question so many received ideas. About Germans. About my own monumental ignorance of the world. About what novels were.'[58] Surely we should not lose sight of the truth of what Richler says about the transforming power of literature in a futile effort to base freedom of speech on a lie, no matter how well-intentioned. To do so would be to misunderstand not only *Ulysses* and the controversy surrounding its publication but also the close and sometimes explosive connection between art and life, a connection that Joyce explored so brilliantly.

Appendix: The Censor's *Ulysses*

The following excerpts from *Ulysses* contain passages deemed obscene or otherwise objectionable by various governmental and editorial authorities between 1918 and 1934. The objectionable passages themselves appear in boldface; text in regular typeface has been added where required to establish a meaningful context. Passages expurgated by the editors of *The Little Review* – all of which were restored in the first edition of the novel – appear in bold within brackets. Unless otherwise indicated, all ellipses in the excerpts are editorial interpolations; all other editorial interpolations appear in regular face brackets. Each excerpt is identified by the appropriate page number(s) and the name of the authority responsible for the objection or expurgation.

Episode I ('Telemachus')

1. Page 12, P 1930; (*U*, pp. 11–12) – US Attorney Martin Conboy[1]

2. Page 13, P 1930; (*U*, pp. 12–13) – US Attorney Martin Conboy

3. Page 14, P 1930; (*U*, pp. 13–14) – US Attorney Martin Conboy

4. Page 17, P 1930; (*U*, pp. 16–18) – US Attorney Martin Conboy

5. Page 21, P 1930; (*U*, pp. 21–2) – US Attorney Martin Conboy

Episode II ('Nestor')

No censored passages

Episode III ('Proteus')

6. Along by the edge of the mole he dawdled, smelt a rock and, from under a [**cocked hindleg pissed against it. He trotted forward and, lifting again his hindleg, pissed quick short at an unsmelt rock. The simple pleasures of the poor. His hindpaws then scattered the sand: then his forepaws dabbled and delved.**] edge of the the mole he dawdled, smelt a rock. Something he buried there, his grandmother. (*LR*, 5:1 (May 1918), p. 41; MS, 3. Proteus, pp. 13–14; *U*, p. 46) – Ezra Pound[2]

Episode IV ('Calypso')

7. A barren land, bare waste. Vulcanic lake, the dead sea: no fish, weedless, sunk deep in the earth. ... A dead sea in a dead land, grey and old. Old now. It bore the oldest, the first race. ... Now it could bear no more. Dead: an old woman's: the grey sunken [**cunt**][3] of the world. (*LR*, 5:2 (Jun. 1918), p. 44; MS, 4. Calypso, p. 7; *U*, pp. 60–1) – Ezra Pound

8.   He felt heavy, full: then a gentle loosening [**of his bowels**]. He stood up
[**, undoing the waistband of his trousers**]. ...
            [**A paper. He liked to read at stool.**]
            In the table drawer he found an old number of *Titbits*. He folded it
under his armpit, went to the door and opened it. ...
            He went out [**through the backdoor**] into the garden ... .
            [**He kicked open the door of the jakes. Better be careful not to get
these trousers dirty for the funeral. He went in, bowing his head under
the low lintel. Leaving the door ajar, amid the stench of mouldy limewash and stale cobwebs he undid his braces. Before sitting down he
peered through a chink up at the nextdoor window. Nobody.**]
            [**Asquat on the cuckstool he folded out his paper, turning its pages
over on his bared knees.**] Something new and easy. Our prize titbit.
Matcham's Masterstroke. Written by Mr. Philip Beaufoy ... .
            [**He allowed his bowels to ease themselves quietly as he read, reading
patiently.**] Life might be so. It did not move or touch him but it was something quick and neat. He read on. Neat certainly. Matcham often thinks of
the masterstroke by which he won the laughing witch who now. Hand in
hand. Smart. He glanced back through what he had read ... .
            [**He tore away half the prize story sharply and wiped himself with it.
Then he girded up his trousers, braced and buttoned himself. He
pulled back the shaky door of the jakes and came forth from the gloom
into the air.**] (*LR*, 5:2 (Jun. 1918), pp. 50–1; MS, 4. Calypso, pp. 14–17; *U*,
pp. 67–70) – Ezra Pound

Episode V ('Lotus-Eaters')

9.   He came nearer and heard a crunching of gilded oats, the gently
champing teeth. **Their full buck eyes regarded him as he went by, amid
the sweet oaten reek of horsepiss.** ... Damn all they know or care about
anything with their long noses stuck in nosebags. Too full for words. ...
**Gelded too: a stump of black guttapercha wagging limp between their
haunches.** Might be happy all the same that way. (*U*, p. 77) – Asst US
Attorney Sam Coleman[4]

10.   Enjoy a bath now ... . He foresaw his pale body reclined in it at full, naked,
oiled by scented melting soap, softly laved. He saw his trunk and limbs
riprippled over and sustained, buoyed lightly upward, lemonyellow [**: saw
the dark tangled curls of his bush floating, floating hair of the stream
around a languid floating flower**]. (*LR*, 5:3 (Jul. 1918), p. 49; MS, 5. Lotus
Eaters, p. 15; *U*, p. 86) – Ezra Pound and/or Margaret Anderson

Episode VI ('Hades')

No censored passages

Episode VII ('Aeolus')

No censored passages

Episode VIII ('Lestrygonians')

11.   Pages 27–50, *LR*, 5:9 (Jan. 1919); (*U*, pp. 151–79) – US Post Office

12.   All kind of places are good for ads. That quack doctor for the clap used to be stuck up in all the greenhouses. ... Strictly confidential. Dr Hy Franks. ... Just the place too. POST NO BILLS. POST 110 PILLS. **Some chap with a dose burning him.** (*U*, p. 153) – Asst US Attorney Sam Coleman

13.   Before the huge high door of the Irish house of parliament a flock of pigeons flew. ... **Who will we do it on? I pick the fellow in black. Here goes. Here's good luck. Must be thrilling from the air.** Apjohn, myself and Owen Goldberg up in the trees near Goose green playing the monkeys. (*U*, p. 162) – Asst US Attorney Sam Coleman

14.   Dignam's potted meat. Cannibals would with lemon and rice. White missionary too salty. Like pickled pork. Expect the chief consumes the parts of honour. Ought to be tough from exercise. His wives in a row to watch the effect. **There was a right royal old nigger. Who ate or something the somethings of the reverend Mr MacTrigger.** ...
        Mr Bloom cut his sandwich into slender strips. *Mr MacTrigger. ... His five hundred wives. Had the time of their lives.*
        —Mustard, sir?
        —Thank you.
        He studded under each lifted strip yellow blobs. Their lives. I have it. It grew bigger and bigger and bigger. (*U*, pp. 171–2) – Asst US Attorney Sam Coleman

15.   Stuck on the pane two flies buzzed, stuck.
        Glowing wine on his palate lingered swallowed. Crushing in the winepress grapes of Burgundy. Sun's heat it is. Seems to a secret touch telling me memory. Touched his sense moistened remembered. ... O wonder! Coolsoft with ointments her hand touched me, caressed: her eyes upon me did not turn away. **Ravished over her I lay, full lips full open, kissed her mouth. Yum. Softly she gave me in my mouth the seedcake warm and chewed. Mawkish pulp her mouth had mumbled sweet and sour with spittle. Joy: I ate it: joy.** Young life, her lips that gave me pouting. **Soft, warm, sticky gumjelly lips. Flowers her eyes were, take me, willing eyes. Pebbles fell. She lay still. A goat. No-one. High on Ben Howth rhododendrons a nannygoat walking surefooted, dropping currants.** Screened under ferns she laughed warmfolded. **Wildly I lay on her, kissed her; eyes, her lips, her stretched neck, beating, woman's breasts full in her blouse of nun's veiling, fat nipples upright. Hot I tongued her. She kissed me. I was kissed. All yielding she tossed my hair.** Kissed, she kissed me.
        Me. And me now.
        Stuck, the flies buzzed. (*U*, pp. 175–6) – Asst US Attorney Sam Coleman

16.   Page 173, RH 1934; (*U*, pp. 175–6) – US Attorney Martin Conboy[5]; Judge Martin Manton[6]

17. Page 60, *LR*, 5:10–11 (Feb.–Mar. 1919); (*U*, pp. 181–2) – Unidentified Official, Translation Bureau, United States Post Office.[7]

Episode IX ('Scylla and Charybdis')

18. Pages 17–35, *LR*, 6:1 (May 1919); (*U*, pp. 197–218) – US Post Office

19. Mrs Cooper Oakley once glimpsed our very illustrations sister H.P.B's elemental.
    O, fie! Out on't! *Pfuiteufel!* **You naughtn't to look, missus, so you naughtn't when a lady's ashowing of her elemental.** (*U*, pp. 185–6) – Asst US Attorney Sam Coleman

20. **—And we to be there, mavrone, and you to be unbeknownst sending us your conglomerations the way we to have our tongues out a yard long like the drouthy clerics do be fainting for a pussful.** (*U*, p. 199) – Asst US Attorney Sam Coleman

21. —The tramper Synge is looking for you, he said, to murder you. He heard you [**pissed**][8] on his halldoor at Glasthule. He's out in pampoe ties to murder you.
    —Me! Stephen exclaimed. That was your contribution to literature. (*LR*, 6:1 (May 1919), p. 19; MS, 9. Scylla and Charybdis, p. 18; *U*, p. 200) – Margaret Anderson

22. The gombeen woman Eliza Tudor had underlinen enough to vie with her of Sheba. **Twenty years he [Shakespeare] dallied there between conjugal love and its chaste delights and scortatory love and its foul pleasures.** (*U*, p. 201) – Asst US Attorney Sam Coleman

23. Love that dare not speak its name.
    —As an Englishman, you mean, … he [Shakespeare] loved a lord. …
    —It seems so, Stephen said, [**when he wants to do for him, and for all other and singular uneared wombs, the office an ostler does for the stallion**].[9] (*LR*, 6:1 (May 1919), p. 21; MS, 9. Scylla and Charybdis, p. 20; *U*, p. 202) – Margaret Anderson

24. Who is the father of any son that any son should love him or he any son?…
    —They are sundered by bodily shame so steadfast that the criminal annals of the world, stained with all other incests and bestialities, do not record its breach: [**Sons with mothers, sires with daughters, nephews with grandmothers, queens with prize bulls.**][10] (*LR*, 6:1 (May 1919), p. 26; MS, 9. Scylla and Charybdis, pp. 25–6; *U*, pp. 207) – Margaret Anderson

25. **—They are sundered by a bodily shame so steadfast that the criminal annals of the world, stained with all other incests and bestialities, hardly record its breach. Sons with mothers, sires with daughters,**

lesbic sisters, loves that dare not speak their name, nephews with grandmothers, jailbirds with keyholes, queens with prize bulls. (*U*, p. 207) – Asst US Attorney Sam Coleman

26.

> *I hardly hear the purlieu cry*
> *Or a Tommy talk as I pass one by*
> *Before my thoughts begin to run*
> *On F. M'Curdy Atkinson,*
> *The same that had the wooden leg*
> *And that filibustering fillibeg*
> *That never dared to slake his drouth,*
> *Magee that had the chinless mouth.*
> **Being afraid to marry on earth**
> **They masturbated for all they were worth.**

(*U*, p. 216) – Asst US Attorney Sam Coleman

27. Page 213, RH 1934; (*U*, p. 216) – US Attorney Martin Conboy; Judge Martin Manton

28.

> *Everyman His Own Wife*
> [*or*
> *A Honeymoon in the Hand*]
> (*a national immorality in three orgasms*)
> *by*
> *Ballocky Mulligan*

(*LR*, 6:1 (May 1919), p. 34); MS, 9. Scylla and Charybdis, p. 35; *U*, p. 216) – Margaret Anderson

29.

> **Everyman His own Wife**
> *or*
> **A Honeymoon in the Hand**
> (*a national immorality in three orgasms*)
> *by*
> **Ballocky Mulligan**
> (*U*, p. 216) – Asst US Attorney Sam Coleman

30. **—O, the night in the Camden hall when the daughters of Erin had to lift their skirts to step over you as you lay in your mulberrycoloured, multicoloured, multitudinous vomit!**
—The most innocent son of Erin, Stephen said, for whom they ever lifted them. (*U*, p. 217) – Asst US Attorney Sam Coleman

31. Page 214, RH 1934; (*U*, pp. 215–17) – US Attorney Martin Conboy; Judge Martin Manton

Episode X ('Wandering Rocks')

32.   Pages 231–3, RH 1934; (*U*, pp. 234–7) – US Attorney Martin Conboy

Episode XI ('Sirens')

No censored passages

Episode XII ('Cyclops')

33.   So they started talking about capital punishment ... .
—There's one thing it hasn't a deterrent effect on, says Alf.[11]
[—What's that? says Joe.
—The poor bugger's tool that's being hanged, says Alf.
—That so? says Joe.
—God's truth, says Alf. I heard that from the head warder that was in
Kilmainham when they hanged Joe Brady, the invincible. He told me
when they cut him down after the drop it was standing up in their faces
like a poker.
—Ruling passion strong in death, says Joe[.]
—That can be explained by science, says Bloom. It's only a natural
phenomenon, don't you see, because on account of the ... [ellipsis
Joyce's]
And then he starts with his jawbreakers about phenomenon and
science and this phenomenon and the other phenomenon.
The distinguished scientist Herr Professor Luitpold Blumenduft tendered medical evidence to the effect that the instantaneous fracture of
the cervical vertebrae and consequent scission of the spinal cord
would, according to the best approved tradition of medical science, be
calculated to produce in the human subject a violent ganglionic stimulus of the nerve centres of the genital apparatus, thereby causing the
elastic pores of the *corpora cavernosa* to rapidly dilate in such a way as
to facilitate the flow of blood to that part of the human anatomy known
as the penis or male organ resulting in the phenomenon which has
been denominated by the faculty a morbid upwards and outwards
philoprogenitive erection *in articulo mortis per diminutionem capitis.*]
(*LR*, 6:7 (Nov. 1919), p. 49; MS, 12. Cyclops, pp. 17–18; *U*, pp. 304–5) –
Margaret Anderson

34.   —The poor bugger's tool that's being hanged, says Alf.
—That so? says Joe.
—God's truth, says Alf. I heard that from the head warder that was in
Kilmainham when they hanged Joe Brady, the invincible. He told me
when they cut him down after the drop it was standing up in their faces
like a poker.
—Ruling passion strong in death, says Joe, as someone said.
...
—The distinguished scientist Herr Professor Luitpold Blumenduft
tendered medical evidence to the effect that the instantaneous fracture

of the cervical vertebrae ... would ... be calculated to inevitably produce in the human subject a violent ganglionic stimulus of the nerve centres, **causing the pores of the *corpora cavernosa* to rapidly dilate in such a way as to instantaneously facilitate the flow of blood to that part of the human anatomy known as the penis or male organ resulting in the phenomenon which has been dominated by the faculty a morbid upwards and outwards philoprogenitive erection *in articulo mortis per diminutionem capitis.*** (*U*, pp. 304–5) – Asst US Attorney Sam Coleman

35.   Phenomenon! The fat heap he married is a nice old phenomenon with a back on her like a ballalley. **Time they were stopping up in the *City Arms* Pisser Burke told me there was an old one there with a cracked loodheramaun of a nephew and Bloom trying to get the soft side of her** doing the mollycoddle playing bézique to come in for a bit of the wampum in her will ... . (*U*, pp. 305–6) – Asst US Attorney Sam Coleman

36.   **Jesus, I had to laugh at Pisser Burke taking them off chewing the fat and Bloom with his *but don't you see?* and *but on the other hand.*** (*U*, p. 306) – Asst US Attorney Sam Coleman

37.   **Gob, Jack made him toe the line. Told him if he didn't patch up the pot, Jesus, he'd kick the shite out of him.** (*U*, p. 314) – Asst US Attorney Sam Coleman

38.   ... Mrs O'Dowd crying her eyes out ... . Couldn't loosen her farting strings but old cod's eye [Bloom] was waltzing around her showing her how to do it. What's your programme today? Ay. Humane methods. Because the poor animals suffer ... and **the best known remedy that doesn't cause pain to the animal and on the sore spot administer gently. Gob, he'd have a soft hand under a hen.** (*U*, p. 315) – Asst US Attorney Sam Coleman

39.   **I declare to my antimacassar if you took up a straw from the bloody floor and if you said to Bloom: *Look at, Bloom. Do you see that straw? That's a straw.* Declare to my aunt he'd talk about it for an hour so he would and talk steady.** (*U*, p. 316) – Asst US Attorney Sam Coleman[12]

40.   —Still, says Bloom, on account of the poor woman, I mean his wife.
      —Pity about her, says the citizen. Or any other woman marries a half and half. ... A fellow that's neither fish nor flesh.
      —Nor good red herring, says Joe.
      —**That's what I mean, says the citizen. A pishogue, if you know what that is.** (*U*, p. 321) – Asst US Attorney Sam Coleman

41.   —A dishonoured wife, says the citizen, that's what's the cause of all our misfortunes.
      —And here she is, says Alf, that was giggling over the *Police Gazette* ..., in all her warpaint.
      —**Give us a squint at her, says I.**

And what was it only one of the smutty yankee pictures Terry borrows off of Corny Kelleher. Secrets for enlarging your private parts. Misconduct of society belle. Norman W. Tupper, wealthy Chicago contractor, finds pretty but faithless wife in lap of officer Taylor. (*U*, p. 324) – Asst US Attorney Sam Coleman

42.   Page 318, RH 1934; (*U*, pp. 323–4) – US Attorney Martin Conboy

43.   So J. J. puts in a word doing the toff about … the Nelson policy … and drawing up a bill of attainder to impeach a nation and Bloom trying to back him up moderation … and their colonies and their civilisation.
       —Their syphilisation, you mean, says the citizen. To hell with them! The curse of a goodfornothing God light sideways on the bloody thick-lugged sons of whores' gets! No music and no art and no literature worthy of the name. Any civilization they have they stole from us. Tonguetied sons of bastards' ghosts. (*U*, p. 325) – Asst US Attorney Sam Coleman

44.   —The European family, says J. J. … [Joyce's ellipses]
       —They're not European, says the citizen. … **You wouldn't see a trace of them or their language anywhere in Europe except in a [*cabinet d'aisance*].**[13] (*U*, p. 325) – Asst US Attorney Sam Coleman

45.   Pages 53–61, *LR*, 6:9 (Jan. 1920) – US Post Office

46.   **And he took the last swig out of the pint, Moya. All wind and piss like a tanyard cat.** (*U*, p. 328) – Asst US Attorney Sam Coleman

47.   **—The French! says the citizen. Set of dancing masters! Do you know what it is? They [were never worth a roasted fart to Ireland].**[14] **Aren't they trying to make an *Entente cordiale* now at Tay Pay's dinnerparty with perfidious Albion? Firebrands of Europe and they always were?…**
       —And as for the Prooshians and the Hanoverians, says Joe, haven't we had enough of those sausageeating bastards on the throne from George the elector down to the … flatulent old bitch that's dead?
       Jesus, I had to laugh at the way he came out with that about the old one with the winkers on her blind drunk in her royal palace every night of God, old Vic, with her jorum of mountain dew and her coach-man carting her up body and bones to roll into bed and she pulling him by the whiskers and singing him old bits of songs about *Ehren on the Rhine* and come where the boose is cheaper.
       —Well! says J. J. We have Edward the peacemaker now.
       —Tell that to a fool, says the citizen. There's a bloody sight more pox than pax about that boyo. Edward Guelph-Wettin!
       —And what do you think, says Joe, of the holy boys, the priests and bishops of Ireland doing up his room in Maynooth in his Satanic Majesty's racing colours and sticking up pictures of all the horses his jockeys rode. …
       —They ought to have stuck up all the women he rode himself. …
       —Considerations of space influenced their lordship's decision. (*U*, pp. 330–1) – Asst US Attorney Sam Coleman

48.   —What is your nation if I may ask, says the citizen.
       —Ireland, says Bloom. I was born here. Ireland.
       —The citizen said nothing only cleared the spit out of his gullet and,
       gob, he spat a Red bank oyster out of him right in the corner. (*U*, p. 331)
       – Asst US Attorney Sam Coleman

49.   His Majesty the Alaki of Abeakuta ... treasured as one of his dearest pos-
       sessions an illuminated bible, the volume of the word of God and the
       secret of England's greatness, graciously presented to him by ... the great
       squaw Victoria ... .
       — ... Wonder did he put that Bible to the same use as I would.
       —Same only more so, says Lenehan. And thereafter in that fruitful
       land the broadleaved mango flourished exeedingly. (*U*, p. 334) – Asst
       US Attorney Sam Coleman

50.   **Goodbye Ireland I'm going to Gort. So I just went round to the back**
       of the yard to pumpship and begob ... while I was letting off my ... load
       gob says I to myself I knew he was uneasy ... in his mind to get off the
       mark ... and when they were in the (dark horse) **Pisser Burke was telling**
       me card party and letting on the child was sick (**gob, must have done**
       about a gallon) flabbyarse of a wife speaking down the tube *she's better*
       or *she's* (ow!) all a plan so he could vamoose with the pool if he won ... .
       (*U*, p. 335) – Asst US Attorney Sam Coleman

51.   —O, by God, says Ned, you should have seen Bloom before that son of
       his that died was born. I met him one day in the south city markets
       buying a tin of Neave's food six weeks before the wife was delivered.
       —*En ventre sa mère*, says J. J.
       —Do you call that a man? says the citizen.
       —I wonder did he ever put it out of sight, says Joe.
       —Well, there were two children born anyhow, says Jack Power.
       —And who does he suspect? says the citizen.
       Gob, there's many a true word spoken in jest. One of those mixed
       middlings he is. Lying up in the hotel Pisser was telling me once a
       month with headache like a totty with her courses. (*U*, p. 338) – Asst US
       Attorney Sam Coleman

52.   —I was just round at the courthouse, says he [Bloom], looking for you.
       I hope I'm not ... [Joyce's ellipses]
       —No, says Martin, we're ready.
       Courthouse my eye and your pockets hanging down with gold and
       silver. **Mean bloody scut. Stand us a drink itself. Devil a sweet fear!**
       There's a jew for you! All for number one. Cute as a shithouse rat.
       (*U*, p. 341) – Asst US Attorney Sam Coleman

53.   I saw the citizen getting up to waddle to the door, ... and he cursing the
       curse of Cromwell on him [Bloom] ... .
       And begob he got as far as the door and they holding him and he bawls
       out of him:
       —Three cheers for Israel!
       Arrah, sit down on the parliamentary side of your arse for Christ'
       sake and don't be making a public exhibition of yourself. Jesus, there's

always some bloody clown or other kicking up a bloody murder about bloody nothing. ... and Jack Power trying to get him [Bloom] to ... hold his bloody jaw and a loafer with a patch over his eye starts singing *If the man in the moon was a jew, jew, jew* and a slut shouts out of her:
    —**Eh, mister! Your fly is open, mister!**
    And says he [Bloom]:
    —Mendelssohn was a jew and Karl Marx and Mercadante and Spinoza. And the Saviour was a jew and his father was a jew. Your God. (*U*, pp. 341–2) – Asst US Attorney Sam Coleman

Episode XIII ('Nausicaa')

54.   Pages 331–55, especially 349–50, P 1930; (*U*, pp. 346–72) – US Attorney Martin Conboy

55.   Pages 42–58, *LR*, 7:2 (Jul.–Aug. 1920); (*U*, pp. 365–82) – US Post Office

56.   Pages 359–64, RH 1934; (*U*, pp. 365–71) – US Attorney Martin Conboy

57.   Pages 42, 43, *LR*, 7:2 (Jul.–Aug. 1920); (*U*, pp. 365–7) – John Sumner[15]: Sumner took particular exception to the following passage:

> ... she knew about the passion of men like that, hotblooded, because Bertha Supple told her once in secret about the gentleman lodger that was staying with them ... that had pictures cut out of papers of those skirt-dancers and **she said he used to do something not very nice that you could imagine sometimes in the bed.**

58.   Page 43, *LR*, 7.2 (Jul.–Aug. 1920); (*U*, p. 365) – Father of the young woman[16]

59.   Page 359, RH 1934; (*U*, pp. 366–7) – Judge Martin Manton

60.   Page 44, *LR*, 7.2 (Jul.–Aug. 1920); (*U*, pp. 367–8) – John Sumner

61.   Page 361, RH 1934; (*U*, pp. 368–9) – Judge Martin Manton

62.   Page 45, *LR*, 7.2 (Jul.–Aug. 1920); (*U*, pp. 368–9) – Father of the young woman who received the unsolicited copy of the July–August 1920 number; John Sumner, who took particular exception to the bold passages below:

Hot little devil all the same. Near her monthlies, I expect, makes them feel ticklish. ... **Where did I put the letter?** ... All kinds of crazy longings. ... That's the moon. **But then why don't all women menstruate at the same time with same moon?** I mean. **Depends on the time they were born, I suppose.** Anyhow I got the best of that. ... Cheap too. **Yours for the asking.** Because they want it themselves. Shoals of them every evening poured out of offices. ... Pity they can't see themselves. A dream of wellfilled hose. ... Mutoscope pictures in Capel street: for men only. ... Do they snapshot those girls or is it all a fake. *Lingerie* does it. **Felt for the curves inside** *her deshabille.* **Excites them also when they're.** Molly.

Why I bought her the violet garters. ... Nuns with whitewashed faces, cool coifs and their rosaries going up and down, **vindictive too for what they can't get. ...**
Ah.
Devils they are when that's coming on them.

63.   Mutoscope pictures in Capel street: for men only. ... **Do they snapshot those girls or is it all a fake?** *Lingerie* **does it. Felt for the curves inside her** *deshabillé.* **Excites them also when they're. I'm all clean come and dirty me. ...**
Ah!
Devils they are when that's coming on them. Dark devilish appearance. Molly often told me feel things a ton weight. Scratch the sole of my foot. O that way! (*U,* pp. 368–9) – Asst US Attorney Sam Coleman

64.   Page 46, *LR,* 7.2 (Jul.–Aug. 1920); (*U,* pp. 369–70) – John Sumner, who objected in particular to the bold portions of the following passage. Ezra Pound had already expurgated '**wet**' from before 'shirt' in the first sentence of the last paragraph.[17]

Scratch the sole of my foot. O that way! O, that's exquisite! Feel it myself too. Good to rest once in a way. **Wonder if it's bad to go with them then. Safe in one way. Something about withering plants I read in a garden. Besides they say if the flower withers she wears she's flirt. ...** When you feel like that you often meet what you feel. ... Dress they look at. Always know a fellow courting: collars and cuffs. Same time might prefer a tie undone or something. Trousers? Suppose I when I was? No. **Gently does it. Dislike rough and tumble.** ... Saw something in me. Wonder what. ... Ought to attend to my appearance my age. ... Still, you never know. **Pretty girls and ugly men marrying.** ... Took off her hat to show her hair. ... **Ten bob I got for Molly's combings when we were on the rocks in Holles street. Why not? Suppose he gave her money. Why not? All a prejudice. She's worth ten, fifteen, more a pound.** ... I think so. **All that for nothing.** ... Funny my watch stopped at half past four. **Was that just when he, she?**
O, he did. Into her. She did. Done.
Ah.
Mr. Bloom with careful hand recomposed his [wet] shirt. O Lord, that little limping devil. Begins to feel cold and clammy. After effect not pleasant. They don't care. Complimented perhaps. ... The strength it gives a man. That's the secret of it. **Good job I let off there behind coming out of Dignam's. Cider that was.** Otherwise I couldn't have. Makes you want to sing after.

65.   Took off her hat to show her hair. **Wide brim bought to hide her face, meeting someone might know her, bend down or carry a bunch of flowers to smell. Hair strong in rut. Ten bob I got for Molly's combings when we were on the rocks in Holles street.** ... Funny my watch stopped at half past four. ... **Was that just when he, she?**
O, he did. Into her. She did. Done.
Ah!

Mr Bloom with careful hand recomposed his wet shirt. O Lord, that little limping devil. Begins to feel cold and clammy. Aftereffect not pleasant. Still you have to get rid of it someway. They don't care. ... **Still I feel. The strength it gives a man. That's the secret of it. Good job I let off there behind coming out of Dignam's. Cider that was. Otherwise I couldn't have.** Makes you want to sing after. ... (*U*, pp. 369–70) – Asst US Attorney Sam Coleman

66. Page 47, *LR*, 7.2 (Jul.–Aug. 1920); (*U*, pp. 370–2) – John Sumner, who objected especially to the bold portions of the passage below.

Suppose I spoke to her. ... Wonderful of course if you say: Good evening, and you see she's on for it: good evening. Girl in Meath street that night. All the dirty things I made her say. Parrots. Wish she hadn't called me sir. O, her mouth in the dark! And you a married man with a single girl. **That's what they enjoy. Taking a man from another woman. French letter still in my pocketbook.** But might happen sometime. I don't think. Come in. All is prepared. I dreamt. ... First kiss does the trick. ... Remember that till their dying day. Molly, lieutenant Mulvey that kissed her under the Moorish wall beside the gardens. **Fifteen she told me. But her breasts were developed. Fell asleep then.** ...
There she is with them down there for the fireworks. **My fireworks. Up like a rocket, down like a stick.**

67. Girl in Meath street that night. All the dirty things I made her say all wrong of course. ... **Parrots. Press the button and the bird will squeak. Wish she hadn't called me sir. O, her mouth in the dark! And you a married man with a single girl!** That's what they enjoy. Taking a man from another woman. ... (*U*, p. 370) – Asst US Attorney Sam Coleman

68. **There she is with them down there for the fireworks. My fireworks. Up like a rocket, down like a stick. And the children, twins they must be, waiting for something to happen.** (*U*, p. 371) – Asst US Attorney Sam Coleman

69. Page 48, *LR*, 7.2 (Jul.–Aug. 1920); (*U*, pp. 371–2) – John Sumner, who objected in particular to the bold portions of the following passage.

Didn't look back when she was going down the strand. ... **Did she know what I? Course. Like a cat sitting beyond a dog's jump.** Woman. Never meet one like that Wilkins in the high school drawing **a picture of Venus with all his belongings on show.** Call that innocence? Poor idiot! **His wife has her work cut out for her.** Sharp as needles they are. When I said to Molly the **man at the corner of Cuffe street was goodlooking, thought she might like, twigged at once he had a false arm.** Had too. Where they get that? ... Bred in the bone. Milly for example ... . Three years old she was in front of Molly's dressing-table ... . Me have a nice pace. ... Young student. Straight on her pins anyway not like the other. **Still she was game. Lord, I am wet. Devil you are. Swell of her calf.**

Transparent stockings, stretched to breaking point. Not like that frump today. A. E. Rumpled stockings. Or the one in Grafton street. **White. Wow! Beef to the heel.**

A monkey puzzle rocket burst ... . And Cissy and Tommy ran out see. ... and then Gerty beyond the curve of the rocks. Will she? Watch! Watch! See! Looked round. **She smelt an onion. Darling, I saw your. I saw all. Lord!**

Did me good all the same. ... **For this relief much thanks.**

70. Three years old she was in front of Molly's dressingtable ... . **Me have a nice face. Mullingar. Who knows? Ways of the world. Young student. Straight on her pins anyway not like the other. Still she was game. Lord, I am wet. Devil you are. Swell of her calf. Transparent stockings, stretched to breaking point.** (*U*, p. 372) – Asst US Attorney Sam Coleman

71. Always see a fellow's weak point in his wife. ... As God made them He matched them. **Sometimes children turn out well enough. Twice nought makes one. Or old rich chap of seventy and blushing bride. Marry in May and repent in December. This wet is very unpleasant. Stuck. Well the foreskin is not back. Better detach.**
Ow! (*U*, p. 373) – Asst US Attorney Sam Coleman

72. Page 50, *LR*, 7.2 (Jul.–Aug. 1920); (*U*, pp. 373–4) – Father of the young woman who received the unsolicited copy of the July–August 1920 number; John Sumner, who objected in particular to the highlighted portions of the following passage.

This wet is very unpleasant.
Ow!
...Very strange about my watch. Wonder is there any magnetic influence between the person **because that was about the time he.** Yes, I suppose at once. **Cat's away the mice will play.** ... Back of everything magnetism. ... **When you hold out the fork. Come. Come. Tip. Woman and man that is. Fork and steel.** Molly, he. Dress up and look and suggest and **let you see and see more and defy you if you're a man to see that and legs, look look and. Tip. Have to let fly.**
Wonder how she is feeling in that region. Shame all put on before third person. Molly, her underjaw stuck out, head back about the farmer in the ridingboots with the spurs. And when the painters were in Lombard street west. Smell that I did, like flowers. It was too. Violets. Came from the turpentine probably in the paint. Make their own use of everything. Same time doing it scraped her slipper on the floor so they wouldn't hear. **But lots of them can't kick the beam, I think. Keep that thing up for hours. Kind of a general all round over me and half down my back.**
Wait. Hm. Hm. Yes. That's her perfume. ... Why did I smell it only now? **Took its time in coming like herself, slow but sure.**

73. Page 357, P 1930; (*U*, p. 374) – US Attorney Martin Conboy

74.　　Back of everything magnetism. ... Magnetic needle tells you what's going on in the sun, the stars. Little piece of steel iron. When you hold out the fork. **Come. Come. Tip. Woman and man that is. Fork and steel. Molly, he. Dress up and look and suggest and let you see and see more and defy you if you're a man to see that and, like a sneeze coming, legs, look, look and if you have any guts in you. Tip. Have to let fly.**

　　　　Wonder how she is feeling in that region. Shame all put on before third person. More put out about a hole in her stocking. (*U*, p. 374) – Asst US Attorney Sam Coleman

75.　　Page 51, *LR*, 7.2 (Jul.–Aug. 1920); (*U*, pp. 374–5) – Father of the young woman who received the unsolicited copy of the July–August 1920 number; John Sumner, who complained in particular the bold portions of the passage below:

　　　　It's like a fine fine veil or web they have all over the skin fine like. ... gossamer **and they're always spinning it out of them, fine as anything, rainbow colours without knowing it. Clings to everything she takes off. Vamp of her stockings. Warm shoes. Stays. Drawers: little kick taking them off.** Byby till next time. **Also the cat likes to sniff in her shift on the bed.** Know her smell in a thousand. ... Wonder where it is really. **There or the armpits or under the neck.** Because you get it out of all holes and corners. ... Dogs at each other behind. Good evening. Evening. How do you sniff? Hm. Hm. Very well, thank you. Animals go by that. ... We're the same. **Some women for instance warn you off when they have their period. Come near. Then get a hogo you could hang your hat on. Like what? Potted herrings gone stale or. Boof! Please keep off the grass.**

　　　　Perhaps they get a man smell off us. What though? ... Breath? What you eat and drink gives that. No. **Mansmell, I mean. Must be connected with that because priests that are supposed to be are different. Women buzz round it like flies round treacle. O father, will you? Let me be the first to. That diffuses itself all through the body, permeates. Source of life. And it's extremely curious the smell. Celery sauce. Let me.**

　　　　Mr. Bloom inserted his nose. Hm. Into the. Hm. Opening of his waistcoat.

76.　　Dogs at each other behind. ... How do you sniff? Hm. Hm. Very well, thank you. **Animals go by that. Yes now, look at it that way. We're the same. Some women for instance warn you off when they have their period. Come near. Then get a hogo you could hang your hat on.** Like what? Potted herrings gone stale or. Boof! Please keep off the grass. (*U*, p. 375) – Asst US Attorney Sam Coleman

77.　　Page 53, *LR*, 7.2 (Jul.–Aug. 1920); (*U*, pp. 377–8) – John Sumner, who objected in particular to the bold portions of the passage below.

　　　　All quiet on Howth now. ... Where we. The rhododendrons. I am a fool perhaps. **He gets the plums and I the leavings.** All that old hill has seen. Names change: that's all. Lover's: yum, yum.

　　　　Tired I feel now. Drained all the manhood out of me, little wretch. She kissed me. My youth. Never again. Only once it comes. Or hers. Take the train there tomorrow. No. Returning not the same. **Like kids your second visit to a house. The new I want.** ... At Dolphin's barn charades in Luke Doyle's house. ... Rip van Winkle we played. ... Then I did Rip van Winkle coming back. She leaned on the sideboard watching. Moorish eyes. Twenty years asleep. All changed. Forgotten. The young are old. **His gun rusty from the dew.**

78.   **Tired I feel now. Will I get up? O wait. Drained all the manhood out of me, little wretch. She kissed me. My youth.** Never again. Only once it comes. (*U*, p. 377) – Asst US Attorney Sam Coleman

79.   Page 55, *LR*, 7.2 (Jul.–Aug. 1920); (*U*, pp. 379–80) – John Sumner, who objected particularly to the bold portions of the following passage.

   Day we went out in the Erin's King ... . Bears in the zoo. Filthy trip. Drunkards out to shake up their livers. Puking overboard to feed the herrings. Nausea. And the women, fear of God in their faces. Milly, no sign of her funk. ... Don't know what death is at that age. **And then their stomachs clean.** ... Loved to count my waist coat buttons. **Her first stays I remember.** Made me laugh to see. **Little paps to begin with. Left one is more sensitive, I think. Mine too. Nearer the heart.** Her growing pains at night, calling, wakening me. **Frightened she was when her nature came on her first.** Poor child!

80.   Page 57, *LR*, 7.2 (Jul.–Aug. 1920); (*U*, pp. 381–2) – John Sumner, who objected in particular to the bold portions of the passages below.

   O! Exhausted that female has me. Not so young now. Will she come here tomorrow? Will I?...
   ...We'll never meet again. **But it was lovely.** Goodbye, dear. **Made me feel so young.**
   Short snooze now if I had. And she can do the other. Did too.

81.   **O! Exhausted that female has me. Not so young now. Will she come here tomorrow? Wait for her somewhere for ever. Must come back. Murderers do. Will I?** (*U*, p. 381) – Asst US Attorney Sam Coleman

82.   **O sweety all your little girlwhite up I saw dirty bracegirdle made me do love sticky we two naughty Grace darling she him half past the bed met him pike hoses frillies for Raoul to perfume your wife black hair heave under embon** *señorita* **young eyes Mulvey plump years dreams return tail end Agendath swoony lovey showed me her next year in drawers return next in her next her next.** (*U*, p. 382) – Asst US Attorney Sam Coleman

Episode XIV ('Oxen of the Sun')

83.   Page 367, P 1930; (*U*, pp. 383–4) – US Attorney Martin Conboy

84.   **Before born babe bliss had. Within womb won he worship. Whatever in that one case done commodiously done was.** (*U*, 384) – Asst US Attorney Sam Coleman

85.   **Young Stephen said indeed to his best remembrance they** [Beaumont and Fletcher] **had but the one doxy between them and she of the stews**

to make shift with in delights amorous for life ran very high in those days and the custom of the country approved with it. Greater love than this, he said, no man hath that a man lay down his wife for his friend. Go thou and do likewise. (*U*, p. 393) – Asst US Attorney Sam Coleman

86.   ... he [Boasthard] fell in with a certain whore of an eyepleasing exterior whose name, she said, is Bird-in-the-Hand and she beguiled him wrongways from the true path by her flatteries that she said to him as, Ho, you pretty man, turn aside hither and I will show you a brave place, and she lay at him so flatteringly that she had him in her grot which is named Two-in-the-Bush or, by some learned, Carnal Concupiscence. (*U*, pp. 395–6) – Asst US Attorney Sam Coleman

87.   ... for that foul plague Allpox and the monsters they cared not for them, for Preservative had given them [a stout shield of oxengut][18] and ... that they might take no hurt neither from Offspring that was that wicked devil by virtue of this same shield which was named Killchild. (*U*, p. 396) – Asst US Attorney Sam Coleman

88.   It is that same bull that was sent to our island by farmer Nicholas ... with an emerald ring in his nose. True for you, says Mr Vincent ..., and a plumper and portlier bull, says he, [never shit on shamrock].[19] ... What for that, says Mr Dixon, but before he came over farmer Nicholas that was a eunuch had him properly gelded ... . So be off now, says he, and do all my cousin german the Lord Harry tells you and take a farmer's blessing, and with that he slapped his posteriors very soundly. But the slap and the blessing stood him friend, says Mr Vincent, for to make up he taught him a trick worth two of the other so that maid, wife, abbess and widow to this day affirm that they would rather any time of the month whisper in his ear in the dark of a cowhouse or get a lick on the nape from his long holy tongue th[a]n lie with the finest strapping young ravisher in the four fields of all Ireland. Another then put in his word: And they dressed him, says he, in a point shift and petticoat ... and rubbed him all over with spermacetic oil and built stables for him at every turn of the road with a gold manger in each full of the best hay in the market so that he could doss and dung to his heart's content. By this time the father of the faithful (for so they called him) was grown so heavy that he could scarce walk to pasture. ... Ay, says another, and so pampered was he that he would suffer nought to grow in all the land but green grass for himself ... . And, says Mr Dixon, if he ever got scent of ... a husbandman in Sligo that was growing as much as a handful of mustard ... out he run ... rooting up with his horns whatever was planted and all by lord Harry's orders. There was bad blood between them at first, says Mr Vincent, and the lord Harry called farmer Nicholas all the old Nicks in the world and an old whoremaster that kept seven trulls in his house and I'll meddle in his matters, says he. I'll make that animal smell hell, says he, with the help of that [good pizzle][20] my father left me. But one evening, says Mr Dixon, ... he discovered in himself a wonderful likeness to a bull ... . In short he and the bull of Ireland were soon as fast friends [as an arse and a shirt.][21] They were, says Mr Stephen, and the end was that the men of the island, seeing

no help was toward as the ungrate women were all of one mind, ... put
to sea to recover the main of America. Which was the occasion, says
Mr Vincent, of the composing by a boatswain of that rollicking chanty:
    –Pope Peter's but a pissabed.
    A man's a man for a' that. (*U*, pp. 399–401) – Asst US Attorney Sam
Coleman

89.   Pages 382–3, P 1930; (*U*, pp. 400–2) – US Attorney Martin Conboy

90.   ... he [Buck Mulligan] had resolved to purchase ... Lambay Island .... **He
       proposed to set up there a national fertilising farm to be named**
       Omphalos **with an obelisk hewn and erected after the fashion of Egypt
       and to offer his dutiful yeoman services for the fecundation of any
       female of what grade of life soever who should there direct to him with
       the desire of fulfilling the functions of her natural.** ... His project ... was
       very favourably entertained ... though Mr Dixon ... excepted to it, asking
       with a finicking air did he purpose also to carry coals to Newcastle. Mr
       Mulligan however made court to the scholarly by an apt quotation from
       the classics which ... seemed to him a sound and tasteful support of his
       contention: *Talis ac tanta depravatio hujus seculi, O quirites, ut matres
       familiarum nostrae lascivas cujuslibet semiviri libici titillationes testibus
       ponderosis atque [excelsis erectionibus]*[22] *centurionum Romanorum
       magnopere anteponunt*: while for those of ruder wit he drove home his point
       by analogies of the animal kingdom more suitable to their stomach, the
       buck and doe of the forest glade, the farmyard drake and duck.
           ... **Mr Dixon, to turn the table, took on to ask Mr Mulligan himself
       whether his incipient ventripotence ... betokened an ovoblastic gestation
       in the prostatic utricle or male womb** or was due ... **to a wolf in the
       stomach. For answer Mr Mulligan, in a gale of laughter at his smalls,
       smote himself bravely below the diaphragm, exclaiming with an
       admirable droll mimic of Mother Grogan (the most excellent creature of
       her sex though 'tis pity she's a trollop):** There's a belly that never bore a
       bastard. (*U*, pp. 402–4) – Asst US Attorney Sam Coleman

91.   Pages 398–9, RH 1934; (*U*, pp. 404–6) – US Attorney Martin Conboy

92.   Ah, Monsieur, he said, had you but beheld her as I did ... . I declare, I
       was never so touched in all my life. ... Would to God that foresight had
       remembered me to take my cloak along! ... Then, though it had poured
       seven showers, we were neither of us a penny the worse. But beshrew
       me, he cried, clapping hand to his forehead, tomorrow will be a new day
       and, thousand thunders, **I know of a** *marchand de capotes*, **Monsieur
       Poyntz, from whom I can have for a livre as sung a cloak of the [French
       fashion as ever kept a lady]**[23] **from wetting.** Tut, Tut! cries le
       Fécondateur, ... my friend Monsieur Moore ... is my authority that in
       Cape Horn, *ventre biche*, they have a rain that will wet through any, even
       the stoutest cloak. **A drenching of that violence ... has sent more than
       one luckless fellow in good earnest posthaste to another world. Pooh! A
       livre! cries Monsieur Lynch. The clumsy things are dear at a sou.** One
       umbrella, were it no bigger than a fairy mushroom, is worth ten such
       stopgaps. **No woman of any wit would wear one. My dear Kitty told me**

today that she would dance in a deluge before ever she would starve in such an ark of salvation for, as she reminded me (blushing piquantly ...), dame Nature, by the divine blessing, has implanted it in our heart and it has become a household word that *il y a deux choses* for which the innocence of our original garb, in other circumstances a breach of the proprieties, is the fittest nay, the only, garment. The first ... is a bath ... [ellipses Joyce's] but at this point a bell tinkling in the hall cut short a discourse which promised so bravely for the enrichment of our store of knowledge. (*U*, pp. 404–5) – Asst US Attorney Sam Coleman

93. I must acquaint you, said Mr Crothers, ... old Glory Allelujerum was round again to-day, an elderly man ..., preferring through his nose a request to have word of Wilhelmina, my life, as he calls her. ... 'Slife, I'll be round with you. I cannot but extol the virile potency of the old bucko that could still knock another child out of her. All fell to praising of it, each after his own fashion ... . (*U*, p. 408) – Asst US Attorney Sam Coleman

94. Singular, communed the guest with himself, ... that the puerperal dormitory and the dissecting theatre should be the seminaries of such frivolity ... .
     But with what fitness ... has this alien ... constituted himself the lord paramount of our internal polity? ... Has he forgotten ... all benefits received? Or is it that from being a deluder of others he has become at last his own dupe as he is, if report belie him not his own and his only enjoyer? ... He says this, a censor of morals, ... who did not scruple ... to attempt illicit intercourse with a female domestic ... . It ill becomes him to preach that gospel. Has he not nearer home a seedfield that lies fallow for the want of a ploughshare? [A habit reprehensible at puberty][24] is second nature and an opprobium in middle life. If he must dispense his balm of Gilead ... let his practice consist better with the doctrines that now engross him. ... this new exponent of morals and healer of ills is at his best an exotic tree which, when rooted in its native orient, throve and flourished and was abundant in balm but, transplanted to a clime more temperate, its roots have lost their quondam vigour while the stuff that comes away from it is stagnant, acid and inoperative. (*U*, pp 408–10) – Asst US Attorney Sam Coleman

95. The gravest problems of obstetrics and forensic medicine were examined ... . The abnormalities of harelip, breastmole ... were alleged by one as a ... hypothetical explanation of swineheaded ... or doghaired infants ... . An outlandish delegate sustained ... the theory of copulation between women and the males of brutes ... . The impression made by his words ... was effaced as easily as it had been evoked by an allocution from Mr Candidate Mulligan ... postulating as the supremest object of desire a nice clean old man. (*U*, p. 411) – Asst US Attorney Sam Coleman

96. I wish you could have seen my queen today, Vincent said, how young she was and radiant ... . she had nought for her teeth but the arm with which I held her and in that she nibbled mischievously when I pressed too close. A week ago she lay ill, four days on the couch, but today she

was free, blithe, mocked at peril. She is more taking then. Her posies too! Mad romp that it is, she had pulled her fill as we reclined together. (*U*, pp. 415–16) – Asst US Attorney Sam Coleman

97. Theodore Purefoy, thou … art … the remarkablest progenitor … . Toil on, … and let … all Malthusiasts go hang. … [**Copulation without population!**]²⁵ No, say I! Herod's slaughter of the innocents were the truer name. (*U*, p. 423) – Asst US Attorney Sam Coleman²⁶

98. Mulligan! Abaft there! Shove ahead. **Keep a watch on the clock. Chuckingout time. Mullee! What's on you?** *Ma mère m'a mariée.* **British Beatitudes!** *Ratamplan Digidi Boum Boum.* **Ayes have it.** To be printed and bound at the Druiddrum press by two designing females. Calf covers of pissedon green. … March! **Tramp, tramp the boys are (attitudes!) parching. Beer, beef, business, bibles, bulldogs, battleships, buggery and bishops. Whether on the scaffold high. Beerbeef trample the bibles. When for Irelandear. Trample the trampellers. Thunderation!** (*U*, pp. 424–5) – Asst US Attorney Sam Coleman

99. Got a pectoral trauma, eh, Dix? Pos fact. **Got bet be a boomblebee whenever he was settin sleepin in hes bit garten. Digs up near the Mater. Buckled he is. Know his dona? Yup, sartin, I do. Full of a dure. See her in her dishybilly. Peels off a credit. Lovey lovekin. None of your lean kine, not much. Pull down the blind, love. Two Ardilauns. Same here. Look slippery.** (*U*, p. 425) – Asst US Attorney Sam Coleman

100. **Every cove to his gentry mort. Venus Pandemos.** *Les petites femmes.* **Bold bad girl from the town of Mullingar. Tell her I was axing at her. Hauding Sara by the wame. On the road to Malahide. Me?** (*U*, pp. 425–6) – Asst US Attorney Sam Coleman

101. What's he got? **Jubilee mutton. Bovril, by James. Wants it real bad. D'ye ken bare socks? Seedy cuss in the Richmond? Rawthere!** [**Thought he had a deposit of lead in his penis.**]²⁷ (*U*, p. 427) – Asst US Attorney Sam Coleman

Episode XV ('Circe')

102. Page 408, P 1930; (*U*, p. 429) – US Attorney Martin Conboy

103. Pages 423, 424, RH 1934; (*U*, pp. 430–1) – US Attorney Martin Conboy; Judge Martin Manton.

104. STEPHEN: **We have shrewridden Shakespeare and henpecked Socrates. Even the allwisest stagyrite was bitted, bridled and mounted by a light of love.** (*U*, p. 432) – Asst US Attorney Sam Coleman

105. *The navvy, swaying, presses a forefinger against a wing of his nose and ejects from the farther nostril [a long liquid jet of snot].*²⁸ (*U*, p. 433) – Asst US Attorney Sam Coleman

106.   THE MOTORMAN: **Hey, shitbreeches, are you doing the hattrick?** (*U*, p. 435) – Asst US Attorney Sam Coleman

107.   BLOOM: ... **Mark of the beast.** (*He closes his eyes an instant.*) **Bit light in the head. Monthly or effect of the other. Brainfogfag. That tired feeling. Too much for me now. Ow!** (*U*, p. 436) – Asst US Attorney Sam Coleman

108.   THE BAWD: **Ten shillings a maidenhead. Fresh thing was never touched. Fifteen. There's no-one in it only her old father that's dead drunk.** (*U*, p. 441) – Asst US Attorney Sam Coleman

109.   Page 434, RH 1934; *U*, pp. 441–2) – US Attorney Martin Conboy; Judge Martin Manton.

110.   THE BAWD: (*Her wolfeyes shining.*) **He's getting his pleasure. You won't get a virgin in the flash houses. Ten shillings. Don't be all night before the polis in plain clothes sees us. Sixtyseven is a bitch.** (*Leering, Gerty MacDowell limps forward. She draws from behind ogling, and shows coyly her bloodied clout.*) (*U*, p. 442) – Asst US Attorney Sam Coleman

111.   BLOOM: (*Meaningfully dropping his voice.*) **I confess I'm teapot with curiosity to find out whether some person's something is a little teapot at present.** (*U*, p. 445) – Asst US Attorney Sam Coleman

112.   MRS BREEN: (*To Bloom.*) **High jinks below stairs.** (*She gives him the glad eye.*) **Why didn't you kiss the spot to make it well? You wanted to.** (*U*, p. 446) – Asst US Attorney Sam Coleman

113.   MRS BREEN: ... (*She fades from his side. Followed by the whining dog he walks on towards hellsgates. In an archway a standing woman, bent forward, her feet apart, pisses cowily. Outside a shuttered pub a bunch of loiterers listen to a tale which their broken snouted gaffer rasps out with raucous humour.*) (*U*, pp. 449–50) – Asst US Attorney Sam Coleman

114.   THE WHORES: **Are you going far, queer fellow?**
How's your middle leg?
Got a match on you?
Eh, come here till I stiffen it for you.
(*U*, p. 450) – Asst US Attorney Sam Coleman

115.   Page 443, RH 1934; *U*, pp. 450–1) – US Attorney Martin Conboy

116.   BLOOM: ... (*He gazes ahead reading on the wall a scrawled chalk legend* **Wet Dream** *and a phallic design.*) (*U*, p. 452) – Asst US Attorney Sam Coleman

117.   BLOOM: ... (*He turns gravely to the first watch.*) ... **Drop in some evening and have a glass of old Burgundy.** (*To the second watch gaily.*) **I'll introduce you, inspector. She's game. Do it in shake of a lamb's tail.** (*U*, p. 456) – Asst US Attorney Sam Coleman

118. BLOOM: (*Behind his hand.*) She's drunk. The woman is inebriated. (He murmurs vaguely the past of Ephraim.) Shitbroleeth. (*U*, p. 457) – Asst US Attorney Sam Coleman

119. MYLES CRAWFORD: (*His cock's wattles wagging.*) Hello, seventyseven eightfour. Hello. *Freeman's Urinal* and *Weekly Arsewiper* here. Paralyse Europe. You which? Bluebags? Who writes? Is it Bloom? (*U*, p. 458) – Asst US Attorney Sam Coleman

120. A VOICE FROM THE GALLERY:

     Moses, Moses, king of the jews,

     Wiped his arse in the Daily News.

     (*U*, p. 459) – Asst US Attorney Sam Coleman

121. PROFESSOR MACHUGH: ... (*The crossexamination proceeds re Bloom and the bucket. A large bucket. Bloom himself. Bowel trouble. In Beaver street. Gripe, yes. Quite bad. A plasterer's bucket. By walking stifflegged. Suffered untold misery. Deadly agony.* (*U*, p. 462) – Asst US Attorney Sam Coleman

122. MRS YELVERTON BARRY: ... He wrote me an anonymous letter ... signed James Lovebirch. **He said that he had seen from the gods my peerless globes as I sat in a box of the** *Theatre Royal* **at a command performance of** *La Cigale.* **I deeply inflamed him, he said. He made improper overtures to me to misconduct myself at half past four p.m. on the following Thursday, Dunsink time.** He offered to send me through the post a work of fiction by Monsieur Paul de Kock, entitled *The Girl with the Three Pairs of Stays.* (*U*, p. 465) – Asst US Attorney Sam Coleman

123. MRS BELLINGHAM: He lauded almost extravagantly my nether extremities ... and eulogized glowingly my other hidden treasures in priceless lace which, he said, he could conjure up. **He urged me, stating that he felt it his mission in life to urge me, to defile the marriage bed, to commit adultery at the earliest possible opportunity.**
THE HONORABLE MRS MERVYN TALBOYS: ... This plebeian Don Juan ... sent me in double envelopes an obscene photograph ... . I have it still. **It represents a partially nude señorita, frail and lovely (his wife as he solemnly assured me, taken by him from nature), [practising illicit intercourse]**[29] **with a muscular torero, evidently a blackguard.** He urged me to do likewise, to misbehave, **to sin with officers of the garrison.** He implored me to soil his letter in an unspeakable manner, to chastise him as he richly deserves, to bestride and ride him, to give him a most vicious horsewhipping. (*U*, pp. 466–7) – Asst US Attorney Sam Coleman

124. Page 458, RH 1934; (*U*, pp. 467–8) – US Attorney Martin Conboy

125. MRS BELLINGHAM: **Make him smart, Hanna dear. Give him ginger. Thrash the mongrel within an inch of his life. The cat-o'-nine-tails. [Geld him.]**[30] **Vivisect him.** (*U*, p. 468) – Asst US Attorney Sam Coleman

126. DAVY STEPHENS: *Messenger of the Sacred Heart* **and** *Evening Telegraph* **with Saint Patrick's Day Supplement. Containing the new**

addresses of all the cuckolds in Dublin. (*U*, p. 469) – Asst US Attorney Sam Coleman

127. THE TIMEPIECE: ... Cuckoo
Cuckoo
Cuckoo

(*The brass quoits of a bed are heard to jingle.*) (*U*, p. 469)–Asst US Attorney Sam Coleman

128. THE NAMELESS ONE: ... **Arse over tip. Hundred shillings to five.** (*U*, p. 470) – Asst US Attorney Sam Coleman

129. Pages 467–8, RH 1934; (*U*, pp. 476–9) – US Attorney Martin Conboy

130. ZOE: **You both in black. [Has little mousey and tickles tonight?]**[31]
(*His skin, alert, feels her fingertips approach. A hand slides over his left thigh.*)
ZOE: **[How's the nuts?]**[32]
BLOOM: **Off side. Curiously they are on the right. Heavier I suppose. One in a million my tailer, Mesias, says.** (*U*, pp. 475–6) – Asst US Attorney Sam Coleman

131. Page 467, RH 1934; (*U*, pp. 476–7) – Judge Martin Manton

132. BLOOM: ... **Rarely smoke, dear. Cigar now and then. Childish device.** (*Lewdly.*) **The mouth can be better engaged than with a cylinder of rank weed.** (*U*, p. 478) – Asst US Attorney Sam Coleman

133. WILLIAM ARCHBISHOP OF ARMAGH: ... Will you ... cause law and mercy to be executed in all your judgements...?
BLOOM: (*Placing his right hand on his testicles, swears.*) **So may the Creator deal with me. All this I promise to do.** (*U*, p. 482) – Asst US Attorney Sam Coleman

134. [**PISSER BURKE**]: For bladder trouble?[33] (*U*, p. 488) – Asst US Attorney Sam Coleman

135. THEODORE PUREFOY: (*In fishing cap and oilskin jacket.*) **He employs a mechanical device to frustrate the sacred ends of nature.** (*U*, p. 491) – Asst US Attorney Sam Coleman

136. DR MULLIGAN: ... Dr Bloom is bisexually abnormal. ... **There are marked symptoms of chronic exhibitionism. Ambidexterity is also latent. He is prematurely bald from selfabuse, perversely idealistic in consequence, a reformed rake, and has metal teeth.** In consequence of a family complex he has temporarily lost his memory and I believe him to be more sinned against than sinning. I have made a pervaginal examination and, after application of the acid test to **5427 anal, axillary, pectoral and pubic hairs, I declare him to be** *virgo intacta.*
(*Bloom holds his high grade hat over his genital organs.*) (*U*, p. 493) – Asst US Attorney Sam Coleman

137. HORNBLOWER: ... And they shall stone him and defile him ... .
      (*All the people cast soft pantomime stones at Bloom. Many bonafide*
      [*travellers and ownerless dogs come near him and defile him*].[34]
      (*U*, p. 497) – Asst US Attorney Sam Coleman

138. Page 488, RH 1934; (*U*, pp. 499–500) – Judge Martin Manton

139. Pages 489–91, RH 1934; (*U*, pp. 499–502) – US Attorney Martin Conboy

140. ZOE: (*Stiffly, her finger in her neckfillet.*) Honest? Till the next time. (*She
      sneers.*) Suppose you got up the wrong side of the bed or [came too
      quick with your best girl].[35] O, I can read your thoughts. (*U*, p. 499) –
      Asst US Attorney Sam Coleman

141. ZOE: ... (*She holds his [Bloom's] hand which is feeling for her nipple*). I
      say, Tommy Tittlemouse. Stop that and begin worse. Have you cash
      for a short time? Ten shillings? (*U*, p. 500) – Asst US Attorney Sam
      Coleman

142. ZOE-FANNY: I let him larrup it into me for the fun of it. (*U*, p. 509) –
      Asst US Attorney Sam Coleman

143. Page 498, RH 1934; (*U*, pp. 509–10) – Judge Martin Manton

144. ZOE: (*... Lynch with his poker lifts boldly a side of her slip. Bare from her
      garters up her flesh appears under the sapphire a nixie's green. She puffs
      calmly at her cigarette.*) Can you see the beauty spot of my behind?
      (*U*, p. 511) – Asst US Attorney Sam Coleman

145. Page 500, RH 1934; (*U*, pp. 511–12) – US Attorney Martin Conboy; Judge
      Martin Manton

146. VIRAG: (*His tongue upcurling.*) Lyum! Look. Her beam is broad. She is
      coated with quite a considerable layer of fat. Obviously mammal in
      weight of bosom you remark that she has in front well to the fore two
      protuberances of very respectable dimensions, inclined to fall in the
      noonday soupplate, while on her rere lower down are two additional
      protuberances, suggestive of potent rectum and tumescent for palpa-
      tion which leave nothing to be desired save compactness. (*U*, p. 513) –
      Asst US Attorney Sam Coleman

147. VIRAG: (*Prompts into his ear in a pig's whisper.*) Insects of the day
      spend their brief existence in reiterated coition, lured by the smell of
      the inferiorly pulchritudinous female possessing extendified pudendal
      verve in dorsal region. (*U*, p. 515) – Asst US Attorney Sam Coleman

148. BLOOM: ... Ocularly woman's bivalve case is worse. Always open
      sesame. The cloven sex. Why they fear vermin, creeping things. Yet
      Eve and the serpent contradict. (*U*, p. 516) – Asst US Attorney Sam
      Coleman

149. ZOE: **There was a priest down here two nights ago to do his bit of business with his coat buttoned up. You needn't try to hide, I says to him. I know you've a Roman collar.**
VIRAG: Perfectly logical from his standpoint. Fall of man. ... Why I left the Church of Rome. Read the Priest, the Woman and the Confessional. ... **Woman, undoing with sweet pudor her belt of rushrope, offers her allmoist yoni to man's lingam. Short time after man presents woman with pieces of jungle meat.** ...
LYNCH: I hope you gave the good father a penance. ...
ZOE: (*Spouts walrus smoke through her nostrils.*) **He couldn't get a connection. Only, you know, sensation. A dry rush.** (*U*, pp. 519–20) – Asst US Attorney Sam Coleman

150. Page 508, RH 1934; (*U*, pp. 519–20) – US Attorney Martin Conboy

151. VIRAG: ... **She sold lovephiltres, whitewax, orange flower. Panther, the Roman centurion, polluted her with his genitories.** (*He sticks out a flickering phosphorescent scorpion tongue, his hand on his fork.*) **Messiah! He burst her tympanum.** (*With gibbering baboon's cries he jerks his hips in the cynical spasm.*) (*U*, p. 521) – Asst US Attorney Sam Coleman

152. Page 509, RH 1934; (*U*, pp. 521–2) – Judge Martin Manton

153. BLOOM: ... **I should not have parted with my talisman. Rain, exposure at dewfall on the sea rocks, a peccadillo at my time of life. Every phenomenon has a natural cause.** (*U*, p. 529) – Asst US Attorney Sam Colemam

154. Pages 522–5, RH 1934; (*U*, pp. 534–9) – US Attorney Martin Conboy

155. BELLO: (*Squats, with a grunt, on Bloom's upturned face....*) ...
Gee up! A cockhorse to Banbury cross. I'll ride him for the Eclipse stakes. (*He bends sideways and squeezes his mount's testicles roughly, shouting.*) **Ho! off we pop! I'll nurse you in proper fashion.** (*U*, p. 534) – Asst US Attorney Sam Coleman

156. Page 522, RH 1934; (*U*, pp. 534–5) – Judge Martin Manton

157. BELLO: **Well, I'm not. Wait.** (*He holds in his breath.*) **Curse it. Here. This bung's about burst.** (*He uncorks himself behind: then, contorting his features, farts loudly.*) **Take that!** (*U*, p. 535) – Asst US Attorney Sam Coleman

158. BELLO: (*Jeers.*) **Little jobs that make mother pleased, eh! and showed off conquettishly in your domino at the mirror behind closedrawn blinds your unskirted things and hegoat's udders, in various poses of surrender, eh?** Ho! Ho! I have to laugh! That secondhand black operatop shift and short trunk leg naughties all split up the stitches at her last rape that Mrs Miriam Dandrade sold you from the Shelbourne Hotel, eh?
BLOOM: Miriam, Black. Demimondaine.
BELLO: ... You were a nicelooking Miriam when you clipped off your backgate hairs and lay swooning in the thing across the bed as

Mrs Dandrade, about to be violated by Lieutenant Smythe-Smythe, Mr Philip Augustus Blockwell, M.P., Signor Laci Daremo, the robust tenor, blueeyed Bert, the liftboy, **Henry Fleury of Gordon Bennett fame, Sheridan, the quadroon Croesus, the varsity wetbob eight from old Trinity, Ponto, her splendid Newfoundland and Bobs, dowager duchess of Manorhamilton.** (*U*, p. 536) – Asst US Attorney Sam Coleman

159. BELLO: ... When you took your seat with womanish care, lifting your billowy flounces, on the smoothworn throne.
BLOOM: **Science. To compare the various joys we each enjoy.** (*Earnestly.*) **And really it's the better position ... because often I used to wet** ... [ellipses Joyce's] (*U*, p. 537) – Asst US Attorney Sam Colemam

160. BELLO: ... The sins of your past are rising against you. ...
THE SINS OF THE PAST: ... In five public conveniences he wrote pencilled messages offering his nupial partner to all strongmembered males. **And by the offensively smelling vitriol works did he not pass night after night by loving courting couples to see if and what and how much he could see? Did he not lie in bed, the gross boar, gloating over a nauseous fragment of wellused toilet paper presented to him by a nasty harlot, stimulated by gingerbread and a postal order?** (*U*, p. 537) – Asst US Attorney Sam Coleman

161. BELLO: (*Satirically.*) **By day you will souse and bat our smelling underclothes, also when we ladies are unwell, and swab out our latrines with dress pinned up and a dishclout tied to your tail.** ...
BLOOM: Thank you, mistress.
BELLO: **You will make the beds, get my tub ready, empty [the pisspots in the]**[36] **different rooms, including old Mrs Keogh's the cook's,** a sandy one. Ay, and rinse the seven of them well, mind, or [lap it up like champagne]. Drink me piping hot. Hop! you will dance attendance or I will lecture you on your misdeeds, Miss Ruby, and [spank your bare bot right well, miss, with the hairbrush]. ... *He bares his arm and plunges it elbowdeep in Bloom's vulva.*) **There's fine depth for you! What, boys? That give you a hardon?** (*He shoves his arm in a bidder's face.*) **Here, wet the deck and wipe it round!** (*U*, pp. 538–9) – Asst US Attorney Sam Coleman

162. Page 526, RH 1934; (*U*, pp. 539–40) – Judge Martin Manton

163. Page 527, RH 1934; (*U*, pp. 540–1) – US Attorney Martin Conboy

164. BELLO: ... Learn the smooth mincing walk on four inch Louis XV heels, **the Grecian bend with provoking croup, the thighs fluescent, knees modestly kissing. Bring all your power of fascination to bear on them. Pander to their Gomorrahan vices.**
BLOOM: ... O, I know what you're hinting at now.
BELLO: What else are you good for, an impotent thing like you? ... Up! Up! Manx cat! What have we here? **Where's your curly teapot gone to or who docked it on you, cockyolly? Sing, birdy, sing. It's as limp as a boy of six's doing his pooly behing a cart. Buy a bucket or sell your pump.**

(*Loudly.*) **Can you do a man's job?** (*U*, pp. 540–1) – Asst US Attorney Sam Coleman

165.   Page 528, RH 1934; (*U*, pp. 541–2) – Judge Martin Manton

166.   BELLO: Die and be damned to you if you have any sense of decency or grace about you. ... **We'll bury you in our shrubbery jakes where you'll be dead and dirty with old Cuck Cohen, my stepnephew I married, the bloody old gouty procurator and sodomite with a crick in his neck, and my other ten or eleven husbands, whatever the buggers' names were, suffocated in the one cesspool.** ... We'll manure you, Mr Flower! ... Byby, Poldy! (*U*, pp. 543–4) – Asst US Attorney Sam Coleman

167.   THE NYMPH: Mortal! You found me in evil company ... . I was surrounded by the stale smut of clubmen, stories to disturb callow youth, ads for transparencies ... . Useful hints to the married.
BLOOM: ... We have met before. On another star.
THE NYMPH: (*Sadly.*) **Rubber goods. Neverrip. Brand as supplied to the aristocracy. Corsets for men. I cure fits or money refunded.** ...
BLOOM: You mean *Photo Bits*?
NYMPH: **I do. You bore me away, framed me in oak and tinsel, set me above your marriage couch. Unseen, one summer eve, you kissed me in four places.** And with loving pencil you shaded my eyes, my bosom and my shame. (*U*, pp. 545–6) – Asst US Attorney Sam Coleman

168.   NYMPH: ... What have I not seen in that chamber?...
BLOOM: ... That antiquated commode. **It wasn't her weight. She scaled just eleven stone nine. She put on nine pounds after weaning. It was a crack and want of glue. Eh? And that absurd orangekeyed utensil which has only one handle.** (*U*, p. 547) – Asst US Attorney Sam Coleman

169.   NYMPH: We immortals, as you saw today, have not such a place and no hair there either. We are stonecold and pure. ... How then could you ...? [latter ellipsis Joyce's]
BLOOM: ... **O, I have been a perfect pig. Enemas too I have administered. One third of a pint of quassia, to which add a tablespoonful of rocksalt. Up the fundament. With Hamilton Long's syringe, the ladies' friend.** (*U*, p. 551) – Asst US Attorney Sam Coleman

170.   THE NYMPH: (*Eyeless, in nun's white habit, ... with remote eyes.*) ... Tranquilla convent. Sister Agatha. ... No more desire. ... Only the ethereal. (*Bloom half rises. His back trousers' button snaps.*) ...
THE BUTTON: Bip!
(*Two sluts of the Coombe dance rainily by ... .*)
THE SLUTS: O Leopold lost the pin of his drawers
                        He didn't know what to do,
                        To keep it up,
                        To keep it up.
BLOOM: (*Coldly.*) **You have broken the spell. The last straw. If there were only ethereal where would you all be, postulants and novices? Shy but willing, like an ass pissing.** (*U*, pp. 552–3) – Asst US Attorney Sam Coleman

171.   THE NYMPH: (*With a cry, flees from him unveiled, her plaster cast cracking, a cloud of stench escaping from the cracks.*) Poli ...! [ellipsis Joyce's]
       BLOOM: (*Calls after her.*) **As if you didn't get it on the double your-selves. No jerks and multiple mucosities all over you.** ... Fool someone else, not me. (*U*, p. 553) – Asst US Attorney Sam Coleman

172.   BLOOM: ... I'm not a triple screw propeller.
       BELLA: (*Contempuously.*) **You're not game, in fact.** (*Her sowcunt barks.*) **Fohracht!** (*U*, p. 554) – Asst US Attorney Sam Coleman

173.   ZOE: (*Lifting up her pettigown and folding a half sovereign into the top of her stocking.*) **Hard earned on the flat of my back.** (*U*, p. 557) – Asst US Attorney Sam Coleman

174.   STEPHEN: ... **Hm. Sphinx. The beast that has two backs at midnight. Married.** (*U*, p. 560) – Asst US Attorney Sam Coleman

175.   LENEHAN: ... Were you brushing the cobwebs off a few quims?
       BOYLAN: (*Seated, smiles.*) Plucking a turkey.
       LENEHAN: A good night's work.
       BOYLAN: (*Holding up four thick bluntungulated fingers, winks.*) **Blazes Kate! Up to sample or your money back.** (*He holds out a forefinger.*) **Smell that.** (*U*, p. 564) – Asst US Attorney Sam Coleman

176.   BOYLAN: (*To Bloom, over his shoulder.*) **You can apply your eye to the keyhole and play with yourself while I just go through her a few times.**
       BLOOM: Thank you, sir, I will, sir. ...
       LYDIA DOUCE: (*Her mouth opening.*) **Yumyum. O, he's carrying her round the room doing it! Ride a cock horse. You could hear them in Paris and New York. Like mouthfuls of strawberries and cream.** (*U*, p. 566) – Asst US Attorney Sam Coleman

177.   Page 551, RH 1934; (*U*, pp. 566–7) – Judge Martin Manton

178.   Pages 552, 553, RH 1934; (*U*, pp. 566–8) – US Attorney Martin Conboy

179.   Pages 555, 556, RH 1934; (*U*, pp. 569–71) – US Attorney Martin Conboy

180.   STEPHEN: (*Gabbles, with marionette jerks.*) ... **Perfectly shocking terrific of religion's things mockery seen in universal world. All chic womans which arrive full of modesty then disrobe and squeal loud to see vampire man debauch nun very fresh young with** *dessous troublants.* (*U*, pp. 569–70) – Asst US Attorney Sam Coleman

181.   STEPHEN: ... (*He points about him with grotesque gestures which Lynch and the whores reply to.*) **Caoutchouc statue woman reversible or lifesize tom-peeptoms virgins nudities very lesbic the kiss five ten times.** Enter gen-tlemen to see in mirrors **every positions trapezes all that machine there besides also if desire act awfully bestial butcher's boy pollutes in warm veal liver or omelette on the belly** *pièce de Shakespeare.* (*U*, p. 570) – Asst US Attorney Sam Coleman

182. THE MOTHER: ... Beware! God's hand! (*A green crab with malignant red eyes sticks deep its grinning claws in Stephen's heart.*)
STEPHEN: (**Strangled with rage.**) **Shite!** (*U*, p. 582) – Asst US Attorney Sam Coleman

183. BLOOM: ... I need mountain air.
(*He hurries out through the hall. ... Bella ... urges on her whores. They blow ickylickysticky yumyum kisses. Corny Kelleher replies with a ghostly lewd smile. The silent lechers turn to pay the jarvey. ... Bloom ... hastens on by the railings ... . After him, fresh found, the hue and cry zigzag gallops in hot pursuit of follow my leader: ...* **Wisdom Hely, V.B. Dillon,** *...* **[Pisser Burke]**[37] *...* (*U*, pp. 585–6) – Asst US Attorney Sam Coleman

184. CISSEY CAFFREY: **I was in company with the soldiers and they left me to do – you know and the young man ran up behind me. But I'm faithful to the man that's treating me though I'm only a shilling whore.** (*U*, p. 587) – Asst US Attorney Sam Coleman

185. PRIVATE CARR: ... What's that you're saying about my king?
(*Edward the Seventh appears in an archway. ...* **In his left hand he holds a plasterer's bucket on which is printed: Défense d'uriner.** *A roar of welcome greets him.* (*U*, p. 590) – Asst US Attorney Sam Coleman

186. RUMBOLD, DEMON BARBER: ... (*He jerks the rope ...: the croppy boy's tongue protudes violently.*)
THE CROPPY BOY: ... (**He gives up the ghost. A violent erection of the hanged sends gouts of sperm spouting through his death clothes on to the cobblestones.** (*U*, pp. 593–4) – Asst US Attorney Sam Coleman

187. PRIVATE CARR: ... **I'll wring the neck of any bugger says a word against my fucking king.** (*U*, p. 595) – Asst US Attorney Sam Coleman

188. **[BIDDY THE CLAP]**[38]: Methinks yon sable knight will joust it with the best.
[CUNTY KATE][39]: ... Nay, madam. (*U*, p. 597) – Asst US Attorney Sam Coleman

189. PRIVATE CARR: ... **I'll wring the neck of any fucking bastard says a word against [my bleeding fucking king].**[40] (*U*, p. 597) – Asst US Attorney Sam Coleman

190. FATHER MALACHI O'FLYNN: (*Takes from the chalice and elevates a blood-dripping host.*) *Corpus Meum.*
THE REVEREND MR HAINES LOVE: (**Raises high behind the celebrant's petticoats, revealing his grey bare hairy buttocks between which a carrot is stuck.**) **My body.** (*U*, p. 599) – Asst US Attorney Sam Coleman

191. PRIVATE CARR: ... **I'll do him in, so help me fucking Christ! I'll wring the bastard fucker's bleeding blasted fucking windpipe!** (*U*, p. 600) – Asst US. Attorney Sam Coleman

192.   PRIVATE COMPTON: (*Tugging his comrade.*) **Here bugger off, Harry.**
There's the cops!...
FIRST WATCH: What's wrong here?
PRIVATE COMPTON: We were with this lady and he insulted us and
assaulted my chum. (*The retriever barks.*) Who owns the bleeding tyke?
CISSEY CAFFREY **(With expection.) Is he bleeding?**[41]
A MAN: (*Rising from his knees.*) No. Gone off. He'll come to all right.
(*U*, p. 602) – Asst US Attorney Sam Coleman

193.   PRIVATE COMPTON: (*Pulling his comrade.*) Here, bugger off, Harry. Or
Bennett'll have you in the lockup.
PRIVATE CARR: **(***Staggering as he is pulled away.***) God fuck old**
Bennett! He's a whitearsed bugger. I don't give a shit for him. (*U*,
p. 603) – Asst US Attorney Sam Coleman

Episode XVI ('Eumaeus')

194.   Thanks, Corley answered. ... I'd carry a sandwich board ... . **I don't**
give a shite anyway so long as I get a job even as a crossing sweeper.
(*U*, p. 618) – Asst US Attorney Sam Coleman

195.   Nevertheless, without going into the *minutiae* of the business, the eloquent
fact remained that **the sea was there in all its glory and in the natural**
course of things somebody or other had to sail on it and fly in the face
of providence though it merely went to show how people usually
contrived to load that sort of onus on to the other fellow like the hell
idea and the lottery and insurance, which were run on identically the
same lines ... . (*U*, p. 630) – Asst US Attorney Sam Coleman[42]

196.   Anyhow in he rolled after his successful libation ... boisterously
trolling...:
—*The biscuits was as hard as brass,*
And the beef as salt as Lot's wife's arse.
O Johnny Lever!
Johnny Lever, O!
(*U*, p. 640) – Asst US Attorney Sam Coleman

197.   **Ladies who like distinctive underclothing should, and every well-**
tailored man must, trying to make the gap wider between them by
innuendo and give more of a genuine fillip to acts of impropriety
between the two, she unbuttoned his and then he untied her, mind
the pin, whereas savages in the cannibal islands, say, at ninety degrees
in the shade not caring a continental. (*U*, p. 646) – Asst US Attorney
Sam Coleman

198.   ... his eyes went aimlessly over the respective captions which came
under his special province, the allembracing **give us this day our daily**
press. (*U*, p. 647) – Asst US Attorney Sam Coleman[43]

199.   **—That bitch, that English whore, did for him, the shebeen proprietor**
commented. She put the first nail in his coffin. (*U*, p. 650) – Asst US
Attorney Sam Coleman

200.   It was a thousand pities a young fellow blessed with an allowance of
           brains, as his neighbour obviously was, should waste his valuable time
           with profligate women, who might present him with a nice dose to last
           him his lifetime. (*U*, p. 656) – Asst US Attorney Sam Coleman

201.   ... it was highly likely some sponger's bawdyhouse of retired beauties ...
           would be the best clue to that equivocal character's whereabouts for a
           few days to come, **alternately racking their feelings (the mermaids')**
           with sixchamber revolver anecdotes verging on the tropical calculated
           to freeze the marrow of anybody's bones and mauling their largesized
           charms betweenwhiles with rough and tumble gusto to the accompani-
           ment of large potations of potheen ... . (*U*, p. 658) – Asst US Attorney
           Sam Coleman

202.   **At the same time he inwardly chuckled over his repartee to the blood**
           and ouns champion about his God being a jew. People could put up
           with being bitten by a wolf but what properly riled them was a bite
           from a sheep. (*U*, p. 658) – Asst US Attorney Sam Coleman[44]

203.   Then the old specimen in the corner who appeared to have **some spark of**
           vitality left read out that Sir Anthony MacDonnell had left Euston for
           the chief secretary's lodge or words to that effect. To which **absorbing**
           piece of intelligence echo answered why. (*U*, p. 659) – Asst US Attorney
           Sam Coleman[45]

204.   **Stephen, who confessed to still feeling poorly and fagged out, paused**
           at the, for a moment ... the door to ... [ellipses Joyce's] (*U*, p. 660) – Asst
           US Attorney Sam Coleman

205.   Bloom looked at the head of a horse ..., **a headhanger, putting his hind**
           foot foremost the while the lord of his creation sat on the perch, busy
           with his thoughts. But such a good poor brute, he was sorry he hadn't a
           lump of sugar but, as he wisely reflected, you could scarcely be pre-
           pared for every emergency that might crop up. (*U*, p. 662) – Asst US
           Attorney Sam Coleman[46]

206.   **The horse, having reached the end of his tether, so to speak, halted,**
           and, rearing high a proud feathering tail, added his quota by letting fall
           on the floor, which the brush would soon brush up and polish, three
           smoking globes of turds. Slowly, three times, one after another, from a
           full crupper, he mired. (*U*, p. 665) – Asst US Attorney Sam Coleman

Episode XVII ('Ithaca')

207.   Which domestic problem ... frequently engaged his mind?
           What to do with our wives.
           What had been his hypothetical singular solutions?
           ... variety entertainments: **commercial activity as pleasantly com-**
           manding and pleasingly obeyed mistress proprietress in a cool dairy
           shop or warm cigar divan: the clandestine satisfaction of erotic irrita-

tion in masculine brothels, state inspected and medically controlled ... .
(*U*, pp. 685–6) – Asst US Attorney Sam Coleman

208.　　　At Stephen's suggestion, at Bloom's instigation both, first Stephen,
then Bloom, in penumbra urinated, their sides contiguous, their organs
of micturition reciprocally rendered invisible by manual circum-
position, their gazes, first Bloom's, then Stephen's, elevated to the
projected luminous and semiluminous shadow. (*U*, p. 702) – Asst US
Attorney Sam Coleman

209.　　　The trajectories of their, first sequent, then simultaneous, urinations
were dissimilar: Bloom's longer, less irruent, in the incomplete form of
the bifurcated penultimate alphabetical letter who in his ultimate year
at High School (1880) had been capable of attaining the point of greatest altitude against the whole concurrent strength of the institution, 210
scholars: Stephen's higher, more sibilant, who in the ultimate hours of
the previous day had augmented by diuretic consumption an insistent
vesical pressure. (*U*, p. 703) – Asst US Attorney Sam Coleman

210.　　　What different problems presented themselves to each concerning the
invisible audible collateral organ of the other?
　　　**To Bloom: the problems of irritability, tumescence, rigidity, reactiv-
ity, dimension, sanitariness, pelosity. To Stephen: the problem of the
sacerdotal integrity of Jesus circumcised (1st January, holiday of obliga-
tion to hear mass and abstain from unnecessary servile work) and the
problem as to whether the divine prepuce, the carnal bridal ring of the
holy Roman catholic apostolic church,** conserved in Calcata, were
deserving of simple hyperduly or of the fourth degree of latria accorded
to the abscission of such divine excrescences as hair and toenails.[47]
(*U*, p. 703) – Asst US Attorney Sam Coleman

211.　　　Did the process of divestiture continue?
　　　... he ... placed his unclothed right foot on the margin of the seat of
his chair, picked at and gently lacerated the protruding part of the great
toenail, raised the part lacerated to his nostrils and inhaled the odour of
the quick, then with satisfaction threw away the lacerated unguical
fragment. (*U*, p. 712) – Asst US Attorney Sam Coleman

212.　　　What did the first drawer unlocked contain?
　　　... a press cutting from an English weekly periodical *Modern Society*,
subject corporal chastisement in girls' schools: ... two partly uncoiled
rubber preservatives with reserve pockets, ... some assorted
Austrian–Hungarian coins: 2 coupons of the Royal and Privileged
Hungarian Lottery, a lowpower magnifying glass: 2 erotic photocards
showing: a) buccal coition between nude señorita (rere presentation,
superior position) and nude torero (fore presentation, inferior position): b) anal violation by male religious (fully clothed, eyes abject) of
female religious (partly clothed, eyes direct) ... . (*U*, pp. 720–1) – Asst
US Attorney Sam Coleman

213.　　　**What considerations rendered it not entirely undesirable?**
　　　**Constant cohabitation impeding mutual toleration of personal
defects.** (*U*, p. 726) – Asst US Attorney Sam Coleman

214.   What advantages were possessed by an occupied, as distinct from an unoccupied bed?
   The removal of nocturnal solitude, the superior quality of human (mature female) to inhuman (hotwaterjar) calefaction, the stimulation of matutinal contact … . (*U*, p. 728) – Asst US Attorney Sam Coleman

215.   What past consecutive causes … of accumulated fatigue did Bloom … silently recapitulate?
   The preparation of breakfast (burnt offering): intestinal congestion and premeditative defecation (holy of holies): the bath (rite of John): … a visit to a house of mourning, a leavetaking (wilderness): the eroticism produced by feminine exhibitionism (rite of Onan): the prolonged delivery of Mrs Mina Purefoy (heave offering) … . (*U*, pp. 728–9) – Asst US Attorney Sam Coleman

216.   What imperfections in a perfect day did Bloom … enumerate?
   A provisional failure … to certify the presence or absence of posterior rectal orifice in the case of Hellenic female divinities … . (*U*, p. 729) – Asst US Attorney Sam Coleman

217.   Page 684, P 1930; (*U*, pp. 732–3) – US Attorney Martin Conboy

218.   Pages 685–9, P 1930; (*U*, pp. 733–7) – Asst Attorney General Joseph B. Keenan.[48]

219.   Envy?
   Of a bodily and mental male organism specially adapted for the superincumbent posture of energetic human copulation and energetic piston and cylinder movement necessary for the complete satisfaction of a constant but not acute concupiscence resident in a bodily and mental female organism, passive but not obtuse. (*U*, p. 732) – Asst US Attorney Sam Coleman

220.   Pages 718–20, RH 1934; (*U*, pp. 733–6) – US Attorney Martin Conboy

221.   By what reflections did he … justify to himself his sentiments?
   The preordained frangibility of the hymen, the presupposed intangibility of the thing in itself: the incongruity and disproportion between the selfprolonging tension of the thing proposed to be done and the self abbreviating relaxation of the thing done: the fallaciously inferred debility of the female, the muscularity of the male:[49] … the natural grammatical transition by inversion … of an aorist preterite proposition (parsed as masculine subject, monosyllabic onomatopoeic transitive verb with direct feminine object) from the active voice into its correlative aorist preterite proposition (parsed as feminine subject, auxiliary verb and quasimonosyllabic onomatopoeic past participle with complementary masculine agent) in the passive voice: the continued product of seminators by generation: the continual production of semen by distillation … . (*U*, p. 734) – Asst US Attorney Sam Coleman

222.   In what final satisfaction did these antagonistic sentiments and reflections, reduced to their simplest forms, converge?
Satisfaction at the ubiquity in eastern and western terrestrial hemispheres, in all habitable lands and islands explored or unexplored (the land of the midnight sun, the islands of the blessed ...) **of adipose posterior female hemispheres, redolent of milk and honey and of excretory sanguine and seminal warmth, reminiscent of secular families of curves of amplitude, insusceptible of moods of impression** or of contrarieties of expression, expressive of mute immutable mature animality. (*U*, p. 734) – Asst US Attorney Sam Coleman

223.   **The visible signs of antesatisfaction?**
An approximate erection: a solicitous adversion: a gradual elevation: a tentative revelation; a silent contemplation. (*U*, p. 734) – Asst US Attorney Sam Coleman

224.   Then?
He kissed the plump mellow yellow smellow melons of her rump, on each plump melonous hemisphere, in their mellow yellow furrow, with obscure prolonged provocative melonsmellonous osculation. (*U*, pp. 734–5) – Asst US Attorney Sam Coleman

225.   **The visible signs of postsatisfaction?**
A silent comtemplation: a tentative velation: a gradual abasement: a solicitous aversion: a proximate erection. (*U*, p. 735) – Asst US Attorney Sam Coleman

226.   What followed this silent action?
Somnolent invocation, less somnolent recognition, incipient excitation, catechetical interrogation. (*U*, p. 735) – Asst US Attorney Sam Coleman

227.   With what modifications did the narrator reply to this interrogation?
Negative: he omitted to mention the clandestine correspondence between Martha Clifford and Henry Flower,... **the erotic provocation and response thereto caused by the exhibitionism of Gertrude (Gerty), surname unknown.** (*U*, p. 735) – Asst US Attorney Sam Coleman

228.   Page 719, RH 1934; (*U*, pp. 735–6) – Judge Martin Manton

229.   What limitations of activity and inhibitions of conjugal rights were perceived by listener and narrator concerning themselves during the course of this ... narration?
By the listener a limitation of fertility inasmuch as marriage had been celebrated 1 calendar month after the 18th anniversary of her birth (8 September 1870), viz. 8 October, and consummated on the same date with female issue born 15 June 1889, **having been anticipatorily consummated on the 10 September of the same year and complete carnal intercourse, with ejaculation of semen within the natural female organ,** having last taken place 5 weeks previous, viz. 27 November 1893, **to the**

birth on 29 December 1893 of second (and only male) issue, deceased
9 January 1894, aged 11 days, there remained a period of 10 years,
5 months and 18 days during which carnal intercourse had been incomplete, without ejaculation of semen within the natural female organ.
(*U*, pp. 735–6) – Asst US. Attorney Sam Coleman

Episode XVIII ('Penelope')

230.   Pages 690–732, P 1922; (*U*, pp. 738–83) – US Attorney Martin Conboy

231.   Pages 724–7, RH 1934; (*U*, pp. 739–43) – US Attorney Martin Conboy

232.   ... Id let him see my garters the new ones and make him turn red looking
        at him seduce him **I know what boys feel with that down on their cheek
        doing that** [frigging][50] drawing out the thing by the hour question and
        **answer would you do this that and the other with the coalman yes with
        a bishop yes I would** ... (*U*, p. 740) – Asst US Attorney Sam Coleman

233.   Pages 724–7, RH 1934; (*U*, pp. 740–4) – Judge Martin Manton

234.   ... he says your soul **you have no soul inside only grey matter because
        he doesnt know what it is to have one yes when I lit the lamp yes
        because he must have come 3 or 4 times with that tremendous big red
        brute of a thing he has I thought the vein or whatever the dickens they
        call it was going to burst** ... (*U*, pp. 741–2) – Asst US Attorney Sam
        Coleman

235.   ... I never in all my life felt anyone had one the size of that to make you
        feel full up he must have eaten a whole sheep after whats the idea
        making us like that with a big hole in the middle of us like a Stallion
        driving it up into you because thats all they want out of you with that
        determined vicious look in his eye I had to halfshut my eyes still he
        hasn't such a tremendous amount of spunk in him when I made him
        pull it out and do it on me considering how big it is so much the better
        in case any of it wasnt washed out properly the last time I let him finish
        it in me nice invention they made for women for him to get all the plea-
        sure ... (*U*, p. 742) – Asst US Attorney Sam Coleman[51]

236.   ... that black closed breeches he made me buy takes you half an hour to
        let them down wetting all myself always with some brandnew fad
        every other week such a long one I did I forgot my suede gloves on the
        seat behind that I never got after some robber of a woman and he
        wanted me to put it in the Irish Times lost in the ladies lavatory D B C
        Dame street finder return to Mrs Marion Bloom ... (*U*, p. 745) – Asst US
        Attorney Sam Coleman

237.   ... my hand is nice like that if I only had a ring with the stone for my
        month a nice aquamarine Ill stick him for one and a gold bracelet I
        dont like my foot so much still I made him spend once with my foot ...
        (*U*, p. 745) – Asst US Attorney Sam Coleman

238. ... he commenced kissing me on the choir stairs after I sang Gounods *Ave Maria* what are we waiting for O my heart kiss me straight on the brow and part which is my brown part he was pretty hot for all his tinny voice too my low notes he was always raving about if you can believe him ... (*U*, p. 745) – Asst US Attorney Sam Coleman

239. Page 731, RH 1934; (*U*, pp. 746–7) – US Attorney Martin Conboy

240. ... you never know what freak theyd take alone with you theyre so savage for it if anyone was passing so I lifted them a bit and touched his trousers outside the way I used to Gardner after with my ring hand to keep him from doing worse where it was too public I was dying to find out was he circumcised he was shaking like a jelly all over they want to do everything too quick take all the pleasure out of it ... (*U*, p. 746) – Asst US Attorney Sam Coleman

241. ... then writing a letter every morning sometimes twice a day I liked the way he made love then he knew the way to take a woman when he sent me the 8 big poppies because mine was the 8th then I wrote the night he kissed my heart at Dolphins barn I couldnt describe it simply it makes you feel like nothing on earth ... (*U*, p. 747) – Asst US Attorney Sam Coleman

242. Page 731, RH 1934; (*U*, pp. 747–8) – US Attorney Martin Conboy

243. ... I wonder will he take a 1st class for me he might want to do it in the train by tipping the guard well O I suppose therell be the usual idiots of men gaping at us with their eyes as stupid as ever they can possibly be that was an exceptional man that common workman that left us alone in the carriage that day going to Howth ... (*U*, p. 748) – Asst US Attorney Sam Coleman

244. ... hes heavy too with his hairy chest for this heat always having to lie down for them better for him put it into me from behind the way Mrs Mastiansky told me her husband made her like the dogs do it and stick out her tongue as far as ever she could and he so quiet and mild ... (*U*, p. 749) – Asst US Attorney Sam Coleman

245. ... there was the face lotion I finished the last of yesterday ... I told him over and over again get that made up in the same place and dont forget it God only knows whether he did after all I said to him Ill know by the bottle anyway if not I suppose Ill only have to wash in my piss like beeftea or chickensoup with some of that opoponax and violet ... (*U*, pp. 750–1) – Asst US Attorney Sam Coleman

246. ... Mrs Langtry the Jersey Lily the prince of Wales was in love with I suppose hes like the first man going the roads only for the name of a king theyre all made the one way only a black mans Id like to try a beauty up to what was she 45 there was some funny story about the jealous old husband what was it all and an oyster knife he went no he made her wear a kind of a tin thing around her and the prince of Wales yes he

had the oyster knife cant be true a thing like that like some of those books he brings me the works of Master François somebody supposed to be a priest about a child born out of her ear because her bumgut fell out a nice word for any priest to write and her a – e as if any fool wouldnt know what that meant I hate that pretending of all things ... (*U*, p. 751) – Asst US Attorney Sam Coleman

247.   ... like the infant Jesus in the crib at Inchicore in the Blessed Virgins arms sure no woman could have a child that big taken out of her and I thought first it came out of her side because how could she go to the chamber when she wanted to and she a rich lady of course she felt honoured H.R.H he was in Gibraltar the year I was born I bet he found lilies there too where he planted the tree he planted more than that in his time he might have planted me too if hed come a bit sooner ... (*U*, p. 752) – Asst US Attorney Sam Coleman

248   Pages 704–5, P 1930; (*U*, pp. 752–4) – Asst Attorney General Joseph B. Keenan.

249.   Pages 738–9, RH 1934; (*U*, pp. 753–5) – US Attorney Martin Conboy

250.   ... it was nice of him to show me out in any case Im extremely sorry Mrs Bloom believe me without making it too marked the first time after him being insulted and me being supposed to be his wife I just half smiled I know my chest was out that way at the door when he said Im extremely sorry and Im sure you were ... (*U*, p. 753) – Asst US Attorney Sam Coleman

251.   yes I think he made them a bit firmer sucking them like that so long he made me thirsty titties he calls them I had to laugh yes this one anyhow stiff the nipple gets for the least thing Ill get him to keep that up and Ill take those eggs beaten up with marsala fatten them out for him what are all those veins and things curious the way its made 2 the same in case of twins theyre supposed to represent beauty placed up there like those statues in the museum one of them pretending to hide it with her hand are they so beautiful of course compared with what a man looks like with his two bags full and his other thing hanging down out of him or sticking up at you like a hatrack no wonder they hide it with a cabbageleaf ... (*U*, p. 753) – Asst US Attorney Sam Coleman

252.   ... that disgusting Cameron highlander behind the meat market or that other wretch with the red head behind the tree where the statue of the fish used to be when I was passing pretending he was pissing standing out for me to see it with his babyclothes up to one side the Queens own they were a nice lot ... I passed outside the mens greenhouse near the Harcourt street station just to try some fellow or other trying to catch my eye or if it was 1 of the 7 wonders of the world O and the stink of those rotten places the night coming home with Poldy after the Comerfords party oranges and lemonade to make you feel nice and watery I went into 1 of them it was so bitting cold I couldnt keep it ... a pity a couple of the Camerons werent there to see me squatting in the

mens place meadero I tried to draw a picture of it before I tore it up like a sausage or something I wonder theyre not afraid going about of getting a kick or a bang or something there ... (*U*, p. 753) – Asst US Attorney Sam Coleman

253. ... that delicate looking student that stopped in No 28 with the Citrons Penrose **nearly caught me washing through the window only for I snapped up the towel to my face that was his studenting hurt me they used to weaning her till he got doctor Brady to give me the Belladonna prescription I had to get him to suck them they were so hard he said it was sweeter and thicker than cows then he wanted to milk me into the tea** well hes beyond everything ... (*U*, p. 754) – Asst US Attorney Sam Coleman

254. ... they want everything in their mouth all the pleasure those men get out of a woman I can feel his mouth O Lord I must stretch myself **I wished he was here or somebody to let myself go with and come again like that I feel all fire inside me or if I could dream it when he made me spend the 2nd time tickling me behind with his finger I was coming for about 5 minutes with my legs round him** I had to hug him after **O Lord I wanted to shout out all sorts of things fuck or shit or anything at all only not to look ugly or those lines from the strain who knows the way hed take it you want to feel your way with a man** theyre not all like him thank God some of them want you to be so nice about it I noticed the contrast he does it and doesnt talk **I gave my eyes that look with my hair a bit loose from the tumbling and my tongue between my lips up to him the savage brute Thursday Friday one Saturday two Sunday three O Lord I cant wait till Monday** ... (*U*, p. 754) – Asst US Attorney Sam Coleman

255. Pages 738, 739, RH 1934; (*U*, pp. 754–6) – Judge Martin Manton

256. Pages 744, 745, RH 1934; (*U*, pp. 759–61) – US Attorney Martin Conboy

257. ... I remember shall I wear a white rose and **I wanted to put on the old stupid clock to near the time he was the first man kissed me under the Moorish wall my sweetheart when a boy it never entered my head what kissing meant till he put his tongue in my mouth** ... (*U*, p. 759) – Asst US Attorney Sam Coleman

258. Page 711, P 1930; (*U*, pp. 760–1) – Asst Attorney General Joseph B. Keenan

259. ... he wanted to touch mine with his for a moment but I wouldn't let him ... **that old servant Ines told me that one drop even if it got into you at all after I tried with the Banana but I was afraid it might break and get lost up in me somewhere yes** because **they once took something down out of a woman that was up there for years covered with limesalts theyre all mad to get in there where they come out of youd think they could never get far enough up** and then theyre done with you in a way till the next time yes **because theres a wonderful feeling there all the**

time so tender how did we finish it off yes O yes I pulled him off into my handkerchief pretending not to be excited but I opened my legs I wouldnt let him touch me inside my petticoat ... he was shy all the same I liked him like that morning I made him blush a little when I got over him that way when I unbuttoned him and took his out and drew back the skin it had a kind of eye in it theyre all Buttons men down the middle on the wrong side of them Molly darling he called me what was his name ... (*U*, pp. 760–1) – Asst US Attorney Sam Coleman

260.   Pages 745, 746, RH 1934; (*U*, pp. 761–2) – Judge Martin Manton

261.   ... he went to India he was to write the voyages those men have to make to the ends of the world and back its the least they might get a squeeze or two at a woman while they can going out to be drowned or blown up somewhere I went up windmill hill to the flats that Sunday morning with Captain Rubios ... I was thinking of him on the sea all the time after at mass when my petticoat began to slip down at the elevation weeks and weeks I kept the handkerchief under my pillow for the smell of him there was no decent perfume to be got in that Gibraltar ... (*U*, p. 762) – Asst US Attorney Sam Coleman

262.   ... Kathleen Kearney and her lot of squealers Miss This Miss That Miss Theother lot of [sparrowfarts][52] skitting around talking about politics they know as much about [as my backside] anything in the world to make themselves someway interesting ... (*U*, p. 762) – Asst US Attorney Sam Coleman

263.   ... I was afraid he mightnt like my accent first he so English all father left me in spite of his stamps Ive my mothers eyes and figure anyhow he always said theyre so snotty about themselves some of those cads he wasnt a bit like that he was dead gone on my lips let them get a husband first thats fit to be looked at and a daughter like mine or see if they can excite a swell with money that can pick and choose whoever he wants like Boylan to do it 4 or 5 times locked in each others arms ... (*U*, pp. 762–3) – Asst US Attorney Sam Coleman

264.   ... yes Ill sing Winds that blow from the south that he gave after the choirstairs performance Ill change that lace on my black dress to show off my bubs and Ill yes by God Ill get that big fan mended make them burst with envy my [hole is itching me always][53] when I think of him I feel I want to ... (*U*, p. 763) – Asst US Attorney Sam Coleman

265.   ... I wish hed sleep in some bed by himself with his cold feet on me give us room even to let a fart God or do the least thing better yes hold them like that a bit on my side piano quietly sweeeee ... (*U*, p. 763) – Asst US Attorney Sam Coleman

266.   ... I wonder what kind is that book he brought me Sweets of Sin by a gentleman of fashion some other Mr de Kock I suppose the people gave him that nickname going about with his tube from one woman to another ... (*U*, p. 765) – Asst US Attorney Sam Coleman

267. ... and the tall old chap with the earrings [I dont like a man you have to climb up to go get at]⁵⁴ ... (*U*, p. 765) – Asst US Attorney Sam Coleman

268. ... a big brute like that that would attack a poor old woman to murder her in her [bed Id cut them off so]⁵⁵ I would ... (*U*, p. 766) – Asst US Attorney Sam Coleman

269. ... of course she cant feel anything deep [yet I never came properly till I was what 22 or so]⁵⁶ it went into the wrong place always only the usual girls nonsense and giggling ... (*U*, p. 767) – Asst US Attorney Sam Coleman

270. Pages 754, 755, RH 1934; (*U*, pp. 768–70) – US Attorney Martin Conboy

271. ... am I ever going to have a proper servant again of course then she'd see him coming Id have to let her know or shed revenge it arent they a nuisance ... (*U*, p. 768) – Asst US Attorney Sam Coleman

272. ... imagine climbing over the railings if anybody saw him that knew us wonder he didnt tear a big hole in his grand funeral trousers [as if the one nature gave wasnt enough]⁵⁷ for anybody hawking him down into the dirty old kitchen now is he right in his head I ask ... (*U*, p. 768) – Asst US Attorney Sam Coleman

273. ... I wont forget that wife of Scarli in a hurry supposed to be a fast play about adultery that idiot in the gallery hissing the woman adulteress he shouted I suppose he went and had a woman in the next lane ... (*U*, p. 769) – Asst US Attorney Sam Coleman

274. ... have we too much blood up in us or what O patience above its pouring out of me like the sea anyhow he didnt make me pregnant as big as he is I dont want to ruin the clean sheets the clean linen I wore brought it on too damn it damn it and they always want to see a stain on the bed to know youre a virgin for them all thats troubling them theyre such fools too ... (*U*, p. 769) – Asst US Attorney Sam Coleman

275. ... wheres the chamber gone easy Ive a holy horror of its breaking under me after that old commode I wonder was I too heavy sitting on his knee I made him sit on the easychair purposely when I took off only my blouse and skirt ... (*U*, pp. 769–70) – Asst US Attorney Sam Coleman

276. Pages 754–6, RH 1934; (*U*, pp. 769–72) – Judge Martin Manton

277. ... I bet he never saw a better pair of thighs than that look how white they are the smoothest place is right there between this bit here how soft like a peach easy God I wouldnt mind being a man and get up on a lovely woman O Lord what a row youre making like the jersey lily easy O how the waters come down at Lahore ... (*U*, p. 770) – Asst US Attorney Sam Coleman

278. ... I ought to go to the doctor only it would be like before I married him when I had that white thing coming from me and **Floey made me go to**

that dry old stick Dr Collins for womens diseases on Pembroke road your vagina he called it I suppose thats how he got all the gilt mirrors and carpets getting round those rich ones off Stephens green running up to him for every little fiddlefaddle her vagina and her cochinchina ... (*U*, p. 770) – Asst US Attorney Sam Coleman

279.   ... I wouldnt let him lick me in Holles street one night ... he slept on the floor half the night naked ... and wouldnt eat any breakfast or speak a word wanting to be petted so I thought I stood out enough for one time and let him he does it all wrong too thinking only of his own pleasure his tongue is too flat or I dont know what he forgets that we then I dont Ill make him do it again if he doesnt mind himself and lock him down to sleep in the coalcellar with the blackbeetles I wonder was it her ... no hed never have the courage with a married woman ... (*U*, p. 773) – Asst US Attorney Sam Coleman

280.   Pages 761, 762, RH 1934; (*U*, pp. 775–7) – Asst US Attorney Martin Conboy

281.   ... grinning all over his big Dolly face like a [wellwhipped childs botty][58] ... (*U*, p. 774) – Asst US Attorney Sam Coleman

282.   Page 725, P 1930; (*U*, pp. 775–6) – Asst Attorney General Joseph B. Keenan

283.   ... often felt I wanted to kiss him all over also his lovely young cock there so simply I wouldnt mind taking him in my mouth if nobody was looking as if it was asking you to suck it so clean and white he looked with his boyish face I would too in 1/2 a minute even if some of it went down what its only like gruel or the dew theres no danger besides hed be so clean compared with those pigs of men I suppose never dream of washing it from 1 years end to the other the most of them only thats what gives the women the moustaches Im sure itll be grand if I can only get in with a handsome young poet ... (*U*, p. 776) – Asst US Attorney Sam Coleman

284.   ... sure you might as well be in bed with what with a lion God Im sure hed have something better to say for himself an old Lion would O well I suppose its because they were so plump and tempting in my short petticoat he couldnt resist they excite myself sometimes its well for men all the amount of pleasure they get off a womans body were so round and white for them always I wished I was one myself for a change just to try with that thing they have swelling upon you so hard and at the same time so soft when you touch it ... (*U*, p. 776) – Asst US Attorney Sam Coleman

285.   Pages 761, 762, RH 1934; (*U*, pp. 776–8) – Judge Martin Manton

286.   ... why cant we all remain friends over it instead of quarrelling her husband found it out what they did together well naturally and if he did can he undo it hes coronado anyway whatever he does and **then he**

going to the other mad extreme about the wife in Fair Tyrants of course the man never even casts a 2nd thought on the husband or wife either its the woman he wants and he gets her what else were we given all those desires for Id like to know I cant help it if Im young still can I its a wonder Im not an old shrivelled hag before my time living with him so cold never embracing me except sometimes when hes asleep **the wrong end of me not knowing I suppose who he has [any man thatd kiss a womans bottom Id throw my hat at him after that hed kiss anything]**[59] **unnatural where we havent 1 atom of any kind of expression in us** ... (*U*, p. 777) – Asst US Attorney Sam Coleman

287.   ... a woman wants to be embraced 20 times a day almost to make her look young no matter by who so long as to be in love or loved by somebody if the fellow you want isnt there sometimes **by the Lord God I was think- ing would I go around by the quays there some dark evening where nobodyd know me and [pick up a sailor off the sea thatd be hot]**[60] **on for it and not care a pin whose I was only to do it off up in a gate some- where or one of those wildlooking gypsies in Rathfarnam** had their camp pitched near the Bloomfield laundry ... **that blackguardlooking fellow with the fine eyes peeling a switch attack me in the dark and ride me up against the wall without a word or a murderer anybody what they do themselves the fine gentlemen in their silk hats that K C lives up somewhere this way** coming out of Hardwicke lane ... and when I turned round a minute after just to see there was a woman after coming out of it too some filthy prostitute then he goes home to his wife after that only I suppose the half of those sailors are rotten again with disease O move over your big carcass out of that for the love of Mike listen to him the winds that waft my sighs to thee so well he may sleep and sigh the great Suggester Don Poldo de la Flora ... (*U*, pp. 777–8) – Asst US Attorney Sam Coleman

288.   ... its a poor case that those that have a fine son like that theyre not satisfied and I none was he not able to make one it wasnt my fault we came together when I was watching the two dogs up in her behind in the middle of the naked street ... (*U*, p. 778) – Asst US Attorney Sam Coleman

289.   ... they have friends they can talk to weve none either he wants what he wont get or its some woman ready to stick her knife in you I hate that in women ... (*U*, pp. 778–9) – Asst US Attorney Sam Coleman

290.   Page 765, RH 1934; (*U*, pp. 779–80) – US Attorney Martin Conboy

291.   ... he could easy have slept in there on the sofa in the other room I suppose **he was as shy as a boy he being so young hardly 20 of me in the next room [hed have heard me on the chamber arrah]**[61] what harm Dedalus I wonder its like those names in Gibraltar ... they had the devils queer names there father Vial plana of Santa Maria that gave me the rosary Rosales y OReilly in the Calle las Siete Revueltas and **Pisimbo and [Mrs Opisso]**[62] **in Governor street O what a name Id go and drown myself in the first river if I had a name like her** ... (*U*, p. 779) – Asst US Attorney Sam Coleman

292. ... Ill get up early in the morning ... I might go over to the markets to see all the vegetables and ... **all kinds of splendid fruits all coming in lovely and fresh who knows whod be the 1st man Id meet theyre out looking for it in the morning Mamy Dillon used to say they are and the night too that was her massgoing** ... Ill start dressing myself to go out ... **Ill put on my best shift and drawers let him have a good eyeful out of [that to make his micky stand for him Ill let him know if thats what he wanted that his wife is fucked yes and damn well fucked too up to my neck nearly not by him 5 or 6]**[63] **times handrunning theres the mark of his spunk on the clean sheet** I wouldnt bother to even iron it out **that ought to satisfy him if you dont believe me feel my belly unless I made him stand there and put him into me Ive a mind to tell him every scrap and make him do it in front of me serve him right its all his own fault if I am an adulteress** ... O much about it if thats all the harm we ever did in this vale of tears God knows its not much ... **I suppose thats what a woman is supposed to be there for or He wouldnt have made us the way He did so attractive to men then [if he wants to kiss my bottom Ill drag open my drawers and bulge it right out in his face as large as life he can stick his tongue 7 miles up my hole]**[64] **as hes there my brown part them Ill tell him I want £1 or perhaps 30/-** I'll tell him I want to buy underclothes then if he gives me that well he wont be too bad ... **Ill let him do it off on me behind provided he doesnt smear all my good drawers O I suppose that cant be helped Ill do the indifferent 1 or 2 questions Ill know by the answers when hes like that he cant keep a thing back I know every turn in him Ill tighten my bottom well and let out a few smutty words smellrump or lick my shit or the first mad thing comes into my head then Ill suggest about yes O wait now sonny my turn is coming Ill be quite gay and friendly over it O but I was forget-** ting this bloody pest of a thing ... Ill have to wear the old things **so much the better itll be more pointed hell never know whether he did it nor not there thats good enough for you any old thing at all then Ill wipe him off me just like a business his omission then Ill go out** ... (*U*, pp. 780–1) – Asst US Attorney Sam Coleman

293. Page 765, RH 1934; (*U*, pp. 780–1) – Judge Martin Manton

294. ... **the sun shines for you he said the day we were lying among the rhododendrons on Howth head in the grey tweed suit and his straw hat the day I got him to propose to me yes first I gave him the bit of seed-cake out of mouth and it was leapyear like now yes 16 years ago my God after that long kiss I near lost my breath yes he said I was a flower of the mountain yes so we are flowers all a womans body** ... and I gave him all the pleasure I could leading him on till he asked me to say yes and I wouldnt answer first ... I was thinking of so many things he didnt know of Mulvey ... and Gibraltar **as a girl where I was a Flower of the mountain yes when I put the rose in my hair like the Andalusian girls used or shall I wear a red yes and how he kissed me under the Moorish wall** and I thought well as well him as another and then I asked him with my eyes to ask again yes **and then he asked me would I yes to say yes my mountain flower and first I put my arms around him yes and drew him down to me so he could feel my breasts all perfume yes and his heart was going like mad and yes I said yes I will Yes.** (*U*, pp. 782–3) – Asst US Attorney Sam Coleman

Notes

Introduction

1. Letter to John Quinn, 17 Nov. 1920, John Quinn Memorial Collection, New York Public Library.
2. *My Thirty Years' War* (New York: Covici, Friede, 1930), pp. 212–13.
3. *LR*, 5:9 (Jan. 1919), p. 27; *U*, p. 151.
4. *LR*, 6:9 (Jan. 1920), p. 55; *U*, p. 330.
5. '"A Trial-Track for Racers": Margaret Anderson and the *Little Review*,' dissertation, University of Wisconsin, 1965, p. 384.
6. *LR*, 7.2 (Jul.–Aug. 1920), p. 43; *U*, pp. 365–6. See Appendix, excerpt 60.
7. *LR*, 7.2 (Jul.–Aug. 1920), p. 48; *U*, p. 371. See Appendix, excerpt 69.
8. John Quinn, letter to Shane Leslie, 21 Jun. 1922, John Quinn Memorial Collection, New York Public Library, p. 2.; letter to Ezra Pound, 21 Oct. 1920, Harley Croessmann Collection of James Joyce, Special Collections, Morris Library, Southern Illinois University at Carbondale, p. 21.
9. John Quinn, letter to Shane Leslie, p. 6.
10. Letter to Joseph B. Keenan, 24 Oct. 1934, File 97–51–7, Dept of Justice Classified Subject Files, Record Group 60, National Archives, Washington, DC.
11. Letter to Frank Budgen, 16 Aug. 1921, *LI*, p. 170.
12. *Working: People Talk About What They Do All Day and How They Feel About What They Do* (New York: Pantheon, 1974), p. xix.
13. *The Handmaid's Tale* (Toronto: Seal Books–McClelland-Bantam, 1986), p. 208.
14. It should be noted that, unlike the trial of Flaubert (and that of the editors of *The Little Review*), the 1932–3 *Ulysses* case was not a criminal prosecution of either Joyce or his representatives but rather a civil proceeding in which *Ulysses* itself was on trial.
15. Marie-Antoine-Jules Sénard, '*Plaidoirie,*' *Madame Bovary* (Paris: Garnier-Flammarion, 1966), p. 389.
16. Sumner, 'Affidavit,' 21 Oct. 1920, 'Exhibit "A",' 'Affidavit and Notice of Motion for the Transfer of Cause from Court of Special Sessions to Court of General Sessions,' 12 Jan. 1921, by John Quinn, Harley Croessmann Collection of James Joyce, Special Collections, Morris Library, Southern Illinois University at Carbondale.
17. Quinn, Letter to Ezra Pound, 21 Oct. 1920, p. 20.
18. '*Ulysses* in Court,' *LR*, 7.4 (Jan.–Mar. 1921), p. 22.
19. (Harmondsworth: Penguin, 1978), p. 5.
20. 'To Whom Does Joyce Belong?: *Ulysses* as Parody, Pop and Porn,' *Light Rays: James Joyce and Modernism* (New York: New Horizon Press Publishers, 1984), p. 29.
21. Ellmann, 'A Chronology of the Life of James Joyce,' *LI*, p. 47.
22. '*Ulysses' in Progress* (Princeton University Press, 1977), p. 170.
23. James Joyce, letter to Grant Richards, 23 Jun. 1906, *LI*, p. 64.
24. *The Art of James Joyce: Method and Design in 'Ulysses' and 'Finnegans Wake'* (New York: Oxford University Press, 1961), p. 35.
25. Ellmann, '*Ulysses*: a Short History,' *Ulysses* (Harmondsworth: Penguin, 1982), p. 717.

1. *Ulysses* at War

1. 19 Dec. 1917, *LII*, p. 414.
2. *My Thirty Years' War*, p. 174.
3. Ibid., p. 175.
4. Ibid., p. 33.
5. Ibid., p. 34.
6. The phrase was used by Jane Heap, *LR*, 4:5 (Sep. 1917), p. 34.
7. 'Announcement,' *LR*, 1:1 (Mar. 1914), p. 2.
8. *A Child of the Century* (New York: Simon & Schuster, 1954), p. 233.
9. 'Preparedness: The Road to Universal Slaughter,' *LR*, 2:9 (Dec. 1915), p. 12.
10. *LR*, 2:9 (Dec. 1915), p. 5.
11. Bryer, 'Trial-Track,' p. 114.
12. 'The Essential Thing,' *LR*, 3.1 (Mar. 1916), p. 23.
13. Leslie Fishbein, *Rebels in Bohemia* (Chapel Hill: University of North Carolina Press, 1982), p. 28.
14. *Masses Publishing Company* v. *Patten*, 244 *Federal Reporter*, 535–45, 24 Jul. 1917 (US Dist. Court, S.D. of New York).
15. *Masses Publishing Company* v. *Patten*, 245 *Federal Reporter*, 102–6, 6 Aug. 1917 (2nd. Cir., Court of Appeals).
16. Zechariah Chafee, Jr, *Freedom of Speech* (New York, 1920), p. 55, as quoted by Peterson and Fite, *Opponents of War* (Madison: University of Wisconsin Press, 1957), p. 97.
17. 'Affadavit,' 23 Nov. 1917, File 49537, Box 165, Office of the Solicitor, Records of the Post Office Department, Record Group 28, National Archives, Washington, DC.
18. 'Brief on Behalf of Complainant in Support of Motion for Injunction Pendente Lite,' *Margaret C. Anderson, Complainant, against Thomas G. Patten, Defendant*, In Equity number E14–379, n.d. (US Dist. Court, S.D. of New York), Beinecke Rare Book and Manuscript Library, Yale University), pp. 32–3.
19. '#335, United States District Court: Southern District of New York. Margaret C. Anderson, Complainant, against Thomas G. Patten, Postmaster of the City of New York, Defendant,' 30 Nov. 1917. Records of the Post Office; see n. 17 above.
20. 'List of Periodicals, Pamphlets, Circulars, Etc., Held to Be Non-mailable, January 18, 1918,' Case File 50839, Records Relating to the Espionage Act, World War I, 1917–20, Office of the Solicitor, Records of the Post Office Department, Record Group 28, National Archives, Washington, DC.
21. 'Pound and Eliot on *Ulysses*: The Critical Tradition,' *James Joyce Quarterly*, 10:1 (1972), p. 8.
22. Letter to John Quinn, 3 Apr. 1918, *The Selected Letters of Ezra Pound to John Quinn, 1915–1924*, ed. Timothy Materer (Durham and London: Duke University Press, 1991), p. 147.
23. Pound's reference is to George Robey (1869–1954), a famous English music-hall comedian.
24. 29 Mar. 1918, *P/J*, p. 131.
25. *LR*, 5:2 (Jun. 1918), p. 39; *U*, p. 55.
26. *LR*, 5:2 (Jun. 1918), p. 44; MS, 4. Calypso, p. 7; *U*, p. 61.
27. The typescript version which Joyce submitted to *The Little Review* has not survived. This and subsequent estimations of Pound's expurgations have therefore been inferred from comparison of the Rosenbach manuscript (*Ulysses: A Facsimile of the Manuscript* (New York: Octagon, 1975)) and the

first Paris edition. My policy has been to identify as Pound's expurgation any controversial passage that appears in both the manuscript and the first edition, but not *The Little Review*. Restored passages are taken from the Rosenbach manuscript.

28. *LR*, 5:2 (Jun. 1918), pp. 50–2; MS, 4. Calypso, pp. 14–17; *U*, pp. 67–70. This version of Pound's expurgations is more accurate than Forrest Read's (*P/J*, pp. 301–2), which includes lines Joyce did not add to 'Calypso' until after its publication in *The Little Review*.

29. *LR*, 5:2 (Jun. 1918), p. 44; *U*, p. 60.

30. *LR*, 5:2 (Jun. 1918), p. 45; *U*, p. 61.

31. Pound is referring here to the urine in the kidney passage as well as Bloom's faeces.

32. Letter to Joyce, 7 Jun. 1918, *P/J*, p. 143.

33. Pound's deletion (if indeed the omission was not caused by a typesetter's error) is shown in brackets. The dog Stephen sees on the strand 'dawdled, smelt a rock and, from under a [**cocked hindleg pissed against it. He trotted forward and, lifting again his hindleg, pissed quick short at an unsmelt rock. The simple pleasures of the poor.** ...] edge of the mole he dawdled, smelt a rock. (*LR*, 6.1 (May 1918), p. 41; MS, 3. Proteus, pp. 13–14; *U*, p. 46).

34. *U*, p. 291.

35. Letter to Joyce, 10 Jun. 1919, *P/J*, pp. 157–8.

36. *Ezra Pound: Politics, Economics, and Writing* (New York: Macmillan, 1984), p. 44.

37. *The Cantos of Ezra Pound* (New York: New Directions, 1983), p. 238.

38. Ibid., p. 196. The ethereal, mystical nature of Pound's eroticism has been elaborately documented by Kevin Oderman, *Ezra Pound and the Erotic Medium* (Durham: Duke University Press, 1986).

39. H. Carpenter, *A Serious Character: The Life of Ezra Pound* (Boston: Houghton Mifflin, 1988), p. 321.

40. *U*, p. 355.

41. *U*, p. 176.

42. *Mimesis* (Princeton University Press, 1974), p. 555. Auerbach also notes that the departure from classical decorum was initiated by 'the story of Christ, with its ruthless mixture of everyday reality and the highest and most sublime tragedy' (p. 555). From this perspective, it is legitimate to say that Joyce's incarnational, egalitarian esthetic is based, however loosely, on Christian foundations.

43. *The Roots of Treason* (New York: Harcourt Brace Jovanovich, 1984), 129. For a fuller account of Pound's Eleusinian interests, see Leon Surette, *A Light from Eleusis* (Oxford: Claredon Press, 1979).

44. Carpenter, p. 167.

45. Ibid.

46. As quoted in *JJ*, p. 615.

47. *The Letters of Virginia Woolf, vol. II: 1912–1922*, ed. Nigel Nicholson (New York: Harcourt Brace Jovanovich, 1976), p. 551; *Diary of Virginia Woolf, vol. II: 1920–1924*, ed. Anne Oliver Bell (London: Hogarth, 1978), entry for 26 Sep. 1922. Like Pound, Woolf was displeased by what she referred to squeamishly as 'the p–ing of a dog' in the 'Proteus' episode (*The Letters of Virginia Woolf, vol. II*, p. 234).

48. As quoted by Foster Damon, *Amy Lowell: A Chronicle* (Boston: Houghton Mifflin, 1935), p. 497.

49. 'Mr. Villerant's Morning Outburst,' *LR*, 5:7 (Nov. 1918), p. 11.
50. Valèry Larbaud's 'James Joyce' and T.S. Eliot's '*Ulysses*, Order, and Myth' belong here as well.
51. Letter to William Carlos Williams, Jan. 1919, as quoted in *P/J*, p. 150.
52. Letter to the Postmaster, 14 Mar. 1919; File 49537, Box 165, World War I Espionage Files, Records of the Post Office Department, National Archives, Washington, DC.
53. In a letter he wrote to Joyce after the war, Pound suggested another explanation for this monitoring of *Ulysses* by the Translation Bureau, claiming that the censors thought *Ulysses* was 'all code' (?July? 1920, *P/J*, p. 182).
54. R.H.C. [A.R. Orage], 'Readers and Writers,' *New Age* (28 Apr. 1921), p. 306.
55. 'Weaving, Unweaving,' in *A Star Chamber Quiry: A James Joyce Centennial Volume 1882–1982*, ed. E.L. Epstein (New York: Methuen, 1982), p. 45.
56. John Middleton Murray, review of *Ulysses*, *Nation & Athenaeum*, xxxi (22 Apr. 1922), p. 124.
57. 'An Irish Revel: And Some Flappers,' review of *Ulysses* (*Daily Express* (25 Mar. 1922): n.p.), *James Joyce: The Critical Heritage*, vol. 1, ed. Robert H. Deming (London: Routledge & Kegan Paul, 1970), p. 191.
58. Extract from '*Ulysses*' (*Quarterly Review*, 238 (Oct. 1922), pp. 219–34), *James Joyce: The Critical Heritage*, vol. 1, p. 207.
59. New York Society for the Suppression of Vice, Annual Report, 1919, as quoted by Paul S. Boyer, *Purity in Print: The Vice Society Movement and Book Censorship in America* (New York: Scribner's, 1968), p. 67.
60. Letter to Sir Horace Rumbold, 11 Apr. 1919, *P/J*, p. 152.
61. As quoted in *JJ*, p. 446.
62. *LR*, 5:9 (Jan. 1919), p. 27; *U*, p. 151.
63. Robert K. Murray, *Red Scare: A Study in National Hysteria, 1919–1920*, (Minneapolis: University of Minnesota Press, 1955), pp. 59–60.
64. See Appendix, excerpt 15.
65. *LR*, 5:9 (Jan. 1919), p. 47; *U*, p. 176.
66. *LR*, 5:10–11 (Feb.–Mar. 1919), p. 60; *U*, p. 182.
67. *LR*, 6.1 (May 1919), p. 21.
68. MS, 9. Scylla and Charybdis, pp. 25–6; *U*, p. 207. Anderson marked the omission of this passage with ellipses, *LR*, 6:1 (May 1919), p. 26. See Appendix, excerpt 24.
69. MS, 9. Scylla and Charibdis, p. 35; *LR*, 6:1 (May 1919), p. 34; *U*, p. 216. See Appendix, excerpt 28. For the other expurgations from the May number, see Appendix, excerpts 21 and 23.
70. 'Trial-Track,' p. 375.
71. See Appendix, excerpts 25, 29.
72. Letter to Ezra Pound, 17 Jun. 1919 (a postscript to letter to Pound dated 16 June 1919), John Quinn Memorial Collection, New York Public Library, p. 8.
73. Letter to John Quinn, 6 Jul. 1919, John Quinn Memorial Collection, New York Public Library, pp. 1, 3.
74. T.S. Eliot, letter to John Quinn, 9 Jul. 1919, John Quinn Memorial Collection, New York Public Library.
75. Reid, *The Man from New York*, p. 406.
76. Quinn, letter to James Joyce, 26 Jun. 1919, Division of Rare and Manuscript Collections, Cornell University Library, p. 5.
77. Letter to John Quinn, 3 Aug. 1919, LII, p. 448.
78. *LR*, 6:7 (Nov. 1919), p. 49; MS, 12. Cyclops, pp. 17–18; *U*, pp. 304–5. Anderson marked the expurgated material with ellipses and an editorial

note: 'A passage of some twenty lines has been omitted to avoid the censor's possible suppression.'
79. See Appendix, excerpt 34.
80. Jane Heap, letter to James Joyce, 9 Jan. 1920, Division of Rare and Manuscript Collections, Cornell University Library.
81. Letter to James Joyce, Jan.–Feb.? 1920, Division of Rare and Manuscript Collections, Cornell University Library.
82. *LR*, 6:9 (Jan. 1920), pp. 54–6; *U*, pp. 330–31.
83. Robert K. Murray, *Red Scare: A Study in National Hysteria, 1919–1920* (Minneapolis: University of Minnesota Press, 1955), p. 239.
84. Murray, *Red Scare*, p. 213.
85. *LR*, 6:9 (Jan. 1920), p. 57; *U*, p. 333.
86. *LR*, 6:9 (Jan. 1920), pp. 57–8; *U*, p. 334.
87. 25 Feb. 1920, *LI*, p. 137.
88. 'Some of the Causes for the Omission of the February Number,' *LR*, 6:10 (Mar. 1920), p. 64.
89. Bryer, 'Trial-Track,' p. 384.

2 *Ulysses* and the Young Person

1. *LR*, 7:2 (Jul.–Aug. 1920), pp. 42–58.
2. Anderson, *My Thirty Years' War*, p. 213.
3. Ibid.
4. Quinn, letter to Ezra Pound, 16 Oct. 1920, with postscript dated 21 Oct. 1920, Harley Croessmann Collection, Special Collections, Morris Library, University of Southern Illinois at Carbondale, p. 6. Unless otherwise indicated, the quotes attributed to Quinn in this chapter are from this letter.
5. As quoted by John Sumner, 'The Truth About "Literary Lynching,"' *The Dial*, 71:1 (Jul. 1921), p. 67.
6. 'Joyce, *Ulysses*, and the *Little Review*,' *South Atlantic Quarterly*, 66 (1967), p. 157.
7. Dickens, *Our Mutual Friend*, ch. 10.
8. *Literature at Nurse, or Circulating Morals: A Polemic on Victorian Censorship*, ed. Pierre Coustillas (New Jersey: Humanities Press, 1976), p. 21.
9. *'Ulysses'*, rev. edn (Baltimore & London: Johns Hopkins University Press, 1987), p. 101.
10. *Three Studies in Twentieth-Century Obscurity* (London: Dufour Editions, 1961), p. 30.
11. *The Secret Museum: Pornography in Modern Culture* (New York: Viking Penguin, 1987), p. 183.
12. *LR*, 7:2 (Jul.–Aug. 1920), p. 43; *U*, pp. 365–6. See Appendix, excerpt 57.
13. *LR*, 7:2 (Jul.–Aug. 1920), p. 48; *U*, p. 371. See Appendix, excerpt 68.
14. *Sylvia Beach and the Lost Generation* (New York: Norton, 1983), p. 76.
15. Kenner, *'Ulysses,'* pp. 61–71.
16. *Joyce the Creator* (Madison, Wisconsin: University of Wisconsin Press, 1985), p. 125.
17. *U*, p. 355.
18. *U*, p. 348.
19. *JJ*, p. 418.
20. 'James Joyce In and Out of Art,' *Four Dubliners: Oscar Wilde, William Butler Yeats, James Joyce, Samuel Beckett* (New York: Georges Braziller), p. 73.

21.   Ibid., p. 76.
22.   *U*, pp. 350–1.
23.   Allen Churchill, *The Improper Bohemians* (New York: E.P. Dutton), p. 187.
24.   Sumner, 'Affidavit,' p. 2.
25.   *My Thirty Years' War*, pp. 218–19.
26.   Quinn identifies these passages in his letter to Ezra Pound, 16 Oct. 1920, pp. 16–18.
27.   Sumner, 'Affidavit,' p. 1.
28.   Ibid., p. 2.
29.   Letter to Shane Leslie, 21 Jun. 1922, John Quinn Memorial Collection, New York Public Library, pp. 2–3.
30.   Ibid., p. 3.
31.   *Regina* v. *Hicklin* (L.R. 3 Q.B. 360).
32.   Quinn, letter to Shane Leslie, p. 2.
33.   Ibid., p. 4.
34.   Ibid., p. 4; Pound's letter to Quinn, 16 Oct. 1920, p. 21.
35.   Letter to Shane Leslie, p. 4.
36.   Letter to Shane Leslie, pp. 4–5. 'Affidavit and Motion for the Transfer of Cause from Court of Special Sessions to Court of General Sessions.'
37.   Letter to Shane Leslie.
38.   Letter to Margaret Anderson, 5 Feb. 1921, Harley Croessmann Collection, Morris Library, University of Southern Illinois at Carbondale, p. 16.
39.   Letter to Margaret Anderson, 8 Feb. 1921, Harley Croessmann Collection, Morris Library, University of Southern Illinois at Carbondale, pp. 1–2.
40.   Ibid.
41.   Anderson, '*Ulysses* in Court,' *LR*, 7:4 (Jan.–Mar. 1921), p. 23; *My Thirty Years' War*, p. 219.
42.   Anderson, '*Ulysses* in Court,' p. 23; *My Thirty Years' War*, p. 219.
43.   Anderson, '*Ulysses* in Court,' p. 23.
44.   Letter to Shane Leslie, p. 6.
45.   Quinn, letter to Shane Leslie, p. 5.
46.   Letter to James Joyce, 13 Apr. 1921, John Quinn Memorial Collection, New York Public Library, p. 8
47.   Anderson, '*Ulysses* in Court,' p. 23; *My Thirty Years' War*, p. 220.
48.   Anderson, '*Ulysses* in Court,' p. 24. Subsequent quotations in this paragraph are from the same source.
49.   Some confusion exists as to who really testified at the Special Sessions trial. In *My Thirty Years' War* Anderson claims that Thayer testified and 'was forced to admit' that he would not have published *Ulysses* in the *Dial* (p. 220). In '*Ulysses* in Court,' however, she indicates that only Powys and Moeller were allowed to testify. I follow Jackson Bryer in preferring the latter account, one which is corroborated by an article in *Publishers' Weekly*, 19 Feb. 1921, p. 522. See Jackson Bryer, 'Joyce, *Ulysses*, and the *Little Review*,' *South Atlantic Quarterly*, 66 (1967), p. 161.
50.   See Quinn, Letter to James Joyce, 13 Apr. 1921, p. 8.
51.   Letter to James Joyce, 13 Apr. 1921, p. 8.
52.   Letter to Shane Leslie, p. 5.
53.   'Improper Novel Costs Women $100,' *New York Times*, 22 Feb. 1921, p. 13.
54.   Anderson, '*Ulysses* in Court,' p. 24.
55.   Ibid.
56.   Ibid.

57. Jackson Bryer claims that Forrester read the offending passages when the Court first convened on 14 Feb. 1921 ('Joyce, *Ulysses*, and the *Little Review*,' *South Atlantic Quarterly*, 66 (Spring 1967), p. 161). I follow the *New York Times* reporter who wrote that the passages were not read then ('Little Review in Court,' 15 Feb. 1921, p. 4).
58. *My Thirty Years' War*, p. 221.
59. 'Improper Novel Costs Women $100,' p. 13.
60. *LR*, 7:2 (Jul.–Aug. 1920), pp. 42–4; *U*, pp. 365–7. See Appendix, excerpts 54–61.
61. *LR*, 7:2 (Jul.–Aug. 1920), p. 46; *U*, p. 353. See excerpts 64, 65. Pound had already deleted the word 'wet' from before 'shirt' in this passage. As he put it to Quinn, 'I did myself dry Bloom's shirt' (letter, 8 Nov. 1920, *The Selected Letters of Ezra Pound to John Quinn, 1915–24*, ed. Timothy Materer (Durham and London: Duke University Press, 1991), p. 202). Pound's laundering did not, evidently, deceive Sumner.
62. *LR*, 7:2 (Jul.–Aug. 1920), p. 47; *U*, p. 354. See Appendix, excerpts 66, 67.
63. *LR*, 7:2 (Jul.–Aug. 1920), p. 48; *U*, 355. See Appendix, excerpts 68, 69.
64. *LR*, 7:2 (Jul.–Aug. 1920), pp. 48–9; *U*, p. 355. See Appendix, excerpts 69, 70.
65. *LR*, 7:2 (Jul.–Aug. 1920), p. 51; *U*, p. 358. See Appendix, excerpts 72–4.
66. Letter to Shane Leslie, p. 6.
67. Quinn, letter to James Joyce, 13 Apr. 1921, p. 8.
68. 'Improper Novel Costs Women $100,', 22 Feb. 1921, p. 13.
69. Quinn, letter to James Joyce, 13 Apr. 1921, p. 8; letter to Shane Leslie, 21 Jun. 1922, p. 7.
70. According to Quinn, Anderson and Heap might even have been sent to prison if he had not assured the judges that the 'Nausicaa' episode was 'the worst in the book' (Letter to James Joyce, 13 Apr. 1921).
71. '*Ulysses* in Court,' p. 24.
72. Ibid., p. 22.
73. Anderson, 'An Obvious Statement (for the millionth time),' *LR*, 7:3 (Sep.–Dec. 1920), pp. 8–9.
74. 'Art and the Law,' *LR*, 7:3 (Sep.–Dec. 1920), p. 7.
75. 'An Obvious Statement (for the millionth time),' p. 10.
76. 'Adult or Infantile Censorship?' *The Dial*, 70:4 (1921), p. 384.
77. 'Joyce, *Ulysses*, and the *Little Review*,' *The South Atlantic Quarterly*, 66 (Spring 1967), p. 163.
78. Augustus N. Hand, Preconference Memorandum, '*U.S. v. Ulysses*', no date, Learned Hand Papers, Harvard Law School Library, p. 3.
79. Letter to John Quinn, 5 Apr. 1921, as quoted by Herbert Gorman, *James Joyce* (New York, Toronto: Rinehart & Company, 1948), p. 280.
80. Sylvia Beach, *Shakespeare and Company* (Lincoln, Nebraska: University of Nebraska Press, 1959), p. 47.
81. Ibid.

3   Making Obscenity Safe for Literature

1. Letter to Grant Richards, 23 Jun. 1906, *LI*, p. 64.
2. 'Letter of Protest,' *Our Examination Round his Factification for Incamination of Work in Progress* (London: Faber & Faber, 1929), p. 191.

3. Introduction, *LI*, p. 37. Sylvia Beach attributes Slingsby's letter to one 'Mrs. Kennedy' (*Shakespeare & Company*, p. 183). I have followed Gilbert as the more reliable authority.
4. Introduction, *LI*, p. 37.
5. Karen LeFévre, 'Literary Censorship and Frances Steloff,' James Joyce Conference, Philadelphia, 1989.
6. Ezra Pound, letter to James Joyce, 29 Mar. 1918, *P/J*, p. 131.
7. James Joyce, letter to Harriet Shaw Weaver, 2 Jul. 1919, *LI*, p. 127.
8. Letter to Stanislaus Joyce, 8 Sep. 1919, *LII*, pp. 451–2. Ironically, even the Japanese seem to have been unwilling to admit *Ulysses* without expurgation. According to Joyce, *Ulysses* appeared in Japan 'with the censor's blanks' (Letter to Paul Léon, 12 Feb. 1938, James Joyce/Paul Léon Papers, National Library of Ireland).
9. Letter to Allen Lane, 12 Sep. 1936, James Joyce/Paul Léon Papers, National Library of Ireland.
10. 22 Dec. 1938, The James Joyce/Paul Léon Papers, National Library of Ireland.
11. *JJ*, p. 88.
12. James Joyce, *Critical Writings* (New York: Viking, 1959), p. 69.
13. [Nov. 1902], *LI*, p. 53.
14. *JJ*, p. 109.
15. *James Joyce and Sexuality* (New York: Cambridge University Press, 1985), p. 152.
16. 'A Portrait of the Artist,' *The Workshop of Dedalus*, edited by Robert Scholes and Richard M. Kain (Evanston, Illinois: Northwestern University Press, 1965), pp. 60–8.
17. Stanislaus Joyce, *The Complete Dublin Diary of Stanislaus Joyce* (Ithaca: Cornell University Press, 1971), entry for 2 Feb. 1904.
18. Ibid, entry for 2 Feb. 1904.
19. *JJ*, p. 165.
20. *JJ*, p. 175.
21. *U*, p. 7.
22. Letter to Stanislaus Joyce, 28 Feb. 1905, *LII*, pp. 83–4.
23. *P*, p. 247.
24. *SH*, pp. 77, 79.
25. *SH*, p. 95.
26. *SH*, pp. 95–6.
27. *JJ*, p. 222.
28. Letter to Stanislaus Joyce, 18 [–20] Sep. 1906, *L II*, p. 162.
29. *JJ*, p. 253.
30. *Here Comes Everybody: An Introduction to James Joyce for the Ordinary Reader* (London: Faber, 1965), pp. 43–4.
31. *Here Comes Everybody*, p. 44.
32. Herbert Gorman, *James Joyce: His First Forty Years* (New York: Huebsch, 1924), p. 58.
33. *JJ*, p. 328.
34. Mary and Padraic Colum, *Our Friend James Joyce* (London: Victor Gollancz, 1959), pp. 101–2.
35. Stewart, 'James Joyce,' *Eight Modern Writers* (New York: Oxford University Press, 1963), p. 443.
36. Levin, Harry, *James Joyce: A Critical Introduction*, rev. edn (Norfolk: New Directions, 1960), p. 48.

Notes

219

37. *P*, pp. 194–203.
38. *P*, p. 203.
39. *P*, p. 205.
40. William T. Noon, *Joyce and Aquinas* (New Haven: Yale University Press, 1957), p. 34.
41. *P*, p. 205.
42. Noon, *Joyce and Aquinas*, p. 35.
43. Theodore Spencer, Introduction, *Stephen Hero* (New York: New Directions, 1944), p. 15.
44. *P*, p. 215.
45. Letter to John Quinn, 14 Oct. 1920, John Quinn Memorial Collection, New York Public Library.
46. *P*, p. 206.
47. *JJ*, p. 135.
48. *P*, p. 8.
49. Ibid.
50. *Elements of Literature*, Canadian ed., edited by Robert Scholes et al. (Toronto: Oxford University Press, 1987), p. 368.
51. *P*, p. 206. As Harry Levin has pointed out, freedom was a primary aim of the symbolist endeavour (*James Joyce: A Critical Introduction*, p. 5).
52. As quoted by Noon, *Joyce and Aquinas*, p. 36.
53. *JJ*, p. 393.
54. 'A History of B.W. Huebsch, Publisher,' dissertation, University of Wisconsin-Madison, 1979, p. 110.
55. Richards's letter is printed in *Studies in Bibliography*, 16, p. 159.
56. This statement applies equally to Joyce's writing of *Portrait*, the final chapter of which Joyce did not complete until November, 1914, some four months after Grant Richards had published *Dubliners* and some nine months after the first instalment of *Portrait* had appeared in the *Egoist*.
57. 30 Sep. 1906, *LII*, p. 168.
58. Giorgio Melchiori, 'The Genesis of *Ulysses*,' *Joyce in Rome: the Genesis of Ulysses* (Rome: Bulzoni Editore, 1984), p. 41.
59. Ibid., p. 45.
60. Ibid., pp. 48, 43.
61. 29 Jul. 1918, *LI*, p. 116.
62. 17 May 1919, *LII*, p. 442.
63. Letter to James Joyce, 26 Jun. 1919. John Quinn Memorial Collection, Rare Books and Manuscripts Division, The New York Public Library.
64. *LI*, pp. 126–7.
65. *LI*, p. 113.
66. Michael Groden, *'Ulysses' in Progress* (Princeton University Press, 1977), p. 4.
67. *'Ulysses' in Progress*, p. 126.
68. Ibid., p. 37.
69. Ibid., p. 34.
70. Quinn informed Joyce of the suppression of the May 1919 number of *The Little Review* in his letter to Joyce of 26 Jun. 1919 (Division of Rare and Manuscript Collections, Cornell University Library). The suppression was also announced in the June number of *The Little Review*.
71. *'Ulysses' in Progress*, p. 44.
72. 8 Sep. 1919, *LII*, pp. 451–2. See also Joyce's letter to Hariet Shaw Weaver, 2 Jul. 1919, *LI*, pp. 126–7.

73. 19 Dec. 1919, *LI*, pp. 132–3.
74. 3 Jan. 1920, *LI*, p. 135.
75. Stanley Sultan, *Ulysses, The Waste Land, and Modernism* (Port Washington, NY: Kennikat Press, 1977), p. 11.
76. A. Walton Litz, 'The Last Adventures of *Ulysses*,' *Princeton Library Chronicle*, 27:2 (1967), p. 10.
77. c. 15 Nov. 1921, *LIII*, p. 53.
78. 26 Nov. 1921, *LIII*, p. 54.
79. Valèry Larbaud, 'James Joyce,' *La Nouvelle Revue Française*, 18 (Apr. 1922), p. 386. The translation is mine. Part IV of this essay was later published in English as 'The "Ulysses" of James Joyce,' *The Criterion*, 1:1 (Oct. 1922), pp. 94–103.
80. Ibid., p. 386.
81. Ibid., pp. 394; 402.
82. Ibid., p. 402.
83. Ibid., p. 407.
84. Ibid.
85. Letter to John Quinn, 3 Sep. 1920, *LI*, p. 145; letter to Carlo Linati, 3 Sep. 1920, *LI*, p. 146.
86. The fourth suppression had not yet occurred, but would soon: eight days after Joyce wrote his letter to Linati, John Sumner would seize the July–August 'Nausicaa' number of *The Little Review*, thus initiating the trials that would end in the suppression of Joyce's novel throughout the English-speaking world. The movement which Joyce believed was being prepared against the publication of *Ulysses* was indeed a reality, not a chimera born of paranoia.
87. Letter to Carlo Linati, 21 Sep. 1920, *LI*, pp. 146–7.
88. See Joyce's letter to Harriet Shaw Weaver, 10 Nov. 1920, *LI*, p. 149.
89. *'Ulysses' in Progress*, p. 52.
90. Michaelmas, 1920, *LI*, p. 147.
91. *'Ulysses' in Progress*, p. 169.
92. Ibid. pp. 169–70.
93. Ibid., p. 52.
94. A. Walton Litz, *The Art of James Joyce* (London: Oxford University Press, 1961), p. 34.
95. *'Ulysses' in Progress*, p. 55.
96. Ibid., p. 60.
97. *'Ulysses' in Progress*, p. 197.
98. *The Art of James Joyce*, p. 48; *U*, p. 78.
99. *'Ulysses' in Progress*, p. 194. Joyce knew of the Court's decision against *The Little Review* by the beginning of April 1921 (see Joyce's letter to Harriet Shaw Weaver, 3 Apr. 1921, *LI*, pp. 160–1).
100. Another event that could easily have reminded Joyce of the vulnerability of his novel to the censor occurred several days after he learned that *The Little Review* had been enjoined from publishing more of *Ulysses*. On 8 April the manuscript of 'Circe' was thrown into the fire by the typist's husband, who found its contents objectionable (see *JJ*, pp. 507–8).
101. 24 Jun. 1921, *LI*, p. 166.
102. 'Spatial Form in Modern Literature,' in R.W. Stallman (ed.), *Critiques and Essays in Criticism* (New York, 1949), p. 325.
103. *P*, p. 212.

104. *P*, p. 206.
105. *The Art of James Joyce*, p. 52.
106. Ibid.
107. Ibid., p. 36.
108. Noel Riley Fitch, *Sylvia Beach and the Lost Generation* (New York: Norton, 1983), p. 119.
109. Mary Nicholson and Jane Lidderdale, *Dear Miss Weaver* (London: Faber, 1970), p. 212.
110. Ibid., pp. 215–17.
111. Anne Lyon Haight, *Banned Books*, 2nd edn (New York: R.R. Bowker Company, 1955), p. 87.
112. James C. Paul and Murray L. Schwartz, *Federal Censorship: Obscenity in the Mail* (Westport, Conn.: Greenwood Press, 1977), p. 46.
113. Samuel Roth, 'Prelude,' *Two Worlds*, 7 Aug. 1927.
114. 'Roth's Magazine Accused: Joyce's *Ulysses* in *Two Worlds Monthly* Called Indecent' *New York Times*, 10 Mar. 1927, p. 2.
115. The role of the Federation of Hungarian Jews in America elucidates Larbaud's perception of the need to state clearly that Joyce's characterizing of Bloom as a Jew of Hungarian descent was *not* anti-semitic (See 'James Joyce,' p. 409).
116. Vice Society records indicate that Samuel Roth and his brother Max, as well as another family member, Pauline, were convicted twice in 1928 and at least four times in 1929. Both Samuel and Max served prison terms in 1929 (Container 4, Papers of the New York Society for the Suppression of Vice, Library of Congress).
117. Ironically, Roth's pirated version of *Ulysses* was used to provided the text for Random House's 1934 edition.
118. John J. Slocum and Herbert Cahoon, *A Bibliography of James Joyce, 1882–1941* (New Haven, Conn.: Yale University Press), 1953, p. 29. See also New York Society for the Suppression of Vice, Annual Report, pp. 9–10.
119. Charles P. Porter, letter to the Chief Constable, Cambridge, 17 Jul. 1926, File HO 144/20071, Records of the British Home Office, Public Records Office, London. Letters quoted elsewhere in this paragraph are in the same location.
120. R.T. Pearson, Chief Constable, Cambridge, letter to [?], 24 Jul. 1926.
121. F.R. Leavis, 'Freedom to Read,' *The Times Literary Supplement*, 3 May 1963, p. 325.
122. Ibid.
123. Ibid. In light of Leavis's troubles, it is hardly surprising that when one J.M. Lask, the son of a miller, requested that the Municipal Library of Stepney acquire a copy of *Ulysses*, the government authorities asked the Post Office to 'keep an eye on any letters which may come to him from abroad' (Letter to R.W. Hatswell, 20 Oct. 1926, File HO 144/20071, Records of the British Home Office, Public Records Office, London.
124. Smiley Blanton, letter to Assistant Collector Stewart, 13 Jun. 1930. See also H.C. Stewart, letter to Commissioner of Customs, Washington, DC, 14 Jul. 1930; and F.X.A. Eble, Commissioner of Customs, Washington, DC, letter to Collector of Customs, New York, 13 Aug. 1930; Commissioner of Customs File 53–14/2, National Archives, Sutland, Maryland. The first copy to be admitted to the USA on the basis of literary merit under the

provisions of Section 305 of the Tariff Act of 1930 seems to have been the French translation imported by Dudley Fitts, then a professor of English at The Choate School, Wallingford, Connecticut. See Dudley Fitts, letter to Mr P. Sheehy, Acting Deputy Collector, Customs Bureau, New York, 26 Apr. 1931; and F.X.A. Eble, Commissioner of Customs, Washington DC, letter to Collector of Customs, New York, 15 May 1931.

125. Letter to R.W. Hatswell, 5 Dec. 1930, File HO 144/20071, Records of the British Home Office, Public Records Office, London.
126. Dudley Fitts, letter to P. Sheehy, 26 Apr. 1931, File 53–14/2, Records of the Commissioner of Customs, National Archives, Sutland, Maryland.
127. Noel Riley Fitch, *Sylvia Beach and the Lost Generation*, p. 132.
128. Beach, *Shakespeare & Company*, p. 133.
129. Ibid., p. 90.
130. The other books were E.R. Curtius's *James Joyce und Sein Ulysses* (1929), Charles Duff's *James Joyce and the Plain Reader* (1932), and Alessandro Francini-Brund's *Joyce Intimo Spogliato in Piazza* (1922).

4   The United States against *Ulysses*

1. Alexander Lindey, memo to Morris Ernst, 6 Aug. 1931, Document 1, *D&C*, p. 77.
2. Ibid.
3. Ben Huebsch, letter to Bennett Cerf, 17 Dec. 1931, Document 6, *D&C*, p. 100.
4. Cerf tells the story in *Contempo*, 3:13 (1934), pp. 1–2.
5. Bennett Cerf, letter to Morris Ernst, 23 Mar. 1932, Document 11, *D&C*, p. 108.
6. Kenneth R. Stevens, '*Ulysses* on Trial,' *Library Chronicle*, 20/21 (1982) p. 92; reprinted, Commentary 17, *D&C*, p. 60.
7. His earlier accomplishments notwithstanding, Ernst would be remembered as 'the lawyer who won the landmark Federal court case that exonerated James Joyce's *Ulysses*' (Alden Whitman, 'Morris Ernst, "Ulysses" Case Lawyer, Dies,' *New York Times*, 23 May 1976, p. 40.)
8. Bennett Cerf, letter to Hellmut Lehmann-Haupt, 21 May 1935, Document 289, *D&C*, p. 480.
9. Bennett Cerf, letter to Paul Léon, 19 Apr. 1932, Document 23, *D&C*, p. 119.
10. *Extracts of Press Notices of 'Ulysses' by James Joyce*, revised version (Harlesdon: Leveridge & Co., Dec. 1922).
11. See Léon's letter to Bennett Cerf, 27 Apr. 1932, Documents 32, 33, *D&C*, pp. 129–31. The bibliographic details are mine.
12. My account of the importation of *Ulysses* is based on Cerf's *At Random* and Ernst's and Lindey's papers (as published in *D&C*). The two sources do not always agree.
13. Bennett Cerf, *At Random*, p. 93; reprinted, Commentary 16, *D&C*, p. 56.
14. H.C. Stewart, letter to Alexander Lindey, 13 May 1932, Document 52, *D&C*, p. 142.
15. T.D. 42907 *A. Heymoolen* v. *United States* (Decided 1 Aug. 1928), Document 53, *D&C*, pp. 142–3. The Customs document refers to the author of *The Law Concerning Draped Virginity* as 'Beuerland.' I prefer 'Beverland' on the authority of Richard Brown (*James Joyce and Sexuality* (New York: Cambridge University Press, 1985), p. 198), who notes that Joyce read the book.

16. Alexander Lindey, letter to I. Fishman, 17 May 1932, Document 56, *D&C*, p. 146.
17. Alexander Lindey, memo to Morris Ernst, 14 Jun. 1932, Document 69, *D&C*, p. 154.
18. Alexander Lindey, memo to Morris Ernst, 30 Jul. 1932, Document 75, *D&C*, p. 157.
19. Morris Ernst, memo to [Lindey], 27 Sep. 1932, Document 80, *D&C* 160; memo to Alexander Lindey, 12 Aug. 1932, Document 76, *D&C*, p. 158.
20. 'Claim,' Document 91, *D&C*, pp. 165–6.
21. 'Claimant's Answer,' 19 Dec. 1932, Document 95, *D&C*, p. 169.
22. The censorship fight began when Cutting, prompted by a friend's inability to import a copy of *Lady Chatterley's Lover*, proposed an amendment to remove all censorship provisions from the existing Tariff Act. Opposed by Senator Smoots of Utah – who declared that *Lady Chatterley* would enter the US over his dead body – Cutting failed to turn his amendment into law, but he did obtain the provision allowing the Secretary of the Treasury to 'admit the so-called classics or books of recognized and established literary or scientific merit … when imported for non-commercial purposes' (Paul and Schwartz, *Federal Censorship*, p. 59). Senator Cutting's fight for reform provides an indirect link between the late and early trials of *Ulysses*. After Cutting's attempt to reform to Tariff Act, Ezra Pound wrote encouraging him to seek reform of Section 211 of the US Criminal Code, under which *Ulysses* had been suppressed in *The Little Review*, 1919–21. Pound's letters to Cutting are in the Bronson Cutting Papers, Library of Congress.
23. H.C. Stewart, letter to Alexander Lindey, 22 May 1933, Document 113, *D&C*, p. 182.
24. Lindey, 'Petition for the Release and Admission of *Ulysses* into the United States on the Ground that It Is a Classic,' 2 Jun. 1933, Document 119, *D&C*, p. 189 [hereinafter 'Petition']. The original document is in File 53-14/2, Records of the Commissioner of Customs, National Archives, Sutland, Maryland. It is reprinted, without copies of the statements made by various prominent figures regarding *Ulysses*, in *D&C*, pp. 186–201.
25. 'Petition,' *D&C*, p. 189.
26. Ibid., pp. 187–8.
27. *Extracts from Press Notices of 'Ulysses'*, original version (Harlesdon: Leveridge & Co., Oct. 1922).
28. Ibid.
29. 'Petition,' *D&C*, p. 192.
30. Kenneth R. Stevens, '*Ulysses* on Trial,' *Library Chronicle*, 20.21 (1982), p. 95; reprinted, Commentary 17, *D&C*, p. 62.
31. Stevens, '*Ulysses* on Trial,' p. 95; reprinted, *D&C*, p. 62.
32. Morris Ernst, memo to Alexander Lindey, 6 Jun. 1933, Document 121, *D&C*, p. 202.
33. Frank Dow, letter to Collector of Customs, New York, 16 Jun. 1933, Document 124, *D&C*, pp. 203–4.
34. Compare James C.N. Paul and Murray L. Schwartz, *Federal Censorship*, p. 59.
35. Alexander Lindey, memo to Morris Ernst, 30 Jun. 1933, Document 129, *D&C*, p. 207.
36. Medalie, as it happened, had already requested the Treasury Department's file on *Ulysses* (See his letter to the Secretary of the Treasury, 1 Jul. 1933,

File 53–14/2, Records of the Commissioner of Customs, National Archives, Sutland, Maryland).

37. Pertzoff, a recent graduate of Harvard University where he had studied *Ulysses* with professor I.A. Richards, had sent Ernst a copy of his graduating thesis to help in the defense of Joyce's novel.

38. Alexander Lindey, memo to Morris Ernst, 5 Sep. 1933, Document 150, *D&C*, p. 222.

39. Alexander Lindey, letter to Judge John Woolsey, 12 Sep. 1933, Document 155, *D&C*, p. 226.

40. I use Ernst's name for the sake of economy; the 'Claimant's Memorandum,' like much of Ernst's defense of *Ulysses*, was also the work of Alexander Lindey.

41. Morris Ernst and Alexander Lindey, 'Claimant's Memorandum in Support of Motion to Dismiss Libel,' 14 Oct. 1933, Document 164, *D&C* pp. 239–41.

42. 'Claimant's Memorandum,' *D&C*, p. 241.

43. '*Ulysses* in Court,' *LR*, 7.4 (1921), p. 22.

44. 'Claimant's Memorandum,' *D&C*, p. 243.

45. Ibid., p. 246.

46. Ibid., p. 248.

47. Ibid., p. 249.

48. Ibid., n. 23, p. 270.

49. *James Joyce's 'Ulysses': A Study* (New York: Knopf, 1930), p. 20.

50. Ibid., p. 21.

51. Ibid.

52. Ibid., p. 22.

53. Ibid.

54. 'Claimant's Memorandum,' *D&C*, p. 252. Ernst cites *Halsey* v. *NY Society* 234 N.Y. 1.

55. 'Claimant's Memorandum,' *D&C*, p. 254. Ernst appeals here to *US* v. *'Married Love'* 48 Fed. (2d) 821.

56. 'Claimant's Memorandum,' *D&C*, p. 253. Ernst cites Magistrate Greenspan's unreported opinion in a case involving Erskine Caldwell's *God's Little Acre*.

57. 'Claimant's Memorandum,' *D&C*, p. 254. Once again Ernst cites Greenspan.

58. 'Claimant's Memorandum,' *D&C*, p. 255.

59. 'James Joyce,' *P/J*, p. 139.

60. 'Claimant's Memorandum,' *D&C*, p. 256.

61. Ibid.

62. Ibid.

63. As quoted in Margaret Anderson, 'JUDICIAL OPINION (Our Suppressed October Issue),' *LR*, 4:8 (Dec. 1917), p. 48.

64. Pound expressed his contempt for this view of the classics in 'The Classics "Escape,"' (*LR*, 4:11 (Mar. 1918), pp. 32–4), perhaps because he objected to its implicit marginalization of works which he believed should vitally influence culture. From this perspective, in conferring on *Ulysses* the status of 'classic,' Ernst was arguably hastening its irrelevance. Ernst, of course, can not be held solely responsible in this regard. As early as 1932 Lewis S. Gannett, literary editor at the *New York Herald-Tribune*, observed that *Ulysses* had already acquired 'the corpselike color of a "classic"' (as quoted in 'Claimant's Memorandum,' *D&C*, p. 268).

65. 'Claimant's Memorandum,' *D&C*, pp. 256–7.
66. Ibid., p. 257.
67. 'Claimant's Memorandum,' p. 257.
68. Ibid.
69. Ibid., pp. 257–8.
70. Ernst's note: *James Joyce's 'Ulysses,'* pp. 27, 28.
71. Ernst's note: *James Joyce's 'Ulysses,'* pp. 160, *et seq.*; 'Claimant's Memorandum,' *D&C*, pp. 258–9.
72. 'James Joyce,' *The New Republic*, 18 Dec. 1929; reprinted, Document 4, *D&C*, pp. 88–9.
73. 'Claimant's Memorandum,' *D&C*, p. 259.
74. As quoted in 'Claimant's Memorandum,' *D&C*, p. 260.
75. Ibid.
76. Ibid.
77. As quoted by Ernst, Ibid., p. 261.
78. Ernst's note here quotes lengthy passages from Herbert Gorman (*James Joyce: His First Forty Years* (New York: B.W. Huebsch, 1924), p. viii) and Paul Rosenfeld (*Men Seen* (New York: Dial Press, 1925), pp. 24–6) in support of his view of the stream-of-consciousness method.
79. 'Claimant's Memorandum,' *D&C*, p. 261.
80. Ibid.
81. Ibid., p. 262.
82. Ibid. Once again Ernst's distinction between literature and obscenity is shown to be less absolute than he would like: both the Library of Congress and the Widener Library shelve works of pornography.
83. 'Claimant's Memorandum,' *D&C*, p. 262.
84. Ibid., p. 264.
85. Ibid.
86. *Peabody Bookshop* v. *United States* (US Customs Court, 2nd Div. Protest 298623–G–556), as quoted in 'Claimant's Memorandum,' *D&C*, p. 265.
87. 'Claimant's Memorandum,' *D&C*, p. 266.
88. Ibid. He also argues that to brand *Ulysses* as obscene would be to place it in the company of 'outright pornography,' which would be like placing 'Dante's *Inferno* in the same category with *Fanny Hill*' ('Claimant's Memorandum,' *D&C*, p. 268). In retrospect it is easy to see that this analogy calls into question Ernst's insistence that pornography and literature are incompatible: some thirty years after Ernst defended *Ulysses*, a Massachusetts court declared that *Fanny Hill* was a work of literary merit.
89. 'Claimant's Memorandum,' p. 267. The quoted passage is from *James Joyce: His First Forty Years*, p. 93.
90. 'Claimant's Memorandum,' *D&C*, p. 267.
91. Ibid., p. 266.
92. Coleman was not the only person in the US Attorney's Office to read *Ulysses*. US Attorney George Medalie looked at it before deciding to proceed with the case, and Coleman passed it around to others, claiming 'that that was the only way his staff could get a literary education' (Alexander Lindey, memo to Morris Ernst, Document 75, *D&C*, p. 157).
93. 'James Joyce,' *Scraps*, 9:11 (12 Dec. 1933), pp. 12–28.
94. Alexander Lindey, memo to Morris Ernst, 6 Sep. 1933, Document 151, *D&C*, p. 223. All quotations in this paragraph are from this memo.

95. 'United States v. "Ulysses,"' Document 184, *D&C*, p. 293. The passage quoted is from Larbaud's 'James Joyce' (see Chapter 3). A copy of Larbaud's article was pasted inside the imported copy of *Ulysses*, to which Atlas undoubtedly had access.
96. 'United States v. "Ulysses,"' *D&C*, p. 295.
97. Ibid., p. 297.
98. *U*, p. 9. Atlas quotes these lines, not quite accurately, in 'United States v. "Ulysses"' (*D&C*, p. 298), and on p. 25 of 'James Joyce' (see n. 93 above).
99. The information about Nicholas Atlas in this and the following two paragraphs was obtained in the author's interview with his son, Judge Jeffrey Atlas, New York City, 14 Jun. 1989.
100. 'Analysis of Books Submitted to Us By the Claimant in the *Ulysses* Case for Comparison,' *D&C*, p. 299.
101. Ibid., p. 302.
102. Ibid., p. 300.
103. Ibid., 304.
104. *New York Herald-Tribune*, 7 Dec. 1933, *D&C*, p. 321.
105. Ibid.
106. Ernst, *The Censor Marches On*, reprinted, Commentary 12, *D&C*, p. 22.
107. According to Susan J. Stabile, the hearing took place on the sixth floor of the Bar Association Building at 42 West 44th Street (*The Trial of 'Ulysses*,' pamphlet accompanying exhibit on the case, New York, 1986, p. 12).
108. 'Ulysses Case Reaches Court After 10 Years,' *New York Herald-Tribune*, 26 Nov. 1933, Document 179, *D&C*, p. 284.
109. Ibid., p. 286.
110. 'Reflections on the *Ulysses* Trial and Censorship,' *James Joyce Quarterly*, 3 (Fall 1965), p. 5; reprinted, Commentary 15, *D&C*, p. 46.
111. *New York Herald-Tribune*, 26 Nov. 1933, *D&C*, p. 285.
112. Ibid., pp. 286–7.
113. Susan J. Stabile, *The Trial of 'Ulysses*,' p. 13. I have not been able to identify Stabile's source for this quote.
114. Ernst, *The Censor Marches On*, reprinted, Commentary 12, *D&C*, p. 22.
115. Ibid.
116. 'News of the Joyce Industry,' *The Literary Essays of Thomas Merton*, ed. Brother Patrick Hart (New York: New Directions, 1985), p. 18.
117. Atwood, *The Handmaid's Tale* (Toronto: Seal Books-McClelland-Bantam), p. 88.
118. Ernst, *The Censor Marches On*, reprinted, Commentary 12, *D&C*, p. 22.
119. Ibid., pp. 22–3.
120. Ernst and Lindey sent Woolsey the 'Claimant's Supplementary Memorandum' on 27 Nov. 1933.
121. Ibid., *D&C*, p. 291.

5   The Well-intentioned Lies of the Woolsey Decision

1. *U.S.* v. *Ulysses*, 5 F. Supp. 182 (District Court, Southern District of New York, 6 Dec. 1933), sec. VI; reprint. Foreword, *Ulysses* (New York: Random House, 1934; 1961); Appendix B, *Ulysses* (London: Bodley Head, 1936); *D&C*, pp. 308–12.

2. *Webster's International Dictionary.*
3. See 'Erotica vs. Pornography,' *Outrageous Acts and Everyday Rebellions* (New York: Holt, Rinehart & Winston, 1983), pp. 219–30.
4. Fiedler, 'To Whom Does Joyce Belong? *Ulysses* as Parody, Pop and Porn,' *Light Rays: James Joyce and Modernism* (New York: New Horizon Press, 1984), p. 29.
5. Fiedler, p. 29.
6. *U.S. v. Ulysses*, 5 F. Supp. 182, sec. II.
7. Forrest Davis, 'Judge Woolsey, Who Searched *Ulysses* But Could Find No Wooden Horses, Has Traits of His Ancestors – George, a Tapster, and Theodore, President of Yale,' *New York World Telegram*, 13 Dec. 1933, D&C, p. 342.
8. Richard Brown, *James Joyce and Sexuality* (Cambridge University Press, 1985), p. 1.
9. Fiedler, p. 30. Paul de Kock, it seems, did not actually write *The Sweets of Sin* (Brown, p. 135).
10. Brown, p. 132.
11. I base my claims about Joyce's reading on Brown, pp. 197–203.
12. Brown, p. 132.
13. Brown, p. 133; *U*, p. 42.
14. *U*, pp. 64, 235–7.
15. Fiedler, pp. 30–2; see *U*, p. 772.
16. Brown, p. 133.
17. Brown, p. 133; *U*, pp. 714–15.
18. *U*, p. 721.
19. *U*, p. 467. The bold portion of this passage was deemed obscene by Asst. US Attorney Sam Coleman. See Appendix, excerpt 123.
20. Fiedler, p. 33.
21. Brown, p. 134; *U*, p. 735.
22. *U*, p. 382. This passage, as the boldface type indicates, was deemed obscene by Asst US Attorney Sam Coleman. See Appendix, excerpt 82.
23. Brown, p. 134; the following example is from *U*, p. 485.
24. Passages in boldface were deemed obscene by the US Attorney's Office in 1932–3. See Appendix, excerpt 14.
25. *U*, pp. 171–2.
26. L.R. Dupuy, *The Strangest Voluptuousness: The Taste for Lascivious Corrections* (Paris: Medical Library, 19–), 'Translated from the French.' A copy of this work is held in Harvard's Widener Library.
27. *Ulysses*, 'Complete and Unexpurgated' (Industry, California: Collector's Publications, 1967).
28. *U.S. v. Ulysses*, 5 F. Supp. 182, sec. III.
29. Ibid., sec. IV.
30. Fiedler, p. 29.
31. *U. S. v. Ulysses*, 5 F. Supp. 182, sec. III.
32. Ibid.
33. Ibid., sec. II, III
34. John M. Woolsey, letter to Manley O. Hudson, 11 Dec. 1933, Manley O. Hudson Papers, Manuscript Division, Harvard Law School Library.
35. *U.S. v. Ulysses*, 5 F. Supp. 182, sec. V.
36. *The Anatomy of Criticism* (Princeton: Princeton University Press, 1957), p. 86.

37. 'Why I Write,' *A Collection of Essays by George Orwell* (New York: Harcourt Brace, 1953), p. 315.
38. Power, *Conversations with James Joyce*, ed. Clive Hart (London: Millington, 1974), p. 69.
39. Power, pp. 53–4
40. Brown, p. 135.
41. *U.S. v. Ulysses*, 5 F. Supp. 182, sec. IV.
42. Ibid.
43. Ibid., sec. V.
44. Ibid., sec. IV.
45. *U.S. v. Ulysses*, 5 F. Supp. 182, sec. VI. For an interesting discussion of the gender bias of Woolsey's decision, see Brook Thomas, '*Ulysses* on Trial: Some Supplementary Reading,' *Criticism*, 33:3 (1991), pp. 371–93.
46. 'L'homme Moyen Sensuel,' *LR*, 4:5 (Sep. 1917), pp. 8–16.
47. 'Reflections on the *Ulysses* Trial and Censorship,' *James Joyce Quarterly*, 3 (Fall 1965), p. 3.
48. *U.S. v. Ulysses*, 5 F. Supp. 182, sec. V, VI.
49. Henry Seidel Canby, editor of *The Saturday Review of Literature*, was connected with this cause. His testimonial letter in defense of *Ulysses* was appended to the claimant's petition to have *Ulysses* admitted to the United States as a classic (Alexander Lindey, memo to Morris Ernst, 7 Dec. 1933, Document 200, *D&C*, p. 317).
50. *U.S. v. Ulysses*, 5 F. Supp. 182, sec. VI.
51. Ibid. Woolsey's distinction between the emetic and the aphrodisiac is in keeping with his tendency to distinguish sharply between 'Joyce's description of a world and his celebration of it' (Brook Thomas, '*Ulysses* on Trial,' p. 373). Anything disgusting or emetic Woolsey excused by appealing to Joyce's truthful description; anything alluring or aphrodisiac – and therefore celebratory – Woolsey simply denied.
52. *U.S. v. Ulysses*, 5 F. Supp. 182, sec. III.
53. Ibid., sec. V.
54. Letter, 16 Aug. 1921, *LI*, p. 170.
55. Beach, *Shakespeare and Company*, p. 90.
56. Margot Norris, 'Modernism, Myth, and Desire in "Nausicaa,"' *James Joyce Quarterly*, 26:1 (1988), pp. 37–50; Jules David Law, '"Pity They Can't See Themselves": Assessing the "Subject" of Pornography in "Nausicaa,"' *James Joyce Quarterly*, 27:2 (1990), pp. 219–39.
57. *U*, pp. 365–7.
58. *U*, pp. 59–60, 63–5, 73–4.
59. '*Ulysses* Unspeakable Filth, Conboy Tells Appeals Court,' *New York World-Telegram*, 17 May 1934, *D&C*, p. 448.
60. Fiedler, p. 29.
61. *James Joyce's 'Ulysses'* (1930), p. 21.
62. *The Classical Temper: A Study of James Joyce's Ulysses* (London: Chatto & Windus, 1961), p. 49.
63. *U*, p. 236.
64. 'Claimant's Memorandum,' *D&C*, n. 23, p. 270.
65. *James Joyce's 'Ulysses'* (New York: Knopf, 1930), p. 20.
66. Ibid., p. 22.
67. 'The "Repeal of Squeamishness,"' *New York Herald-Tribune*, 8 Dec. 1993, *D&C*, p. 6.

68. Lewis Gannett, 'Books and Things,' *New York Herald-Tribune*, 9 Dec. 1933, *D&C*, p. 330.
69. Forrest Davis, 'Judge Woolsey, Who Searched *Ulysses* But Could Find No Wooden Horses, Has Traits of His Ancestors,' *New York World-Telegram*, 13 Dec. 1933, *D&C*, p. 341.
70. *George Washington Law Review*, 2 (May 1934), p. 517.
71. 'Another Repeal,' *The Nation*, 20 Dec. 1933. Significantly, Morris Ernst approvingly quotes this passage (which he believed to have been written by Joseph Wood Krutch) in his 'Brief for the Claimant-Appellee,' *D&C*, pp. 414–15.
72. Paul Boyer, *Purity in Print* (New York: Scribners, 1968), p. 272. The works destroyed in Berlin included those by Einstein, Freud, Marx, Gide, Proust, Mann, Zola, Wells, Remarque, Hemingway, Jack London, Upton Sinclair, Margaret Sanger and Helen Keller.
73. Ernst, Foreword to *Ulysses*, 11 Dec. 1933 (New York: Random House, 1934), p. v.
74. Manley O. Hudson, letter to John M. Woolsey, 8 Dec. 1933, Manley O. Hudson Papers, Manuscript Division, Harvard Law School Library.
75. Lewis Gannett, 'Books and Things,' *New York Herald-Tribune*, 9 Dec. 1933, *D&C*, pp. 330, 332.
76. Heywood Broun, 'It Seems to Me,' *New York World-Telegram*, 9 Dec. 1933, *D&C*, p. 332.
77. Bennett Cerf, 'Publishing *Ulysses*,' *Contempo*, 3:13, p. 2.
78. As quoted in *JJ*, p. 667.
79. In fact, as we shall see, Joyce seems never to have regarded the Woolsey decision as a criticism of *Ulysses*.
80. Letter to Constantine P. Curran, *LI*, p. 338.
81. Conboy is listed as an officer in the Society's 1929 Annual Report.
82. Letter to the Attorney General, 9 Feb. 1934; letter to the Attorney General, 23 Feb. 1934, Department of Justice Files, National Archives, Washington, D.C.

6   Late Encounters with the Enemy

1. Martin Conboy, letter to the Attorney General, 5 Mar. 1934, File 97–51–7, Record Group 60, Department of Justice Files, National Archives, Washington, DC.
2. Conboy's page references here are to the eleventh (1930) printing of the first edition. See Appendix for corresponding pages in the 1961 Random House edition.
3. *U*, p. 13.
4. Morris Ernst, 'Reflections on the *Ulysses* Trial and Censorship,' *James Joyce Quarterly*, 3 (Fall 1965), p. 5.
5. Joseph B. Keenan, 'Memorandum for the Solicitor General,' 6 Mar. 1932, File 97–51–7, Record Group 60, Department of Justice Files, National Archives, Washington, DC., p. 2.
6. 'Memorandum for the Solicitor General,' p. 3.
7. Ibid., p. 3.
8. Ibid., p. 4.

9. Ibid., pp. 2–3.
10. Ibid., p. 4.
11. 'Brief for the Libellant-Appellant,' no date, Document 258, *D&C*, p. 374.
12. Conboy's page references here are to the 1934 Random House edition. See Appendix for the corresponding pages in the 1961 Random House edition.
13. 'Brief for the Claimant-Libellant,' *D&C*, p. 375.
14. Ibid.
15. Gerald Gunther, *Learned Hand: The Man and the Judge*, with a Foreword by Justice Lewis F. Powell, Jr (New York: Alfred A. Knopf, 1994), p. 333.
16. 'Conboy Opens U.S. Appeal to Bar *Ulysses*,' *New York Herald-Tribune*, 17 May 1934, Document 266, *D&C*, p. 446.
17. 'Conboy Opens U.S. Appeal,' Ibid.
18. Ibid.
19. Ibid., p. 447.
20. '*Ulysses* "Unchaste and Lustful," No Lunchtime Story for 3 Judges,' *New York World-Telegram*, 16 May 1934, Document 264, *D&C*, p. 443.
21. 'Conboy Recites from *Ulysses* and Girl Flees,' *New York Daily News*, 18 May 1934, Document 268, *D&C*, p. 449.
22. '*Ulysses* "Unchaste and Lustful,"' p. 444.
23. 'Conboy Opens U.S. Appeal', p. 446.
24. 'Is Conboy's Face Red as He Reads *Ulysses* in Court,' '*New York Daily News*, 17 May 1934, Document 265, *D&C*, p. 444.
25. '*Ulysses* "Unchaste and Lustful,"' p. 443.
26. 'Conboy Opens U.S. Appeal,' p. 446.
27. *U*, p. 742. See Appendix, excerpt 234.
28. Ibid. See Appendix, excerpt 235.
29. *U*, p. 749. See Appendix, excerpt 244.
30. *U*, p. 754. See Appendix, excerpt 254
31. *U*, pp. 760–1. See Appendix, excerpt 256.
32. *U*, p. 763. See Appendix, excerpt 261.
33. *U*, p. 780. See Appendix, excerpt 288.
34. *U*, pp. 780–81. See Appendix, excerpt 288.
35. 'Conboy Recites from *Ulysses* and Girl Flees,' *New York Daily News*, May 18, 1934, Document 268, *D&C*, p. 449.
36. '*Ulysses* Fate Up to Court as Arguments End,' *New York Herald-Tribune*, 18 May 1934, Document 269, *D&C*, p. 450.
37. '*Ulysses* Fate Up to Court,' p. 451.
38. Gunther, *Learned Hand: The Man and the Judge*, p. 336.
39. Learned Hand, Pre-Conference Memorandum, '*U.S.* v. *Ulysses*,' 6 Jul. 1934, Learned Hand Papers, Harvard Law School Library.
40. Learned Hand, Pre-Conference Memorandum.
41. Ibid.
42. Augustus N. Hand, Pre-Conference Memorandum, '*U.S.* v. *Ulysses*,' no date, Learned Hand Papers, Harvard Law School Library.
43. Augustus N. Hand, Pre-Conference Memorandum. All quotes in this paragraph are from this source.
44. Augustus Hand, Pre-Conference Memorandum.
45. Manton, Pre-Conference Memorandum, *U.S.* v. *Ulysses*, Learned Hand Papers, Harvard Law School Library.
46. Cecil Maitland, 'Mr. Joyce and the Catholic Tradition,' *New Witness*, 20 (4 Aug. 1922), pp. 70–1; reprinted *James Joyce: The Critical Heritage*, ed. Robert

H. Deming (London: Routledge & Kegan Paul), pp. 272–3. Chesterton responded that the Catholic Church was hardly to be held responsible for Joyce's depiction of sexuality in *Ulysses* ('At the Sign of the World's End: An Extraordinary Argument,' (*The New Witness*, 18 Aug. 1922)).

47. This view is confirmed by John R. Horan, son of Francis H. Horan, the US Attorney who assisted Conboy in the government's appeal from the Woolsey decision: 'Judge Manton was a staunch and political Catholic. ... If two Catholic judges had been sitting, the result could have been different' (Letter to the author, 28 Jun. 1990).
48. Gunther, *Learned Hand: The Man and the Judge*, p. 333.
49. Augustus N. Hand, *U.S.* v. *Ulysses*, 72 F. 2d 705 (2nd Circuit 1934); reprinted Appendix B, *Ulysses* (London: Bodley Head, 1936); Documents 270, 271, *D&C*, pp. 452–62.
50. *U.S.* v. *Ulysses*, 72 F. 2d 705, *D&C*, p.453.
51. Ibid.
52. Ibid., pp. 453–4.
53. Ibid., p. 454.
54. Ibid.
55. Ibid.
56. Ibid., p. 456.
57. See *The Republic*, Books 2, 3, 10.
58. Ibid., p. 458.
59. Ibid.
60. Ibid., p. 460.
61. Ibid.
62. Ibid.
63. Ibid., pp. 460–1.
64. Ibid., pp. 461–2.
65. Martin Conboy, letter to Attorney General Homer S. Cummings, 31 Aug. 1934, File 97–51–7, Record Group 60, Department of Justice Files, National Archives, Washington, DC.
66. Harry S. Ridgely, 'Memorandum for the Solicitor General,' 10 Sep. 1934, File 95–51–7, Record Group 60, Department of Justice Files, National Archives, Washington, DC.
67. Ridgely, p. 3.
68. Ridgely, p. 7.
69. Ibid., p. 8.
70. Ibid.
71. John S. Sumner, letter to Homer S. Cummings, with attachment, 18 Oct. 1934, File 95–51–7, Record Group 60, Department of Justice Files, National Archives, Washington, DC.
72. John S. Sumner, letter to Joseph B. Keenan, 24 Oct. 1934, File 95–51–7, Record Group 60, Department of Justice Files, National Archives, Washington, DC.

Conclusion

1. The British (Bodley Head) editions also included the decision of the Court of Appeals.
2. Bennett Cerf, letter to Robert Kastor, 22 Mar. 1932, Document 9, *D&C*, p. 103.

3. Cerf, letter to Paul Léon, 13 Oct. 1933, Document 163, *D&C*, p. 234.
4. Paul Léon, letter to Bennett Cerf, 21 Oct. 1933, Document 170, *D&C*, p. 278.
5. *JJ*, p. 702. Joyce's reluctance may also have reflected his belief that 'readers would be better off without such cues, that the book was better experienced than skeletalized' (Hugh Kenner, review of *Ulysses on the Liffey*, *James Joyce Quarterly*, 2 (Winter 1973), p. 278). Kenner's view, incidentally, harmonizes with Joyce's decision to publish *Ulysses* without its Homeric chapter headings.
6. Alexander Lindey, letter to Judge Woolsey, 19 Dec. 1933, Document 232, *D&C*, p. 351.
7. *James Joyce's 'Ulysses'* (New York: Knopf, 1930), p. v.
8. *James Joyce's 'Ulysses'* (New York: Vintage, 1955), p. ix.
9. *U*, p. 61.
10. James Joyce's 'Ulysses' (1955), p. 136.
11. *U*, p. 86.
12. James Joyce's 'Ulysses' (1955), p. 158.
13. *James Joyce's 'Ulysses'* (1930), p. v.
14. *James Joyce's 'Ulysses'* (1955), p. ix.
15. *James Joyce's 'Ulysses'* (New York: Vintage, 1987). The quote is from an article in the *Saturday Review*.
16. *The Lifetime Reading Plan*, 3rd. edn (New York: Harper & Row, 1978), p. 78.
17. Martin Joos, 'Verbal Parallels and Recurrent Images,' *Word Index to James Joyce's 'Ulysses,'* by Miles A. Hanley (Madison: University of Wisconsin Press, 1951), p. 389.
18. Ibid., p. 390.
19. Ibid., *U*, pp. 68–9.
20. *U*, p. 70.
21. Joos, p. 390; *U*, p. 376.
22. 'James Joyce's *Ulysses* Seized in Morality Squad Raid Here,' *St Louis Post-Dispatch*, 1 Jul. 1959, p. 1.
23. Michael William Adams, *Censorship: The Irish Experience* (University, Alabama: University of Alabama Press, 1968), p. 172.
24. Peter Coleman, *Obscenity, Blasphemy & Sedition: 100 Years of Censorship in Australia* (Sydney: Angus & Robertson, 1974), pp. 18–20.
25. '*Ulysses* Comes Out of Hiding,' *Vancouver Sun*, 13 Apr. 1950, p. 12; (see also Blair Fraser, 'Our Hush-Hush Censorship: How Books Are Banned,' *Maclean's*, 15 Dec. 1949, p. 24.
26. 'James Joyce,' *Encyclopedia Americana* (International Bicentennial edn, 1987).
27. *Ulysses on the Liffey* (New York: Oxford University Press, 1972), p. 16.
28. Review of *Ulysses on the Liffey*, *James Joyce Quarterly*, 10.2 (1973), p. 277.
29. Ibid. Subsequent quotes in this paragraph are from the same source.
30. See *JJ*, pp. 502–4.
31. *JJ*, p. 503.
32. *JJ*, p. 6.
33. *JJ*, p. 513.
34. Arthur Power, *Conversations with Joyce*, ed. Clive Hart (Millington, 1974), p. 32.
35. *JJ*, p. 459. James Joyce, letter to Frank Budgen, 19 Jul. 1919, *LI*, p. 126.
36. *JJ*, pp. 362–3.
37. As should be clear by now, Ellmann was not the best person to introduce Michael Moscato's and Leslie LeBlanc's *The United States vs. One Book*

Entitled Ulysses. Ellmann's preface to that work repeats the same misleading, and in many places inaccurate, view of the censorship of *Ulysses* presented in the first (1959) edition of *James Joyce.*

38.   Richard Brown, *James Joyce and Sexuality* (Cambridge, 1985), pp. 1–2.
39.   Vincent J. Cheng, '"Goddinpotty": James Joyce and the Language of
       Excrement,' *The Languages of Joyce*, ed. by R. M. Bollettieri Bosinnelli, *et al.*
       (Philadelphia/Amsterdam: John Benjamins, 1992), p. 85.
40.   Anne Freedgood, letter to the author, 4 Nov. 1987.
41.   Gerald Gunther, *Learned Hand: The Man and the Judge* (New York: Knopf,
       1994), p. 334.
42.   Edward de Grazia, *Censorship Landmarks* (New York: Bowker, 1969),
       pp. 94–6.
43.   Harold C. Gardiner, S.J., 'Moral Principles for Discerning the Obscene,' *The
       Catholic Theological Society of America: Proceedings of the Ninth Annual
       Convention* (Montreal, June 1954), p. 128.
44.   Ann Ilan Alter, 'An Introduction to the Exhibit,' in *Censorship: 500 Years of
       Conflict*, The New York Public Library (New York, Oxford: Oxford
       University Press, 1984), p. 23.
45.   Paul S. Boyer, *Purity in Print: The Vice-Society Movement and Book Censorship
       in America* (New York: Scribner's, 1968), p. 253.
46.   'A Thoroughly Dangerous Law,' *Quill & Quire* (Aug.–Sept. 1959), p. 12.
47.   Ira Glasser, Executive Director, American Civil Liberties Association, letter
       to Friends of the Association, no date, p. 2.
48.   This paragraph is based on Nat Hentoff, 'Saying No to Molly Bloom,'
       Village Voice, 9 Jul. 1987, p. 42; and Robert L. Corn, 'The F.C.C. Cleans Up
       the Airways,' *The Nation*, 5 Dec. 1987, pp. 679–80.
49.   'Saying No to Molly Bloom,' *Village Voice*, 9 Jul. 1987, p. 42.
50.   *The New York Review of Books*, 39:9 (14 May 1992), p. 31.
51.   *P*, p. 206.
52.   Ibid.
53.   George Steiner is useful here. See *Real Presences* (Chicago: University of
       Chicago Press, 1989), pp. 141–2.
54.   As quoted by John Garvey, 'Don't Be Offended: Correct-Think on Culture,'
       Commonweal, 117:16 (28 Sep. 1990), p. 535.
55.   Arthur Power, *Conversations with James Joyce*, p. 69.
56.   'Freedom of Interpretation,' *Politics of Interpretation*, ed. W.J.T. Mitchell
       (University of Chicago Press, 1983), p. 55.
57.   'Human Personality,' *Simone Weil: An Anthology*, ed. and intro. Sian Miles
       (New York: Weidenfeld & Nicolson, 1986), p. 76.
58.   *All Quiet on the Western Front*, 'A Book-of-the-Month Club Classic Reissued
       by the club in celebration of its 60th anniversary, A new introduction by
       Mordecai Richler,' 1986.

Appendix: the Censors' *Ulysses*

1.   Conboy's objections to the Paris edition of *Ulysses* figure in his letter to US
      Attorney General Homer S. Cummings, 23 Feb. 1934. See Chapter 6.
2.   As previously mentioned, Ezra Pound's and Margaret Anderson's expur-
      gations have been inferred from comparison of the Rosenbach manuscript
      (*'Ulysses': A Facsimile of the Manuscript*) and the first Paris edition. My
      policy has been to identify as an intentional expurgation any controversial

passage that appears in both the manuscript and the first edition but not *The Little Review*. Restored passages are from the Rosenbach manuscript.

3. Pound substituted 'belly.'

4. Assistant US Attorney Sam Coleman's objections to various passages in *Ulysses* appear in the margins of the copy of the Shakespeare & Company edition of the novel (Paris 1930) imported by Morris Ernst, seized by US Customs, and admitted as the sole piece of evidence in *U.S. vs. 'Ulysses.'* The book is held in the Rare Books Library, Columbia University.

5. Conboy's objections to the 1934 Random House edition of *Ulysses* are recorded in his 'Brief for the Libellant-Appellant.' See Chapter 6.

6. Judge Manton's objections to specific pages of *Ulysses* can be found in *U.S v. Ulysses*, 72 F. 2d 705, *D&C*, pp. 457–62. See Chapter 6.

7 Letter to the Postmaster, 14 Mar. 1919; File 49537, Box 165, World War I Espionage Files, Records of the Post Office Department, National Archives, Washington, DC. See Chapter 1.

8. *LR* substituted '......'

9. Anderson substituted ellipses for the deleted passage and included the following explanatory note: 'The Post Office authorities objected to certain passages in the January installment of "Ulysses," which prevents our mailing any more copies of that issue. To avoid a similar interference this month I have ruined Mr. Joyce's story by cutting certain passages in which he mentions natural facts known to everyone.'

10. For the expurgated passage, Anderson substituted '......'

11. Anderson marked the expurgation of the following passage with ellipses and an editorial note: 'A passage of some twenty lines has been omitted to avoid the censor's possible suppression.'

12. Coleman's marginal notation here is a vertical line and 'Bloom [illegible word],' not his usual mark of objection.

13. The bracketed portion was underlined by Coleman.

14. The bracketed portion was underlined by Coleman.

15. Sumner's objections to various pages of *Ulysses* in *The Little Review* are recorded in the affadavit he swore before Judge Corrigan, City Magistrate, 21 Oct. 1921 (see Chapter 2). His objections to particular passages are ennumerated in John Quinn's letter to Ezra Pound, 16 Oct. 1920, pp. 16–18.

16. The objections of the father of the young woman who received the unsolicited copy of the July–August 1920 number of *The Little Review* are recorded in John Sumner's article, 'The Truth About "Literary Lynching."'

17. As Pound later explained to Quinn, he 'made one or two deletions' in the July–August 1920 instalment of 'Nausicaa': 'I did myself dry Bloom's shirt' (letters, 31 Oct. 1920 and 8 Nov. 1920, *The Selected Letters of Ezra Pound to John Quinn, 1915–24*, ed. Timothy Materer (Durham and London: Duke University Press, 1991)), pp. 198, 202.

18. The bracketed portion was underlined by Coleman.

19. The bracketed portion was underlined by Coleman.

20. The bracketed portion was underlined by Coleman.

21. The bracketed portion was underlined by Coleman.

22. The bracketed portion was underlined by Coleman.

23. The bracketed portion was underlined by Coleman.

24. The bracketed portion was underlined by Coleman.

25. The bracketed portion was underlined by Coleman.

26. Coleman's marginal notation here consists of a vertical line and an arrow pointed at the text, not his usual mark of objection.
27. The bracketed portion was underlined by Coleman.
28. The bracketed portion was underlined by Coleman.
29. The bracketed portion was underlined by Coleman.
30. The bracketed portion was underlined by Coleman.
31. The bracketed portion was underlined by Coleman.
32. The bracketed portion was underlined by Coleman.
33. The bracketed portion was underlined by Coleman.
34. The bracketed portion was underlined by Coleman.
35. The bracketed portion was underlined by Coleman.
36. The bracketed portions were underlined by Coleman.
37. The bracketed portion was underlined by Coleman.
38. The bracketed portion was underlined by Coleman.
39. The bracketed portion was underlined by Coleman.
40. The bracketed portion was underlined by Coleman.
41. Coleman's usual marginal annotation is incomplete.
42. Coleman's marginal notation next to this passage consists of a vertical line, not his usual mark of objection.
43. Coleman placed a parenthesis, not his usual mark of objection, on either side of this passage.
44. Coleman placed parentheses around this passage, not his usual mark of objection.
45. Coleman placed parentheses around this passage, not his usual mark of objection.
46. Coleman placed parentheses around this passage, not his usual mark of objection.
47. Coleman marked the second bold portion of this excerpt with a vertical line, not his usual mark of objection.
48. Keenan's objections to the Paris edition are recorded in his 'Memorandum for the Solicitor General,' 6 Mar. 1934. See Chapter 6.
49. Coleman placed two marks of objection next to this passage.
50. The bracketed portion was underlined by Coleman.
51. Coleman placed two marks of objection next to this passage.
52. The bracketed portions were underlined by Coleman.
53. The bracketed portion was underlined by Coleman.
54. The bracketed portion was underlined by Coleman.
55. The bracketed portion was underlined by Coleman.
56. The bracketed portion was underlined by Coleman.
57. The bracketed portion was underlined by Coleman.
58. Coleman underlined the bracketted passage; he did not use his habitual mark of objection.
59. The bracketed portion was underlined by Coleman; he did not place any mark in the margin.
60. The bracketed portion was underlined by Coleman.
61. The bracketed portion was underlined by Coleman.
62. The bracketed portion was underlined by Coleman.
63. The bracketed portion was underlined by Coleman.
64. The bracketed portion was underlined by Coleman.

Index